MOSHE DAYAN

Moshe Dayan

Shabtai Teveth

Steimatzky's Agency
together with
Weidenfeld and Nicolson

Weidenfeld and Nicolson
5 Winsley Street   London W1

Weidenfeld and Nicolson Jerusalem
19 Herzog Street   Jerusalem

Translated from the Hebrew by Leah and David Zinder

ISBN 0 297 99522 7

Printed in Israel by Keter Press, Jerusalem, and bound
by Wiener Bindery, Jerusalem, 1972

CONTENTS

FOREWORD

Following the Six-Day War, Minister of Defense Moshe Dayan became a political and public figure of utmost importance. Rarely has a people placed such profound trust in a single man. This phenomenon would be extraordinary anywhere and is so much more so in Israel, where the public votes for more than nine different parties and is sharply divided on a number of ideological issues concerning the future of the country's existence. Nonetheless, Dayan commands the complete trust of the majority of Israelis, and their attitude has endowed him with a unique status. At times—such as during the "missile crisis" of August 1970—it seemed as though the fate of the government rested in his hands alone. To the Jews of the world— and perhaps not only to them—he has become the symbol of a tiny country that continues to exist by virtue of its courage in a sea of enemies forever threatening to destroy her.

Dayan believes that Israel has yet to reach its "rest and peace" and must intensify its drive for Jewish settlement, and a parallel can legitimately be drawn between the history of that settlement and his own life. The return of the Jewish people to its homeland was accompanied by a steady escalation of the hostility between Arabs and Jews. Dayan lived out that escalation and was even one of its creators. One might say that he traversed the span of time from the Stone Age—weapons of his youth—to the Electronic Age—the sophisticated arms of the Superpowers, now his responsibility as Israel's Minister of Defense.

But war was only one side, the unexpected and perhaps even compulsory side, of working the land in the era of Jewish settlement, while the actual endeavor of settlement was from the outset the cornerstone of the reemergence of Jewish life in Palestine. The history of this settlement movement is the second major leitmotif in Dayan's life, from his birth in Degania, the mother of kibbutzim, to his childhood and adolescence in Nahalal, the first moshav, to his term as Minister of Agriculture (1960-5). Just as agriculture was the bridge to Jewish-Arab cooperation in his youth, after the Six-Day War, when he assumed responsibility for the Administered Territories, it became a prime factor in his efforts to establish neighborly relations between the two peoples. It is entirely characteristic, therefore, that only two kinds of people can relate the story of Dayan's life: Arabs and Jews, farmers and soldiers, men of peace and men of war.

ACKNOWLEDGMENTS

Because of the nature of a biography about a living personality and due to certain restrictions, such as military censorship and the Israel Archive Law, I could make only limited use of documented information, and most of the source material for the composition of this work was therefore gathered through over one hundred recorded interviews, during which I was also allowed to look through personal papers—documents, letters, diaries, notes, and photocopies. Meshulam Halevi allowed me to make a copy of Moshe Dayan's diary from the fifth grade, and I was also permitted to read the manuscript of Shmuel Dayan's autobiography, edited by Shmuel Gilai, and of the third volume of Dr. Yehudah Slutzky's *History of the Haganah,* which deals mainly with the period of struggle to establish the State of Israel. In addition, Noah Dagoni allowed me to read his diary from the period of his imprisonment in the Acre Fortress. My thanks to all these men for allowing me access to these unpublished works.

The correspondence between Shmuel, Dvorah, and Moshe Dayan constitutes an important source for chapters 1-10. All the family letters in print were published by Shmuel Dayan. Scattered among his publications are his letters and those of members of his family, and a posthumously published selection of her articles contains an appendix of 108 of Dvorah Dayan's letters. Shmuel Dayan's autobiography contains others of his wife's letters, letters from Moshe, and his own replies to some of their previously published letters.

Moshe Dayan granted me nine extensive recorded interviews between January 1970 and January 1971 and replied to the various questions I addressed to him in person and by telephone. These interviews shed much light particularly on his childhood, youth, the early stages of his military career in the Haganah and Zahal, and his parents and other personalities in his life. Nahman Betser and Benjamin Zarhi were very helpful on the period of Dayan's childhood in Nahalal, and Mrs. Shulamit Dagan (née Dayan) described to me in great detail the family background of the early years.

For the period of the Haganah and early years of Zahal, particularly regarding the War of Independence, I am indebted to former Prime Minister and Minister of Defense David Ben Gurion, Deputy Prime Minister Yigal Allon, and ex-Chiefs-of-Staff Lt. Gens. (Res.) Ya'akov Dori, Yigael Yadin, Mordechai Maklef, Chaim Laskov, Zvi Zur, Yitzhak Rabin, and Chaim Bar-Lev. Important contributions toward my understanding of the Jerusalem period were provided by Lt. Col. (Res.) Hillel Fefferman and especially Maj. Gen. Meir Zorea. In describing the pre-C-o-S period, Maj. Gen. (Res.) Uzi Narkiss was a faithful and perceptive source of information and an eye witness with a sense of humor, and I owe him special thanks. In writing on the period of Dayan's term as C-o-S I was aided by Mrs. Neora Bar Noah (née Matalon), Brig. Gen. Shlomo Gazit, and Col. (Res.) Mordechai Bar-On. Their perspicacity enabled me to approach the events as though I had witnessed them myself. I owe a special debt of gratitude to Maj. Gen. Israel Tal, who read the manuscript and commented on the military matters therein.

For the period after Dayan's term as C-o-S and his entry into politics, Avraham Ofer, MK, who clearly remembers the days of the "Youngsters" in Mapai, Minister of Communications Shimon Peres, and Deputy Minister of Transport Gad Ya'akobi were of great assistance. I also thank the latter for reading the two final chapters of the manuscript and helping me maintain the accuracy of some of the details. I am also very grateful to the late Zalman Aranne for his help in clarifying the position of the Mapai veterans in their struggle with the "Youngsters."

I wish to thank Chaim Israeli, Director of the Minister of Defense's Office, who generously allowed me to exploit his extensive knowledge of the history of the defense services. I also express my gratitude to my colleague Avraham Schweitzer for reading the entire manuscript and offering his comments and corrections and to Gershom Schocken, the editor of Ha'aretz, who read the work with great care and commented on both details and major sections.

In preparing the English edition of this book for publication, I was faced by the challenge of tailoring the work for a readership outside of Israel, and I have consequently tried to select out certain passages which I believe to be of less vital interest to the non-Israeli reader. Most of the written sources referred to in the preparation of the book were, of course, in Hebrew, and I have therefore deleted the long bibliography and many bibliographical notes contained in the Hebrew edition. Finally, I wish to thank Ina Friedman of Weidenfeld and Nicolson Jerusalem for her close collaboration with me in preparing the final version of this edition for publication.

TEL AVIV

May 1972

Shabtai Teveth

"My self has significance as long as I remain myself."

Chief-of-Staff Moshe Dayan in a note to Minister of
Defense Pinhas Lavon

1   SHMUEL AND DVORAH

If a boy, they would call him Moshe. Apart from their love, this was the only certainty in Shmuel and Dvorah Dayan's life when, on May 2, 1915, Dvorah felt the first contractions of labor. Everything else was cast in doubt.

To begin with, this was to be the first birth at Degania and was not at all according to plan. Not only were facilities for childbirth totally lacking, but the members of Degania had even taken it upon themselves to forestall such an eventuality. In the autumn of 1914, Shmuel himself had demanded that marriages be temporarily banned in the settlement. The members' experience with Gideon—the only other child at Degania (born to Yoseph and Miriam Baratz at the Scottish Mission Hospital in Tiberias)—had taught them that babies were an obstacle to physical labor, one of the sacred tenets of the new kvutza.* A pregnant woman, Shmuel claimed, could undertake only limited work, and after the birth she would be kept fully occupied nursing and caring for the child. He proposed that the members of the kvutza "be allowed to marry only five years after the settlement established itself economically and consolidated itself socially." A few weeks later Shmuel learned that Dvorah was pregnant and that in marrying her he would be the first to break his own resolution. This was not to be the last time Shmuel failed to practice what he preached.

The wedding took place with due ceremony on a crisp Friday morning in 1914, probably in September. From Shmuel's description of the event, it was apparently carried out with some haste. One of the settlement's carts was pressed into service to collect the litter scattered about the farm. A second cart was dispatched to Tiberias to bring wine, almonds, and fruit. A third was driven wildly to the neighboring settlement of Menahamiya to bring the shochet,** who would conduct the ceremony. The courtyard was thoroughly swept and the dining hall decorated with flowers and tendrils of vine. Dvorah sat in her room sewing her wedding dress. "At times," Shmuel wrote, "the cloth grew damp with tears of longing for her parents." That evening the shochet blessed Shmuel and Dvorah under

---

* "Group" in Hebrew but at the time a term meaning the members of a communal settlement, the farm itself, and the idea that lay behind the new community. It preceded the term "kibbutz" as the name of a collective farm.
** Ritual slaughterer, allowed by Jewish law to conduct marriages.

an improvised wedding canopy—a blanket tied to orchard staves on the banks of the Jordan.

Dvorah's pregnancy was not the only problem facing the Dayans. There was also the question of her integration into the *kvutza*. When she arrived at Degania in 1913, the members rejected her application for membership for they felt she was not strong enough to endure the hardships and was not "a working force." Furthermore, they claimed, she was "alien" and "not fully involved in Zionism." The rejection was mutual, for while farming inspired and exalted the members of Degania, Dvorah wrote to Shmuel: "It's boring here, deadly boring. So much so that I have become the very embodiment of boredom." She did not share the vision behind the establishment of Degania. Dvorah wanted "to see the world" and wrote: "I am not inclined to philosophizing, nor do I presume to found my life upon new values." She did little to improve her knowledge of Hebrew and derived complete spiritual satisfaction from Russian literature, particularly Chekhov and Tolstoi. And while Dvorah believed that nothing could rival the joys of literature, the *kvutza* felt that nothing could rival the exalted virtue of physical labor.

The Dayan's personal problems were compounded by political developments. At the time, the fate of the entire Yishuv* hung in the balance, for the First World War had broken out and the Turkish Government in Palestine regarded the Jewish community as a potential—if not active—ally of Great Britain. In a rapid series of decrees, the authorities expelled the Jews from Tel Aviv and Jaffa, sending them north to the Galilee. These deportations emphasized the tenuous position of the Zionist foothold in Palestine and were a very real threat to the security of the new settlements in the Galilee. One way to avoid deportation or exile was to acquire Ottoman citizenship and become a subject, rather than an "enemy alien." The leaders of the Yishuv urged the Jews of Palestine to be "Ottomanized." Among the first to do so were the farmers, who wanted above all to remain on their land. In November and December 1914, the members of Degania applied for Turkish citizenship at the district office in Tiberias.

The *kvutza* also fared badly. Those who were not conscripted were forced to pay a large ransom to the Turkish authorities, and the Turkish Army confiscated mules, oxen, sacks of grain, carts, even clothes and undergarments. The authorities also levied a heavy tax upon the settlement, and the members of Degania were warned that failure to meet the payment would entail the confiscation "of anything the authorities see fit." Shmuel feared that they might have to abandon Degania.

---

* Collective term for the Jewish community in Palestine.

As though all this were not enough, one day in April a teeming, yellow cloud blotted out the sun over Palestine. Locusts had come to the Jordan Valley. They gathered and destroyed the larvae and plowed over the soil before the pupae emerged; but to no avail. The locusts were everywhere. The men tried placing large round tins around the trees and smearing the trunks with a sticky paste, but the locusts leaped over the tins directly to the tops of the trees. Finally, they covered the trees with cloth bags, tightly tied at the trunks. The white-shrouded orchard looked like rows of dead men silently overlooking Degania and boding little good. The locusts remained in the Jordan Valley for three months. As soon as one swarm flew off, another immediately replaced it. The combine bundled the insects in the hastily harvested sheaves (three-quarters of a bale to the usual three); men and beasts trampled them underfoot. At night the settlers were often too exhausted to notice the locusts crawling over them and shook them off only when they rose the next morning.

There were two stone buildings in Degania at that time: a two-story building with eight rooms for living quarters, two halls, a small office, and four balconies; and a single-story building containing the dining hall, kitchen, bakery, a storehouse and showers. Shmuel and Dvorah's room, in the lower story of the main building, was prepared for the birth. The shutters were firmly closed and the door locked to keep out the locusts. The settlement nurse cleaned and polished every corner of the room and looked after the expectant mother. Water was boiled and everyone anxiously awaited a sign from the nurse. But Dvorah's labor continued for two days, while her moans could be heard through the shuttered windows. When no news came, Shmuel asked one of the men to relieve him of guard duty in the fields and returned to the house. As Dvorah's pains grew more intense, the nurse agreed to let him enter the room. At dawn on May 4, 1915, the baby's first cry was finally heard.

The main reason for choosing the name Moshe was the Dayan's desire to perpetuate the memory of Moshe Barsky and was the last link in a chain of absurd and tragic events. One night, when Shmuel was guarding wheat on the threshing floor, a mosquito flew into his ear and caused an inflammation. After the local doctor failed to cope with the complications, Shmuel decided to make his way to Beirut, but the only result of the operation he underwent there was to cause his nose to bleed profusely whenever he engaged in strenuous physical labor. One Saturday in November 1913, nothing could be done to stop the bleeding, and nineteen-year-old Moshe Barsky offered to ride to the neighboring settlement of Menahamiya to bring a coagulant. In the evening his mule returned alone, and after a search his body was found near the Jordan River. The police subsequently learned that he had been attacked by six Arabs in an attempt to steal the mule. Barsky had struggled fiercely until one of them shot him in the back. His grave in the olive grove was the first in Degania. Thus the infant Moshe inherited with his very name a direct association with the struggle between Jews and Arabs which would characterize the rest of his life.

Moshe Dayan's birth in Degania was to prove a distinct asset to his political fortunes. The settlement became an aristocratic family; nowhere in the Jewish Labor movement—which became the dominant sociopolitical force in the Yishuv and later in the state—could a more "exclusive" and select club be found. Of all the early Jewish settlements in Palestine, only Nahalal and Ein Harod (both established in 1921) managed to approach Degania's preeminence in the Labor movement. While prominent leaders of the Yishuv were often at pains to establish their ties with Degania, Moshe belonged to it by birth, the delight and pet of the founders of the first kibbutz. As the settlers were all young, with little or no experience in raising children, they all took an active part in his education. Moshe was therefore raised by many of the founding fathers of the Labor movement in Palestine.

In 1915, however, Degania was a far cry from the aristocratic family or exclusive club of later years. Furthermore, when Moshe was born Shmuel and Dvorah were not even certain of where they would make their permanent home, and they were equally unsure of their ultimate goals in life. Dvorah still dreamed of "seeing the world" and could not yet accept the new doctrine of manual labor as the path to spiritual redemption. Shmuel was no more at ease with his conscience. Ostensibly he was sustained by the fervent spirit of the Second Aliyah,* whose motto was "conquest by labor." Shmuel seemed to be constantly running from his father's house in Zaskow to Uman, from Uman to Odessa, and from Odessa to Jaffa, arriving in Palestine in June 1908 to continue from Jaffa to the agricultural settlements of the coastal plain. "Conquest by labor" meant, first of all, preparing oneself for the physical hardships of farming. Shmuel did so first as a hired hand, then as a member of an organized group of agricultural workers. He worked on farms throughout the country and finally arrived at Degania. Now he asked himself whether Degania would be the end of his journey. Was he finally to stop running and settle on the kibbutz, or was he still a "conqueror by labor" who must move on to clear new lands for the redemption of his people? Conflicting ambitions made the decision a difficult one.

The transition from life in Russia to the rigors of Palestine was

*Second wave of Jewish immigration to Palestine, 1904-14.

easier for Shmuel than for Dvorah. Zaskow, in the district of Kiev, was a poor town inhabited by a few hundred Jews who depended mainly on horse trading for their livelihood. Shmuel's family, among the poorest in the town, nonetheless enjoyed some measure of distinction. On his mother's side he was a distant descendant of Rabbi Pinhas of Koritz, one of the great Hassidic leaders of the eighteenth century. On his father's side he was a Levite and fourth generation descendant of Reb Eliyahu, who served as a *dayan* (religious judge) in the "court" of the well-known Hassid Aryeh Leib, the "Grandfather of Spola."

It was Reb Eliyahu the *dayan* who gave the family its name and bequeathed the status of *dayan* to his sons and their descendants. Reb Pinhas, Shmuel's grandfather, was a *shochet* and *bodek** in Zaskow, respected by the local Jewish community both for his advice on matters of dietary law and as an arbitrator in domestic or commercial disputes. But Pinhas's son, Reb Avraham (Shmuel's father), was plagued by misfortune all his life. While still a child, he was permanently maimed when a cow stepped on his foot. When the time came for him to be married, a match was arranged with a poor orphan. Reb Avraham also managed to break the traditional slaughtering knife, was disqualified as a *shochet,* and lost the inherited position of *dayan* to one of his three brothers. When he tried his hand at trade, he was equally unfortunate. One of the many business ventures he attempted was the sale of raisin wine to the poor, but it involved frequent trips down to the cellar. Mortally frightened of the ghosts and spirits he believed inhabited the dark recesses, Reb Avraham would send his ten-year-old son Eliyahu to bring up the bottles of wine. One day a goat wandered unnoticed into the cellar. Walking down the steps, Eliyahu suddenly found himself face to face with a veritable devil, complete with horns and a beard. The child shrieked so that his father nearly fainted. Courage can hardly be counted among the qualities that Reb Avraham bequeathed to his grandson Moshe.

Reb Avraham became dependent upon his children early in their childhood. When he worked as a *commissionnaire* (a traveling salesman of the time), eleven-year-old Eliyahu became his full-time assistant. By the age of fourteen, Eliyahu's commercial acumen earned him a position as a clerk in Odessa. Reb Avraham therefore moved the entire family to Odessa in 1898, but on the day Eliyahu was to have opened a new chapter in his family's fortunes, the shop went bankrupt. He then went to work as a day laborer in a match factory and sold pretzels in the street after work hours. Two years later the family returned to Zaskow and Eliyahu again became

* One who examines meat to decide if it is kosher.

a *commissionnaire*. Shmuel, born in 1890 and seven years younger than Eliyahu, now joined his elder brother on trips.

Shmuel's formal education began in a *heder*.* He was an obstinate child and on one occasion so angered the rabbi that he received a slap which knocked out two of his teeth. He was subsequently transferred to another *heder*. Although the family's poverty affected his schooling, Shmuel learned to read and write Hebrew and Russian. His fine, clear hand often gained him work as a scribe, writing "pleas" from local farmers to the district authorities.

In Odessa Eliyahu had come under the influence of the nascent Zionist movement and transmitted much of his zeal to Shmuel. Both brothers were independent, strong-willed, and resourceful. After years of hard work, Eliyahu had managed to save 600 rubles, and in 1908 he left his wife and children in Zaskow and set out for Palestine, together with his sister Beileh and his brother Shmuel. Eliyahu was one of the few pioneers of the Second Aliyah who came to Palestine with sufficient means to tide him over difficult times. He soon established a farm in Ein Gannim and then returned to Zaskow to send his wife and children to Palestine. He himself remained in Russia to raise money for the farm. In 1912 he returned to Palestine accompanied by his sister Bat-Sheva.

Unlike his younger brother, Eliyahu resolutely turned his beliefs into practice. He refused to engage in political activities and zealously upheld the principle of independent labor.** Shmuel, on the other hand, was attracted by politics and public affairs. Even before the end of his first year in Palestine, he held a meeting in support of *Hapoel Hatzair*, the newspaper of a left-wing party of the same name. Barefoot and wearing the one "Sabbath shirt" he had brought from Russia, he walked from Ein Gannim to Jaffa, and handed the editors of the newspaper the small sum he had gathered together with a protocol of the meeting.

This short mission marked a turning point in Shmuel's life. It brought him in contact with Y.H. Brenner, the writer and ideologist of the Hebrew Labor movement; Yoseph Sprinzak, the Secretary of the Hapoel Hatzair Party; and Yoseph Aharonovitch, the editor of *Hapoel Hatzair*, who invited him to write for the paper. At this point in his life, however, public affairs and journalism occupied relatively little of his time. The Jaffa alley where *Hapoel Hatzair* had its dismal offices offered none of the fascination, activity, and heady sense of breaking new ground that were to be found in

* Jewish equivalent of a primary school in Eastern Europe. It was run by individual rabbis who taught children of mixed ages.
** One of the principle ideals of the pioneers of the Second Aliyah. Socialist in concept, it deplored the use of hired labor and extolled the redemptive power of personal contact with the soil.

pioneering. There was irresistible romance in the wild, open country, the wandering groups of pioneers living in the fields, working on the land, suffering, dancing. This spirit was epitomized by the men of Hashomer (The Guard), romantic Jewish heroes mounted on horses in traditional Arab dress. They were the ideal image of the renewed contact with the ancient homeland of the Jewish people. At that time striking roots in the country meant resembling the inhabitants of the land. The men of Hashomer studied the Arab ways and tried to pattern their own lives according to these ancient customs.

About a year after his arrival in Palestine, Shmuel bought a pistol and an ammunition belt in Jaffa. He wore them during the day and kept them close by his pillow at night. Possession of such a weapon was a justifiable means of self-defense. Far more important, however, the pistol and five bullets were the trademark of the highest order of pioneers—the men of Hashomer. After hearing of an Arab attack on Kfar Tabor, Shmuel decided to leave the coast and go north to the Galilee. Together with three friends, he made his way toward the beleaguered Jewish settlements, hoping "to plow and sow" and assist Hashomer. He got as far as Yavniel, where he was hired as a farmhand by Ya'akov Sahin and was faced with the first and most important lesson of "conquest by labor": proving to the farmers of the Jewish settlements that a youngster from the Ukraine could work in the fields like an Arab fellah. In Petach Tikva, Shmuel had worked picking fruit and building houses. At Yavniel, Sahin ordered his Arab hand to teach the new man how to plow. Shmuel adjusted with difficulty to farm work and never ceased to marvel at the old Arab's stamina and perseverance.

Sahin put Shmuel up in the stable, a lodging that enhanced his status for two reasons: first, to be on hand and feed the oxen at night, and secondly so that he would be able to guard the farmyard and the house. Though guard duty was in fact the automatic responsibility of anyone who slept in the loft, Shmuel wasted no time fitting himself out with the obligatory Hashomer outfit. The glamour was short-lived, however, for six months after his arrival at Yavniel, he contracted malaria. Sahin took pity on him and brought him into the house to recuperate, but made up his mind that the Jewish youth would never be able to take the place of a good Arab fellah. When Shmuel recovered he found that his place in the loft had been given to an Arab.

He did not leave the Galilee, however. Instead he went to the "national farm" at the settlement of Kinneret, near the Sea of Galilee, where he joined a group of pioneers who divided their time between work and endless ideological disputations. Shmuel proved to be a fierce debater and was soon voted onto the editorial staff of *Hashfifon,* the pioneers' satirical publication. With him on the staff was the poetess Rachel Blubstein. She was slight, delicate, and sensitive, with soft eyes and a preference for solitude. He was drawn to her by the same delicate frame and poetic nature that later attracted him to Dvorah, but his love was not requited. In 1911 he moved from Kinneret to the newly established settlement of Degania.

In 1905 the Jewish Colonization Association (ICA) purchased the lands of Daleika and Um-Jouni from their Arab owners. In June 1908 the Jewish National Fund founded a farm on part of these lands, whose cultivation was undertaken by the members of Horesh, the first organization of Jewish agricultural workers in the Galilee. Within a few months, however, relations between the members of the Horesh group and the JNF-appointed manager of the farm became strained and the project was abandoned. In December 1909— the official date of the founding of Degania—a contract was drawn up between a group of six men and one woman and the Palestine Land Development Company. According to the terms of this agreement, the PLDC was to retain ownership of the farm, but the settlers would manage it independently and receive a monthly salary of 45 francs each, with net profit being divided equally between them and the company. Should the farm incur any losses, however, the PLDC would cover them.

Although the group proved itself capable of running an agricultural farm, the original members dispersed only ten months and ten days after the start of the experiment. In October 1910 a new contract, similar to the first, was drawn up between the Hadera Commune and the PLDC. This was the real beginning of the *kvutza* at Um-Jouni, named Degania by the new settlers after the five kinds of cereal (*dagan,* in Hebrew) they sowed on their lands.

Until 1922 the *kvutza* of Degania was composed of two groups: members of the commune and hired workers. The former lived a truly communal life, sharing everything equally and fully. In 1911, when Shmuel came to the settlement as a hired worker, there were eleven members in the commune. They moved into the mud huts that had been abandoned by the former Arab tenant farmers. The members of the commune were the backbone of the *kvutza* and were somewhat less than fond of Shmuel. They disliked the way he pushed himself into prominence and forced his way into the management of the farm. At the group's general meetings, he opposed the members of the commune on many issues relating to the social and agricultural structure of the settlement. His desire to become a representative of the group made it quite clear that he would never be completely satisfied merely working in the fields, but he was often hampered by his inability to express ideas clearly and forcefully. Sometimes without even realizing it, and fully believing that his thoughts were original, Shmuel expressed the ideas of other members, rewording them in his own high-flown rhetoric. He seemed like a bit-part actor who would be satisfied with nothing less than a lead.

Shmuel organized an opposition group within the *kvutza* and held long meetings with his supporters in the vineyards or on the threshing floor. Once consolidated, this group emerged into open conflict with the leaders of the *kvutza*. At one of the general meetings, they demanded that Yoseph Bussel be replaced as farm manager by Shmuel Dayan. The issue was not put to a vote at that meeting, but was finally resolved when Shmuel stormed into the *kvutza* office with some of his followers and demanded that the safe and account books be made his responsibility. This unprecedented act aroused the wrath of many members, and it was not to abate in Shmuel's lifetime. He finally achieved his aim of sharing the management of the farm with Bussel. Although they handled the social and agricultural affairs of the *kvutza* together, Bussel—one of the pillars of the commune—retained the real leadership and power. Nevertheless, by the time Dvorah came to Degania in 1913, Shmuel was undoubtedly a central figure there.

It is hard to imagine a more unlikely match for Shmuel. Dvorah was born in the small Ukrainian village of Prochorovka on September 23, 1890. Although their native villages were not far from one another, Shmuel and Dvorah came from different worlds. Unlike Zaskow, with its active Jewish life, synagogues, and schools, Prochorovka had only one Jewish family, the Zatulovskys. Dvorah's grandfather, Yehoshua Zatulovsky, was the Rabbi of Squira, and her uncles were rabbis in neighboring communities. Her father, Yehi'el Ze'ev Zatulovsky, was a scholar, avid student of the Hebrew language and culture, and the successful manager of a large lumber business. He was also an author of some note for his book *The History of the Jews in the Days of Chmielnicki*, which dealt with the defense of the Jewish population in the Ukraine during that period of pogroms. Dvorah's background was therefore more distinguished than Shmuel's.

Dvorah and her brother grew up on an estate that consisted of two stone houses situated on the banks of the Dnieper. Until the age of eight, she studied at home with a private tutor. After that the village priest, Father Ippolyte, persuaded her enlightened and liberal father to allow Dvorah to study at the church school, where she was the only Jewish student. It was there that she first learned Russian, for until then she had only spoken the Ukrainian dialect. Upon completing her studies there, she went on to a Russian secondary school in Kremenchug, then entered the Department of Pedagogy at the University of Kiev. Strangely enough, she shared neither her father's love for the Hebrew language nor his Zionist fervor. Many years later, writing about this period in her life, Dvorah noted that she had fallen in love with the great expanses of Russia, its people, language, and literature. During the abortive 1905 Revolution, while still at secondary school, she devoted herself to the movement for the emancipation of the proletariat. Unmindful of the dangers involved, Dvorah joined the Narodniks and visited workers' homes and factories, helped the needy, and became known as "daring Virotchka, always ready for action." She joined the students' faction of the Social Democratic Party and sympathized with the suffering of the poor. She became deeply attached to Professor Rossov of the Department of Pedagogy and joined him first in a study of slum children in Kiev and then on a study tour of Caucasia and the Crimea. According to Miriam Baratz, her close friend at Degania, she even entertained thoughts of marrying him.

Literature was her greatest love and Tolstoi the idol of her soul. In 1910, when news came of his death, she hurried to the railway station with many of her student friends to board a train to Yasnaya Polyana. There she joined the long line, a motionless parade of thousands, and passed the white birch trees, reached the house, slowly advanced up the stairs, and finally entered Tolstoi's study. Her pain at the loss of Tolstoi was so great that she found herself unable to leave, and she spent a few days at the Tolstoi Commune in Tillyatinsky. Twenty-five years later, on the farm at Nahalal, she was to write: "In every person's life there comes a moment when he wishes to bid the sun stand still. That was my moment."

In the fall of 1911, Bulgaria—supported by Russia—attacked Turkey. This marked the beginning of the Balkan Wars that were to divest Turkey of all her European holdings. Against her parent's wishes, Dvorah volunteered as a nurse and left Prochorovka for the Bulgarian front to devote herself to aiding and comforting the soldiers (her unrequited love for Professor Rossov may also have played a part in her decision). It was on this hazardous mission that she was assailed by doubts about her real nationality. For the first time she began to question whether this was really her war, or the Russians really her people. Who were her people? Where were their masses, their laborers, soldiers, and farmers? These doubts and her parent's heartbroken letters from Prochorovka prompted her to return to the Ukraine.

Dvorah resumed her university studies and took on a part-time post with the local authorities in Kiev, but she found no answers to the questions that had gnawed at her in Bulgaria. One night, during a gay students' party in her room, she fell into a mood of restless melancholy, and gazing at the animated faces of her friends she could not shake off a sense of estrangement. "I have discovered a grave error in my life. The people to whom I wish to devote myself are not my people, and I am a stranger amongst them." That same night she decided that she must "begin everything anew." She packed her bags and in the morning took the first riverboat down the Dnieper, returning to her father's house.

Dvorah searched for the answers to her questions in her father's library. There she discovered scores of books written in Hebrew. Although she did not understand the language, she sensed that the solution to her dilemma was to be found in them. She did not return to the university but spent the winter of 1912 at her father's desk, looking through the many letters he had received from Palestine. One day she came upon a letter written in Russian from Ze'ev Tiomkin, the representative of Hovevei Zion in Palestine describing the latest developments in the Yishuv. As she read her excitement mounted and an idea flashed in her mind: "That is where the workers of my people are. I shall join them!"

Though Zionists at heart, Dvorah's parents were dismayed by their daughter's decision to emigrate to Palestine. Apart from their natural reluctance to see her leave their house, they felt that the trip was dangerous. After all, she was still only a young woman and would be traveling on her own to a desolate, disease-ridden country inhabited by Arabs, who were thought to be savages. Her only defense on this trip was a letter from a friend addressed to Israel Bloch of Degania, asking him to meet Dvorah at the port of Haifa. She sailed from Odessa in January 1913 aboard the steamship *Princess Olga,* which also carried a few hundred Russian pilgrims.

A week later, on a rainy Saturday morning, Dvorah stepped down from the ship into a small boat that took her to the harbor, where her papers and luggage were examined by the Turkish authorities. Everything went smoothly, except that Israel Bloch failed to appear. She simply stood waiting, not knowing where to go, and then decided to follow a passenger who had been met by her family. Walking alongside them, she came to a hotel. A short while later, a bearded, middle-aged man approached her and asked what she was doing in Palestine. She learned from him that Israel Bloch had gone to Damascus to buy cows for the Degania dairy. The friendly stranger, Israel Betser, had been a member of the first group of settlers at Degania. He now lived with his family in Merhavya. Dvorah took an immediate liking to him and gladly accepted his invitation to stay with his family until Israel Bloch returned. The following day she set out for Merhavya with Betser, who later became one of the founders of Nahalal and a close friend of the Dayans. When word was received that Bloch had returned, she took the train to Zemakh and then walked to Degania.

Upon her arrival at the settlement in the spring of 1913, the members saw "a charming girl, with a bright, smiling and wonderfully fresh-looking face. Two long braids crowned her head. Her eyes were deep and dark, always open wide to face a world which seemed so beautiful and promising. Very feminine and high-spirited, she laughed readily, but her happiness would often give way to a sudden seriousness." They nevertheless turned down her request for membership in the *kvutza*. According to Miriam Baratz: "In 1913 three girls came to us. Two were beautiful and the third was plain. When the two beauties came, most of the men (poor things) flocked round them. Dvorah was the more beautiful of the two, hers being a profound and delicate beauty. Shmuel Dayan, the *"tzaddik"* [righteous man], declared that the two beautiful girls must be sent away from Degania because the men had stopped working and neglected the farm." Actually, Miriam Baratz claims, the majority of the members had little to do with the decision to turn down Dvorah's request. The prime mover was none other than Shmuel himself, who engineered her rejection in order to get her away from his rivals. Had Dvorah remained in Degania, Miriam insists, it is doubtful whether Shmuel would have won her. Dvorah later accepted this version of the story, though perhaps only in jest. Be that as it may, this was the story Moshe heard from his mother and often recounted to friends in his youth.

In 1913 Shmuel looked every inch a pioneer. He spoke heatedly of a lofty vision, managed the farm at Degania, wrote for *Hapoel Hatzair,* worked in the fields, and guarded the settlement as a mounted watchman. In response to a request from Hashomer, Degania sent Shmuel and another member to help guard the fields of Merhavya. He was one of twenty guards and helped drive away the local Arabs who tried to harvest wheat in the settlement's fields. He also took part in a number of skirmishes with Arab bands. During his stay in Merhavya, Shmuel wrote to the "new girl" at Degania and romantically described his experience as a guard.

Meanwhile, Dvorah was treated like a new recruit in Degania and given the less honorable farm chores. For a time she patched together old sacks; later she graduated to more prestigious work, rooting up weeds and working on the threshing floor. One day she was given a truly responsible task: baking bread for the fifty people in the *kvutza*. Her fingers grew stiff, her back ached, and she shifted her weight from one foot to the other, but finally, with what she later described as superhuman effort, she managed to bake the required number of loaves. To the members of the *kvutza,* only results mattered; the efforts required to achieve them were unimportant. Dvorah worked side by side with Miriam Baratz, who carried sacks of wheat, milked the cows, worked even when feverish with malaria, and baked bread for fifty people with something less than superhuman effort. Dvorah's education and enlightened mind were of little relevance to life at Degania.

She did not attend the general meeting in which her application for membership was discussed, but she could hear the voices in the next room through the thin walls. Though the discussion was in Hebrew and she could not understand everything that was said, the general drift was painfully clear. She was being criticized for not speaking Hebrew or Yiddish, for not being fully involved in Zionism, and for not being a "working force." What the *kvutza* required above all was work, total involvement in farm affairs, industriousness, and complete identification with the group's ideals. The list of her failings went on: she was over-educated, would not eat their food, and though cheerful enough during the day, she wandered off alone at night. One remark remained engraved in her memory: "She came to us from a different environment. Our ideals and interests are alien to her." Of the trials that attended her integration into Degania, Dvorah wrote: "I came to them and said: 'I belonged to a different society, one perhaps opposed to your own. But I did not find the truth there and came to find it among you. I wish to drink deeply of your sanctity.' And they replied, 'But you are alien to us.' What anguish I underwent during that period of my life."

Dvorah decided to remain in Degania until after the threshing. When the work was done, she went to the ICA farm at Sejera, hoping to find work and to study. At first the manager of the farm refused to employ her, claiming it did not become a woman like her "to mess about with garbage" and "work clothes are not made of silk." She wrote to Shmuel of this incident saying that "such reasoning might well reduce a person to starvation." Nevertheless, she managed to get work on the farm on alternate days and had time to go to the settlement school. She spent much of her spare time talking with the Russian-Orthodox wife of the Hebrew teacher, and often, when the other girls went out to work, Dvorah would read to her from Chekhov.

When Dvorah moved to Sejera, her correspondence with Shmuel became more intense, and they often signed their letters "Yours" or "With kisses." Shmuel visited Sejera frequently. He was a handsome, deeply tanned man, with strong, angular features and soft, coal-black hair. Stubbornness, perseverance, and forcefulness were among his most prominent traits. His lack of grace lent him an air of gravity. Shmuel understood her problems and admired her intellectual qualities. His presence calmed her. "The members do not see in you a capacity for work," he wrote. "I see an entire world in you." She believed in every word he said, in each facet of his forceful personality. It seemed that his actions were a true reflection of his convictions, and she saw in him a hero and a prophet. Because he spoke Hebrew fluently, she seems also to have regarded him as her cultural superior, with the power to draw her out of her old world and be her support and guide in the new one. According to Miriam Baratz, Dvorah was trying to overcome her involvement with the Russian professor as quickly as possible. Therefore, Shmuel was a savior in more ways than one.

After the mosquito-in-the-ear incident, Shmuel went to Beirut, where the doctors operated on his nose. Early one morning Dvorah suddenly burst into his hotel room in tears and embraced him tightly. With neither proper clothes for the journey nor friends to advise or help her, she had spent all her money on a one-way ticket to Beirut. During his stay in the hospital, she spent as much time as she could by Shmuel's bedside and slept in a cheap hotel. They returned to Degania an engaged couple. This time the members of the *kvutza* accepted Dvorah with open arms, and for the first time she began to regard Degania as her home. But the two had little time to enjoy their new-found happiness, for both fell ill soon after their return from Beirut. Since the best doctors in the Levant had failed to cure Shmuel's problem and his suffering increased from day to day, he asked the *kvutza* to help him seek medical aid in Vienna. At about the same time, Dvorah contracted malaria and then bronchitis. The couple agreed that she should return to her parent's home to recover, while he went to Vienna for treatment. Later, he would join her in Prochorovka and they would announce their engagement.

The expenses involved in Shmuel's proposed trip to Vienna were too great for the *kvutza,* and the members turned down his request for a loan. He decided to go to Austria on his own and borrowed five louis d'or from Eliyahu. Elegantly attired in a new jacket and boots ordered in Tiberias, with the rest of his belongings in a wooden chest, Shmuel sailed from Jaffa in December 1913. Dvorah's parents sent part of the money she needed for her trip and Shmuel provided the rest.

With the help of the local Zionist Federation in Vienna, he was accepted for treatment at a private Christian hospital. The two corresponded regularly. Dvorah advised Shmuel to use his time to read and even sent a list of recommended books, while he exhorted her to begin her convalescence immediately: " . . . You must become a farmer. We shall soon return to our work on the land. Our plans to 'see the world' can easily tear us away from the land. The city has many attractions . . . But we shall not abandon the land, for there can be no meaning to our lives without our work on the soil."

On board ship to Russia, Dvorah suffered a relapse of malaria. She arrived at Odessa in January 1914, pale, weak, and exhausted.

She was immediately taken to a doctor, but one illness followed another until April. The doctor forbade her to return to Palestine, but Dvorah was adamant. She wrote to Shmuel: "In Palestine there is a reason to rise in the morning, there is something to live for. Here I am like a caged bird. Let us go back soon, soon!" Nevertheless, the memory of her first love was apparently still alive, for she made a special trip to Kiev to say good-bye to Professor Rossov and perhaps prove to herself that she was now immune to his attractions.

Dvorah then began to prepare for the return trip to Palestine. In her free time she put the finishing touches to a short story about the street urchin Vovka, but then decided not to have it printed because she no longer wished to publish anything in Russian. All the while, she waited impatiently for Shmuel to join her at her parents' home. But Shmuel was delayed by problems. In 1910 he was supposed to have reported for military service in the Czarist Army, and now he faced punishment as well as compulsory conscription. He had taken the precaution of leaving Palestine under an assumed identity by borrowing a passport from Eliyahu Golomb. While he had faced no problems entering Russia, leaving was going to be a different matter. For Golomb, then nineteen years old, was also obliged to report for military service. Shmuel reached his parents' home in Zaskow without incident. There he began growing a beard to disguise himself as an old man and be able to leave Russia with a second false passport. He wrote Dvorah and asked her to acquire the necessary passport; then he set out for Prochorovka, covering 30 kilometers of a snow-bound road on foot. Describing his reception at the Zatulovsky home, Shmuel wrote in his autobiography: "Love and heartwarming joy immediately filled the house. It was a night of happiness for the new family and remained a joyful memory for the entire forty-three years of our life together."

At the end of July 1914, Shmuel and Dvorah sailed from Odessa to Haifa. They left just in time, for while they were still at sea Germany declared war on Russia and France: the First World War had begun.

2   DEGANIA (1915-1920)

Dvorah gave herself completely to her child. She spent hours watching him, noting every expression and sound he made, and Shmuel often found himself a mere onlooker. Miriam Baratz, the first mother among the members of the *kvutza,* was so dedicated to her work in the cowshed that she often took her son Gideon with her, laid him down in a feed trough, and, while flies covered his face, milked the cows. But Dvorah was reluctant to take her child with her to the fields; she wanted to devote all her time to him alone. The *kvutza* opposed such a notion for it meant a waste of working potential. Miriam Baratz suggested to Dvorah a form of cooperative motherhood: one of them would go out to work while the other cared for the two children. Dvorah agreed to look after the children, and this was the first instance of communal child care in the kibbutz movement. "Two weeks later, despite the fact that Gideon was an easy child, Dvorah came to me and said, 'Miriam, I can't do it. I want to be everything to my child: nurse, teacher, university. I don't want to complicate matters by being nurse to someone else's child.' And that was the end of the first cooperative child-care scheme." Moshe was regarded as a difficult infant because of his incessant crying. Miriam Baratz recalls that "he was a screamer second to none," and Dvorah would often take him down to the Jordan at night so that his crying would not wake the weary settlers.

By the summer of 1916, there were four children in Degania, all of whom became infected with trachoma. Dvorah contracted the disease from Moshe, and they began a period of constant trips to doctors throughout the country. In July 1916 Dvorah took Moshe by cart to Shmuel's sister Beileh Hurvitz, who had settled in the village of Nahalat Yehudah, about a´ kilometer and a half north of Rishon le-Zion. By the time Dvorah reached the village, her vision had so deteriorated that she could hardly see. The treatment she received was not immediately effective, and it was some time before her eyesight returned. But before she was completely cured of trachoma, she came down with a high fever. Despite her discomfort, she rode alone to Jaffa to see Dr. Chaim Hissin, who diagnosed a liver disease but could not admit her to his hospital because of the many typhoid cases there.

By the time Dvorah and Moshe returned to Degania—both of them still sick—the war had spread. In the beginning of 1917, the Turks uncovered the pro-British spy ring called "Nili" and initiated widespread searches to round up its members. The "Nili" ring was actually much smaller than the Turks suspected, and their search for members even reached Degania. All the men were detained and later taken to Kinneret for lengthy interrogations. But at least the women and children of Degania miraculously escaped the plagues that spread through the war-torn country, and after a while, all but one of the men returned to Degania.

Then the Turkish authorities expropriated the two stone houses in the settlement and used them as lodgings for German pilots. Some of the members set up new quarters in the loft of the cowshed, while others moved into the partitioned sections of the empty granary. The month of November 1917 was cold and wet, and the few warm corners in the improvised quarters slowly disappeared, leaving only an expanse of cold, damp ground. The kitchen had been taken over by the Germans, and the settlers were left without a place to warm themselves. Winds raced through the gaps in the partitions, chilling them to the bone and extinguishing the improvised lamps.

One day in the summer of 1918, Moshe came down with a high fever. A few days later, fearing for their child's life, Shmuel and Dvorah took him to Dr. Pokhovsky in Tiberias, who informed them that the child had pneumonia. There was no hospital in Tiberias, so Shmuel and Dvorah took a room on the second floor of the Weingart Hotel and stayed by Moshe's bedside in shifts. With no ice to cool the stifling room, they waved wet towels over his bed, but Moshe remained motionless for nine days. One morning Shmuel woke his wife to take over the morning shift saying, "Listen." She bent over her child and heard Moshe say, "Mother, they're singing." Then she too heard the voice of the muezzin from the minaret of the nearby mosque, summoning the faithful to their morning prayers.

The summer at Degania, 200 meters below sea level, is long and hot. Temperatures around 96° are normal, and 104° is not out of the ordinary. Dr. Pokhovsky suggested that Moshe be taken to a cooler place for convalescence. Dvorah took him to Metulla, high in the cool Upper Galilee, but their stay there was not a restful one. Though far from the trials of war, word reached them of the deportations, the scarcity of food, and the spreading plagues. In Metulla, Dvorah experienced "days of despair and hope. First sleepless nights and days of fear; then days filled with joy at the sight of the recovering child . . . He laughed and played again." Finally, the time came for them to return to Degania. A cart was sent from the *kvutza* at night so that they might leave Metulla early in the morning and avoid the midday heat. As the cart made its way down the winding road to the Huleh Valley, however, the horses suddenly started and reared up violently, breaking the harness shaft. The driver set about repairing the damage, while the sun climbed high in the sky and the cool morning gave way to the white-hot glare of noon. Dvorah saw that the repairs would take longer than expected and decided that she must take Moshe out of the sweltering heat of the Huleh Valley. She picked him up and set off in the direction of Rosh Pinna, 20 kilometers to the south. Cutting across the fields, she walked without stopping, and as the sun beat down upon them, Moshe's breathing became labored. Her strength drained away and she longed to lay down the child, whose weight seemed to double from moment to moment. Only the urgency of reaching safety projected her forward. In the distance she saw red-tiled roofs and the figure of a woman approaching. What followed seemed to be a dream. She handed the child to a woman and felt cool drops of water on her face. She did not know how she entered the house, but later, when she regained consciousness and looked around, she discovered herself lying with Moshe on a cool floor covered with straw mats, a jug of cold water by their side. The image of Dvorah carrying her child across the trackless field characterized the first five years of Moshe's life.

All this time Moshe continued to suffer from trachoma and was subjected to incessant but inadequate treatment. The persistent disease reinfected Dvorah. Moshe could not be cured in Degania or Tiberias; proper treatment could only be had in Jaffa or Jerusalem, but these two cities were completely cut off from the Galilee. In December 1917 the British and Turkish armies faced each other across a front that extended from Jerusalem to Jaffa. Ten months were to pass before Allenby crushed the Turkish forces in the decisive battle of Megiddo.

After their defeat, the Turks beat a hasty and disorderly retreat in the direction of Damascus. The members of Degania fled the settlement and went into hiding, for anyone unfortunate enough to cross the Turks' path was immediately taken prisoner and forced into carrying equipment for the troops. The soldiers raided Degania, setting fire to anything they could not transport, but they fled the settlement before the destruction was complete. The local Bedouin then seized the opportunity and galloped into Degania, shooting wildly and taking whatever was left.

The British conquest of Palestine reunited the country and brought great changes in the Yishuv, but the Dayan family found neither rest nor peace. The prolonged bout with trachoma resulted in the contraction of Moshe's left eye, causing Dvorah great concern. Her only desire was to find a permanent cure for both herself and her child. It was believed that a change of climate might be of help and open the rapidly closing eye. So Dvorah and Moshe left Degania again, this time for Kibbutz Gan Shmuel; but the change of climate brought neither of them respite from the disease. Dvorah made preparations to go to Jaffa, where she consulted Dr. A. B. Krinkin, the first—and in fact only—opthalmologist in Jaffa. His diagnosis was that both mother and child were suffering from a severe case of trachoma and that an operation would be necessary on Moshe's left eye. He agreed to administer the prolonged treatment, but the fee he demanded was astronomical: £1 for each visit.

From Jaffa, Dvorah wrote to Shmuel that she was going on to Jerusalem. "There is hope that they will accept us both at a hospital there, and the treatment will be much less expensive. It is impossible to say how long we will have to stay. When will there be an end to these strange and never-ending ailments?" She was referring not only to trachoma, for before leaving for Jerusalem she also complained of increasingly severe headaches. She wrote to Shmuel that they had reached "terrible proportions and have taken their toll of my strength. Very often I fall into despair. Will these illnesses never end?"

Dvorah and Moshe spent the early part of 1919 in Jerusalem. Moshe was admitted to Dr. Aryeh Feigenbaum's hospital, which comprised thirty beds and where patients were treated, for the most part, either free of charge or for a minimal fee. Dvorah entered the Rothschild Hospital, which had been donated by the famous family that year. The physician who examined her found that she was suffering from an inflammation of the kidneys, in addition to trachoma, and insisted that she be hospitalized for treatment. Dvorah agreed but went to Dr. Feigenbaum's hospital for treatment in order to be close to Moshe. "They tell me that Moussik misses me very much and wakes up at night crying, 'Where is my mother?'" Dr. Feigenbaum told Dvorah that Moshe's case was severe and would take some time to cure. But he offered her the consolation that an operation would not be necessary and the contracted eye would return to its normal size once the trachoma was cured. Meanwhile, the treatment he prescribed was daily massages of the eye with copper sulfate.

When Dvorah finally left the hospital, she began looking for work to support the two of them. But jobs were scarce in Jerusalem and she considered leaving Moshe and going to Jaffa to earn their living. The plan did not materialize, however, and she remained in Jerusalem, struggling to make ends meet. Shmuel sent food as often as possible and even managed one trip to Jerusalem. His letters to Dvorah were full of complaints about his weakness from malaria and his need for a rest. Even while she was still in the hospital he ceaselessly exhorted her to prepare herself for work in the fields and to study Hebrew "for Moshe, so that he won't surpass you in his knowledge." He urged her to recover quickly and "return to Degania with renewed strength." These letters became increasingly rhetorical and often sounded like Hapoel Hatzair convention resolutions. One of them ended as follows:

. . . My darling, sing to our dear Moshe songs of hope, for there is hope, my love! Let us not betray the vision, nor lack faith. Let us live in the great hope that lights the path of our nation and find strength together with the young people who have pitched their tents upon the final hope, in this our country that our hands shall conquer.

Dvorah and Moshe returned to Degania in the summer of 1919. Dvorah's eyes were completely cured, but Moshe's still required treatment. Apart from the warmth and love Dvorah bestowed upon him, Moshe derived another benefit from the constant, close contact with his mother: she told him many fascinating and instructive stories and even taught him the Hebrew alphabet while she learned it herself. By the age of four he could already read and write somewhat and had earned his father's praise for his handwriting.

When the war was over and life returned to normal, a controversy arose at Degania over whether the *kvutza* was a "settlement group" or a "conquest group"; in other words, whether the members should remain in Degania to develop the settlement on a permanent basis or leave this task to others and go on, as pioneers, to conquer the wilderness. Shmuel regarded Palestine as a desolate, uninhabited land. He saw about him only "weeds, thorns and thistles, wild grass, sands and marshes, rocks and stones." He considered the Arabs part of this wilderness, not unlike the mosquitoes, insects, and wild animals. As such, they were transitory. Just as the wild grasses and thorns would be burnt away and the marshes drained, so the starving, disease-ridden Bedouin tribes and land tenants would be dispersed.

In the discussions at Degania, Shmuel demanded that the *kvutza* leave the settlement to others and settle the 100,000 dunams of land in the Horan Mountains east of the Jordan, which belonged to Baron Edmond de Rothschild. This land fired the imagination of those who believed in the perpetual spirit of pioneering, "To be alone on the land and far from the cities, to be few among many thousands of Arabs and Bedouin, to lay the foundations for the future of the Yishuv," in Shmuel's words. He and his supporters backed their demand with the following reasoning: "Have we now completed our duty as pioneers? Can we now sit back like landlords in this large house and carry on our quiet work, while out there 100,000 dunams of land are lost to us forever?" Yoseph Bussel and Tanhum Tanpilov, two pillars of the commune, objected: "What is this talk of ownership, of profits, and a quiet life in this blazing valley that saps our strength with malaria and the constant danger of Bedouin attacks? We have staked a claim on this land. Here we shall take root and bring sons and daughters into the world."

This difference of opinion over the national duty of the *kvutza* was attended by another, even more bitter dispute about the group's way of life. The concept of collectivism, which lay at the very core of the *kvutza,* was questioned. In 1919 Eliezer Yaffe published an article in *Hapoel Hatzair* entitled "For the Establishment of Workers' Moshavim."* Yaffe had studied agriculture in America before immigrating to Palestine and belonged to what was known as the "American Commune," which had worked at Kinneret and other settlements in the Galilee. His article suggested that the moshav be composed of equal individual farms and be based upon two principles: national ownership of the land and independent labor (hired help would be forbidden).

That year the annual Hapoel Hatzair convention was to be held in June at the Kinneret farm. As the date drew near, opinions were sharply divided for and against the moshav. Its proponents, including Shmuel, claimed that the *kvutza* limited individual freedom, while the moshav was the best way to serve both personal and national needs. The defenders of the *kvutza* in Degania were astonished to find in their midst members who favored the moshav. The Hapoel Hatzair convention passed a resolution calling upon the party to take practical steps toward the establishment of a moshav, and The Organization for the Establishment of the First Moshav was founded. Shmuel, Israel Bloch, and several other members of Degania joined the new organization. After the convention Yoseph Bussel demanded that Shmuel and his companions be ousted from the *kvutza.* He claimed that "the existence in our midst of a group opposed to the *kvutza* prevents us from improving conditions on the farm."

Shmuel's departure from Degania was, in his own words, "attended by great pain." It was preceded by a long discussion with Dvorah, "whose doubts about leaving Degania were greater than my own." Soon afterward Dvorah wrote from Tel Aviv: "In Degania, Moshe and I felt happy and free . . . It was cold and it rained. Moussik does not have proper clothes, and his shoes are torn." By his own account, however, Shmuel felt a need to obey the inner voice that urged him to continue "the conquest," and "logic and long discussions were of no avail. Higher powers had decreed it."

The impression Shmuel left in Degania does not bear him out. Although not all of the members supported Bussel's proposal to expel Shmuel, he was nevertheless bitterly criticized by the veterans for the way he clashed with the leaders of the *kvutza.* Many held this against him for the rest of his life. So deep was their resentment that they publicly dissociated themselves from the book he wrote for

---

* Moshav, concept of settlement based on equal parcels of land divided between, and cultivated by, individual members who shared only marketing, water, and other services.

Degania's twenty-fifth anniversary celebrations and accused him of exploiting the occasion to enshrine his own memory. They also omitted his name from the official *Jubilee Book*. Obviously, the members of Degania regarded Shmuel's departure with something less than "great pain." Negative opinion about Shmuel's character, which was to follow him for the rest of his life, had already begun to crystallize. He was thought to be stubborn, cantankerous, egoistic, ambitious, and often insincere. Later on, he was even labeled a "Jesuit." His virtues, according to the members of Degania, were his intelligence, courage and tenacity of purpose. Dvorah, on the other hand, was remembered in Degania with deep affection. Her full name appeared in the *Jubilee Book* (others were listed only by their initials) and her contributions to communal education in the *kvutza* were described at length.

Shmuel gave the following description of their departure from Degania: "We left quietly and unobtrusively, with a few poor bundles, a pillow, and a cushion in our hands." Two and a half years were to pass before the establishment of Nahalal, the first moshav. Meanwhile, "excited and stimulated by the prospect of great deeds," Shmuel wandered across the country with his family. They settled first in Tel Aviv, but as Shmuel's missions on party affairs became more frequent, Dvorah sent Moshe to Miriam Baratz at Degania. When the Agricultural Committee of Hapoel Hatzair asked Shmuel to help prepare the land for a new *kvutza* near Degania—to be called Degania B—Moshe visited Degania every day and sometimes even slept there.

Before the main body of settlers arrived at Degania B, a group of twenty pioneers—mostly men—came to the site. They immediately began laying the foundations for the farm buildings and started work on the stable. Until the first house was completed, they all slept in a large British Army surplus tent, setting up their beds in two long crowded lines. By January 1920 the fields were sown and red tiles had been laid on the roof of the first house.

Every day, Moshe went to the kindergarten at Degania A. Together with the two Amiad sisters, Bat-Ami and Shlomit, he often rode to the kindergarten on the cart that left Degania B to draw water from the Jordan near Degania A. On days when the cart did not make the trip, the children walked the short distance. Bat-Ami, nine months older than Moshe, and Shlomit, two years his junior, were both afraid to walk along the path on their own. On either side they could see Arabs plowing the fields. As Moshe did not share the girls' timidity, it was his duty to accompany them and calm their fears. The two sisters kept close to their protector and felt secure in his presence, but Moshe loved to tease them. The moment they were out of sight of the adults, he would race down the path toward Degania A. The girls invariably burst into tears and ran for their lives, trying in vain to catch up with him.

Bat-Ami also remembers the time Moshe fell into the small pond in front of the kindergarten. The teacher asked him why he was so wet, and he replied curtly, "It's none of your business." Later he composed a ditty which he would recite with his two charges when he deigned to escort them to the kindergarten:

> Ha-ha-ha,
> On his way to the school,
> Our Moshe fell into a pool.
> How did he ever get into this mess?
> It's none of your business.

At Degania B, Shmuel directed the work, dug ditches, plowed the fields, and even found time to go out on missions for the party. Dvorah baked bread for the settlers and cooked their meals on a stove set up in the courtyard. "The first year at Degania B was a hard one," Shmuel wrote in his autobiography, "particularly for Dvorah, who also had to care for four-year-old Moshe. It was an abrupt change from the settled routine of Degania to a life of tents, huts, laundry, cooking on wood fires, and water brought in barrels from the Jordan." Sometimes Dvorah's weakness and susceptibility to illness exasperated him and led him to think of her as an obstacle in his path. A hint of the tension between them appears in a few passages of a letter Dvorah wrote to him, later included in his autobiography:

> The night is finally over, and as always the sharp pain has abated, but in my heart something aches without respite. I feel that I cause you nothing but sorrow and that you haven't known a single moment's happiness with me. I know I am wrong . . . but I cannot forget the expression on your face yesterday, which I read as saying: "You're never satisfied, always complaining. There will never be an end to it." And I began to wonder if there wasn't some truth in this. Then I thought that I give you only trouble.

Writing to Dvorah between Hapoel Hatzair meetings or in the offices of the Zionist Organization in Jaffa or Jerusalem, Shmuel again urged her to strengthen herself for work in the fields and to study Hebrew. Once she replied: "I summoned the last of my strength to finish my work. Moussik returned from Degania in the evening and I took him to our room. I washed and caressed him, lavishing love upon him, kissing each of his tiny fingers. We spoke of you all the time, and I so wanted us to have not only our Moussik, but other children. Moussik hugged me close and we fell asleep."

Moshe's earliest childhood memories are of the suffering caused him by the hot climate of the Jordan Valley, the dust blown up by the dry east wind, and the disease in his eyes. He remembers Degania of those days as clouds of eye-clogging dust which made breathing difficult. Among his greatest pleasures were the trips to Zemakh. With its railroad station, shops and stalls, and a population of a few thousand Arabs, the village seemed like a bustling city. Shmuel and Dvorah often treated him to iced lemonade, brightly colored sweets and *halva*. When there was no money for such delicacies, Moshe wandered through the streets of Zemakh "window-shopping." His most vivid recollection of this period is riding on a cart pulled by a wildly galloping horse and looking back at Degania B going up in flames. Two separate events seem to have merged in his memory, since the women and children of Degania B were evacuated to Degania A a day or two before the Arab attack on the settlement. As the two kibbutzim were only a kilometer apart, the children actually watched the flames from the relative safety of Degania A.

At the time there was a noticeable awakening of anti-Zionist Arab nationalism in Palestine. It was occasioned, among other things, by the Balfour Declaration of 1917,* the peace talks of 1919, the Anglo-French agreements on the division of the defunct Ottoman Empire, and the commencement of British civil rule in the country. One of the chief manifestations of this new movement was armed attacks on Jewish settlements in the Galilee.

From March 1920 Arabs began roaming the Galilee in large bands, mounted or on foot, raiding even Arab villages for loot. Later, when these bands of Bedouin were joined by Arab nationalists from the villages, the raids gradually became politically oriented. A major attack was planned for April 24, 1920 against an Indian contingent of the British Army bivouacked in Zemakh. Prior to the attack itself, rumors spread through the Jewish settlements that the Arabs were about to mount large-scale raids on the Jewish community in Tiberias and the settlements of the Jordan Valley. Degania B was particularly vulnerable as it was the newest of the kibbutzim in the area and contained only twenty men. Heeding the persistent rumors, the men began to prepare the defenses. Shmuel was appointed commander of the settlement and immediately began organizing the digging of trenches and preparation of bunkers. He applied to the British District Commissioner in Tiberias for additional weapons, only to be ordered to arrange for the evacuation of the settlement, since "large forces are planning an attack on Degania B."

Indeed, two days before the attack on Zemakh, Degania B came under heavy fire. Only then were the women and children evacuated to Degania A, while the men remained to defend the settlement, three

---

* In which His Majesty's Government viewed "with favour the establishment in Palestine of a National Home for the Jewish people."

to a trench. Shmuel had provided them with "clean rifles and an adequate supply of bullets" and ordered them to remain at their posts even if two of the three fell. The nearby settlement of Menahamiya had also been under attack for two days, and two of its members had been killed in the fighting. Only ten men remained to defend the settlement against further raids; the rest had fled west to Yavniel.

On the morning of April 24, the British authorities sent a machine-gun unit from the Indian contingent at Zemakh to reinforce the defenders of Menahamiya. Catching sight of the masses of Arabs galloping toward Zemakh, the Indian soldiers turned in their tracks and fled to their camp. The sight of the fleeing British unit greatly encouraged the attackers, who advanced steadily toward Degania B and Zemakh. They approached to within a few hundred meters of Degania B. Shmuel ordered his men into the trenches, enjoining them to fight to the last man. Later, however, he wrote: "The descent into the trenches was accompanied by serious misgivings on the part of the men." In Shmuel's account of the event, a former officer in the Czarist Army explained that it was impossible for fifteen soldiers to repulse so many troops. "His argument seemed logical to the men, and they began leaving the trenches." Shmuel had to decide between forcing the men to fight and calling a retreat. As the Arabs drew closer, his decision could no longer be delayed. He ordered a retreat.

As the last to leave the settlement, Shmuel described the final moment in Degania B:

I felt a desire to remain in the courtyard and shoot anyone who approached the house. Instead I ran to the tent, took out a tin of kerosene, poured its contents on the wall of the wooden building, and ignited it. I managed to jump on the black horse and ride away before the fire spread. I fired in the direction of the raiders, and my horse reared under me as I turned to face an Arab mounted on a white horse who had come up on me from behind. We finally lost each other in the sea of rupe wheat. It all happened at nine o'clock in the morning. Thus defeated in battle, I could not face the men. A fierce pain burned in me.

Shmuel's self-reproach was sharpened by the knowledge that ten men had saved Menahamiya by fighting back tenaciously and refusing to retreat or abandon their village, while Degania B went up in flames.

The British authorities estimated the Arab force attacking Zemakh at five thousand men, mounted and on foot. The Indian troops held their ground well. Then two RAF planes began bombing the attackers and the tide of the battle turned dramatically. The Arabs fled in panic, and the Indian cavalry went after the stragglers, driving the entire force far from Zemakh. It was this last minute reversal that saved Degania A.

In the evening, the men of Degania B returned to the smoking ruins of their home. They spent the night in Degania A and set up temporary quarters in the courtyard. As the Arab attacks continued sporadically for about a week, though considerably diminished in force, the men went out to harvest the fields in pairs, one standing guard while the other worked.

A year after the first group of settlers came to the farm, Shmuel turned Degania B over to Levi Eshkol. The members of the second Degania were no better disposed toward Shmuel than those of the first. They could no more forgive him his faults and made no mention of him in the official history of the settlement. In his autobiography, Shmuel deplored their attitude: "Neither in the Jubilee anthology, nor anywhere else [did they mention] the first group that laid the foundations. Why? Because of their desire to be regarded the sole founders? Or was it because the real founders later became members of moshavim?" This passage also illustrates how deep the conflict was, at least in Shmuel's mind, between the *kvutza* and the moshav.

In the summer of 1920, the Dayans moved to Tel Aviv to await the establishment of the first moshav. They lived in the basement of a house belonging to the poet Ya'akov Fichman. Dvorah found work in Hapoel Hatzair's Bureau for the Location of Relatives, tracing the whereabouts of new immigrants and delivering letters to them. Shmuel took on a number of positions but worked mainly on the Agricultural Committee of the party. On their way to work in the morning, they would leave Moshe in a nearby nursery. In the afternoons he remained alone in the basement flat until their return. Afraid that he might try to leave the house and wander about the city on his own, they always locked the doors and windows when they left. They had reason to fear, for Moshe was fond of neither the city nor the nursery. One day he broke all the windows in the flat in an unsuccessful effort to escape. Shmuel punished him with a slap, but afterward took the precaution of having iron bars placed on every one of the windows.

The family spent little time together. Shmuel was frequently away from home on party affairs, devoting much of his time to the organization of the first moshav. In 1920 he left Palestine for Kishinev to visit his parents, who had fled Zaskow during the pogroms that followed the civil war in Russia. Shmuel remained in Eastern Europe even after his parents immigrated to Palestine. The elderly couple appealed to Dvorah to urge his return, but despite their pleas Shmuel did not hurry back. On his return, he stopped in Constantinople to visit groups of pioneers on their way to Palestine and help "prepare them for their new life in the country." He even planned to extend his mission and go to Russia to "inculcate the Hapoel Hatzair spirit in the thousands of Jews languishing there with no news of the land of hope," but the trip did not materialize.

By Shmuel's own account, Dvorah and Moshe were left behind with hardly a penny. She did not even have enough money to pay the fare from Tel Aviv to Ein Gannim or Nahalat Yehudah in order to visit Shmuel's parents. "It's difficult not having a place of my own," she wrote to Shmuel, "but what could I do? When you left I could not bear to remain in the basement any longer." First she sent Moshe back to Degania and a short time later she left her few belongings in Fichman's house and joined him there. Before his trip, Shmuel had apparently contemplated becoming a full-time party worker and moving to Tel Aviv permanently. Dvorah implied as much in a letter written from Degania: "In the fields and among the trees, it is so much easier than among the stones of Tel Aviv . . . My darling, we cannot remain in the city, we cannot." Of the two, Dvorah seems to have become more attached to village life.

Shmuel returned in April 1921 and joined the teams of road builders on the Haifa-Jedda road. He immediately became involved in the organization of Nahalal and made trips to the British Army base of Sarafend, near Tel Aviv, to buy surplus supplies. Moshe stayed with the Baratz family in Degania until the summer of 1921. Dvorah joined Shmuel at the road builders' camp, but decided to leave as soon as she received word that her parents were on their way to Palestine. She refused "to accept the notion that [her parents'] first home in Palestine would be a road." She traveled with Moshe to Haifa and found a house there. "It was a special arrangement," she wrote. "A friend of mine who taught in a school in Haifa gave us permission to use the school building during the summer vacation. It was a large, old, Arab building, and we had to create an illusion of a 'home' in order to receive my parents there. Despite the joy of the reunion, those were hard times." To add to the difficulties of caring for her parents, Moshe suffered a relapse of malaria.

Yom Kippur [the Day of Atonement] arrived. Worshipers used the school as a synagogue . . . The sounds of prayer filtered through to our room. My heart was bitter, and my prayer different from theirs. I decided to check his temperature once more, then take the child and move out of the building that same day. And that is what we did. The child was weak and pale but did not have fever. We decided to leave immediately. We were ashamed lest the men at prayer see us pass with our bundles, [so] we lowered them from one of the windows, mother and father each gave a hand to the child, and we bid Haifa farewell.

It was therefore on the Day of Atonement that their life in Nahalal began.

3   NAHALAL (1920-1925)

"A bright, light-filled period began for me when we moved to Nahalal. There was no dust, no dry winds, and even my eyes improved slightly," said Dayan, recalling his childhood. It was also at Nahalal that the family's wanderings finally came to an end. But this is Nahalal seen in retrospect. In the autumn of 1921, the proposed lands for the moshav looked like a wasteland. The Organization for the Establishment of the First Moshav sent three of its members to survey the area in the foothills of the Nazareth mountains, near the Arab village of Ma'alul. The latter was identified as the Mahalul mentioned in the Jerusalem Talmud and the biblical Nahalal of the books of Joshua and Judges.

Arriving at the spot, Shmuel and his two companions were greeted by "an expanse of land completely submerged in water. The water covered the land with no outlet. A kind of crust covered the entire area, and mosquitoes buzzed in the air. Arab shepherds drawing water from a well with ropes and pails filled the nearby clay and wooden troughs to water their sheep. I stand there among the milling sheep, contemplating the marsh. Should we not drain it?" From the Nazareth road, it was 2 kilometers along a muddy path to the lands allotted them. "We lose our boots in the mud and the mule sinks under its burden."

Shmuel later gave a picturesque description of their encounter with Ma'alul-Mahalul-Nahalal:

On our way we met one of the local inhabitants, an old man.
"Granddad, what are those ruins?"
"An abandoned village."
"What kind of village was it?"
"A German one."
"And where are its inhabitants?"
"Dead."
"Do you remember the village?"
"It all happened in my childhood."
"And since then no one has come to settle here?"
"There was a second village after the first, an Arab village."
"Where is it?"
"Abandoned, too."
"And the people, where are they?"
"Dead, all dead," he replied, turning to leave.
"Why is it impossible to live in this place?"

"Bad spirits and bad water. He who drinks of these waters, his belly swells and he dies within three days."

With the old man's words echoing ominously in their ears, the three continued on their way, asking themselves, "If two settlements died here, why should the fate of the third—ours—be any different from the first two?"

After extensive bargaining with the Arab landowners over a number of years, the JNF finally purchased lands in the Jezreel Valley, trying wherever possible to ease the pain of displacement for the Arab tenants. It bought the lands of Mahalul and the vicinity from the wealthy Sursuk family of Lebanon. According to the terms of purchase, the Arabs of Mahalul—who retained some of the land in the area—were cut off from their traditional sources of water. The JNF therefore agreed "to give the fellaheen a strip of land 700 meters wide between the road and [the spring of] Ein Beida. Water for their cattle and sheep will be supplied to the Arabs by pipes from the two springs, Ein Beida and Ein Madura." A third spring, Ein Sheikha, also became the sole possession of the JNF, but no arrangement was made to share its water with the local Arabs.

While arrangements were made to give the villagers of Mahalul access to water sources, no such arrangement was made with the Bedouin tribe of Arab el-Mazarib, nomadic shepherds who grazed their flocks without regard for boundaries and lived on sheep raising and their talent for theft. In time, however, both the agreement with Mahalul and the absence of such an agreement with the Arab el-Mazarib tribe resulted in endless friction between the local Arabs and the settlers of Nahalal.

The Twelfth Zionist Congress, held at Karlsbad in September 1921, had on its agenda approval of a budget for the establishment of Nahalal. On behalf of the future moshav, Eliezer Yaffe requested 37,500 Egyptian pounds for a village comprising eighty families, and he asked for half this amount immediately. There was little money in the treasury of the Zionist Organization, however, and some delegates were opposed in principle to the concept of a moshav. The Congress approved only 32,000 Egyptian pounds to be provided from the beginning of the following fiscal year. In the end, even this amount was not transferred in full to the new moshav. On November 16 Yaffe wrote to his fellow-settlers of the Congress's disappointing decision and suggested that they nonetheless "settle in Mahalul as soon as possible."

The members of The Organization for the Establishment of the First Moshav were scattered throughout Palestine and were by this time weary of uncertainty and their seemingly endless state of transition. They decided to settle Nahalal at once, despite the budget question. A group of seven men spent the night of Saturday, September 10, 1921, near the place where Nahalal was to be established. To protect themselves against possible attack, they pitched their tents at the foot of Samunia Hill (later known as Shimron Hill), did not light fires, and discussed their plans for the following day in whispers. The next morning they cleaned the hill of layers of sheep dung and pitched their tents on the top. Later on September 11, 1921, the date that had been set for the establishment of the moshav, they saw a convoy of carts bearing the first settlers of Nahalal. The twenty men gathered there began cutting down reeds, surveying, clearing the area, and bringing water from the springs and bread from Haifa.

Shmuel was in the first group of seven that came to Mahalul. Ten days later he brought Dvorah and Moshe from Haifa. They took the train to Tel Shmam (now Kfar Yehoshua) and from there, carrying their bundles, walked to Shimron Hill. From afar, it looked like an army camp: two large tents and seven smaller ones, all the equipment, and even the settlers' clothes had been purchased from British Army surplus.

When Moshe came to "Conquest Hill," as the site of settlement was called, there were twenty-six adults there. The families lived in the small tents. One of the larger tents housed the kitchen and dining room in one half and an office and "clubhouse" in the other; the second large tent was used as a stable for the horses and the Indian mules. Each family tent contained two beds and an upturned barrel that served as a table. Moshe was the only child in the camp, apart from a baby girl who was born in one of the tents. For amusement he would walk alone to the Nazareth road and watch the few cars that passed or climb to the top of the hill and look out over the valley. When additional families joined the settlement, Moshe ceased to be the only child. All his friends were the children of pioneers whose lives had followed a pattern similar to the Dayans'.

As the area was still infested with typhus and malaria, there were settlers who felt that the women and children should be brought only to a permanent settlement and not to the makeshift camp at Conquest Hill. As winter approached, they added to their arguments the hardships of spending the winter on the bare hill, open to wind, rain, and frost; and when the first winter rains came the lands around Nahalal turned into a sea of mud. They further strengthened their case by pointing out the danger of possible Arab attacks. Yet those who claimed that Nahalal was their home and could not fully be so without the women and children finally swung the decision in their favor. Israel Bloch, the spokesman of this group, claimed that the families should share their fate in all things. In any case, he said, if the families separated for reasons of security, the break might well last forever. The issue was finally resolvèd quite suddenly. In the words of one of the first women settlers:

On Thursday I came to Nahalal with the children, and on Friday we awoke to the sounds of shots. I hid with the children under the bed. As soon as the shooting was over, a very agitated Eliezer Yaffe entered our tent and said that under these circumstances the children and I could not remain any longer. The following day the situation was discussed and it was decided to take us to Nazareth.

Strange as it may seem in retrospect, the Arab city of Nazareth served as a haven for the families of Nahalal. Arab nationalism was still in its infancy, and there was scant cooperation between the city Arabs, the Bedouin, and the fellaheen, all of whom were often at odds with each other. In contrast to the Bedouin, the villagers of Mahalul and Majdal accepted the settlers of Nahalal with indifference. When they realized that the new Jewish settlements would bring them profit (the settlers bought goods in the Arab shops and milled their grain at Majdal), they even tended to cooperate with their new neighbors. The willingness to cooperate was even greater among the notables, landowners, and merchants of Nazareth. For the women and children of Nahalal, the city had other advantages that recommended it as a refuge. First of all, it was the seat of the district government, and its security forces were under the command of British officers. Secondly, the majority of its inhabitants were Christians, and the city was only a two-hour walk from Nahalal. "Our meeting with the Arabs of Nazareth was very cordial," Dvorah wrote. "They tried to help us find flats and proved extremely friendly." Unlike Dvorah, who experienced Arab cordiality at first hand, Shmuel regarded the women and children as "prisoners among Arabs."

A few days before November 2 (Balfour Day), half of the men of Nahalal went to Nazareth to protect the women and children in the event of disturbances, while the other half remained in Nahalal to defend the camp. Their fears were soon dispelled, however. The Arabs attacked neither the men at Nahalal nor their families in Nazareth. In fact, it was not until 1934 that blood was shed in conflicts between the settlers of Nahalal and their Arab neighbors.

The fifteen children and their mothers remained in Nazareth for eight months. Time dragged interminably, for they lived in constant tension. Every day, accompanied by Dvorah, Moshe went to the municipal clinic for "treatment with the blue stone," and in those eight months in Nazareth the last traces of trachoma finally disappeared. A kindergarten and first grade were organized. The teacher "locked herself up with the children" and devoted considerable time and talent to her work. Accompanied by some of the other women, she took them on frequent outings around the city, and Moshe discovered a new world—a large Arab city, the bustle of large crowds, high stone churches, and the constant sound of bells. " . . . He's so big now," Dvorah wrote to Shmuel, "and I sometimes feel he does not need me any more. I long for the days when Moussik was young and needed me so much." (Dvorah now wrote to Shmuel in Hebrew, telling him that she "no longer wished to write in Russian.")

Moshe's first year of formal education began in Nazareth. He displayed a flair for drawing, and while his friends—both older and younger than he—were still learning the alphabet, he could read and write with ease. His adjustment to life within a social framework, however, was ambivalent. His friends noticed that he tried and genuinely wished to be part of the group, but at the same time he tended to be withdrawn and self-enclosed. When Moshe did not care for a game, he would suggest another, but would eventually join in once play had begun. "Even in matters that did not suit his temperament or were not to his liking, he joined the rest. Whatever game was played, he took part; he never stayed out of a game." Moshe often proposed picking a fight with the Arab children who taunted the Nahalal children as they walked about the town in pairs. "Moshe was never afraid to start fights with Arab children, even those older than himself," recalls his cousin Shulamit.

Two months after their arrival, the settlers of Nahalal came down from Conquest Hill and established their permanent settlement on a low hill in the center of their lands. In reply to a letter from Moshe begging to be allowed to return to Nahalal, Shmuel wrote:

My dear child,
    I greatly desire to speak to you, to watch you studying, to have you follow me behind the plow. But this cannot be at the moment. We will not be able to build a house for ourselves in Nahalal until the summer, so for the present you will have to remain in Nazareth. Write to me of your life at school, and I shall tell you of my life here. This morning, I walked behind the plow with the knowledge that this land was being plowed for the first time in its history with a European plow, and that is what made the plowing difficult. And when was this land plowed by Jews? A great many years ago. Do you know how much one hundred is? Twenty times one hundred years ago, that is two thousand years ago, the Jews were driven out of this land and went into exile. Since then they have not dared to return to our country, and it is only during the past one hundred years that Jews in different parts of the Diaspora have begun to think about rebuilding the ruins of this land. They began to understand that we must, before all else, return to work the land in Palestine.
    When I was your age and learned about the towns and villages of the Jezreel Valley, I never dreamed that I would one day settle in one of these towns. I yearned to be in the land to which Moses brought the Jews but which he himself could not enter. I yearned for this land, to conquer it

once again; and when I grew up and reached the age of seventeen, I came to this land. And here we slowly began to conquer the soil, not by war but by plowing and hard work. We have plowed the border between the Arabs of the village and ourselves. We plow within our borders and they within theirs, and thus the land will remain ours. When you grow up we shall work the land together and never leave it. If all the Jews and their children do so all over the country, it will surely be ours once again and forever.

Warm kisses to you, my dear child,

Yours,
Father

Shmuel, like other early pioneers, tended to give an ideological lecture when asked to tell the story of his life. Thus from his earliest childhood, Moshe was raised on the teachings of Zionism and its historical justification.

While the lands of Nahalal were being prepared for cultivation, the settlers were regarded as hired hands of the landowner, the JNF, and received a daily wage which had to suffice for their families as well. Maintaining two households—in Nazareth and in Nahalal—rapidly ate up their meager salaries. Like others at Nahalal, Shmuel visited Nazareth every Saturday and sometimes in the middle of the week. Whenever he could, he came by cart, bringing a sack of coal, a sack of potatoes and, if there were a few pennies left over, a sack of white flour. He returned to Nahalal with the clothes that Dvorah had washed and ironed for him.

Dvorah's burden of separation and lack of money were aggravated by pains in her leg. She wrote to Shmuel: "I am consumed by the need to be strong, to overcome the scarcity of everything," and "I'm so sick and tired of being ill." She began to fear that the hardships and her perpetual illnesses would lead to her end: " . . . The thought of death does not frighten me, but what of you, and Moussik? I cannot go near my little child without tears in my eyes." Dvorah did not go to Haifa to have her leg treated. She had come to Nazareth pregnant and was trying to save every penny for the birth and the baby. She did not yet know where she would give birth. For routine examinations she went to a mission hospital in Nazareth and was treated by a French-Arab doctor who communicated with her in Russian and treated her devotedly. One day he showed her the room he had prepared for the birth in the small hospital, and Dvorah almost consented to have the child in Nazareth. "Suddenly I looked about me," she later wrote, "and saw a picture of Jesus Christ over the bed intended for me. I was engulfed by a sense of alienation. I left the doctor that day knowing I would never return to him."

As she neared the end of her pregnancy, Dvorah asked Shmuel to borrow the three pounds she needed for the journey to Haifa. No one in the camp at Nahalal had that amount to spare, and she had to ask her brother in Haifa to fetch her by cart. Packing for the trip, she carefully included the bundle of clothes she had washed and ironed for Shmuel. They had agreed to meet on the Nazareth-Haifa road so that Shmuel could see Dvorah on her way and take Moshe back to Nahalal. Shmuel arrived at the meeting place early and lay down to rest by the roadside. His working day began at 4:30 and continued until the hay had been brought into the stable for the night. In the evenings, he turned to the affairs of the new moshav and the party. He often fell asleep in the leaking tent fully clothed. When Shmuel awoke from his nap, Dvorah's cart had already passed on its way to Haifa. He returned to the camp "in despair," not knowing whether Moshe had gone to Haifa with Dvorah or returned to Nazareth on his own. To his joy, he saw a familiar figure approaching from the direction of Shimron Hill, his six-year-old son. Dvorah was certain that Shmuel was delayed and asked Moshe to wait for him. Unaware that his father was sleeping soundly a little further down the road, Moshe waited patiently. With darkness approaching rapidly and no sign of Shmuel, he set off in the direction of the camp. Shmuel made up a bed for him in the tent and later wrote to Dvorah: "He sleeps with me and we are both enjoying ourselves." Moshe went out to the fields with his father, kicking up the freshly turned earth in the furrows. Soon after, he returned to Nazareth, where Dvorah's mother, who had come from Haifa, looked after him.

In Haifa, Dvorah's expectations soon gave way to disappointment. First she learned that her pregnancy was not as advanced as she and the Nazareth doctor had thought. Then she discovered that there was no room for her at the small Haifa maternity hospital. She was told to return in a week, when it might be possible to add her name to the waiting list. She nonetheless decided to remain in Haifa with her brother and registered with a midwife. Shmuel sent her food and suggested that she remain in Haifa for at least a month after the birth, to rest and recover her strength, " . . . and then, if all goes well, we'll build a hut and settle down with the children."

On February 21, 1922 Dvorah gave birth to a daughter, Aviva. Complications that developed after the birth forced her to remain in bed. She was beset by guilt for remaining in bed while the members of Nahalal struggled on the land. Shmuel found it difficult to visit Dvorah in Haifa, and as her illness lingered his visits became less frequent. He did not forgo his party work, however, and traveled to Jerusalem to participate in a meeting of the Hapoel Hatzair delegation to the Elected Assembly. He too was troubled by a guilty conscience and wrote to Dvorah that he had intended to visit her but could not find "the few pennies necessary, because there is no money in the entire camp."

At Passover the women and children returned to Nahalal, this time for good. Dvorah arrived soon afterward with her infant daughter, but she had not fully recovered and conditions in Nahalal made convalescence impossible. As their hut was not yet built, the four Dayans crowded into the small tent. During the cold nights Dvorah was unable to sleep and often got up to cover the baby. As she described those days in the tent: "Bathing the baby is particularly difficult. If I close the flaps it becomes unbearably stuffy and I am covered with perspiration. If I leave them open, a strong wind blows through the tent. By the time I finish washing and feeding the baby, my legs are weak, my back aches, and my head is spinning."

She began running a fever, and the doctor who was called in from Haifa diagnosed an infection of the breast and the beginning of an abscess. There was no choice but to take her to a hospital in Jerusalem and then to the rest home in Motza, on the outskirts of the city. When she returned to Nahalal, she appeared to have regained her health, but the abscess continued to grow and in 1924 she underwent a second operation in Jerusalem. From then on, Dvorah was never to be completely healthy again.

When she returned to Nahalal in the summer of 1922, Dvorah found the beginnings of a farm: field crops, a vineyard, and a vegetable garden. Shmuel had first sown broad beans, then wheat and hay. Next to the tent he erected a stable for their animals: two mules, a young cow with swollen udders about to calve, another young cow (also with calf), and a calf. There was also a nursery, which supplied beetroot for fodder. After a short time, the family moved into a wooden hut built near the stable. It enabled them to guard the livestock and left room on their plot for the stone house they would eventually build. In this temporary dwelling, the family lived in somewhat close proximity to the animals. The hut was built in stages, beginning with the kitchen and one room, then another room and a porch. When Moshe was eight years old a cubicle was added on for him. This last addition was unusual for Nahalal and was made upon Dvorah's insistence; it remained Moshe's room until his wedding. Chickens had free run of the house and laid eggs in every reasonably comfortable corner, while turkeys gobbled under the beds. Dvorah was nonetheless particular about the appearance of her house, decorating it with tablecloths and curtains made of simple fabrics. She took great pride in the flowers planted in neat beds outside the hut. Outside Moshe's room she planted a rose bush which slowly wound around his window.

The farm was based on field crops. Each settler in Nahalal was given 80 dunams of land, divided into four 20-dunam plots in different parts of the moshav's lands. The plots were divided according to the quality of the land and their distance from each settler's house. A four-year cycle of crop rotation was instituted: wheat, barley, corn, and hay. It was only after 1935 that mechanized farming was introduced into Nahalal. Until then the fields were plowed with oxen and mules. Like the other settlers, Shmuel took his son out to the fields with him. At first he was taken aback by the child's reaction to his work. He often referred to it as an example of "Moshe's pessimism." Moshe sat by the cart watching his father plow. Each time Shmuel came near, he called out, "What are you plowing for? Nothing will ever grow here!" Shmuel replied, "What do you mean? Of course we will grow things here!" And the next time Shmuel approached the cart, Moshe called out again, "Father, why are you working so hard?" The boy persisted in his nagging until Shmuel angrily sent him home.

Despite this pessimism, Moshe eventually joined his father in believing that the fields would bear fruit. He helped Shmuel by preparing seeds for sowing and being generally cooperative. Shmuel brought his grain to be milled in the Arab village of Majdal, and trips to the mill became pleasure jaunts for Moshe. While his father haggled with the miller, Moshe waited in the cart, whip in hand, guarding the load from the village urchins. Afterward he helped his father load sacks of flour and groats onto the cart, and toward sundown the two would return home.

On these trips to Majdal and Mahalul, Moshe met the children of Nahalal's Arab neighbors. Shmuel explained that the villagers were, for the most part, tenants and hired laborers whose working conditions were highly primitive and to whom "this land is a source of slavery and suffering." He stressed the wretchedness of the Arab village so as to highlight the superiority of Nahalal.

Shmuel's lectures, however, achieved the opposite of their aim. Instead of hating the Arabs and being permanently prejudiced against them, Moshe took pity on them. In his first years at school, he often sketched the bent bodies and wind-scarred faces of the sharecroppers as they worked behind the simple plows on their pitiful lands. Moshe did not condemn them for their wretchedness, but admired them for their endurance, perseverance, and ability to subsist on the barest necessities. He often met Arab and Bedouin children in the fields. They had never seen a European plow and stared with amazement at the pairs of mules that Jews used for their plowing. One of the Bedouin children who came more often than any other was Wahash Hanhana, one of the Arab el-Mazarib camped in black tents at the foot of Shimron Hill. Wahash, who was two years older than Moshe, found it difficult to believe that a mere boy could handle the amazing new plow. He would stand by the field where Moshe was working and gradually draw near. Once he asked Moshe to let him try holding the plow, and Moshe agreed. While Shmuel rested in the shade of the cart, Moshe and Wahash plowed the field together, one holding the reins, the other guiding the plow. His visits to Moshe and Shmuel became more frequent, and soon he was a regular guest both behind the plow and at the simple meals they ate near the cart. This was the beginning of a friendship between the two boys.

In Nahalal, Shmuel was once again torn by conflict. For two years he worked virtually alone to build up and consolidate the farmstead. He was the first to build a chicken coop and planted larger vegetable plots than any of the other settlers. Yet he still burned with the ambition to become a public figure. A short while before Passover in 1924, while awaiting her second operation, Dvorah wrote to Shmuel and tried to delay him from giving his "explosive pressures" the desired outlet by going to Jerusalem on a party mission. In those days it was considered bad form to assume public positions of one's own free will, for there was no higher, more exalted calling than to guide a plow through the fields. The party functionaries were at pains to project the image of men sentenced to forced labor. Shmuel offered Dvorah the excuse that he eventually bowed to the relentless pressure of Hapoel Hatzair, and as soon as she returned to Nahalal in the summer of 1924 he left for the party offices in Jerusalem, even though he was well aware that the burden of the farm was a heavy one, especially for his wife. He dwelt upon his guilty conscience, offering it to Dvorah as compensation for her suffering:

> . . . I listen to the yearning of my heart, questioning again and again, grieving over the hardships of our life. Where does deliverance lie? How easy life is here in Jerusalem by comparison! Those who live in the city squander their money, for they earn easily and their lives are easy. Do they not realize that they remain uncreative, that without pioneering life has no value? At midnight I finally went to sleep in a single bed, with a strange man, in a remote corner of town. He left in the morning. At night I dreamed I was standing near our cow Humma and how she sighed . . . My heart longs for you, my darlings. I am reminded of the hardships of your life, the burden of work you must bear, and the empty pockets. Here the party treasury is empty. I received a few pennies in coupons for my expenses.

Shmuel's party mission in Jerusalem appears to have established the pattern of his relationship with Dvorah in the years that followed. It became increasingly clear that nothing could stand in the way of his political aspirations—neither the needs of a struggling farm, nor a sickly wife and young children. The only consolation he offered Dvorah were his pangs of conscience. In a letter dated August 17, 1924 he wrote:

... Naturally I must first of all return to the farm and ease your heavy burden, but at the moment I cannot get away. I have no peace, and I am as a mourner among the revelers. It is strange, but I also find satisfaction in the fact that things here are not easy for me: self-castigation, pleasure in torment, walking about harassed, ill-dressed, and sleeping in the rooms of strangers. I think of the want at home and see the waste here. It cuts deep into my soul.

Shmuel had found a formula: in confessing his guilt, he rid himself of it and felt purged and vindicated.

A great deed performed in the service of the nation has been known to atone for injustice rendered to a family. Seeking just such an extraordinary deed, Shmuel revived his notion of settling the Rothschild lands on the Horan plateau in Transjordan. He raised the idea and defended it heatedly at the Jerusalem branch of Hapoel Hatzair, demanding that a group of settlers be sent to the Horan as soon as possible. The party appointed a special committee to examine the practical aspects of the idea and organized a survey mission to the Horan, which Shmuel headed. The committee then met with the directors of ICA and tried to win them over to their idea, but with little success. Finally, Shmuel composed a memorandum in the name of the Hapoel Hatzair Party and submitted it to members of the World Zionist Executive. When Dr. Chaim Weizmann visited Nahalal, Shmuel tried to persuade him to support the scheme, but Weizmann seemed skeptical, as the entire concept of settling the Horan was too complicated politically. However, Weizmann did promise to study Shmuel's plans and give them further thought. On September 26, 1924, when they met again, Weizmann tried to withdraw from the situation by suggesting that Shmuel go to Paris to present his idea to the Baron himself.

Shmuel had to wait some time before a meeting could be arranged with Baron de Rothschild. He returned to Nahalal, but regarded it merely as a base from which to leave on his various sorties. His attitude developed into a pattern which was to endure for many years. Suddenly his luck changed: he was to go abroad and see Baron de Rothschild in person.

Shmuel left for Europe in the middle of August 1925. In Vienna he met Dr. Chaim Weizmann again and was given a noncommittal letter of introduction to the Baron. But the Baron, or perhaps his secretary, read between the lines of Weizmann's note, and on their way to Paris, Shmuel and another member of the original mission were informed that the Baron was ill, out of town, and receiving no one. Nevertheless, Shmuel remained in Europe on behalf of the JNF and did not return to Nahalal until April 1926—a full nine months after his departure—by which time Dvorah had already given birth to their third child and second son, Zohar.

Now and then Shmuel considered leaving the moshav and settling in the city. Just before his trip to Europe, he was offered a position in the Agricultural Center of the Histadrut* in Tel Aviv. He wrote to Dvorah: " . . . Among my greatest doubts is the question of Moshe. How will he be brought up in a city? It really frightens me . . . to move him and ourselves into the city for a year or two." While he rejected the idea of moving his family to Tel Aviv, he did not abandon the notion of working there himself. On his way to Vienna in August 1925, he warned Dvorah that the question of working in the Agricultural Center would become acute upon his return: " . . . I do not want to go, but am obliged to. I know duty will prevail." He entertained no illusions about the hardships the family would have to endure, but after three months in Europe his plans changed. On November 1, 1925 he wrote to Dvorah from Warsaw that news of Zion was not reaching the Jewish people in the Diaspora and that everyone he met told him, "Surely you will not be content with only a few months of JNF work before disappearing once again." In short, it had been suggested that he extend his mission to Poland on behalf of the party for at least another year. "I haven't agreed," he wrote, "but they give me no peace."

Initially, Dvorah reconciled herself to Shmuel's mission as an ordeal she must endure for the sake of the nation. But soon after his departure she learned that she was pregnant. She informed Shmuel of her state, but refrained from asking him to cut his trip short. A crippled relative helped her with the housework and a hired hand helped with the farm chores. To some extent ten-year-old Moshe also helped on the farm. But Dvorah's pregnancy weakened her, and she was in dire financial straits.

Gradually, her descriptions of the state of the farm and family became more pointed. The tomatoes and eggplants were rotting in the fields and the hired hand left. Swallowing her pride, Dvorah applied to the village committee and requested "mutual aid," which meant receiving help from one of the men of the moshav. "I left the committee meeting with a heavy heart," she wrote to Shmuel. "From afar I could hear Viva weeping. She was wandering about the dark courtyard crying, 'Where's Mother? Where's Father?' I pitied our little one so. We slept together in the same bed. Viva fell asleep next to me with a smile on her face; I was in tears."

Dvorah borrowed money for seeds and medicines and wrote Shmuel that she had no idea how she would be able to repay all the debts. She was unable to sell the ton and a half of grain that remained in the loft or the hay. Her work day gradually lengthened, beginning at 4 a.m. with the first milking and ending at nine in the evening. De-

---

* General Federation of Labor, founded in 1920.

spite the long hours, however, she was unable to cope with all the work. She suffered from recurrent headaches and constant fatigue, and since her first hints to Shmuel failed to bring him home, she became more explicit. In a letter dated October 25, she wrote that the winter was setting in and she had no clothes for the children, adding, "Without you, the children feel like orphans." Their letters crossed, and she received a letter written from Grodno on October 16 which turned out to be an unintentionally ironic reply to her own: " . . . In half an hour, I shall be standing before an audience of a thousand people in the municipal theater and I shall speak once again. In the morning I shall be speaking at the large synagogue . . . in the afternoon before members of Hehalutz and Hapoel Hatzair and in the evening . . . "

At first, Moshe was pleased with the honor his father's trip brought the family and eagerly anticipated his gifts. He wrote to Shmuel reporting his activities and news of the farm. In one of his letters he describes going to synagogue with his mother and sister on the Day of Atonement: "I prayed from a prayer book and fasted for half a day." Among the gifts Shmuel sent was a box of carpenter's tools and a finely bound book of Psalms. "I received your presents with great pleasure," Moshe wrote, "and a few days later I had already completed a chair and a sofa for Aviva's dolls. And how nice the book of Psalms is! Every evening I sit down and read from it." He also sent his father a copy of an essay written for the children's newspaper. It was not the only piece he contributed to the paper, but it was the only one he sent his father because "You shall read the rest when you come home, and I hope you'll come home soon."

Moshe felt his father's absence keenly and was even more sensitive to his mother's hardships. He also began hinting to Shmuel that it was about time he returned. In September he wrote: " . . . I just came back from watering the trees. I ate supper and read the book about Bar-Kokhba.* You are now on your way to France, and I can't imagine how we can stay here on our own for five months." As Shmuel prolonged his stay in Europe, Moshe's hints also became more unreserved. In November 1925 he wrote: "Hanukkah is approaching, and I'm sure you will send us something, but it will not take your place. A holiday without a father is not a holiday."

Moshe was then in the fifth grade at primary school and at the suggestion of his teacher had begun keeping a diary. During his father's absence, the boy's handwriting became perceptibly smaller and he made many more spelling mistakes than usual. The entry for Thursday, November 3, 1925, contains many such mistakes, as well as a number of sentences that have no apparent connection with those

---

* Leader of the Second Jewish Revolt against Rome, AD 132-135.

immediately preceding or following them: " . . . I received a book from Father. When I remember him—my nice father—how we used to play together in the mornings, how he would explain difficult verses in the Bible for me, how he taught me to plow, how he would read books to me, how he would correct my mistakes, and how, and how . . . "

When Dvorah received Shmuel's letter stating his intention to remain in Europe for another year and suggesting that she and the children join him, she could no longer contain herself. On November 2, the anniversary of the Balfour Declaration, she expressed her feelings quite clearly: "Writing to you on November 2, I hope that your visa has expired and that you will be forced to leave Poland and perhaps, perhaps, finally come home"—fine sarcasm, implying that perhaps only the Balfour Declaration and the related return to Zion could induce her husband to return from the Diaspora. Dvorah rejected out of hand Shmuel's plan for them to live in Europe.

Still, Shmuel did not hasten home. He spent the month of December in Warsaw, while one of the cows died, its calf was slaughtered for meat, and the second cow began feeding from her own udders because Dvorah had no money to buy fodder. Moshe contracted malaria, and once the rains came Dvorah continued working in the muddy, damp garden. "It is extremely difficult for me to bend down now, and my feet hurt especially. I must have hot baths, but I cannot prepare them alone," she wrote as she neared her ninth month of pregnancy. To relieve her suffering, Shmuel again suggested that she come to Europe for a year, but Dvorah again refused. Shmuel then wrote, " . . . Perhaps you will also understand that it isn't necessary to work all the time," suggesting that she work less and rest more. Ironically enough, at about the time this letter was received, Dvorah was expecting the hatching of 450 eggs in the chicken coop, but most of them were spoiled because she and Moshe were unable to maintain a constant watch by the incubator. Shmuel did not return home for Passover and he was still in Europe on April 8, 1926, when his son Zohar was born, and on May 4, when the child was circumcised.

By this time, Dvorah realized that she had no choice but to support Shmuel's political ambitions, and the only way to do so was by strengthening the family's position in Nahalal. When Dvorah embarked upon her marriage, she probably envisioned Shmuel as a laborer, rooted in the soil and shouldering the burden of agricultural work, while she—with her love of literature and natural inclination toward self-expression—would be a devoted wife and mother. But the opposite turned out to be the case. By the time Shmuel returned to Palestine in the summer of 1926, it was clear that Dvorah—

the delicate, fragile woman who had been so attracted to the world of the spirit and the intellect, the young girl whom Shmuel had constantly urged to prepare herself for the physical rigors of life on the land—now carried the entire burden of the farm on her own shoulders. The young woman who dreamed of doing something "extraordinarily great" and wanted to "see the world" was now the farmer deeply bound to the land, while Shmuel was the one involved in affairs of the mind. Many of their friends were surprised by this reversal of roles. Leading figures in the Labor movement considered Dvorah a far more gifted and impressive personality than Shmuel. Zalman Aranne once remarked that Dvorah's relation to Shmuel was like a "poem that found its way into a book of arithmetic exercises." Miriam Baratz insisted that Dvorah would have left Shmuel had they remained on the kibbutz, and only the family's constant wanderings and the precarious conditions of their life in Nahalal prevented a divorce.

Whether still bound to Shmuel by love or guided by wisdom alone, Dvorah became resigned to the fact that her family's happiness depended on her firmly supporting Shmuel in his public life. To achieve this, she willingly denied her own ambitions and suppressed her talents. It was only in 1929 that she began publishing short sketches in *Dvar Hapoelet* that were written with sublety, a fine sensitivity, a discerning eye, and an understanding heart.

4 MESHULAM'S CLASS

(1925-1929)

One evening in the autumn of 1922, an innocent-looking young man entered the village office of Nahalal carrying all his worldly possessions: a bundle of clothes and a flute. He introduced himself as the new teacher, Meshulam Halevi, thirty-one years old. He had several good references and later, when he met the leaders of the moshav, explained that he was an exponent of liberal education. Only a few of the settlers understood what he meant, but most of them were impressed.

Meshulam (as everyone addressed him) was born in a village in Byelorussia. He attended a *heder* and a *yeshiva,** then studied secular subjects and supported himself by giving private lessons. At the age of twenty he was accepted by the Pedagogic Course in Grodno, a kind of Jewish teachers' seminary. He also taught himself to play a number of musical instruments, including the flute (at which he excelled). When he was conscripted into the Russian Army, this talent saved him from serving at the front, as he was posted to a regimental orchestra as a flutist. After the Revolution and a period as headmaster of the Jewish school in Bobruisk, he emigrated to Palestine in 1920.

Studies in Nahalal got under way immediately. Meshulam divided the children into three age groups. He taught the oldest group in his tent and later in his hut. The younger groups had to wait until the infirmary hut could be converted into two classrooms, after which they studied there for a year. There was no floor in the hut, nor were there tables and chairs, so the children laid out mats and studied on the floor. The hut was surrounded by marshes, thorns, and swarms of gnats, and fires were often lit outside to keep the gnats away. In the summer the tin roof turned the room into a blazing oven and field mice scuttled about freely; in the winter rain dripped through the roof into pails and basins and a cold wind whistled through the cracks in the wall.

Eventually a proper school was built in the settlement, but the initial difficulties stimulated Meshulam and crystallized his concept of liberal education. In drawing up the syllabus, he chose to disregard the country-wide "Curriculum for Municipal Schools," published by the Education Committee of the Jewish Agency, for he regarded it as unsuitable for Nahalal. The essence of his first

---

* Institute for higher education in Jewish religious studies.

conversation with the settlers served as his guideline: the primary aim of the curriculum must be to educate the children toward life on a moshav. It therefore seemed pointless to prepare the children for formal higher education. He gave priority to Bible studies, followed by nature and geometry.

The third group, numbering seven girls and nine boys, of whom Moshe was the youngest, began their studies as the second grade. In accordance with Meshulam's concept of liberal education, each child studied the subject that interested him. Those who wanted to study Bible sat on the sofa, as though they were reading a book at home; those interested in arithmetic sat at one of the tables near the wall. Communal activities—like the painting of sackcloth curtains for the classroom—took place round the center table. When the class held discussions or listened to a story, they all sat in a circle on the floor. Classwork took the form of discussions, meetings, telling stories, and individual work. Meshulam believed that the children's society had every right to impose obligations on its members, but the teacher had no right to force a child to study against his will. From the outset he held meetings, discussions, and elections, established committees, and founded the *Village Children's Newspaper,* all aimed at arousing a desire for creative study. When the third group had reached the fifth grade, the children were encouraged to keep private diaries and maintain an exchange of letters among themselves.

Meshulam apparently sensed something remarkable in Moshe, for he kept the child's fifth-grade diary for many years. One of his reasons for doing so was an entry from March 9, 1925. He had promised the children that their diaries were placed in his cupboard for safekeeping only and he never read them. He was therefore taken aback when he read these lines in Moshe's diary:

No. Impossible. I see that if I wish to be one of the diligent pupils, I must not devote all my time to writing compositions or drawing. I must devote myself to one thing only, because I can always find time for essays. The days are simply not interesting. I come, do a few lessons, write. At night I go either to a rehearsal or a meeting. There are things that are worthwhile writing and talking about, but it's not worthwhile bringing them out into the open. That's why I don't write about them—I'm afraid someone will read this. Goodbye.

By developing his writing ability, Moshe could, as he implies in the above passage, excel among his classmates. He drew extremely well and wrote exceptional poems and essays. Meshulam and his pupils invested a great deal of time, love, and energy in the class newspaper. The single copy that appeared periodically was finely bound and passed from one child to another. Its pages were illustrated with paint and India ink and contained a number of regular features, the most important of which were articles on the Bible and notes on the children's experiences. The editorial board was composed of the entire class, and essays or pieces submitted to the newspaper were read aloud before it. A poem submitted by Moshe in 1925 was rejected at its first reading. The class misunderstood the first line and consequently could not make sense of it. Meshulam intervened, explained the line in question, and expressed his opinion that it was a very fine poem. He then read it out again:

"The Song of the Harp"

He plucked the harp so slow,
He plucked a song of woe.
He sat in the tent alone,
In the tent, the wanderer's home.
The tree above his head
Bowed too, as mourning the dead.
The trees all swung and swayed,
By the light of the stars, bright-rayed.
And the harp still played and played,
Begging, alone and afraid.

As might be expected, the editorial board agreed unanimously to include the poem in the paper. In time it became quite popular, and the girls in the class would recite it with great feeling.

Nahman Betser, Moshe's classmate, relates that the day would often begin with a discussion, and if the majority of the children agreed that it was a fine day they would waive the schedule and go out for a walk, spending the day identifying plants and animals. Meshulam began taking the children on outings from his first year at Nahalal. He would often suggest that they have their lessons out in the field. He always went equipped with a magnifying glass and a botanical handbook. Just as he taught the children to speak correct Hebrew, he instilled in them a profound love for the flora and fauna of their country. Another aim of these excursions was to become acquainted with the Arabs. At the time, Nahalal was still quite isolated. The only other Jewish settlements in the area were Merhavya to the east and Yagur to the west. The children of Nahalal met Arab children near the springs in the area. They learned a few words of Arabic and could soon converse. Later, the children frequently went unaccompanied to even distant Arab villages. As the frequency of their outings increased, so did the distances that the children covered. Some were afraid to go far without Meshulam or one of the adults, and only the most daring, including Moshe, reached places that were considered "out of bounds." The official school hikes gradually lengthened to three or four days. The crowning hike, which lasted a week and ended with a visit to Jerusalem and the Wailing Wall, was always reserved for the graduating class of the primary school. The hiking enthusiasts among the children, including Moshe, formed a geographical society, and one of their many excursions took them to Geder, east of the Jordan.

Moshe's classmates and fellow-members of the geographical society noted the ease with which he befriended the Arabs. "He especially loved the hard-working Arab fellah," one of them recalled. "We all deeply respected men of labor, but Moshe reserved a special feeling for them." He carefully studied the customs of the fellaheen and the Bedouin and would embark on imaginary trips across vast deserts in the company of Arab horsemen.

In 1925 Moshe published a long story in this romantic vein in the school paper. Its heroes are two Arabs, Ali and Mustapha, whom Moshe and his friends join in a mounted expedition across the dessert. He knows at a glance they are Bedouin. Galloping on their horses, at first they cannot tell whether the Bedouin are friends or enemies, so they sit "glued to their saddles. In one hand we hold the reins and in the other . . . a pistol." All dressed in the long, flowing robes of the Orient, the boys race each other on horseback, feast together by the fire, and become friends. Then a battle ensues (Moshe gives no clear hint against whom) and Ali, Mustapha, Moshe, and his friends fight side by side. Next they encounter a fierce sandstorm, after which Moshe writes:

I remember that blood ran from my nose, my mouth, darkness, I lost consciousness, I see red circles . . . I see as though through a mist: date palms, Mustapha, Ali, Arabs dressed in white . . . What is this? A dream? An hallucination? . . . Then sleep once again . . . A few days later they told me that they found me unconscious. (Ali and Mustapha were saved because they knew there was an oasis nearby.) . . . I lay there for twenty days. And now, with the help of Allah and his Prophet Muhammad, I was saved. I thanked my saviors seventy times.

Although the circumstances surrounding his rescue are unclear, the point of the boy's story is that Arabs saved him from certain death.

Meshulam devoted a great deal of time and energy to the choir and orchestra. He taught the children to play the violin, flute, clarinet, trumpet, and cymbal and accompanied the choir on a concertina. From the very first rehearsals of the choir it became clear that Moshe, like the rest of his family, was simply tone deaf. But this in itself was not sufficient reason for exempting him entirely from the musical activities of the class. While most of the children belonged to the choir and the orchestra, Meshulam allowed Moshe to belong only to the orchestra. His instrument was the whistle. The cuckoo-like sound it emitted was an important part of the orchestra's rendition of Haydn's "Toy Symphony," but Moshe played the whistle with a pronounced lack of talent.

Although he excelled in writing, drawing, and nature and Bible studies, Moshe was not one of the teacher's pets. One of Meshulam's favorites was Dov Yermiyah, who was also well liked by the entire class—especially the girls. According to his teacher and classmates, Dov, two years older than Moshe, was a gentle, good-looking, gifted, and musical boy who played the violin at school parties. Meshulam's fondness for Dov certainly provoked Moshe's anger and envy. Meshulam recalls that in the winter of their first school year Dov's father would carry him to school on his shoulders, so that his clothes would not become soiled. Dov wore outfits made of soft corduroy, and everyone admired his cleanliness, good looks, curls, and rosy cheeks. But as soon as his father had deposited him on the relative safety of the mat and gone on his way, Moshe—in clothes made from his father's discarded outfits—would jump on him and beat him. Even though Dov was the older, he would fall back and allow himself to be beaten until Meshulam intervened. If his father did not arrive punctually to fetch him at the end of the day, Dov would remain at the school until Meshulam took him home, for fear of being attacked by Moshe.

Meshulam has been criticized for a serious shortcoming: fomenting inequality between the Nahalal children and those recently arrived from abroad, or at least doing little to bridge the gap between them. The Nahalal children sensed Meshulam's respect for their origins and largely took it for granted. Yet his approval of their status made it all the more natural and official. The children of Nahalal's founders readily attest to their feeling of superiority. Nahman Betser recalls: "I think our parents instilled in us this feeling of being 'chosen.' Nahalal was the first moshav, so our group felt as though we were superior to everyone else. The children of Merhavya, Balfouria, and Tel Adashim used to call us 'pure olive oil.' And Meshulam nurtured this feeling of superiority in us."

According to his former classmates, this sense of superiority was more highly developed in Moshe than in others. As proof, they point out his efforts to assume leadership over the class. The children opposed Moshe for they believed each of them was the son of someone who figured prominently in the annals of "conquest by labor." Moreover, some felt that the status of their families was superior to Moshe's because they were devoted to their farms and lands and refused to leave the soil and become involved in politics (politicians were not very highly thought of in Nahalal). Moshe's innate desire for preeminence and the general atmosphere fostered by Meshulam encouraged competition and haughtiness.

The generally recognized leaders were Moshe Betser and Amnon Yannai from the senior class and Dov Yermiyah from the junior class. Until his death on board a British troopship in 1943, Moshe Betser was considered the most impressive personality in the group, and to a great extent he created the mold in which his and future Nahalal generations were cast. Yehoshua Palmon, who came to Nahalal from Tel Aviv only in 1930, found a uniformity of behavior in the Nahalal children. Asked on one occasion who were the spokesmen of the group, he replied: "When I say 'spokesman,' I must smile, for at that time strength was measured by silence. People were impressive when they were silent, and even when pressed they would express their views with great reservation, in a very English, noncommittal manner. They reflected a great deal, struggled with their souls—the more one struggled the better—and pondered the nature and direction of the path their lives would follow." Ruth Dayan (then Shwarz) came to Nahalal in 1934 and recalls discovering a "Nahalal type": "Tough, introspective, and not very talkative." One may assume that Moshe, the bright, alert child, who "loved to surprise people with a beautiful word" and excelled in expressing himself, found it difficult to conform to the pattern exemplified by Moshe Betser. But under the circumstances he had no choice; to be accepted he had to imitate the other children.

Moshe Betser had three brothers and three sisters. His younger brother Nahman was a classmate of Moshe's and was often described as "a prince." In his youth, he too became one of the children's leaders. Like his brother and father, Nahman was endowed with deep-rooted moral values and was extremely considerate. When the group of boys grew older, he became their collective conscience.

The second of the three leaders in the group was Amnon Yannai. He was a handsome boy and the outstanding pupil in the class. Meshulam was forever praising his many talents. Amnon radiated benevolence, comradeship, and understanding, and all the girls doted on him. Teacher and pupils alike expected great things of him. When the group discussed their future and tried to guess which one of them would become "a great man," they invariably chose Amnon. Not one of the pupils thought that Moshe had a future as a soldier and statesman.

Amnon's best friend was Dov Yermiyah. Of all the children in the younger class, he was Meshulam's favorite. "Meshulam would have been much happier if Dov had become a great man," Shulamit Dayan remarked. Dov was an outstanding pupil and outshone all the other children in music. Above all, he was the girl's idol. They were divided into two groups—those who merely loved Dov and those who were "crazy about him." As a child, Moshe envied

Dov the special attention he received from Meshulam, and as a youth he resented the girls' love for him.

One of the exceptional boys in the group was Avino'am Slutzky. Though not outstanding in leadership and influence, he was a wildly inventive practical joker. Many of his escapades were so extraordinary that his friends found even the label "wild man" inadequate. Despite the boy's mischievousness, Meshulam was fond of Avino'am and tried to help him mend his ways. Avino'am responded by taking up the clarinet. Nevertheless, he caused Meshulam many trying moments. The teacher became so accustomed to the boy's pranks that he believed Avino'am capable of anything. A typical instance occurred in 1927, when a strong earthquake shook Palestine, destroying several houses in Safed and Nablus. The tremor was felt in Nahalal a few moments after Avino'am left the class to take a drink of water from the tap in the courtyard. For a moment Meshulam was at a loss as the schoolhouse suddenly began swaying and pictures dropped from the walls in rapid succession. Then comprehension dawned and he rushed out to the courtyard shouting "Avino'am! Stop that at once!" Avino'am was one of the founders of "Habibi," an organization dedicated to the perpetration of practical jokes. "Habibi" was an acronym for "The Society of Jewish Ruffians in Palestine," and Moshe was an active member.

In 1929 the youth of the village were permitted to share the guard duty with their parents. Moshe carried a double burden, for at the end of 1929 Shmuel went to the United States and left his son to take his place. The boys guarded the courtyards, armed with spears fashioned by the village blacksmith, and Moshe earned a reputation for bravery when he extended his nightly round beyond the courtyard to behind the cowsheds.

To realize his ambitions for class leadership, Moshe had to fight on a number of fronts and contend with the preeminence of several children. Moshe Betser was an immovable fortress of spiritual, moral, and social authority in the school. Amnon Yannai and Dov Yermiyah were loved for their beauty, kindness, sociability, and musical talents. As for practical jokes and athletic prowess, Moshe had to contend with no less a prankster than Avino'am Slutzky. But on July 5, 1926, he nonetheless exulted: " . . . I want to organize a party . . . Altogether I feel that once again I am in the center of things and that I now lead the children."

Heartened by his growing sense of power, Moshe set out to tackle Meshulam. Some time after the above entry was written, he recorded the following assessment of his position: " . . . I now feel more and more that the children are like clay in my hands. I feel that I am not the same Moshe, that I am a different child. Meshulam also treats me better. Altogether everything is good." Moshe's buoyant spirits can no doubt be attributed, among other things, to his parents' return to Nahalal. Shmuel was back from Europe and Dvorah from the rest home near Jerusalem. But this sense of triumph and control over the class was short-lived.

It was, of course, hopeless to try to challenge Meshulam's standing in the class. As for the others, an eleven-year-old boy could hardly undermine the unqualified leadership of thirteen-year-old Moshe Betser. There were also children in the village who had turned fifteen and regarded him as a mere brat. Moshe was unsuccessful even within his own class. When Meshulam instituted elections, Moshe did not receive as many votes as the others. In this respect, his position in the class remained unchanged throughout primary school and for several years afterward. Unable to beat Amnon and Dov, he tried to join them in the hope of forming a triumvirate, but failed again. The two boys not only rejected him, but even confided to the others that they could not bear his company. Moshe began to "fawn on them in an undignified way," but to no avail. The children explained his rejection by the fact that good, sociable Amnon and Dov "could not stand anyone who derides his inferiors, teases, offends, and annoys." His envy for Dov was an important element in Moshe's social conduct as a child.

Moshe fared best—though not always well—against Avino'am, and the competition between them lasted for years. Some of the children thought they were opponents, while others were under the impression that they were the best of friends. Avino'am does not recall Moshe ever having been a close friend, and Moshe himself said, "I don't recall being especially close to anyone." Moshe played hard, was a stubborn competitor and a bad loser. Once, to regain face, he challenged Avino'am to a fight. Avino'am was older, taller, and stronger than Moshe and his arms were particularly long and powerful, but Moshe offset these disadvantages by reckless bravery, nimbleness, and cunning, and the fight ended in a draw.

There is no knowing what the children's attitude toward Moshe would have been were it not for his undisputed talents in writing and drawing. His sketches, essays, and poems reflected great sensitivity. Drawing a lonely pine bowed by the winds, he seemed to pity the tree for its pain; when he sketched an Arab trudging behind a wooden plow, it was as though he shared the man's hardships. His classmates all acknowledged his superiority in reading and thinking. Moshe pursued these pastimes in the privacy of his tiny room, far from their company. He loved to read by the light of a kerosene lamp or "to lie under my warm blanket and think," as he wrote in his diary. In the twenties and thirties, books in Hebrew, especially for youth, were scarce. Most of them were translations of French and Russian classics. Moshe read the works of Dostoyevski, Tolstoi,

Pushkin, and Chekhov (his mother's mentors) in Hebrew. As he was an avid reader, he had no choice but to take up books for adults. He even glanced through works by the Hebrew writer Y.H. Brenner, which is difficult reading even for an educated adult.

As early as primary school, his classmates discerned in Moshe a complex character. To describe him only as a bidder for class leadership, a bad loser, cruel at games, or scornful of the weak is a distortion of his personality. One would have to add—as his friends did—the "poetic" side of his nature. When one of the girls came to his room to borrow E.L. Winitch's novel *Gadfly,* Moshe was still engrossed in the last few pages. Tears rolled down his cheeks as he read of the bitter fate of the Gadfly, the Italian revolutionary Arturo, who wrote to his mistress Jima: "Tomorrow at dawn they will shoot me." Two lines remained deeply engraved in his memory:

> I am a happy butterfly
> If I live or if I die.

When he submitted his story about Ali and Mustapha to the *Village Children's Newspaper,* he illustrated it with a drawing of three long-stemmed anemones. "We were so taken with this drawing," Bat-Ami recalls, "that we copied it from the newspaper and embroidered [the pattern] on all the curtains in our house. My girl friends did the same, and Moshe's anemones could be seen in a number of homes." While the other children wrote about daily events at school or in the village or merely reported what they had heard during lessons, Moshe wrote stories that grew out of his rich imagination. The following appeared in the ninth children's newspaper in June 1927:

Part of "The Hangman"

The hangman walks, his mind full of thoughts, and he remembers . . . as though it happened just this moment . . . He was then eight years old, and it was a time of rioting, and the king . . . was cruel to his subjects, and the people desired a republic . . . and his father too was among the rebels. One day as he was lying in bed half asleep, his father came to his bedside, kissed his forehead, looked piercingly into his eyes, and asked: "Shall you renounce your father's teachings?" And he was young then and could not understand. Now he is a hangman. Hangman! The words crush and stab . . . he was twenty years old, arrested for having murdered a man, and sentenced to death . . . and he agreed to be a hangman . . . But what is the matter? A stone is pressing upon his heart, pressing and bearing down upon him, and he goes into a tavern to drink. Inside, everything is dirt and squalor, vomiting drunkards, and he drinks. The drink is strong, but his emotions are sevenfold stronger.

There was no tavern in Nahalal or anywhere in Palestine, but Dvorah had told Moshe about the drunken villagers of Prochorovka, and he had read of alehouses and drunkards in books.

Contradictory qualities existed side by side in Moshe. In his contact with the children at school—especially with the girls—he was not only young but childish. The same was true of his behavior at home. He was still very close to his mother, and eagerly awaited the Russian legends she would tell him every night. Moshe remembers her as a superb storyteller. Her tales opened up the rich world of the Russian humanistic culture which he could not yet find in Hebrew. To this day, he attributes his love of Russian literature to his mother's influence. To the same extent, though, he used these stories to maintain the warm, intimate contact he had enjoyed with his mother throughout early childhood.

Though he was intellectually developed well beyond his years, Moshe was highly vulnerable. When offended he would draw in his lips and cry silently. The only sign of his distress would be the tears that welled in his eyes. As a grown man he retained this habit. In 1939, when he was twenty-four years old and a prisoner in Acre, the sight of his wife and baby daughter moved him to tears. And to this day, as Minister of Defense, Moshe Dayan is incapable of remaining dry-eyed at a military funeral. Despite his sensitivity, however, he was extremely independent as a child, and when his father was in Poland and his mother in Jerusalem recovering from her operation, Moshe remained on the farm alone.

Moshe was also an unusually hospitable boy. The children often spent the Sabbath in the fields surrounding the village and at sundown they would all meet at one of their homes. Most of the parents were reluctant to play host to fifteen or twenty children at a time. Dvorah, however, always kept an open house for Moshe's friends and would serve them hot tea, fresh bread, and her homemade grape jam. When they were older, Moshe often read poetry or played records for them.

Hospitality notwithstanding, he frequently made fun of his friends. He was as skilled at unearthing their weak points as he was at turning them into barbs to be used against them. His barbs were so devastating—especially those directed at Avino'am—that one day the class joined forces and excommunicated him. It is difficult to determine precisely which incident prompted so drastic a step. Nevertheless, one day Moshe's classmates all jumped on him, threw him on the ground, and thrashed him. Then they vowed not to speak to him for a month.

Moshe's "excommunication" was the culmination of ever-growing friction with his classmates. Until then, he had always managed to reintegrate himself into the group after each unpleasant incident. He managed to avoid being too personal in his quarrels, and there was no one who especially disliked him or was not on speaking terms with him. What provoked the class's ire, one of his classmates recalls, was "the Dayan trait of haughtiness, contempt for others. We all shared a feeling of superiority, but it was more pronounced in Moshe. We never let him become the class leader . . . because of his ambition. His very attitude provoked opposition." Another classmate recalls: "He was uncompromisingly aggressive. If he fought a boy, it was not enough merely to beat him. If there was mud on the ground, for example, he wouldn't rest until he had plastered the boy's face with it." The children laughed at his clever ditties and acknowledged his sense of humor but could not forgive him for mocking the weaker children. One of the girls in the class said: "Our boys were known for their honesty, their straightforwardness; their word was sacred. Everyone thought that Moshe and his family were none too honest. I reacted to him as I did to all the Dayans. At the time, I thought they were rather sly. The Dayan family had been traders in Russia; perhaps that's where it came from. The children inherited some of it from their parents."

Evidently, the founders' attitude toward Shmuel influenced their children's attitude toward Moshe. A girl who was fond of him related that "just as everyone thought him brave, talented, and extraordinarily bright, they also thought he was dishonest. His father had become a politician, and politicians become dishonest . . . His mother also did not say what she really thought. She may have been even less honest than Shmuel." Avino'am Slutzky recalls: "During our childhood and adolescence, he was not a leader and was often rejected by the group. There was something unpleasant about him, something of the Dayan traits. They were quite capable of weaving intrigues in order to achieve what they wanted. Shmuel was not a pleasant character. A person who could say in 1929, this is *my* rifle, then fortify his own barn and care only about his own farm, was bound to be disliked. He was also unpopular as a public figure because he was dishonest." Even Moshe's close friend and second cousin, Binya Zarhi, felt that the attitude toward the family as a whole was projected onto Moshe. Of the excommunication, Binya says: "It was the outcome of his independence, his sense of superiority. This haughtiness was a Dayan trait. When I analyze it, the Zatulovskys did not have it. Shmuel was respected, but not liked. At one time he served on the council for three years in a row, and many of the men resented this."

In an intimate, closely knit village such as Nahalal, the families, no matter how large, were regarded as homogeneous units. The children were identified by their kinship, and Moshe was always "Shmuel Dayan's son." His neighbors viewed Shmuel as one who had gained prominence and widespread recognition not through the fulfillment of his ideals and hard work on the land, but through politics and public activities. Moreover, during his many absences from the farm, he was forced to hire a farmhand, and thus betrayed one of the founding principles of the moshav—independent labor. In the twenties, such a deviation from moshav ideology was tantamount to dishonesty. Added to this was the fact that he was not without other failings and was by no means a sociable man.

Apparently, the settlers also begrudged Shmuel political recognition. Nahalal was famous in Palestine and abroad as the standard-bearer of a new way of life, equality and justice, and the renewed settlement of the people of Israel in their ancient homeland. All the founders of Nahalal wished to share this distinction equally, and they may well have felt that Shmuel enjoyed more credit than he deserved. Visitors to Nahalal wanted to meet and study the younger generation of the first moshav, and Shmuel invariably introduced them to Moshe. The other founders of Nahalal undoubtedly felt that their homes were no less deserving of high-ranking visitors. If they sensed in Shmuel, justly or otherwise, traits such as haughtiness and superiority, they must surely have transmitted this feeling to their children.

The terms "dishonest" and "sly," however, were relative to the scale of values in Nahalal. In fact, what the settlers of Nahalal meant by these terms was something closer to not practicing what one preaches. To extol the virtues of work on the land while abstaining from working oneself was, in their eyes, a mark of dishonesty. The values of the Nahalalites were absolute, not unlike those of a religious faith. In such an orthodox society, anyone who did not observe the basic tenets was bound to be severely criticized.

Shmuel's ambivalence found its expression in the kind of education Moshe received at home. The fact that his parents had given him a room to himself was extremely unusual. Since the aim of the founders of Nahalal was to raise a generation of farmers, the Dayans' explanation that the boy needed the room for reading and thinking was received with much skepticism. To what purpose is a hard-working farmer required to think or read? The doubts about Shmuel and Dvorah's covert intentions were reinforced when it became known that they were allowing Moshe to study English privately. The teaching of foreign language in the school had already encountered opposition from the farmers. Many of them claimed that such studies were unnecessary and that Jews had had their fill of speaking foreign languages during the years of exile. In any case, they said, it was difficult enough to study Hebrew. They feared that anyone who learned English would leave Nahalal—to see the city, the world—and would never return to his farm. Shmuel himself came out against higher education, and although Meshulam tried to explain the importance of a second language, the council refused to approve the funds necessary for hiring an English teacher.

Dvorah saw things in a different light. Unlike Shmuel and the other founders, she recognized the intrinsic value of knowledge and feared that without a broader education and more comprehensive knowledge, the children of Nahalal would regard themselves as the very center of the world. Dvorah suggested that English be taught privately to those who were interested, and a teacher was found to work for a monthly fee of one Palestinian pound. When it concerned his own son, Shmuel shelved his opposition to private tutoring in English and did not repeat his line about "the city that beckons with a thousand deceitful lights." To the Nahalites, his reversal was a clear indication of dishonesty. Soon after Moshe began studying English, he aggravated the criticism by telling his friends that when he grew up he would "see the whole world."

Moshe's friends did not openly accuse him of cheating. On the contrary, it was well known that he never lied and was always honest with himself. But he was not entirely frank on many occasions, and by Nahalal standards this was tantamount to dishonesty or cunning. He was also able to plan two or three moves in advance, while other, less sophisticated children only saw what lay immediately ahead. When it became clear to the other children that he was capable of turning events to his own advantage by his foresight, they began to accuse him of intrigue, cunning, and dishonesty.

Moshe's attitude toward farm work was another target of attack. In a society like Nahalal, founded on total dedication to agriculture, public opinion was severely critical of anyone who treated this "sacred" undertaking with indifference. The children also ranked dedication to work highest in their scale of values. Of all Moshe's failings, as his friends assessed them, the most serious was the feeling that he was not "a serious worker." As soon as Moshe satisfied his curiosity in a new area of work, he lost interest and grew impatient with its endless repetition. Watching a mule consume a portion of barley, for example, could hold his attention for only a few moments. For the majority of Nahalalites, young and old, it was a profound and memorable experience to watch their animals eat their own barley for the first time. They even held a special celebration to mark the event. First they harvested the barley, then brought it in ceremoniously and placed it in neat stacks on the threshing floor. The idea was that the mules would be tied to stakes and the entire village would then watch with pride as the animals munched on the first sheaves of barley grown in Nahalal. Each child was given the honor of leading the mules to his "family stake," and all the children did so, except Moshe. His parents were deeply shamed: "Every other child knew where his stack was, but Moshe could not find our stack of barley and tie the mule to the stake." Shmuel even considered punishing the boy. He noted with a heavy heart that "Moshe did not even seem excited by what was happening."

Moshe was fond of watching cows giving birth. "Mother would send me out to watch the cows give birth or see the plants sprouting," he related. "I was fascinated by these things—how the cow goes into labor, gives birth, then licks the newborn calf. I loved watching the animals, watching the creation of life." He also liked to invent names for the farm animals, a habit which irritated his father. But for all his interest in naming the cows, he was by no means eager to milk them. Shmuel noted sadly that "he did the farm work, but with little joy."

Other Nahalal children took up the burden of farm work long before he did. Israel Betser's children sat on the threshing sledge at the age of five, while Moshe "was unenthusiastic about work." At nine, Nahman Betser was a worker to be reckoned with: "Along with our studies, my brother and I worked on the farm every free moment we had." In his free moments, Moshe liked to read, reflect, hike. In 1925, when Shmuel was in Europe, word of Moshe's attitude to work on the farm got to the other children by way of the Dayan's hired hand. He related that he once asked Moshe to hoe a plot of ground in the orchard, and for a while Moshe worked hard; but he soon became bored and his pace slackened. Then he spread the earth he had already hoed over the rest of the plot to make it look though he had completed the entire area. When the children heard this story they pronounced it "a dreadful act of deceit."

When Baruch Nigos came to the Dayan farm in 1929, Shmuel warned him before leaving for the United States, "Don't expect much help from Moshe." According to Nigos, Moshe did work, but without enthusiasm. On the other hand, he was an avid reader of books and newspapers, and instead of helping with the work he inundated Nigos with general information and politics. After the 1929 riots, Britain sent a Royal Commission to Palestine to study the situation. It heard testimonies concerning the riots in Hebron and at the Wailing Wall and received wide coverage in the local press. Moshe followed the Commission's progress in the two papers that arrived at the house, *Davar* and *Hapoel Hatzair*. Nigos recalls that he knew many of the testimonies by heart "and would quote everything that had been said at the Royal Commission, adding his own comments on who testified well, which testimony might cause harm to Jewish interests and which might benefit them. He lived the entire affair." As lodgers in the house, Nigos and his wife were a captive audience for the boy.

Moshe invested his talents, energy, and diligence only in work that captured his interest. At the time he was fascinated by grafting. Avraham Galutman, the village expert on fruit orchards, spoke highly of Moshe's work, but the notion of Moshe as a hard worker was sceptically received by his classmates. One day, however, this estimation was confirmed by none other than Israel Betser, who told his son that he was amazed by the high standard of Moshe's grafts and added, "Just look at the eagerness and talent he devotes to work that interests him." Moshe built his own grafting shed and later started his own apple nursery. The nursery eventually won high praise and his seedlings were in great demand.

The general opinion of Moshe among his Nahalal classmates later influenced his fortunes as a military man and politician. His friends dispersed throughout the country in the Haganah, in kibbutzim, Wingate's Night Squads, and the political institutions of the Yishuv, and many of them were asked for and gave their estimations of the man.

Moshe's *bar mitzva* was held in May 1928. He was still very close to his mother, and Shmuel wrote that she was "the one person who found ways to his heart." He also thought there was a physical resemblance between mother and son. "Their expressions would shift from tenderness to hardness. Suddenly there would be an attractive, captivating smile, and then an overly serious expression would cloud their faces." Moshe's friends believe that he was fond of his father as well. Shmuel was actually on close, friendly terms with his son. The two of them often played together and wrestled. One of their games was to see who could tie whom to the table with a belt. Shulamit Dayan recalls her surprise upon entering the Dayan household and seeing Moshe tying Shmuel to the table leg.

Moshe read from the Torah. Like many of his classmates, he went to synagogue on the festival of Simhat Torah. The children would stand on the benches to see the scroll, and, imitating the adults, touch it and then kiss their fingers. The Nahalal synagogue was filled mainly with the founders' parents. Shmuel's father, Reb Avraham, gave Moshe *tfillin* (phylacteries) as a *bar mitzva* gift and taught him how to wind them on his hand, arm, and forehead. Moshe was not unusual in this respect. After the reading from the scroll, there was a reception at the Dayan's house. This was the only birthday Moshe ever celebrated, for Shmuel objected to birthday parties in principle.

5   YOUTH (1930-1933)

On April 7, 1926 the Agricultural School for Girls in Nahalal was officially opened, with Hannah Meisel-Shochat as its first headmistress. In his address at the opening ceremony, Dr. Chaim Weizmann mentioned that 1,500 girls had applied for the forty places available in the first class. The school's importance to the development of agriculture in Palestine was indisputable, and its local importance in Nahalal soon became apparent. "Naturally, the school was a great attraction for the boys of the village," Shmuel wrote. "They sought the company of the new girls. New faces every year . . . attracted the boys, and they became frequent guests at the Girls' School." Indeed, one would be hard put to find a more pleasing gift to the boys of any village.

In 1926, however, Moshe and his companions were as yet unable to enjoy this promising addition to Nahalal, since the school offered a two-year course for girls aged eighteen and over. The first contact between Meshulam's class and the girls was therefore made through characteristic "Habibi" activities: throwing stones at the girls on their way to the privacy of the threshing floor with the village youth. On Friday nights Moshe and his friends would steal into the school kitchen and gorge themselves on the puddings and cakes that had been prepared for the Sabbath or make off with choice plums and apples from the school orchards. The headmistress repeatedly complained about these thefts to the village committee. On one occasion the members of "Habibi" were caught red-handed, confined to their homes, and forbidden to enter the school grounds. Moshe wrote a skit based on this incident. It was a parody of *Chains*, a play by Gorki that had been performed by the Habimah Theater. Soon after the incident, the skit was staged at the youth clubhouse, and one of the ditties Moshe composed to a Russian tune from *Chains* became something of a local hit. The refrain ran:

> Gone are the good old days,
> The puddings, the pies all forgotten.
> Since we were all arrested,
> The garden's bright apples lie rotten.

The Girls' School played a more significant role in the children's lives in 1929, when Moshe's class completed primary school and the pressing question of their secondary education had to be faced.

Though the parents in Nahalal were generally pleased with Meshulam, they were not entirely satisfied with the children's over-all proficiency, mainly because the school lacked teachers expert in each subject. It was therefore suggested that the children continue their studies at the Girls' School, but the experiment met with little success. Only a few of Moshe's classmates remained to complete the special course of studies arranged for them.

Over the years a legend has developed that Moshe was the only male pupil in the Girls' School. Shmuel himself was among those responsible for its perpetration, as he was fond of repeating the story and even wrote about it in his autobiography. In fact, almost all the boys and girls of the second and third classes began their secondary studies at the Girls' School in the autumn of 1929. The arrangement proved inconvenient, however, as studies were disrupted whenever the sons were needed on the farm. While many of the children left school permanently, Moshe, who had a craving for knowledge and was encouraged by his parents, was one of the few who persevered. He had to exert considerable effort to keep up his secondary studies, for soon after he entered the school, in September 1929, Shmuel left on a mission to the United States, leaving a great part of the farm work to his son.

Shmuel described the circumstances of this trip in his autobiography: " . . . after the riots of 1929, the Executive Committee of the Histadrut asked me to go to the United States . . . I abandoned my nest and left my country, for I had been summoned to raise a great, bitter cry, to rally the nation, to rouse it from its complacency . . . " Shmuel wrote to Dvorah from Alexandria before embarking for France, from the *Franconia* as he was crossing the Atlantic, and from America. In reading the correspondence between husband and wife, one has a sense of *déjà vue*. His emotional, guilt-ridden letters monotonously reiterate the words and tone of the Zionist movement's leadership. Even the lands of the Horan are mentioned, for Shmuel went to Washington and met Judge Louis Brandeis to discuss the possibility of buying 100,000 dunams of land in Transjordan for "half a pound a dunam." Brandeis rejected the idea.

Moshe read his father's letters carefully and learned about the United States, American Jewry, and its importance to the Zionist endeavor in Palestine. Shmuel traveled from coast to coast, then on to Canada, and finally back to New York, making speeches in Yiddish, holding press conferences, and publishing articles on Nahalal in the Yiddish newspaper *Der Tag*.

At first Dvorah resigned herself to this mission and to Shmuel's absence. On the eve of the Day of Atonement, October 11, 1929, she wrote to him: " . . . It would have been better had you not gone on this trip, but you must not think of returning before your mission is completed. In my most difficult moments, I have frequently thought of asking you to return, but each time I resolved anew—one must be strong and endure." At first she wrote only "half the truth" about her hardships at home with the three children and the farm work, but gradually she began to give detailed accounts of the situation. "The beetroot came up nicely but the birds are destroying it"; "the field is all mud and I do not know how we'll go up there tomorrow to bring the vegetables down"; "Aviva and I have no shoes"; "we have no rubber boots"; "the clover has not sprouted"; "on rainy days I did not read or write anything . . . I only mended our 'royal vestments' "; "nothing was done in the garden before the rains . . . the fence is broken and the chickens eat the plants"; "we have done nothing in the chicken coop as yet."

Dvorah's physical condition was poor, and Moshe had suffered a relapse of malaria. On March 23, 1930, she wrote to Shmuel:

He feels weak now. If only he wouldn't wander about at night he would recover. But he is totally under the influence of the "martial law"[a reference to the Haganah,* which the boys of Nahalal joined after the riots of 1929]. He is the only boy of his age there. I am greatly distressed by this, and for this reason too I eagerly await your return . . . Almost every night he comes home at midnight, and that also wears him out.

The family's financial distress was acute, as 1930 was a bad year for the farmers of the Jezreel Valley. Dvorah ran into debt at the village store and wrote to her husband: "The first anniversary of my father's death is approaching, and he still does not have a headstone."

This time, however, unlike 1925-6, Dvorah refused to sacrifice herself completely on the altar of Shmuel's career. She began to satisfy her own aspirations as well. In 1929 she published her first article in *Dvar Hapoelet,* entitled "My Immigration." On the strength of this and subsequent articles, the editors of the periodical offered her a position on the editorial board. She was nominated as a candidate to the Histadrut's Sick Fund Conference and became a delegate to the Women's Labor Council and the Hapoel Hatzair Conference. She felt that Shmuel's trip set back her own ambitions and added frustration to her financial difficulties and physical weakness. Once in a while she did indulge herself by going to Tel Aviv, but for lack of choice she took the younger children with her. Describing these trips to Shmuel, she wrote: "I pitied Moussik for remaining alone in the house . . . I couldn't hold back my tears when we parted . . . "

Shmuel's replies to Dvorah followed the same pattern as before. He described New York as a veritable Sodom—bright lights, licen-

---

*Underground national Jewish defense organization which functioned until the establishment of the Israel Defense Forces on May 25, 1948.

tiousness, revelry, orgies, and a universal preoccupation with trade and commerce—which caused him deep spiritual anguish. Nonetheless, he again prolonged his stay abroad. He extended his tour of the United States to include the West Coast and Canada. Then he decided to attend the annual session of the Zionist Executive as an observer, and finally, he informed Dvorah that he intended remaining abroad after the session itself.

In an effort to hasten his return, Dvorah wrote him of the criticism leveled against him at the village meetings, but even this failed to impress Shmuel. Eight months after his departure, Moshe and Dvorah both wrote to him threatening that they would not write again unless he replied that he was coming home. Shmuel answered this "ultimatum" in a letter dated April 23, written in Chicago:

> . . . Alone in my room, in this elegant hotel, my soul is cast down . . . A few hours ago I read your short letter—one page, half filled with something written by both of you, only two lines from Moshe . . . and you seem to be informing me that you will not write again, that I shall receive no more letters from you. All this while I know that I shall be here for three more weeks. How can you leave me without a word from you? I do not understand the real reason behind this dark mood of yours.

It was apparently during this period of his life that Moshe's feelings about his parents began to crystallize. To begin with, he developed certain reservations towards his father, which may have been the source of his later impatience with all minor politicians and functionaries and his dislike of party politics. He also began to notice that his mother's feelings—which he sensed were more profound then Shmuel's—were always contained. "I don't remember seeing Mother cry, not even at funerals. She never lost control; she never raised her voice. Father, on the other hand, did so often. And she had good reason to raise her voice; what with difficulties at home and ill-health, she should have rent heaven and earth with her cries. But she kept everything inside." Rather than complain about Dvorah leaving much of the farm work to him, Moshe was deeply impressed by her decisiveness and daring.

> Even as a child I understood that [Father] talked in formulas, like most of the Hapoel Hatzair leaders. When a son discovers his father talking nonsense, he begins to disrespect him. There was no point in arguing with him because he never developed his thoughts logically. Arguments with him were not of the kind in which one side or the other could be convinced. Father would trot out truisms, and that was that. With Mother, one could discuss things and argue. She could prove to you that you were wrong or admit that you were right.

When Shmuel left for the United States, Baruch and Bella Nigos were hired to help Dvorah on the farm. Originally, Dvorah thought she might also be sent abroad, in which case the couple would take charge of the children as well. Her trip did not materialize, but Dvorah still retained the couple to enable her to go to Tel Aviv or to convalesce away from home. Dvorah gave the couple her bedroom and moved into the next bedroom with Aviva and Zohar; Moshe remained, as always, in his own tiny room. The small house soon became overcrowded, and differences of opinion began cropping up between Dvorah and the hired couple. Behind the friction lay the distress caused by Shmuel's prolonged absence and Dvorah's dissatisfaction with the Nigos's work.

Dvorah's difficulties became so acute in 1930 that she broke one of the cardinal rules of the moshav and sold produce privately, instead of through the marketing services of the village. An Arab peddler often came to Nahalal to sell vegetables, and the settlers generally bartered with him, offering eggs or a chicken in return for his goods. The village committee repeatedly warned the settlers that anyone found doing business with the peddler would be punished, and the village dairy would not accept his milk. Dvorah's bartering was discovered one day, and the dairy refused to accept the milk she brought. In protest, she took all the cans she had with her and poured every drop onto the pavement in front of the dairy. Those who witnessed the incident related that she did so with a calm expression on her face. This impressive demonstration confirmed the villagers' opinion of Dvorah as a woman of great daring. After all, she had to rise every morning at four o'clock to milk the cows, and every liter was worth one *grush**—a considerable sum in those days. While Moshe helped on the farm, he did so with little enthusiasm and very often at the wrong times. He would promise faithfully to wake up "as the ox grazes," but unless Dvorah woke him he would sleep well into the morning.

When Shmuel returned from America, he brought Moshe a gift which greatly enhanced the boy's social standing in Nahalal: a gramophone and several records, including cantoral music by Meir Herschman and Yossele Rosenblatt, light music (such as "Eine Kleine Nachtmusik" and "The Persian Market") and a number of Viennese waltzes. These were apparently the first gramophone and records in Nahalal and certainly the first in Moshe's circle. The were regarded as a marvel of cultural progress and were an irresistible attraction. With their help, Moshe's house became a center of social activity. He would play the records on Friday nights and Saturday afternoons or evenings, and all his friends— including Dov Yermiyah and Amnon Yannai—would come to listen.

*Or piastre, 1/100 of a pound.

After a time, the boys knew all the melodies by heart and often walked through the village singing them loudly in unison. Moshe sometimes supplemented the "musical afternoons" with readings. While Dvorah served tea and jam, he read passages from *Rocks of Chaos* by Avraham Shlonsky. Eventually, this became a social event that no youth in Nahalal could afford to miss. It also gave Moshe the opportunity to make overtures to his first girlfriend—Chaya Rubinstein.

She was called "Jule" from the day one of the teachers remarked that she spoke as though she had a mouth full of *julim* (marbles). When the school year began, the boys of Nahalal would crowd about the gates to look over the new girls. When sixteen-year-old Jule first appeared in the courtyard, her blue eyes, curly brown hair and tall, full figure immediately earned her the title of distinction, *Futchra,* which in Nahalal slang was a girl thought most desirable for dances, walks, and company. Moshe's and his friends' chances of dancing with the eighteen- and twenty-year-old girls were slim, for the older boys were well-built, fine-looking young men. Though he loved to dance, Moshe never dared ask any of the girls, for they were all much older than he. Of all the girls, he was attracted to Chaya-Jule, but his bashfulness left him standing on the side, gazing longingly as crowds of admirers thronged about her.

Though undoubtedly piquant, the legends about Moshe as the only male pupil in the Girls' School—a lone rooster among the pullets— are unfortunately untrue. Far from lording it over the female bounty at the school, he was bashful and hesitant even with Chaya-Jule and for a long time was too shy to approach her. His chance to reveal his feelings finally came when Gideon Baratz came on a visit from Degania and told Moshe that he was related to Jule. With Gideon's help, Moshe took the first step of asking her for notes of some of the lessons he had missed. He then asked her if they might prepare their lessons together. She was a good student and known for her conscientiousness. After that, it was but a step to inviting her home to his musical afternoons. One afternoon, while the others were absorbed in the music, he mustered up courage and whispered in Jule's ear, "Let's go for a walk," only to receive a prompt lesson in manners from the city girl. "If you want me to come for a walk with you, you have no choice but to ask me properly if I would like to." Moshe was acutely embarrassed but managed to do as he was told. To his surprise, she accepted the invitation.

The two went out for long walks and talked for hours. Moshe told Chaya about the books he read and lectured her about Zionist policies and personalities. One Sabbath evening in the winter, Chaya fell and broke her arm as she was racing on her bicycle. There was no doctor in Nahalal, and she had to wait until the following morning before being taken to the doctor at Kfar Yehoshua. Moshe stayed at her bedside in the school dormitory until lights out. He was finally asked to leave the room but maintained his vigil in the courtyard throughout the night, shivering in the cold. The following morning he took her in his cart to Kfar Yehoshua. He frequently spoke to her about the virtues of chastity, fidelity, and devotion, stressing the necessity of overcoming one's desires. At first Chaya approved, but later she wished he were more demonstrative. Moshe never said "I love you," or tried to "start anything," in Nahalal slang.

The problems of his own social adjustment also came up in their conversations. Moshe was generally thought to be tough, witty, and dry, and he complained of this to Chaya, saying that the other youth thought him cruel. She was amazed to discover that this was true: "They said terrible things about him—that he was a liar, conceited, ambitious . . . and boastful. In spite of this, they still respected him." Why he was regarded in this light was the subject of many long conversations. Moshe was deeply hurt by his friends' criticism, and Chaya believed that this was the reason he read so many books on social theory: It was as if he wanted to discover his place in the group and learn why he was attacked.

One evening he was unable to meet Jule as arranged and had difficulty explaining why. Finally, he promised to reveal "the biggest secret in the whole wide world," swore her to secrecy, and told her that the Haganah had begun to operate in Nahalal and that "it is the most precious, important thing in the country and in the world."

It was only after the riots of 1929 that Nahalal joined the Haganah organization and began receiving arms and military instruction. The boys of the moshav were brought in on the secret. First they were posted as sentries and charged with warning the adults should the police approach; later they were given lessons in judo and pistol shooting. The handling of live weapons was of secondary importance; belonging to the Haganah was a far more coveted prize for the boys of Nahalal. Most of them had handled weapons of one sort or another from their early childhood. Moshe recalled: "As far back as I can remember, there was a rifle with ammunition in the house. Knowing about weapons was like knowing about farm work. Just as I can hardly remember when it was that I began milking cows, so it's hard to remember the exact time I first began handling Father's carbine." The German carbine was kept hidden in the house, carefully wrapped in an oiled cloth. At first Moshe could only watch his father clean his rifle, then he was allowed to clean it and after that Shmuel allowed him to load it. Moshe remembers firing the carbine when he was ten. He used empty bottles and tins for targets. It was only many years later that he acquired a weapon of his own.

Until 1932 the villagers of Nahalal lived peacefully with their Arab neighbors. The Haganah weapons were kept hidden in the houses, and the boys were given no special tasks. Their only activity—which later became important from a security point of view—took place outside the framework of the Haganah and sprang naturally from Nahalal's circumstances. Yehudah Mor, Moshe's uncle, organized a band of horsemen to help with the guard duty in the fields. At the time, disputes over grazing lands and property rights were the only points of friction between Nahalal and its Arab neighbors, but the boys also partipated in the fights that broke out when the JNF began clearing new lands for nearby settlements.

There were five riders in Yehudah Mor's band: Avino'am Slutzky, Nahman Betser, Amnon Yannai, Dov Yermiyah and Moshe Dayan. Two Nahalalites volunteered to teach the boys proper military equestrianship. Both Nahum Havinsky and Yoseph Dromi had been in the Czarist Army, the former with a Cossack regiment and the latter with a unit of the Russian cavalry. On Saturdays and holidays the boys and their teachers rode out bareback to the fields. Dromi and Havinsky did teach the boys how to mount and dismount at full gallop and how to hobble their mounts during a foot maneuver, but the two self-styled teachers spent a much greater part of their time telling the boys tall tales of their illustrious past. One of Dromi's favorite stories was of the time his *polkovnik* (colonel) wanted to settle an account with him and gave him a wild horse that no one in the entire regiment was able to tame—no one, that is, except Dromi. He simply gave the horse its head, "released all it's speed," and rode him. One day, as he was galloping wildly on the horse, a farmer's cottage suddenly loomed up directly ahead of them. He hesitated for only a moment, and then cried out "À la barrière!" Pulling the reins tight, he flew with the horse right over the cottage. While in the air, Dromi told them, he managed to see a farmer below him crossing himself. Dromi taught the boys "proper" equestrian figures as practiced by Czar Nikolai's cavalry. He had the boys build a barricade so that they could practice the order "À la barrière!" None of them knew what the French words meant, but they all leaped the obstacle with ease.

Havinsky liked to tell his cadets the story of one of his more celebrated charges. It occurred during a war—the exact nature and date of which were never made clear—and he, alone on his charger, conquered a hill single-handed. He taught the boys the principles of a cavalry charge. Among other things, he demanded that they shout "Hurrah! Taken is the hill!" as they galloped up the hill chosen for the maneuver. The riders ranged their steeds in a straight line, then galloped wildly up the slope, waving their stick-swords. Though all five of them shouted at the top of their lungs, Havinsky's cries could be heard above them all. Galloping over the fields like Cossack horsemen became part of Moshe's world of imagination. He had been reading *The Flood* and *By Fire and By Sword* by Henrik Senkievic, whose heroes' names were all but unpronounceable. There was Jan Skrzetuski; Pan Wolodyjowski, the stocky cavalryman who was a swordsman *par excellence*; Prince Czilichowski; one-eyed Zagloba; and the giant Lithuanian, Longinus Podbipienta, who lifted his sword—the Zervikaptur—with one hand while everyone else required two. In his tiny room, by the light of a kerosene lamp, Moshe read about Anna Borzobohata-Kresinska, who came from Rozlogi-Siromhi on her way back from the Czerkes; and about Jan Skrzetuski's love for the beautiful Helena Kurtzivcovna. The wars between the Cossacks and the Lakhs, the Ukrainians and the Polish landowners and their Jewish agents, Bogdan Chmielnicki and his companions took place in the second quarter of the seventeenth century in places that were familiar to him from stories of his parents' childhood. He even found mention of the village of Prochorovka, his mother's birthplace.

Moshe knew he should admire the Poles who took the Jews under their patronage and should by the same token despise Chmielnicki's Cossacks, who raided Jewish villages and slaughtered their inhabitants without mercy. Indeed, as he read Senkievic, his responses tended that way. But Havinsky and Dromi had served in Cossack cavlary regiments, which were, by their account, far superior to the Lakhs. Thus, galloping up a hill, fired by Havinsky's trumpeting cries of "Hurrah! Taken is the hill!" Moshe and his friends seemed the incarnation of the dreaded Cossacks, and in later years Levi Eshkol often derogatively invoked this image of Moshe.

The first task Yehudah Mor gave the young horsemen was to help drive away the flocks that the Bedouin grazed on the wheat fields of Nahalal after the harvest. As the fame of the mounted guard spread, they were often asked to come to the aid of nearby Kfar Yehoshua and other settlements as far north as Yokne'am. All the boys in the group were strong and daring, but Moshe's superior alertness and courage became increasingly evident. Avino'am Slutzky once remarked that for Moshe, courage was a physical trait. Just as someone may have a physical deficiency, such as one leg shorter than the other, Moshe was simply "deficient" in fear.

The main reason for fighting between the Arabs and the horsemen was the trespassing of flocks on Nahalal fields. The minority of the Arabs came from the Nahalal area, while the majority inhabited the arid regions of Transjordan. For generations these tribes of nomadic shepherds had grazed their flocks throughout the summer in the lush Jezreel Valley. They were slow to adjust to changes, new political boundaries, and the establishment of Jewish settlements in the valley.

As soon as the harvest began, they would bring thousands of cattle and sheep to their traditional summer grazing lands. As a rule, they pitched their black tents near the water sources and the springs on the east bank of the Kishon River.

Armed with whips (except for Avino'am, who used a thick rubber hose with metal bands wound round one end), Yehudah Mor and his young horsemen would ride out to chase off the shepherds and their flocks. Occasionally they also rounded up a few cows and brought them back to Nahalal. Arabs who came to retrieve their cows were fined and given stern warning that the next time they trespassed on Nahalal lands, their cattle would not be returned. According to Mor, riding after the shepherds and their wildly fleeing cows was an art, especially as the group usually rode out at night. After a while, the watchman of Kfar Yehoshua joined the riders and set out after the dark-robed Turkoman shepherds. He dealt differently with the Arabs: on an order from him, the boys would catch one of the shepherds, tie him up with his feet in the air, and then whip the prisoner across the soles.

Moshe had a natural talent for combat leadership, and Avino'am recalls that "it always felt good to go out to fight with Moshe. He was very daring. He never looked twice; he simply ran forward. We all noticed that nothing seemed to frighten him, nor did he seem to care a whit what might happen to him. And in fights he knew no mercy." The boys of the moshav, who had never accepted his leadership in any other field, gradually learned to respect his unique gift for combat leadership.

There was no lack of fights with the local Arabs, particularly with the shepherds of the Arab el-Mazarib tribe. Since the establishment of the moshav, the ownership of certain plots of land in the area had remained unresolved. The el-Mazarib shepherds brought their flocks onto the Nahalal lands, cut down the eucalyptus trees planted by Meshulam's pupils, and often harvested Nahalal corn for themselves. When the horsemen appeared, the shepherds usually fled, leaving their flocks behind. One day the boys were surprised to see a shepherd stand his ground. First they threw stones at him from a distance, while Moshe cracked his whip over the sheep's heads. Riding out ahead of the others, he approached the shepherd and raised his whip high over his head. Before he could bring it down, however, he recognized the shepherd as Wahash, his childhood friend, now grown to manhood. The Arab looked Moshe in the eyes and reproached him for his behavior. Nahman Betser recalls:

Not only did we let Wahash go, but he even shamed us. After all, we had been his friends, especially Moshe. We used to meet, eat, and drink at each other's homes. And now his friend, Moshe, throwing stones at him . . . raising a whip against him. From his point of view he hadn't stolen anything from Moshe's house. He had only grazed his sheep on a field of stubble, and he didn't consider this trespassing because the el-Mazarib had always brought their sheep to graze on these lands.

Moshe wheeled his horse and galloped off toward Nahalal with his friends, leaving Wahash and his sheep where he had found them.

By 1930 Nahalal was no longer the only Jewish settlement in the Jezreel Valley. During the twenties an increasingly dense network of Jewish settlements formed on the western side of the valley. Yet the youth of Nahalal remained aloof and self-enclosed, an island unto themselves. This might have been the case in the other settlements as well had it not been for the formation of pioneer youth movements on a country-wide basis. One of the first of these was Hanoar Ha'oved (founded in 1924), the youth arm of the Histadrut. When the representatives of this movement tried to establish a branch in Nahalal, however, they came up against unexpected difficulties.

The youth of Nahalal opposed Hanoar Ha'oved primarily because of their sense of superiority. Bat-Ami relates: "We felt that Hanoar Ha'oved was for city children, and their reasons for belonging meant nothing to us." Their resistance was staunch, and the few youth who did try to start the movement in Nahalal failed. The leaders of the Labor movement were very concerned over the fact that the youth of the first moshav had chosen to alienate themselves from the Histadrut's official youth movement, and they feared that the youngsters of other moshavim would follow suit. They therefore sent Israel Galili (one of the founders of Hanoar Ha'oved) to persuade the youth and village committee to accept the movement. This was apparently the first time Moshe met Galili, for he was among the youth of Nahalal who opposed the establishment of Hanoar Ha'oved in the moshav.

When the failure to establish the movement in Nahalal became indisputable, one of the local boys who had led the effort published an article in the movement's journal, Bama'aleh, accusing Nahalal youth of "lack of character, general indifference, . . . absence of public-mindedness," lack of independence from the generation of founders, and "destructive negativism." A month later, on September 25, 1931, Moshe published an answer to these accusations in the same journal, defending the "spirit of Nahalal." The letter placed him in the position of an official spokesman of Nahalal youth and of moshav youth around the country.

In retrospect, Moshe's opposition to the establishment of Hanoar Ha'oved in Nahalal may be seen as a first instance of his aversion to party institutions and to participating in their activities. Furthermore, his stance placed him in direct opposition to men who were to become highly influential in the Haganah and the Palmach,* two organizations with which he was to become involved in later years. At the same time, however, he remained loyal to the village leadership of Nahalal, who opposed Hanoar Ha'oved for fear of kibbutz influence, so that his stance cannot really be described as rebellious.

* The elite corps of the pre-State defense force.

6 HIKING AND FIGHTING

(1933-1935)

On the night of December 22, 1932, the settlement of Nahalal was rocked by a loud explosion and a scream. The settlers rushed into the rainy winter night to discover that a bomb had been thrown into the Ya'akobi house. Eight-year-old David was killed outright, and his father, Yoseph, was fatally injured. He died at dawn. There had been several attacks on Jewish settlements in the Jezreel Valley during that year before the Ya'akobi murders, but despite these warning signals the members of Nahalal were taken by surprise. Since the establishment of the settlement twelve years before, they had experienced nothing more serious than occasional altercations with Arab shepherds and quarrels over property rights.

After six months of intensive investigation by the Haganah Information Service in Haifa, and with the help of the police—especially two Arab police officers—Ahmed el-Gala'eini, a nineteen-year-old blacksmith, and Mustapha el-Ali, a forty-three year old Arab farmer from the village of Zippori, were arrested. Their detention led to the subsequent arrest of three other suspects. All five had a distinctive feature in common: a wild, unkempt beard. This sign brought about the disclosure of a terrorist organization known as "The Bearded Sheiks," better known as the "Kassamai'in" after their leader Az-el-Din el-Kassam.

Born in Syria, el-Kassam taught in an Arabic school in Haifa, served as a preacher in a mosque, and was the secretary of the Young Men's Moslem Association. He found recruits among the workers in the quarries and the railroad stores, as well as mechanics and blacksmiths in town and anyone who had access to explosives or any knowledge of metalwork. The latter made it possible for his organization to specialize in the manufacture of homemade bombs. El-Kassam was a religious zealot who was prepared to lay down his life for Allah. Before sending his men out on a mission, he would read them passages from the Koran. He also forbade them to shave their beards. Initiates into the organization had to take a religious oath, and during the few months of basic training Sheik el-Kassam schooled them in *Shihada,* death in the war for the faith.

At the end of 1933 the Haifa District Court sentenced Mustafa el-Ali to death and Ahmed el-Gala'eini to fifteen years' imprisonment, and el-Kassam subsequently ordered a temporary halt to all activities. It was only in September 1934 that "The Bearded Sheiks" renewed their activities, "fighting for our religion and homeland, murdering Englishmen and Jews because they are taking over our land." After a series of murders and acts of sabotage and blackmail, el-Kassem led twenty-three of his men into the mountains of Jenin to prepare for a major attack on Kibbutz Beit Alpha. On November 7, 1935 some of them killed a Jewish police sergeant. A police unit went out to track down the murderers and ten days later, on November 17, made its first contact with the Kassamai'in and opened fire. In the ensuing battle near Jenin, three of el-Kassam's men were killed before he himself fell, mortally wounded. After a fifth was seriously wounded, the remaining men surrendered. The second half of the original force managed to evade the pursuing police and set up a base camp in the Nablus mountains. This small group became the nucleus of the "Kassamiya" movement, after its martyred founder.

El-Kassam's heroic death left a deep impression on the Arab community in Palestine. His exploits became legend, and his funeral procession in Haifa—attended by ten thousand school-children—turned into a mass demonstration of Arab nationalism. His death attracted the attention of the Jewish community as well. David Ben Gurion observed:

> In the days of el-Kassam we discovered that we were facing a new phenom-enon among the Arabs. This was not Nashashibi or the Mufti,* nor was it a question of political careerism or avarice. In Sheik el-Kassam we dis-covered a zealot who was willing to lay down his life for his faith. And now we face not one but scores and perhaps even thousands like him, supported by the entire Arab nation.

To a certain extent, the Kassamai'in were the seeds from which al-Fatah and other terrorist organizations would later sprout.

In Nahalal, Moshe disagreed with his father on the issue of the Kassamai'in. Shmuel had raised Moshe to believe that the Arabs were innately evil, which was why they robbed, plundered, and instigated pogroms and riots. Like many other Jews in Palestine, Shmuel called the Kassamai'in bases "murderers' nests." From his viewpoint, the men who killed Ya'akobi and his son were "dirty criminals." He saw the course of events as completely clear-cut and simple: we, the Jews, help the Arabs, bringing them prosperity and progress; and they respond by killing us, killing one another, and even killing the British. What kind of human beings are they? According to Shmuel, Moshe related, the balance was heavily weighted in the Jews' favor, and the Arabs "had no case." As Moshe

---

* Raghr eb-Bey Nashashibi, Mayor of Jerusalem, leader of moderate faction of Arab nationalist movement; Haj-Amin el-Husseini (the "Mufti"), British-appointed religious leader of the Arabs of Palestine and the leader of the extremist Arab nationalists.

remarked later, "a tremendous gulf developed" between his father and himself. Moshe tried to see the Arabs as they saw themselves, and not "through the eyes of a Russian Jew."

I understood then that they do have national motivation. Until that time I had been raised on the stories of the Hashomer guards about the most famous thief of all—an Arab named Abu Jilda—and other Arab bandits. The case of el-Kassam was the first time I began to regard the gangs as part of a national structure with nationalistic motivation. Individually, the Kassamai'in were virtuous men, exceptional idealists.

In September 1933, Shmuel went to Prague to participate in the Eighteenth Zionist Congress. By this time he had become a seasoned politician, returning to his farm only on weekends. Dvorah also began devoting more time to public work. With both parents away most of the time, the bulk of farm work fell to Moshe. "He was always bitter about the fact that he had to work the farm himself, that he couldn't ask his mother to share the burden. He was never free to do as he pleased, to study, pass his matriculation, and continue his education. He was very bitter about it, but also very devoted to his family, especially to his mother." This was the impression of Yehudit Wigodsky, Moshe's new girlfriend. His relationship with Chaya-Jule was broken off in the spring of 1932 because, according to Jule, as soon as he put on long trousers, he began eyeing other *futchras*.

Yehudit, known by her nickname Yuka, was easily the most beautiful girl in the Girls' School but was never "one of the gang." She was delicate, gentle, modest and self-effacing. In Nahalal she was regarded as a rare, Nordic beauty. The technique Moshe had employed to win Chaya-Jule's affections would not do with Yuka, and their romance began quite differently. Every week one of the second-year students was sent to the pine nursery at Kfar Hahoresh to bring back seedlings for the school. The trip was made by cart, hired for the purpose from one of the farmers in the village. Moshe arranged things so that whenever Yuka's turn came, it would be his turn to drive the cart. During these trips to Kfar Hahoresh, which Moshe dragged out to last the entire day, they began to discover their feelings for one other. Yuka recalls how Moshe would often stray off the road to "pick some apricots and plums for the trip." This was strictly forbidden, but Moshe's daring both shocked and attracted her.

On Friday nights, the girls were allowed to stay out until midnight. As they grew closer, Moshe and Yuka took to going out to dance at the Nazareth-Haifa crossroads. They strolled through the fields holding each other tightly, and although they kissed, that was as far as their self-imposed limit allowed. "Moshe was very considerate,"

Yuka related. "He dared not go any further. We both agreed that we must remain chaste. Perhaps he had to make an effort to control his desires. For me it was easier, because it was natural. I had had a very puritanical upbringing." On the whole, Yuka describes Moshe's attitude toward her as "chivalrous." During this period in Moshe's life, rumors spread in Nahalal that all was not well between Shmuel and Dvorah. Moshe was deeply hurt by the gossip and told his cousin Shulamit that for him the sanctity of family life was the highest virtue.

As a result of his wide reading, Moshe developed a far greater cultural awareness than did his friends. He was always thrilled by discoveries that opened doors to mysterious new worlds. His sophistication made him conscious of the inherent ambivalence of life. This was a concept totally foreign to the thinking of the pioneers, and in this respect Nahalal was no exception. The youth of the Yishuv were raised on clearly defined values based upon unalterable concepts of good and evil. Once Moshe alarmed Shulamit by telling her that "one doesn't always have to tell the truth; at any rate, not the whole truth." Shulamit recalls being profoundly shocked by this heresy, and Moshe's friends, who failed to discern his subtleties, regarded his ambivalence as the equivalent of dishonesty.

Unlike Moshe's classmates and his seniors, the younger boys of Nahalal, particularly those in the fourth class, regarded Moshe as a leader and a paragon of the finer virtues. The general consensus among them was that Moshe was an honest person who never evaded the truth and had a lively sense of humor, which made him fascinating company. Despite their fondness for him, they never grew close to him, as is often the case with young children and an older instructor. Their attitude was one of awed respect rather than love.

Moshe became active in the youth groups, presiding over meetings and organizing other activities in the youth center. Among the younger children were some of Moshe's students from the signals course he gave in Nahalal. According to Binya Zarhi, Moshe's qualities of leadership began to emerge from the time he joined the Haganah. Membership in the defense organization placed Moshe and his friends and rivals in an entirely new sphere of competition, in which rules imposed from the outside replaced the closed, intimate rules of the youth group or the class. Sociability was accepted as a virtue in the Haganah, but certainly did not bestow as much status as it had in Meshulam's class. The Haganah placed a far higher value on ingenuity and courage.

At the beginning of the summer of 1933, Mapai members in Nahalal tried to persuade the boys of the second and third classes to join the party. Nahman Betser recalls that Moshe had many reservations about doing so. "Just as he examined everything else thoroughly, asking the why's and the wherefore's of everything, so he often examined and criticized the Mapai platform." Nahman himself was not overeager to join Mapai, for the youth of Nahalal regarded parties and public affairs as synonymous and equally distasteful. Nevertheless, despite the boy's reservations about party involvement, and without consulting them, *Hapoel Hatzair,* now the official organ of Mapai, published in its June 9, 1933 edition an announcement that the Nahalal youths were enrolled in the party.

Nahman Betser openly refused to join Mapai. In his own words, he "rejected it," if only for the fact that his membership had been announced without his permission. Though Moshe did not take so drastic a stand, he refrained from becoming involved in any party activities. On the other hand, he willfully joined the Histadrut from a similar sense of obligation. He was highly critical of the political parties of the Yishuv and their affiliated youth movements. In fact, he became involved in party affairs only after the loss of his eye, when he believed his military career was at an end. In 1933, however, he had only one ambition—to study.

The opportunity to widen his horizons and continue his studies came unexpectedly. In 1932 Nahalal received a loan from the United Jewish Appeal to replace the original huts with permanent housing. The work was planned in two stages: the first forty houses were to be built from 1933 to 1935, and the rest from 1935 onward. The project was handed over to a contractor and an engineer named Avraham Papper, who had devised a new technique for single-casting concrete. Papper, who was Amnon Yannai's uncle, suggested that the boys of Nahalal organize a construction gang that would specialize in his technique and work with him on the houses of Nahalal. The boys gladly accepted the offer, for the agricultural economy of the moshav was still shaky and money was scarce due to the country-wide economic crisis of 1933. Papper's offer seemed a good way to earn some extra money, especially after he suggested that the boys establish a proper construction gang that would also build houses in Tel Aviv according to his system.

As the boys did piecework and wanted to earn as much money as possible, they worked themselves to the brink of exhaustion. Dvorah wrote to Shmuel about Moshe's new venture: "Moshe is working in building. It is extremely hard work, and he practically never has a break in the afternoon. We need you here. Aviva is in a bad mood and Moshe is also irritable and tired." Moshe was so tired that on Saturdays he would remain in bed all morning and even missed a number of lectures to the youth group. He was somewhat disappointed by the wages received for his efforts and wrote to his father: "It would seem that the daily wages in building are not worth the effort." His fatigue was probably caused by the fact that in addition to working with the construction gang, he continued working on the farm.

Tel Aviv tempted the boys with the prospect of earning more money. They organized themselves into a construction gang and left Nahalal for the big city. Dvorah asked her son to remain in Nahalal, at least until Shmuel's return from Prague. A disease had broken out in the chicken coops, and there was a danger of drought in the vineyards. Moshe's refusal to remain on the farm provoked a lengthy quarrel with his mother, but he prevailed in the end and joined his friends.

Papper's offer was attractive for another reason: the boys would be able to use their earnings to study at one of the night schools in the city. It was this plan, above all else, that convinced Moshe to join the group and leave Nahalal. While the others left behind relatively well-established farms tended by fathers and brothers, however, Moshe was leaving a struggling farm with no help. Aviva was twelve at the time and Zohar was only eight. Dvorah, who was by now well involved in public affairs, was left to work the farm with the help of a single hired hand.

Moshe's insistence on leaving, despite the obvious hardships Dvorah would have to endure, was in keeping with a family tradition that justified the fulfillment of personal ambitions even at the expense of the family. This philosophy implies a pale of individual responsibility whose limits are defined by the individual himself. Within its bounds, the individual is totally responsible for everything he and others must do; beyond them, "everything will take care of itself," for better or for worse. Within the limits of her self-imposed responsibilities, Dvorah did what was necessary on the farm and was left with a sense "of wholeness and justice." After completing all she felt necessary, if the children's shoes were still torn or the chickens still suffered from disease, she did not grow indifferent, but neither did she indulge in any form of self-recrimination. Above all, such misfortunes never prevented her from fulfilling her own ambitions. Moshe apparently adopted this outlook on life early in his youth. Within the bounds of the responsibilities he defined for himself, he did everything he had to do, and although one could criticize the limits as being too narrow or too broad, none could fault the quality of the work done within them. Just as one of her children's illnesses did not prevent Dvorah from attending a meeting of the editorial board of *Dvar Hapoelet* in Tel Aviv, so an outbreak of Newcastle disease in the chicken coop, or drought in the vineyards, or Shmuel's absence did not prevent Moshe from fulfilling his wish to study.

In the autumn of 1933, after completing the first forty houses in

Nahalal, the seven boys left for Tel Aviv, where they were joined by two others: Avraham Yaffe (later OC Southern Command and a division commander in the Six-Day War) and Yehoshua ("Yosh") Palmon (later Director of the Arab Department of the Jewish Agency and Ben Gurion's Adviser on Arab Affairs). Half of the group stayed at Yaffe's father's house, while the others shared a flat in the old commercial center of the city. In the evenings they studied at two different schools: the Technion Night School, where Moshe studied geometry, algebra, and draughtsmanship; and the Popular University, a branch of the Hebrew University, where the boys attended lectures in literature and Hebrew grammar.

During his stay in Tel Aviv, Moshe sat for a portrait of himself in a photographer's studio. He wore a white shirt, his hair was neatly brushed, and his eyes were bright and alert. He was so pleased with the result that he gave copies to all his friends. The inscription on the copy sent to Yuka read: "To Yuka—in spite of everything, with love, Moshe. January 7, 1934." At that time their relationship was undergoing a crisis. The fact that Moshe was far from Nahalal intensified their feelings for one another to the point of love. In the summer of 1933, Yuka graduated from the Girls' School and returned to her parents' home in Rishon le-Zion. After work, Moshe would often travel to the village by bus to take Yuka into Tel Aviv; in the evening he would travel back with her to Rishon le-Zion and then take another bus back to Tel Aviv. Four trips, each an hour long, were no obstacle to his love. He would often spend the weekend at the Wigodsky home. In Tel Aviv, the couple went to the cinema or strolled through the city or along the beach, talking for hours. Sometimes they wandered through the village and fields in Rishon le-Zion.

Within a short time, Moshe proposed to Yuka. His love for her was only one of his reasons for doing so. He told Yuka that he was tired of "traveling back and forth and being alone all the time"; he wanted "to settle down" somewhere, and he didn't particularly care where. He had discussed new ways of life and new ideas of pioneering and adventure with his friends in Tel Aviv. Among these was the idea to establish a fishing cooperative on Lake Kinneret. In fact, within a year his friends established their own settlement near Nahalal—Kvutzat Shimron.

In Moshe's circle, it was almost unheard of for a boy under twenty to want to marry. Moshe may have exhausted the will power needed to conquer his desire. While several of his friends in the group were living with their girlfriends in Tel Aviv, Moshe was still a virgin. True as ever to his belief in the sanctity of family life, he felt that only marriage could provide a solution for him. Yuka accepted his proposal in principle but wanted to postpone their marriage until an unspecified date in the future. She felt they were too young to marry and that she, at any rate, was not ready to assume the burden of family life. At this point their relationship reached an impasse. Although Yuka knew that Moshe's friends "dared more and were happier," she grew angry with Moshe for making demands that were not in keeping with her principles of chastity. She rejected the notion of premarital sex and wanted to return to the beautiful, spiritual evenings they had spent walking hand in hand. She clearly remembers the evening on the beach when Moshe gave her an ultimatum: either marriage or love-making, and if neither, then they must part. In the end, they agreed to delay the final decision and stop seeing each other to test whether they could bear being apart, really wanted to marry, or should resume their relationship on the old basis. The inscription on the photograph was an allusion to this state of affairs. Yuka, as well as some of Moshe's friends, believed that one of the main motives for his wish to marry so young was his desire to leave his parents' house. Israel Gefen, who later married Aviva, described the Dayan household as oppressive. Shmuel preached incessantly and Dvorah always walked about the house despondently, "the very embodiment of suffering on the face of the earth." Yuka did not believe that Moshe was destined to achieve fame. She was certain that he would be a farmer, and she saw no reason to surrender her youth so soon and join him in the endless drudgery of farm life. These were her thoughts when she rejected his proposal.

During the harvest months of 1934, the construction gang returned to Nahalal to help their parents. In September a new group came to the Girls' School. Among them was Ruth Shwarz, who in less than nine months was to become Moshe's wife.

Autumn, the interval between the summer harvest and the winter sowing, was a favorite time for hikes and outings. As the years went by, the Nahalal hikes became increasingly ambitious. Far from being haphazard outings, they were carefully planned expeditions designed to teach the youth of the village about their country as systematically as possible.

When the boys of the construction gang returned home, the youth of Nahalal were in the midst of preparation for the hike along Lake Kinneret, which was to end with a climb up Mount Hermon. Though the mountain was not in Mandatory Palestine (it was then partly in Syria and mostly in Lebanon), it could be climbed without a passport or an entry permit. The excitement that preceded the proposed hike was crushed when the outing was canceled for reasons of security. The growing tension between the Arabs of Palestine and the Jewish community made hiking dangerous in areas far from Jewish settlements. The hiker far from home faced other problems as well. In the summer of 1934, the first organized attempt was made to bring large numbers of illegal immigrants into Palestine. A country-wide manhunt after illegal immigrants was begun, and the press carried detailed accounts of its progress.

Moshe fought the cancellation of an earlier hike to Mount Hermon, and the argument soon became a matter of personal prestige. If the others accepted Moshe's opinion, it would prove that they acquiesced to his will and tacitly acknowledged his supremacy over them. They steadfastly refused, and Moshe, unwilling to give up the hike he had so eagerly anticipated, turned to the younger class and asked if anyone was prepared to join him. Two of the boys agreed— Binya Zarhi and Baruch Zemel. But by that time Moshe had changed his plans and proposed a far more ambitious and daring expedition: to hike south from Beisan along the Jordan River to Jericho, then along the shores of the Dead Sea south to Sodom, and from there westward to Hebron, Beersheba, and finally Gaza on the Mediterranean. The latter three cities were notorious for their hostility to Jews.

When the details of Moshe's plans became known, the youth and adults of Nahalal raised an outcry. They asked the security authorities in the moshav to forbid the boys to go out on so hazardous an outing. The hikers would roam dangerously far from home, and the route they suggested passed through large areas of Palestine inhabited only by Bedouin. The warning that they might be caught and stripped naked was odd, but not far from the truth. The three boys nonetheless prepared to leave. They equipped themselves with two canteens each, and the crossed straps gave them a rather military aspect, which they thought quite dashing. They were warned that the first thing the Bedouin would do was take their canteens—and then what would they do without water? Each boy took five Palestinian pounds, and they had one camera between them. The money constituted their entire savings, and Baruch Zemel's camera was a rare thing in those days.

They paid little heed to the warnings and soon after the Jewish New Year set out by bus for Beisan. From the Arab town they walked down to the Jordan and began the first leg of their hike. In their knapsacks were hard-boiled eggs, tins of sardines, and extra clothes. Moshe took a map as well. On the very first day, they had trouble with water. The month of September is known for its hot, dry eastern winds, and because of their constant need for water, the boys had to walk close to the riverbed. But they ran into many obstacles: thick, almost impassable vegetation, thorns, and deep ravines. Nevertheless, as long as they kept to the channel, their water supply could always be replenished. Toward evening, as they neared the Damiya Bridge, they caught sight of a large Bedouin encampment pitched right on the river bank. Circling west to avoid it, they reached the main road through the Jordan Valley long after sunset, with very little water left in any of the six canteens. To conserve both strength and water, Moshe decided that they should sleep where they were, alongside the road, rather than look for a place off the road free of thorns, snakes, and scorpions. They agreed to rise at dawn, rejoin the riverbed on the other side of the Bedouin camp, and continue on their way south. But even before they fell asleep they finished the last of their water.

Two hours later they awoke with parched tongues. Moshe's watch showed midnight. The dry, choking air was utterly still, and they feared that without water they would not last the night. Moshe suggested that they go back to the river and risk the danger involved in passing the Bedouin camp. As slowly and quietly as they could, the three boys stole toward the riverbed. Suddenly, the night was shattered by the raucous barking of dogs, and the boys discovered that they had inadvertently stumbled into the middle of the·encampment. In the pitch-black night they had been unable to discern the black tents. Their first impulse was to run for their lives, but Moshe stopped them, saying that "it wouldn't be nice to run away." Instead, the three stood up and called out, *"Ya zalame, ya zlam, ya nass!"* (Oh men, oh man, oh people). Their self-confidence apparently alarmed the Bedouin, who had no idea who had broken into their encampment in the middle of the night and were afraid to reply to the call. Everything was still for a few moments, and then a candle was lit in one of the tents. With the leather canteen straps across their chests, the boys looked like officials or policemen. In the dim light of the candle they caught sight of an old Arab—"a hundred years old" according to Binya—standing nearby and shaking with fear. They asked him for water. Staring fixedly at the crossed leather straps, he poured a trembling stream of water into their canteens.

Returning to the road, the boys slept soundly. When they awoke, the sun was shining brightly over the Gilead Mountains east of the Jordan. As they ate breakfast, Moshe told his friends about an argument he had with Dr. Theodor Herzl in a dream. "Listen to this," Moshe said. "I told him that I was angry at him for preceding me and being the first to conceive of a Jewish State."

Since they had no desire to return to the Bedouin camp after the previous night's incident, and thinking of visiting the spring and stream of Wadi Far'ah, they left the Jordan Valley and struck out westward toward the Jiftlik Valley. The three marched on singing until they lost their way. Moshe's map was of little help, for it was not a topographical one. Later they learned that they had entered Wadi Fatsa'el.

Their predicament now was much more serious than before.

They had very little water, were far from the river, and had no idea
where water could be found in the area. The heat and the long walk
had worn them out. When an Arab appeared, as if out of nowhere,
they hesitated, uncertain of their next move. To their surprise, the
Arab did not call for help or try to attack them with his club. Instead
he took them to a large Bedouin camp, where they were asked to wait
in one of the tents while a curious crowd gathered around them. After
a short time, they were invited into a large, ornately decorated tent
and found themselves face to face with Emir Diab. At first the Arab
scowled at them, then rebuked them for coming to a part of the
country which did not belong to them. He also pointed out that
"there is a feud between us." Moshe replied on the boys' behalf.
He began by wishing the Emir well and blessing him in the traditional
Arab manner. Then he added that the three hikers had heard of
the Emir's famous hospitality and were therefore not afraid to be
found in the tribe's territory after they had lost their way. They
hoped that the people of his tribe would show them the way to
their destination, Jericho. The Emir responded with *"Tfadalu"*
(Welcome) and invited them to spend the night as his guests and
partake of food and drink. Baruch Zemel's camera, which aroused
great curiosity, helped to break the ice and doubtlessly enhanced
their welcome. The Emir had his photograph taken three times—
each time with two of the three boys. Moshe offered to send him
copies, and the last of the barriers between them fell. The boys
drank bitter coffee around flickering campfires, then lay down on
soft camel's-wool mattresses for a good night's sleep. In the morning
their host provided them with cakes of dried camel's milk, blessed
them, and bade them farewell. He also put at their disposal an ass
driver who was on his way to Jericho to bring flour.

The hospitality displayed by Emir Diab made a profound
impression on Moshe. Many years later, as Minister of Defense and
governor of the territories conquered by Israel in the Six-Day War,
this experience played an important part in the formation of his
liberal policies. Years after the event he often said that he personally
had "never come up against any reprehensible conduct on the part
of the Arabs." Listening to him talk of his childhood, one cannot but
sense that his attitude toward the Arabs is imbued with a love for
their culture and way of life; that it was only the quirks of history and
the bitter destiny of the Jewish people that placed him at the head of
troops who recurrently fought the Arabs.

Packing their knapsacks on the asses, the boys set off toward
Jericho. But no sooner had they reached the main road than fresh
trouble loomed in the form of two Arab policemen from Nablus.
The sight of an Arab ass driver in the company of three Jewish boys
was odd and aroused their suspicion. First the policemen separated

them, then proceeded to beat the Bedouin so that he would know who was boss. After that they turned to the three boys, first searching their clothing and packs and then asking where they were from. Suspecting them to be illegal immigrants, they prepared to take the boys to the Nablus police station.

Moshe refused to go and told the policemen in Arabic that he and his friends were not illegal immigrants. His initial gambit of speaking Arabic did not convince them, so Moshe asked one of the policemen his name, and the Arab told him—Jabber. Was he any relation to Jabber of the Nahalal police? To the boy's surprise, he replied that he was none other than the man's brother. This revelation cleared all suspicions and they exchanged greetings and warm handshakes. The ass driver, watching these proceedings from a respectful distance, could not believe his eyes. When they continued on their way, he said they must certainly be armed, for otherwise the incident was beyond comprehension. Moshe told him he was right and added—in Hebrew—to his friends, "We must make them believe that Jews never walk about unarmed. When other hikers come their way, this Arab and his friends will know they have weapons and will take care not to harm them." The ass driver wanted to know where they had hidden the pistol. "Between the bread and the olives," Moshe told him.

The boys parted from the ass driver at a crossroads near Jericho. The Arab continued to the town, while the boys struck out toward Kalya on the northern shore of the Dead Sea. In the work camp there, they met a man who had been the baker at Degania. The adventures that had befallen the boys only whetted their appetites for more. They told their friend that they intended going south from Kalya through Ras Feshkha to Sodom on the southern shore of the Dead Sea. The baker, who at first greeted them warmly and gave them food and drink, was shocked when he heard their plans. He told them that a large group of hikers had recently taken the same route, lost its way, and had not been found since. He so feared for them that he called in the supervisor of the work camp, who forcibly put the three boys on the camp bus to Jerusalem.

Rather than put an end to their plans, the unexpected trip to Jerusalem merely modified them. They decided to travel from Jerusalem to Hebron by bus, then on foot down to Ein Gedi and the southern region of the Dead Sea. They stayed the night in the city and the following morning took an Arab bus to Hebron, where they wished to visit the Cave of the Machpela (the traditional burial place of Abraham, Isaac, and Jacob) but were not allowed to enter. After wandering through the city, they stopped by a flour mill where a caravan of camels was about to set for the south of the Dead Sea, and they expressed the wish to join it. For some reason, at the very last moment Moshe became suspicious. "I don't like them, we're not going with them," he told his friends. Instead of going to the Dead Sea, they took an Arab taxi to Beersheba. Then they traveled on a crowded bus to Gaza and went directly to visit the old port. Before they could see very much, Arab policemen arrested them and brought them to the local police station for interrogation. Once again they were suspected of being illegal immigrants. Binya Zarhi and Baruch Zemel were amazed at the courage Moshe displayed. He refused to be interrogated in Arabic and tried to intimidate the policemen by requesting the name of the interrogating officer, writing the name with a flourish in his notebook. He also wrote down the number of the policeman who arrested them.

Once again the sweet smell of publicity, which he had sampled a few months before with the publication of his first article in *Bama'aleh*, tempted Moshe. He told his friends that in the public interest they "must" report all that had befallen them on their way. They too would benefit, he added, as the publicity would enhance the entire adventure in the eyes of Nahalal. Arriving in Tel Aviv in the evening, Moshe took his friends to the offices of *Davar*, but when they arrived he informed his surprised companions that he would not enter the building. He told them to go in and ask for Zalman Shazar (later third president of the State of Israel), one of the editors of the paper and a close friend of the Dayans. Moshe explained that he did not want to go in because of a large pimple that had sprouted on his chin and marred his appearance. The real reason may have been his characteristic reluctance to talk about himself. He finally prevailed and the two boys went in without him. Shazar was amazed to hear that Moshe was waiting out in the street and had not come up to see him. Nevertheless, he listened to their tale and then wrote a news story which was published on the front page the following day, September 17, 1934.

The boys spent the fifth night of their adventure in Tel Aviv. Moshe divided what was left of the camel's milk cakes among his friends as a memento of their adventures. By the time the three returned to Nahalal, the morning edition of *Davar* had already been passed from hand to hand and they had become celebrities.

Before the end of 1934, Moshe enjoyed even greater fame and distinction, this time as the result of a battle. The JNF lands bordering on Wadi Shimron, part of which were given to Nahalal for cultivation, had formerly served as grazing lands for the villagers of Mahalul and the Bedouin of Arab el-Mazarib. Although thirteen years had passed since the establishment of Nahalal and an even greater interval since the sale of these lands, the former tenants, as well as the local Bedouin, continued to bring their flocks to their

traditional grazing lands. Quarrels over land were common throughout Palestine, but only rarely did they develop to the point of
bloodshed.

Afraid that the Arabs would claim right of possession over these
lands by their continued presence, the JNF watchman suggested
that the entire area be plowed and sown for "political" purposes.
On December 20, 1934 the young men of Nahalal, led by Binya
Zarhi, drove eight pairs of mules hauling large plows into the
disputed land and began plowing. Following the plows with
sack in hand, Moshe, the only sower, scattered the seeds. Slowly
at first, then in rapidly increasing numbers, the Bedouin gathered
on the slopes of the wadi. For a while they watched; then they began
throwing stones at the sower and the men behind the plows. This
move was answered by a hail of stones from the Nahalalites. During
the exchange Moshe continued sowing, completely exposed. When
he reached the top of the slope, according to one account, an Arab
suddenly appeared and struck him over the head with his club. Moshe
fell to the ground, blood flowing over his face.

Yehuda Mor, who supervised the entire operation astride his
horse, ordered the men of Nahalal to stop plowing. He sounded
an alarm and sent men to Nahalal and the neighboring kibbutzim
to summon help. The Bedouin began their own alarm to bring
reinforcements from camps in the area and the village of Mahalul.
Meanwhile, the wounded were evacuated to Nahalal. Moshe
recovered consciousness as soon as he was brought to the village and
walked to the village council. Only after reporting that he had
"completed his mission" did he agree to have his wound attended.
He was taken from the infirmary to his parent's house and ordered
to remain in bed for fear of concussion.

The fight and its casualties remained in the headlines for a week
after the event. Moshe did not even know who brought the club
down on his head. He thought then, and still does today, that it was
his friend Wahash. An Arab who witnessed the fight, Abed of the
Abeidat family, stated that it was Abdullah Mustapha who had struck
Moshe. When he was allowed out of bed, Moshe was still weak from
loss of blood. At the docter's insistence, he was sent to recuperate at a
rest home. Five months later, in May 1935, Moshe invited the notables of Arab el-Mazarib, as well as his young Arab friends Wahash
Hanhana and Abdullah Mustapha, to his wedding. According
to Abed, a messenger came on horseback to the el-Mazarib encampment bringing Moshe's invitation. At first the members of the tribe
were afraid to come. Abed recalls the event: "The tribe sat in council
and discussed the matter. The younger men said, 'Nahalal still has a
feud with us, they will beat us,' while the elders said, 'What's the
matter with you? Would they invite us to a wedding in order to beat

us up? Nothing will happen.'" And indeed, the entire tribe came to the wedding. Abed continued:

In the tribe, Moussa was spoken of as a hero. The Bedouin judge a man by his daring. We saw that he was a man who goes fearlessly ahead, in front of everyone else, and unarmed, too. Two years later, at the end of the harvest, there was a famine, and our tribe was poor. People searched for food, picking one stalk of wheat here, one there, and did not regard it as stealing. Abdullah Mustapha went down to the wheat fields of Nahalal to gather the residue. Suddenly he saw Moussa watching over the fields on horseback. But instead of shouting at him, instead of striking him or chasing him away, Moussa greeted him, dismounted and helped Abdullah gather some wheat, then sent him on his way.

7 THE HAGANAH

(1935-1938)

On September 1, 1934 the new school year began at the Agricultural School for Girls. In the evening, the boys of the village crowded around the school to survey the new crop. This first meeting was always one of glances. According to one of the boys, "They gazed at us, and we stared back at them until everyone, more or less, had found a partner." At the very least, by the time the glances were over, it was clear who was going to invite whom to dance on Friday night at the youth center. On this occasion, Moshe's glance met that of a girl named Ruth Shwarz.

Ruth was totally caught up in her enthusiasm for the kibbutz, so much so that she abandoned her secondary school studies. She told her parents that there was no sense in continuing as "there are already too many Jewish scholars." Her only aim in life was to live on a kibbutz, and she would therefore be much better off studying agriculture. When Ruth left for Nahalal she promised her friends that the *only* thing she would acquire in Nahalal was an education in agriculture.

At first Ruth and Moshe danced together at the Nazareth crossroads and went for walks and rides in an ox-drawn cart. Then Ruth, for whom English was a second language, began giving Moshe private lessons. After the clash with the Bedouin in Wadi Shimron, Ruth accompanied Moshe to a rest home, where they were photographed together for the first time. From there they went on to Jerusalem, and Ruth introduced Moshe to her parents. On July 12, 1935 they were married. At twenty, Moshe was the first boy in his class to take a wife.

Ruth was born in Haifa on March 6, 1917 to Rachel and Zvi Shwarz. Both her parents had been in the third graduating class of the Herzliya Gymnasium, the first Hebrew-language secondary school in Palestine. The Shwarzes first taught at the school at Merhavya and then, during the First World War, Zvi helped Rachel's father, a wealthy man, in running "Atid," the first vegetable-oil factory in Palestine. In 1920 the family left Palestine for England, where Zvi entered the London School of Economics and obtained an M.A. degree in Social Sciences, while also studying at the rabbinical institute, Jew's College, and serving as a Hebrew-English translator for the directors of the London offices of the Keren Hayesod. They returned to Jerusalem in 1925. Zvi was appointed secretary to the directors of the Keren Hayesod. In

1930 he began studying law and in 1934 joined the law firm of Dr. Dov Yoseph, later becoming one of its partners. By 1935 the Shwarz house in Jerusalem had become a meeting place for the Labor Zionist, Anglo-Jewish, university, British Zionist, government, and Jewish Agency elites of Jerusalem.

It may be said that the marriage of Moshe and Ruth was a society match between children of prominent members of the Second Aliyah intelligentsia and the communal settlement on the one hand, and the political, English-speaking elite, on the other. The Dayan-Shwarz wedding was a unique event. It was unusual for agricultural settlements to celebrate weddings with lavish ceremony, and Ruth's parents added to the settlers' feeling of strangeness by hiring a special bus to bring prominent Jerusalemites and national personalities to Nahalal. And as if that were not enough, Moshe invited the entire Arab el-Mazarib tribe (Arabs at a Jewish wedding were a rare sight indeed). Only Ruth's friends from the Mahanot Ha'olim movement boycotted the wedding to protest her "betrayal" of the kibbutz.

The ceremony took place at 6 p.m. under a walnut tree in the Dayans' yard. The groom worked until the last minute arranging the refreshments. The Dayans supplied grapes and boiled corn in large tubs, while Rachel Shwarz brought a carload of cakes, drinks, cold cuts, and sausages—great delicacies in those days. Ruth remembers that as soon as the ceremony was over, she rushed to the house, took off her wedding dress, put on shorts and a working shirt, and ran to the barn, because in the excitement "everyone had forgotten that it was milking time." When Ruth returned from the barn to the festive singing and folk-dancing, the Bedouin of Arab el-Mazarib danced the *debka* and rode wildly on their horses, firing in the air in the best tradition of the Arab *fantaziya*. Abdullah Mustapha shook Moshe's hand in a formal *sulha,* the traditional peace-making ceremony.

Ruth thought highly of Moshe's ability both as an organizer and a speaker. She remembers that she sensed in him a paradoxical blend of toughness and sensitivity, easy good nature, and relentless ambition, all combined with shrewd common sense. In the eyes of her parents, however, Moshe was above all a young man lacking an education. They therefore decided that their wedding gift would be a study trip to England: boat tickets and a monthly allowance of £15 a month (generous for those days) for as long as the young couple remained abroad.

Zvi wanted Moshe "to increase his knowledge of English, because we—my wife and myself—were greatly influenced by English culture." Dvorah also felt that the trip would be beneficial. Although Shmuel was opposed to both the trip and the proposed studies, the family majority carried the day, and on June 19, 1935 Moshe took out a British-Palestinian passport in which he was described as a farmer, 5' 8" tall, with black hair and brown eyes.

Zvi Shwarz asked friends in England to help Moshe receive a scholarship to one of the better universities. Lady Erleigh, the daughter of Alfred Mond (Lord Melchett) invited the young couple to stay at her estate and tried to secure a place for Moshe at one of the Oxford colleges; through his association with Harold Lasky, Zvi tried to arrange a place for him at the London School of Economics; Dr. Chaim Weizmann did his share by applying on Moshe's behalf to Cambridge—a rather impressive range of choices for a graduate of the two-year course at the Nahalal Girls' School.

These efforts and contacts are indicative of the great new world of opportunity that Moshe entered through his marriage into the Shwarz family. Both the Dayan and Shwarz families were well known and had many wide-ranging connections. Had Moshe chosen a career in politics or law, he could not have hoped for a better start. It soon became clear, however, that Moshe was to go his own way without making much use of his family's connections. The principal contribution of the Shwarz family to Moshe's progress lay in teaching him how to dress properly in a jacket and tie and the social graces that enabled him to mix easily in sophisticated company. He even learned (and loved) to dance the waltz and the tango. Although he "danced like a bear," as Ezer Weizman put it, he eagerly attended the afternoon tea-dances at the King David Hotel in Jerusalem. The Shwarzes would have accomplished much for their son-in-law even if they had only helped him overcome his farmer's awkwardness in high society. But their contribution did not stop there, for they also helped him broaden his cultural horizons. The trip abroad left its stamp on him. He was on his way to the great city of London, while most of his friends on the moshav had never sailed even as far as Cyprus. In brief, his marriage to Ruth Shwarz must be regarded as an important turning point in Moshe Dayan's life.

That things did not turn out as planned is another matter. "From the very first day, Moshe hated London. He was not a great lover of abroad and wanted to return home immediately," Ruth recalls. Among the reasons for his unhappiness were primarily the language problem (for he learned English very slowly) and his discomfort in a suit and tie. He finally rebelled, removed his tie, and refused to wear an overcoat, reverting naturally to the more comfortable Palestinian style of dress and even wearing sandals instead of shoes. With Moshe on his bicycle in trousers and an open-collared shirt, and Ruth behind him in a skirt and blue, youth-movement shirt, the two were a bizarre sight as they pedaled through the streets of

London. Finally there was the English weather. Soon after they arrived it turned cold, and Moshe had no choice but to wear shoes again. He also resorted to an overcoat, but wore it directly over his shirt without a jacket. In short, on his first visit to a large city in a foreign country, Moshe suffered from the depression that afflicts so many Israelis upon leaving their small, new country for distant lands.

In the meantime, Harold Lasky's and Chaim Weizmann's connections bore fruit. Moshe was registered at the London School of Economics and offered the opportunity to study agriculture at Cambridge on condition that he pass entrance examinations at some time during the course of his studies there. Far from raising his spirits, however, these prospects only served to deepen his despondency. News from home aggravated the situation: his parents wrote depressing letters about the state of the farm, the endless mud, diseases in the cowshed, and the fact that they were constantly "dead tired." Moshe began feeling guilty about the leisurely life he was leading in London with a comfortable, work-free income while his family suffered at home. News of political developments in Palestine was no better: riots had broken out throughout the country in 1936, and Nahalal was shocked by a murder. The London winter added its own dismal tones to an already bleak picture. Ruth, who wanted to stay on in England, tried to persuade him to take the university entrance examinations, but Moshe had already made up his mind. After six months in London, they returned to Nahalal. Commenting on this trip, Moshe said:

I went to England without a matriculation certificate and without knowing a word of English. I didn't even spend a single day at Cambridge. Being abroad depressed me. To this day I hate going abroad. Every trip is a burden. I stayed there for six months and nothing came of it. I learned only enough English to make conversation. I soon realized that the correspondence courses I took at LSE were worthless and the few lectures I attended were of little interest. The riots in Palestine were a good enough excuse to come back. The political situation in the country worried me most, and helped me make up my mind. Today I think that if I had gone to England with a matriculation certificate and begun regular studies, the tension in Palestine might not have been enough to make me come back. But since our stay in England seemed futile anyway, I returned to the farm. I wanted very much to study, but it didn't work out.

Upon his return Moshe faced two important decisions. The first concerned the function he would fulfill during the riots; the second was where he would settle and make his home. While he was in England, seventeen of his exclassmates founded the Shimron Group, and he was undecided whether to join them or live and work on his parents' farm.

The first of these problems was quickly solved. In 1936 the Haganah began working in cooperation with the British Army against the Arab terrorist gangs. One of the first manifestations of this cooperation was the assignment of Haganah guides to British Army units. One of the requirements for guides was a working knowledge of English, and Moshe's stay in England made him an obvious choice. He was posted to the regiment that was guarding the Iraqi oil pipeline. In retrospect, this assignment may be regarded as the first stage of Moshe's military career, although at the time he himself regarded it as only a temporary post and was much more concerned with the question of finding a place to settle down.

The founding of the Shimron Group by the youth of Nahalal in 1935 was their attempt to strike out on their own in an independent settlement framework and thereby avoid falling into the ready-made pattern established by their parents. Initially the youngsters had no idea of what kind of social framework they desired. The group was first called simply "Shimron," the definition *kvutza* being added only later. The Nahalal village council reacted calmly to the establishment of the group and graciously offered them 380 dunams of land around Shimron Hill. The founders evidently hoped that their children would see the folly of their ways and soon return to toe the Nahalal line. Eventually, several girls from the Agricultural School, as well as a youth-movement nucleus of Polish and Rumanian immigrants, joined the original Shimron Group, and in 1938 they established Kibbutz Hanita on the Lebanese border.

Moshe decided to throw in his lot with the majority, after reaching the conclusion that he and Ruth belonged with their friends. But his own willingness to join the Shimron Group was not enough; he still had to be accepted into the group—and that, it transpired, was not as easy as he had thought. His application for membership was received coolly, and some members of the group openly doubted his suitability for life in a kibbutz. They knew that he was not always easy to get along with, and three members of the group demanded that he be given only provisional status until the group could decide whether or not to accept him as a full member. The nature of the kibbutz is such that sociability is a crucial factor.

This virtual rejection would have been a slap in the face for Moshe even if he had not struggled for leadership throughout his childhood. Nahman Betser advised him to accept the provisional membership, and on his camp bed in Afula, he wrote to Betser on August 12:

After thinking over your suggestion that I accept provisional membership in the Shimron Group, I began to understand just how impossible such a thing is for me. Just imagine my position as a candidate for membership. If a total stranger is a candidate, it means the others have to get to know him before deciding whether or not to accept him. But when I am the candidate, it means exactly the opposite . . . I'm given a period of "grace" to change and become something else; only then will they accept me. I cannot and do not wish to be in the position of being tested. On the one hand, I won't be able to take part in the discussions on Shimron affairs, important issues, because I shall always feel as though I am a nonmember. On the other, I will have to go to extremes of counterfeit for my three (or more) opponents, so that they can make up their minds whether or not I have changed for the better.

If you wish to trust me to a certain extent (the same degree of trust, by the way, that each one of you enjoyed in the beginning until you were accepted by the group), if you believe in my capability and good will—fine. If not—then not. I may not succeed in conforming to the ideal you have set for yourselves, though personally I don't think that should be necessary. What is important is that one sincerely wishes to live an honest life within the group, that one should support the continuing development of the society and the settlement, work hand in hand with the others, not look for the easiest work or the best position, and that one should be frank and open with everyone. That, in fact, is all.

Keep well,
Moshe

This letter indicates that Moshe's views on the relationship of the individual to society had already crystallized, and they have not changed much since then. The latter part of the letter delineates several principles that were to guide him in the future. Sociability was not among them; nor was the emotional partnership that became so vital a principle in kibbutz life. In effect, what he was saying was that an individual should be allowed to integrate into a society, even on the purely superficial level of carrying out his duties and refraining from exploiting that society. Beyond that, the individual should be given leave to do as he sees fit.

In 1936 this credo was unpalatable to Moshe's friends in Shimron. By that time, the kibbutz had become a venerated social ideal that attracted the cream of the pioneering youth. Sociability and the sharing of experiences were the ties that bound the members together. The individual was called upon not only to carry out the duties imposed on him by his society, but also to bare his soul to the others. Moreover, and perhaps most important of all, each individual in the kibbutz was accorded an equal measure of respect, regardless of his capabilities, talents, or status in fields of competitive achievement.

In time, reality modified these concepts somewhat, and many youngsters who saw in the kibbutz an ideal way of life discovered after a year, or perhaps twenty years, that they were unable to live happily within the kibbutz framework. Of the many who proudly bore the banner of the kibbutz movement, only a select few remained to realize its promise. In some cases, for every member who remained on a kibbutz, one hundred left. The remarkable thing about twenty-one year old Moshe was his levelheadedness—later to be regarded as a highly developed sense of reality—in all that concerned his companions' ideals. From the outset he took into account the possibility that he might not find his place in the kibbutz, while they embarked upon their new venture untroubled by any such doubts. As it turned out, only one Nahalal-born member of the original Shimron Group remained in Hanita.

It was typical of Moshe that after refusing to join the group on a trial basis, he backed down and agreed. Thus he joined the group provisionally for a six-month period, while Ruth was accepted unconditionally from the outset. When the trial period was over, a ballot was taken, and Moshe was accepted as a member of the Shimron Group, a social framework that did not particularly appeal to him. But the young Dayans remained in Shimron for two years, and Moshe did his best to participate in all the group's social activities.

One aspect of kibbutz life that proved to be an unavoidable source of conflict was the fact that important functions within the kibbutz were delegated on the basis of popularity, rather than merit or aptitude. This was painfully highlighted when the question of electing a local commander for the settlement arose. Although it was abundantly clear that Moshe was best suited for the position, the Haganah district council appointed Nahman Betser. Their explanation was that apart from being knowledgeable in security matters and having a flair for leadership, a local commander also had to be well liked. There may have been another reason for this choice. In the egalitarian kibbutz society, the authority of the local commander over the other members of the settlement was an exception, and the members of Shimron were reluctant to give Moshe any such advantage over them.

Nahman Betser was the backbone, conscience, and compass of the Shimron Group. As a direct result of this appointment, Nahman's relationship with Moshe grew increasingly complex. On the one hand, a deep friendship existed between them; but there was also a keen rivalry which, in Moshe's case, even developed into envy, for the position of local commander carried a special bonus: participation in the Haganah platoon leaders' course to be held in the summer of 1937. Once Nahman completed that course, he outranked Moshe in the Haganah. For a while, the rivalry overshadowed the friendship. In his capacity as commander, Nahman was in charge of the settlement guards. The orders were all in English, and Nahman had difficulty with the language. Moshe, who knew the language better, frequently mocked Nahman's mistakes in English and was very often undisciplined. He could not forgive Nahman for taking the position he deserved.

To make matters worse, Ruth struck up a friendship with Nahman. She felt she could trust and confide in him, and to a certain extent he was a haven for her in her difficulties. Nahman was the incarnation of all that was good in the kibbutz, and she was not the only one who regarded him as a guiding light and moral support. The unhappy triangle did not break up immediately. Matters became increasingly uncomfortable until April 1938, when Nahman packed his bags and left Shimron for a kibbutz in the Beisan Valley. There were several reasons for this sudden decision, but his strained relations with Ruth and Moshe undoubtedly played an important part in it.

On November 4, 1938 the Shimron Group moved to its permanent settlement at Hanita. Two months earlier, however, Moshe and Ruth had left the kibbutz, together with the majority of the Nahalal-born members.

Moshe and Ruth had lived in Shmuel and Dvorah's home before joining the Shimron Group, and they returned there for a short time after leaving it. In 1936 a proper concrete house replaced the wood-frame hut. Moshe and Ruth then moved into a hut of their own, where they lived until 1944. While they stayed at the Dayans' house, however, the young couple occupied Moshe's tiny room. Ruth soon entered the normal backbreaking pace of work at Nahalal, but as is often the case, the joint household of elder and younger Dayans was not altogether successful. At first the problems seemed trivial. Ruth liked to knit in the afternoon hours of rest, and Dvorah feared that her daughter-in-law had taken leave of her senses, while Shmuel dismissed the pastime as a *petit bourgeois* habit that had to cease. If Ruth wanted to sew a dress in the evenings, she would again arouse the elder Dayans' anger for wasting her time on frivolities, rather than making cheese or butter. Another point of friction was the gifts Ruth received from her parents: a washing machine that worked on kerosene and a radio set. The last straw was a boxer bitch Ruth received from relatives in Vienna. Moshe loved the dog and named it Lava, but to Shmuel doting on a dog seemed the epitome of *petit bourgeois* decadence, and one day before dawn he shot the dog. At first Dvorah eagerly anticipated Ruth's arrival in the house, for she hoped that the younger woman's help would free her of some of the farm responsibility and enable her to devote more time to her public work. But she soon came to the conclusion that two women on one farm were one too many, and she left Nahalal to spend a year in Jerusalem managing a women's farm.

In the summer of 1936, Moshe became involved in the Haganah and met two of the three people who, in his estimation, excercised the greatest influence on his character and thinking: Yitzhak Sadeh and

Captain Orde Charles Wingate. The third, David Ben Gurion, was to enter the picture only at a later stage.

In the Yishuv, the events of 1936-9 became known as the "Bloody Riots," while British circles referred to them as the "Arab Revolt." This was a period of both pain and achievement for the Yishuv, but the price of achievement was high: 550 dead and 2,500 wounded. Nonetheless, the accomplishments were impressive. Legal and "illegal" immigration (beyond the quota allowed by the Mandatory authorities) continued unabated, and 63,000 Jews entered Palestine. Counting natural increase, death, and emigration, the population of the Jewish community grew from 385,000 to 460,000, an increase of 19.4%.

More important, and pertinent, is the fact that the Haganah grew in strength and numbers. Many of its units underwent military training for the first time, initially as militia and later as proper field troops. The official history of the Haganah describes the riots of the period as the great struggle for the determination of the national character of Palestine. The leaders of the Yishuv regarded the riots as a series of preliminary skirmishes in the battle for the establishment of the Jewish State.

One of the most vulnerable and politically spectacular targets for the Arab attack was the Iraq Petroleum Company's pipeline, which was regarded as one of the life lines of the British Empire. Buried only one meter underground, the pipe was extremely accessible. The technique employed by Arab saboteurs was very simple: they uncovered the pipe at a given point and punctured it with rifle fire; then, from a distance, they threw a flaming, weighted sack on the oil-saturated ground; and within seconds the entire area around the break burst into flame. Such fires often raged for days, and by the time soldiers appeared on the scene the saboteurs were nowhere in sight. In fact, until the autumn of 1938, when Orde Wingate and his Special Night Squads put an end to this practice, Arab terrorists sabotaged the pipe at will and inflicted heavy losses on the oil company.

The anti-British nature of the Arab Revolt temporarily linked the British authorities and the Jewish community in a common cause, initiating a period of cooperation between the Mandatory Government and the Haganah that lasted until the publication of the White Paper in May 1939. The first manifestation of this new policy was the British Army's request for guides acquainted with the mountain paths around the Arab villages in the vicinity of the pipeline.

Moshe served as a guide for eight months and received a salary of 8 Palestinian pounds a month. He lived in a tent at the company camp in Afula, working first with units of the King's Own Scottish Regiment and then with units of the Yorkshire

Rifles. He was issued the uniform of a "ghaffir," and his duties consisted of guiding the units on regular patrols along the pipeline. According to Moshe, his experience as a guide with the British Army taught him "the limitations of an army functioning within a rigid routine." On leave at Shimron, he told his friends that he was not very impressed by the military proficiency of the Regular Army and gave severely critical accounts of its methods of operation: the soldiers were inadequately trained in fieldcraft and their uniforms were too cumbersome for their missions; patrols were carried out in a slipshod manner; and ambushes were prepared carelessly. The soldiers, he recounted, did not really care about guarding the pipeline. In fact, he claimed, the British units were merely maintaining a presence in the area and seemed to be satisfied with no more than just that. These observations emphasized the importance of proper training in fieldcraft, and during those eight months in Afula the outline of a military-training manual began to take shape in his mind.

The policy of the Jewish Agency toward the Arab Revolt was one of restraint and cooperation with the British. One manifestation of cooperation was the Jewish Settlement Police, a Jewish militia composed of Haganah members and subject to regulations that allowed the Mandatory Government to reinforce army or police units. The establishment of the JSP meant official sanction for the possession of firearms and training in the use of small arms by the Haganah. By June 1936 there were 1,300 JSP's and by July 1939, 22,000 (including supernumerary policemen in towns and villages). Moshe joined the JSP in the spring of 1937, after relinquishing his post as a guide, and served in the Nahalal District.

The policy of restraint aroused sharp controversy in the Jewish community. According to its critics, it placed the Yishuv in the position of a ward that had to turn to the British for its defense. Thus, although it accomplished much in terms of the opportunity for training and consolidating the ranks of the JSP, the policy ultimately had a destructive effect on Jewish communities in Palestine and abroad. The lot of European Jewry was deteriorating from year to year. The Jews of Nazi Germany were persecuted and killed indiscriminately; yet when European Jews looked to Palestine for hope, they saw an all too familiar sight—Jews leaving the blows of their persecutors unanswered.

Several Haganah officers grew very bitter about the military implications of restraint because it necessitated passively waiting to be attacked and then holding out as well as possible. A course of action had to be devised to enable the Jewish community to maintain restraint, while achieving limited but effective retaliation. The official history of the Haganah describes the creation of Sadeh's

"Flying Squad" unit as "a revolution in the entire tactical thinking of the Haganah." This unit was soon succeeded by the Mobile Guards of the Jewish Settlement Police. In 1937 Moshe was appointed commander of one of the three Mobile Guards (known as MG's) in the Nahalal District. This appointment testifies to his success in the early stages of his military career. His MG consisted of six policemen on a small truck, a sizeable force for that time. The MG's were the most active and experienced of all the Haganah units at the time and became quite famous throughout the Yishuv.

By the spring of 1939 there were sixty-two MG's, each numbering between eight and ten men. Their standing orders were the sum total of experience these units gained during the riot years. They stated that there should be one MG for each bloc of settlements and that its size should be determined by specific local needs. Its duties were "a) to prevent attack and any form of terrorist activity against Jewish settlers or vehicles, b) to serve as immediate reinforcements in case of attack."

In the execution of their duties, the JSP's were forced to assume a split personality, as they were under the direct command of both the British authorities and the Haganah, which called upon them for special duties. For the Haganah, the most important JSP function was to train other Haganah members. Like many others Moshe was both an MG commander and a Haganah instructor. He received his own training from official courses of the British Army and those given by the Haganah. The British Army instructors instilled many of their military manners in the men of the Mobile Guards, and as a result a strict discipline of drill, dress, and inspections was instituted in the JSP. These rules and conventions caused Moshe the greatest difficulties. Spit and polish, parade, drill, and military neatness did not come easily to him, and his friends claimed that such things were simply against his nature. He nonetheless did his best to have his unit excel in drill and dress. Binya Zarhi recalls that when Moshe returned from the course at Sarafend, "he took drill very seriously. He would take his men out to the main road with clean rifles and polished shoes and drill them until they excelled at it, even though he personally hated all of it."

It was as the commander of an MG that Moshe first displayed his tendency toward disobedience. His commanding officer, Lee Marshall, ordered him to gather all his constables and rush to the Nazareth mountains to help put out a forest fire. Marshall's motives for the order were simple humanity and good citizenship; but something rebelled in Moshe, something not at all clear or understandable, and he refused to obey the order. The only explanation he could offer for this insubordination was: "I didn't want to. There were no political reasons. Perhaps it was hot and I thought it irrational to

go and find my constables, who received only 6 pounds a month."
Whatever the reason for his failure to act, he was punished and
temporarily demoted from sergeant to private. This was the first of
the two demotions in Moshe's military career.

As a Haganah instructor, he devoted all his efforts to training the
members of the Shimron Group and the younger boys of Nahalal.
By 1937 he had his own well-formed ideas on fieldcraft and used the
boys of Nahalal to test them. Ahya Ben-Ami recalls:

[He] began giving his lessons in fieldcraft in Nahalal. It was a great turning
point in the Haganah . . . Before that we had only learned how to handle
weapons or routine drill . . . Did we love him? Yes and no. Actually,
we respected him. We were always ready to follow him as a leader, but I
couldn't possibly define our feelings for him as love. He was never aloof
from us, and we could always go up and talk to him; yet somehow he
remained distant.

In 1938 Moshe was appointed commander of an NCO course held at
Kibbutz Alonim. By that time he had already compiled a personal
manual of fieldcraft, which later developed into the first proper,
ordered manual of field training in the Haganah. The bulk of Moshe's
booklet was devoted to criticism of the external mannerisms that
were an integral part of the British Army and had been adopted by
the JSP. He was firmly against drill, cumbersome uniforms, and
"square" formations. Instead, he offered rules devised on the basis
of his observations of men and topography, giving advice on how to
guard more effectively, shoot more accurately, steal up to an objective unnoticed, find effective firing positions, throw grenades further,
wear lighter clothing that facilitated crawling, and crawl faster.

In this campaign against routine, Moshe did not content himself
with merely writing a training manual; he used a favorite trick to
demonstrate his theories: taking his MG men and penetrating an
area defended in the traditional Haganah manner. One night he
penetrated the defenses of Ju'ara, a Haganah base which was a
veritable fortress; anyone entering it without prior notice and express
permission was in danger of being shot on sight. The commanders
of the base were proud of the foolproof security arrangements they
had instituted to conceal the base from the British authorities. Some
of his men hesitated when Moshe suggested that they try a live
exercise and penetrate Ju'ara without notifying anyone. But Moshe
and those who believed in his concepts of fieldcraft managed to persuade the rest, and one dark night they carried out their extraordinary exercise. He felt certain that anyone who approached Ju'ara
from an unexpected direction, crawled properly, and entered the
perimeter fence itself would succeed in penetrating the base without
much trouble. And that is exactly what happened: the entire unit

entered the base without a single shot being fired. The officers in charge of the security of Ju'ara later complained that entering under the fence was "not fair." As far as Moshe was concerned, fairness was not a standard that applied to war; results were all that counted. Ingenuity, tenacity, a practical approach to problems, and an iron will emerged as Moshe's distinctive traits. When he was given command of a course, for example, he chose his instructors personally, rejecting anyone he did not know or who had yet to prove his worth. This practice of choosing men on the basis of individual qualification, rather than political affiliation—which was a common criterion— made him unique among the young commanders of the Haganah. He often went to Haganah HQ in Tel Aviv so that he could choose only those instructors he thought were the best in their field.

Nineteen thirty-eight was an important year in the welding of the Haganah into an army, for it was then that Sadeh's special Field Companies and Orde Wingate's Night Squads were formed. Although both units were short-lived, they had a formative influence upon the character of the Haganah.

The renewed outbreak of the Arab Revolt in 1938 brought about the formation of the Field Companies and the Night Squads. The four and a half months between the middle of June and the end of October 1938 were the most painful for the Yishuv in terms of casualties, with 223 men killed. This meant a monthly average of fifty deaths (higher, both relatively and absolutely, than the average monthly casualty rate during the "War of Attrition" fought along the Suez Canal between 1968 and 1970).

The Field Companies—known by their Hebrew initials as FOSH— were an offshoot of Sadeh's "Flying Squad." For the most part, the FOSH units were built on the basis of existing Mobile Guards, which were subordinate to other military or police frameworks, but with the creation of Wingate's Special Night Squads, the FOSH was relegated to the status of a poor relation. The Night Squads had a dynamic unified command, elite manpower, a proper budget, and a large supply of weapons. The SNS became the main striking force employed against the Arab gangs of the Galilee and the Jezreel Valley, while the FOSH was reserved for actions in the south. The few units that remained active in the north often went out with Wingate's SNS.

During the relative lull in the rioting, between December 7, 1936 and May 13, 1937, sixteen new Jewish settlements were established in the Beisan, Jordan, and Menashe valleys. This period of calm came to an abrupt end on Sunday, September 26, 1937, when the District Commissioner of the North, Lewis Andrews was killed in Nazareth and the Mandatory Government dissolved the Arab

High Committee. In October the Arab Revolt flamed up with a vengeance and the steady spread of Jewish settlement had to be suspended. The movement was renewed with the establishment of Hanita on March 21, 1938, an event which the official history of the Haganah describes as "heroic." The establishment of Hanita was primarily a political act. Toward the end of 1937, the Jewish community felt that partition of Palestine, a prelude to the establishment of a Jewish State, was imminent. The borders of this state, it was believed, would be determined by diplomatic bartering, and there was reason to fear that the Western Galilee, which had no Jewish settlement of any form apart from the resort town of Naharia, would be severed from the projected Jewish State. Ben Gurion believed "four or five Jewish settlements along the northern border will strengthen our hold on the Upper Galilee," and against the objections of the Mandatory Government, Hanita was founded. Actually, the Haganah held the spot for eight months, for it was only on November 4 that the Shimron Group moved to the new kibbutz.

Ninety men from various settlements were chosen for the "conquest group" of Hanita. The Haganah organized a supporting force of 400 men, including 110 MG's from all over the country. According to the official history of the Haganah, the covering force left for Hanita "under the command of Yitzhak Sadeh and his two young deputies for the action, Yigal Allon and Moshe Dayan." The establishment of Hanita was the largest operation the Haganah had undertaken up to that time, and the battles waged for the settlement were a high point in the armed conflicts of that period.

During the month that Sadeh's force remained in Hanita, Moshe served as commander of the armored car (a standard truck covered with a layer of steel plates) used to transport men from Naharia to the new settlement. This seemingly minor point is significant, for it was the sum total of Moshe's experience in an armored or motorized unit when he was appointed commander of a mechanized battalion in 1948.

According to Moshe, Sadeh and Wingate influenced him "very, very much" in the same direction—breaking down conventions:

I remember that on the first night, when Hanita was attacked, Sadeh begged the OC, Dori, to let him go out and attack the Arabs, but permission was refused. At the time it was regarded as sheer irresponsibility to think of taking thirty men beyond the fence of a barely established settlement on the Lebanese border. Sadeh taught us that kind of "irresponsibility," which really means breaking the rules of what can be done.

"One night a taxi came to Hanita and an extraordinary figure stepped out. He carried two rifles, a dictionary, and some Hebrew newspapers. We gazed at him in amazement. His daring at coming up to Hanita alone at night astonished us and made a tremendous impression." Thus Dov Yermiyah recalls Wingate's arrival in Hanita. The Scottish Artillery Captain Orde Charles Wingate, who is said to have had a far-reaching influence on shaping the resourcefulness and fighting spirit of the Israeli soldier, arrived in Palestine in September 1936 and two years later undertook a survey of the methods used by the Arab terrorists. In the course of his work, he met and gained the complete confidence of many Haganah and Jewish Agency leaders and in turn became an ardent Zionist. At one point he even drew up plans for the establishment of a Jewish army which was to play a decisive role in the Middle East as an ally of the British Empire in the event of a world war.

It was during his study of the activities of the Arab gangs that Wingate came to Hanita. After surveying the settlement, his first remark was, "Why don't you go out beyond the fence and build positions outside?" When the members of Hanita explained their system of fortification, he retorted angrily that fortifications were useless and that defenders must "go out and meet the enemy." Within the bounds of his authority to carry out a survey on the Arab gangs, Wingate led a group from Hanita on patrols across the border into Lebanon. Long-range patrols such as these had never been carried out by the Haganah. What Sadeh had begged for permission to do and had been dismissed as "irresponsibility" was now being taught by a professional soldier and accepted by HQ.

On June 5, 1938 Wingate submitted a memorandum to his commanding officer on "the possibility of night movements by armed forces of the Crown with the aim of putting an end to the terror in North Palestine." It was here that he first proposed the creation of the Special Night Squads which he was soon to lead. The proposal was accepted and implemented soon thereafter. Three Special Night Squads were formed. The first, which Wingate himself commanded most of the time, camped at Kibbutz Ein Harod and comprised eighteen British soldiers, one British officer, and twenty-four Haganah men, most of whom he "stole" from Hanita.

The main duty of the Squad was to guard the oil pipeline. Until then, the night had been the exclusive realm of Arab terrorists, and Wingate's audacity lay in his belief (which he proved to be correct) that a European-born soldier would be able to take better advantage of the dark than an Arab. Thus in 1938 he laid down one of the important principles of the Palmach and Zahal*—fighting at night. Wingate's qualities of orientation in the field ("He read a map like

---

* Hebrew acronym for Zva Haganah l'Yisrael, the Israel Defense Forces, officially established on May 25, 1948.

others read a children's book"), leadership, resourcefulness, and daring, as well as his many idiosyncrasies, impressed both his men and the Haganah. He loathed inspections, his only interest being that the soldiers' weapons be kept clean, and his men brought their rifles to him personally without the ceremony of a parade drill. He is described in the Haganah annals as an eccentric, a genius, a man more religious than rational, given to great pathos, a firm believer in the Bible, and fired with a sense of the special mission of the Jewish people. Everything he did evoked wonder and amazement in the Haganah and the Yishuv.

Wingate became legend overnight, and his "boys" liked to tell of his ingenious exploits, such as putting the taillights on the front of the Squad's cars to confuse the enemy as to the direction in which they were traveling, and how he always drank last when he and his man came to a well or spring. His lectures always began with the statement: "We are the best night fighters and the Arabs are scared stiff of the night." Wingate's military doctrine—using small, highly mobile forces for large-scale attacks, exploiting the night and every trick of deception and diversion to carry out daring surprise raids—greatly influenced the development of the elite combat units of the Haganah. The efficacy of his methods was demonstrated by the fact that in his time no further damage was caused to the Iraqi pipeline.

Wingate met Moshe Dayan in 1938, while he was still carrying out his survey of the Arab gangs. He turned up at Shimron one day in a dilapidated old car. Moshe invited the Captain to give a lecture on his method of mobile ambushes. After the lecture, Wingate led the men of Shimron on a night patrol in the Nazareth mountains, and it created a sensation. To begin with, he sent ahead two scouts who were well acquainted with the area. Not satisfied with the pace they set, he urged them on and finally took over the lead himself, "leaving everyone else panting for breath behind him." For the purposes of his demonstration patrol, he marked out the objective on the map some 6 kilometers from Shimron. Moshe related:

I could have reached the spot with my eyes closed. Still, he took the lead and played the part of the scout. He would stop the column at intervals and listen to the left and right. He bumped into bushes and obstacles, and the going was hard. He was not very strong, physically, yet ... the English artilleryman who had come from the Sudan and was unfamiliar with the local terrain led the way, walking sensibly and well, listening, and choosing his route and place of ambush wisely. It was quite a surprise for me, and I was deeply impressed.

Wingate met Dayan several times after that. When he became commander of the Night Squads, he often brought his deputy to these meetings, first at Nahalal and then at Shimron. "As for military matters, I thought him a genius, an innovator and nonconformist," was Moshe's assessment. In this respect, he and Yitzhak Sadeh were kindred spirits. Wingate was a superb military man and perhaps instilled in Moshe the realization that an army can be more than merely a hollow, routine framework.

Wingate carried out one of his better-known operations with the help of Moshe and his Mobile Guard. On the outskirts of the small village of Lid el-Awadin, a large Bedouin encampment served as a transit camp for members of the Galilee terrorist gangs and for arms shipments to the gangs in Samaria. The village served as a base for plunder, sabotage, arson, and armed attacks. Wingate received word that a gang numbering forty members was camped in the village, and he decided to take them by surprise. He therefore took his Ein Harod Squad on a full patrol eastward along the oil pipeline, instead of westward toward Lid el-Awadin, as might have been expected. He also spread the rumor that he and his men were on a routine march and had no intention of undertaking any special action. Wingate brought his men back to Ein Harod at nine in the evening without giving them the slightest inkling of what awaited them. As they approached their camp, he ordered them to remain on the patrol cars and await further orders. When the time came, he instructed the drivers to head for Haifa. As they drove along the road that winds through a deep, arc-shaped ravine, he ordered his men to jump off the moving cars, while the drivers continued in the direction of Haifa. Hidden by the deep ravine, Wingate and his men continued on foot to Kibbutz Sarid, where they were joined by Moshe and the eight men of his Mobile Guard.

At dawn on the following day, after a forty-five minute march through the fields, Wingate and his force approached Lid el-Awadin and laid an ambush in a wide semi-circle covering all the northern and some of the southern approaches to the village about 500 meters from the peripheral houses. Simultaneously, Wingate's deputy, Lieutenant Bredin, left the Afula base on foot with two platoons, one Ulsterman and one Jewish. They took up positions closing off the southeastern side of the village. In the first light of dawn a truck appeared on the dirt road that ran parallel to the railway tracks and ended about 800 meters from the village. This was the bait—six of Moshe's MG's dressed as railway workers, jumped off the truck and began working on the tracks. Hidden in the back of the truck were several more men, with two Lewis machine guns. The tailgate was set so that the slightest touch would open it.

Everything went exactly according to plan. The terrorists in the village caught sight of the six workers and were sure they would be easy prey. Several of them ran toward the tracks waving their rifles.

When they came to within 100 meters of the truck, the tailgate was pushed open and the two Lewis guns cut them down on the spot. The surprise was complete. The sudden sound of gunfire caused panic in the village and the nearby Bedouin encampment. The members of the gang immediately turned tail, heading first northeast, where they ran into the ambushes Wingate had laid, then southeast toward Jenin, where Bredin and Nahman Betser were waiting for them. Wingate watched the proceedings from a nearby hill. At the appropriate moment he ordered Brenner to lead the men from the ambushes into the village to clear it and round up remaining terrorists.

According to Zvi Brenner, who was Wingate's close associate and confidant, "Wingate was tremendously perceptive and could tell a born soldier when he saw one. He had great respect for Moshe, because he too hated repeating the same operation twice and always tried innovations. A year later, in 1939, when we were in the Acre prison, Wingate sent Moshe and myself gifts—copper plates—and corresponded with us."

Moshe later returned to Lid el-Awadin on a retaliatory attack. In the beginning of 1939, a JSP from Nahalal was killed in an ambush and mines were laid between Kfar Yehoshua and Nahalal. The trail of both the murderers and saboteurs led to Lid el-Awadin, and the Haganah ordered Moshe to capture the *mukhtar* (head of the village), dead or alive, and blow up his house. He received reinforcements from the NCO course at Ju'ara; Yigal Allon, who commanded the course at the time, became his second-in-command. Moshe's plan called for the Haganah men to disguise themselves as British soldiers, complete with uniforms, helmets, English cigarettes, and British Army bully beef, so that they would not only look but also smell like British soldiers. They drove up to Lid el-Awadin in army trucks, giving orders in English, and gathered all the men of the village onto the threshing floor. Yigal Allon, who knew very little English at the time, tried a little Yiddish: "Take positions *arum* and *arum*" (Yiddish for "around and around"), he told the men. The two-story house belonging to the *mukhtar* was demolished, though the *mukhtar* himself, away for the day, escaped unscathed.

Another retaliatory raid in which Moshe participated took place following the murder of two afforestation workers near Kfar Hahoresh. Moshe asked for volunteers from the younger boys of Nahalal, and Binya Zarhi, Ahya Ben-Ami, and Oded Yannai agreed to come along. Moshe also asked Yehudah Mor to help them, and although the raid did not have official Haganah approval, Mor sent a car to obliterate the raiding party's tracks. Moshe and his men broke into the house of the man they thought was responsible for the killings and shot him. Recalling the incident, Ahya Ben-Ami said: "I took part in that action as one of the most active Haganah members in Nahalal. I did not hesitate . . . for a moment. But afterward I was left with a sour taste in my mouth. From a personal, moral point of view, and perhaps even from a political one, I felt that this was not the right way."

Reflections of this sort were part of the rigorous life in store for the generation that later carried the burden of the War of Independence. Moshe never expressed his feelings about any of the retaliatory raids, but the concept of retaliation itself did not seem wrong to him, as was later amply demonstrated by the many raids carried out by Zahal while he was Chief-of-Staff.

8   ACRE   (1939-1940)

October 1939 to June 1941 was perhaps the most crucial period in the molding of Moshe Dayan's future, personality, and image. He tasted imprisonment and life at its lowest ebb, was unexpectedly released and could appreciate the meaning of liberty, went out on a daring combat mission which won him fame, lost his left eye, and felt certain that he had lost everything and would never again lead men into battle.

In 1939 the British Government began to consider seriously the possibility that the Axis Powers would exploit the dispute in Palestine to gain the support of the Arabs in the Middle East. An immediate consequence of this evaluation was that the Colonial Office, which sought the Arabs as allies for Britain, increased its influence. The end of the Arab Revolt, therefore, also marked the end of cooperation between the Zionist movement and Great Britain. On May 17, 1939 the British Government issued a White Paper severely limiting Jewish immigration to Palestine and Jewish purchase of Arab lands in large areas of the country. The Mandatory Government and its security forces abandoned their former policy of cooperation with the Haganah and began to curtail its activities. One of the first manifestations of this turnabout was the imprisonment of forty-three Haganah men.

Fearing British surveillance over the bases at Ju'ara and Kfar Vitkin, Haganah HQ moved its Tenth and Eleventh Platoon Leaders' Course to Yavniel. Moshe Dayan and Yigal Allon were among the six hand-picked instructors at the Yavniel course, ostensibly a physical education program run by the Hapoel Sports Federation. The first course at Yavniel—the tenth by Haganah count—encountered no difficulties. But during the second one, which began in the latter half of August 1939, a surprising incident occurred. On October 3, two British officers from the Tiberias Police Force visited the camp quite unexpectedly and inspected the lecture hall and the living quarters, where they discovered rifles hidden under the mattresses. The incident was immediately reported to Haganah HQ in Tel Aviv, and it was decided to evacuate the camp at once.

Preparations began for the transfer of the course to Kibbutz Ein Hashofet. The men were divided into two groups: a large one numbering forty-three men led by the commander and his deputy, Moshe Carmel, and a smaller group of seventeen, led by Yigal Allon. Yigal Allon and his men made their way safely to Ein Hashofet. The

"Forty-three' as they later became known, were not as fortunate. The group's departure, which had been set for midnight, was postponed because of the time needed to collect all the weapons from the "slicks" (weapon caches) and the precautions that had to be taken in case the base was under observation.

The unexpected delay turned out to be the Forty-three's undoing. At 6 a.m., on its way into Wadi Bira, the group encountered a unit of the Transjordanian Frontier Force, about twelve to fifteen men strong, riding on three or five pickups. This small Arab force surrounded and captured the larger Jewish one. The men were detained, British authorities were notified, and that day the Forty-three were taken in custody to the Acre prison. The incident brings to light the difference between the Haganah and its later manifestation as Zahal. Standards of fighting and the fighting spirit of the Jews in Palestine rose to increasingly higher levels over the years as a result of objective circumstances; they were never inbred traits of the Yishuv that could be taken for granted.

The prevalent view in the Yishuv was that the arrest of the Forty-three resulted from a misunderstanding and from the fact that there were Arabs serving in the Frontier Force. Everyone believed that this misunderstanding would be cleared up in a matter of hours and that the problem would soon be put right. The sight of the prison—the Fortress of Acre—shocked the Haganah men. It was a formidable stone building, built into the city walls in the eighteenth century by the local Turkish pashas. The British had turned it into a prison.

Hands on each other's shoulders, the men were taken to a spiral staircase and climbed the worn steps in the dark. At the top they were herded into a darkened, narrow, stone-walled hall with high, vaulted ceilings. They were given water, food, and mattresses and then left on their own. Before they could fall asleep, however, the lights suddenly came on again and policemen entered. The men were ordered to rise and stand in line, then asked who knew English. It turned out they were being prepared for a night interrogation.

In his book *Forty-three Letters from a Hebrew Prisoner* (1942), Moshe Carmel writes that the prison authorities tried to intimidate the Forty-three. While one of the men was being interrogated in an adjacent room, "a bony hand, holding a club" was seen in a small window that opened onto the hall. The hand waved the club up and down, right and left, while "a gruff voice could be heard through the window, muffled and breathing heavily, saying 'Death! Death!,' repeating the same word over and over again in a sing-song cadence."

The four men who said they knew English, Zvi Brenner, Moshe Dayan, and two others, were interrogated first. According to Brenner, the commanders of the course had not given any instructions on how to act during an interrogation. Before being taken into the room, he recalled a lecture given by a Haganah lawyer who suggested that if caught and questioned a Haganah man must state only his name and then demand to see a lawyer. Carmel confirms that Course HQ had not given any directives on behavior in case of capture and interrogation, but, he added, there was an accepted procedure in the Haganah—which was not far removed from a standing order—that one was to give no information whatsoever and ask to see a lawyer. According to Noah Dagoni, however, Carmel's order "not to say a word at the interrogation . . . [to] give only our name and our age" was given in the field.

Zvi Brenner was taken for interrogation at one o'clock in the morning. His companions in the darkened hall could hear sounds and a few words from the nearby room. As he walked in, Brenner was placed up against a wall with a spotlight trained on his face. Three men dressed in civilian clothes and holding batons fired questions at him in turn. The men in the hall heard sounds of blows, kicks, groans, questions, then once again blows, kicks, groans, and a cry of pain. Throughout the interrogation Zvi Brenner repeated only a single sentence—without a lawyer he would not say a word.

Brenner claims that the British wanted to find out, among other things, whether the men belonged to the Haganah or to the "Irgun,"* whose members had killed a British police officer a short time before. When Brenner refused to talk, they beat him until he lost consciousness, poured water over him, and beat him again. It is likely that Brenner's interrogation was deliberately held within earshot of his friends, so that they might be more prone to talk when their turn came. A door opened, lights were turned on for a moment, and Zvi Brenner was brought in staggering but still on his feet. He asked for water, drank some, then fell down on a mattress. Moshe was then taken into the room for interrogation and the lights were switched off again.

In one respect Moshe underwent a far crueller interogation for, according to Brenner and Carmel, the interrogators threatened to leave his young daughter, Yael, an orphan. Of the four men interrogated, Moshe was the only one who was married and had a family. The possibility of execution was not inconceivable. According to the Emergency Regulations of the British Mandate, originally designed to aid the administration in its fight against Arab terrorism, illegal possession of firearms was a crime punishable by death. Years later Brenner wrote: "Moshe Dayan was told that these were his last moments and that his secret would never go beyond the heavy walls of

---

* Irgun Zvai Leumi, a militant, dissident resistance movement led by Menahem Begin.

the Acre Fortress. His family would merely be informed that he was executed like any other criminal.''

From Carmel and Brenner's descriptions, it is quite clear that Moshe had no intention of following Brenner's example. Instead he immediately told his interrogators about his family. He felt there were some things he was allowed to reveal, and, far from doing harm, they might be of help to himself and his companions. Following this line of reasoning, he told the interrogators that the Forty-three were members of the Haganah and that they had been on their way from Yavniel to Moledet for training. To questions about the source of their rifles or about Haganah activities, he replied, "I don't know." He insisted that the Haganah was not a terrorist organization and was not fighting the British. On the contrary, he said, many of his friends, and he himself, had cooperated with the British Army.

When the interrogators threatened to beat him, Moshe warned them that if they continued to beat and torture the prisoners, he would get word of it to his Jewish friends outside, and "they will know how to take care of torturers." According to Noah Dagoni, "It was only after Moshe's warning that the torturing ceased." His decision to speak out brought the interrogations to an end that night after only two other men had been questioned.

It was typical of Moshe to try and find a way out of his predicament through initiative and resourcefulness before putting his will power and physical stamina to the test. This strategy developed into a pattern of behavior: acting tough when given no choice, but being flexible if there was any chance of emerging victorious without a clash. To a great extent his actions constituted direct assumption of leadership and responsibility for the group. In Moshe's opinion— and lacking explicit directives—it was pointless to conceal the Forty-three's association with the Haganah. On the contrary, he felt that the truth could only be of service to the men. At the trial the defense employed a similar line of reasoning by claiming that the Haganah men had been in training in order to be of aid to the British Army in its war against Germany. Quite clearly, Moshe spared his friends from further interrogation and torture.

The majority of his companions, especially Zvi Brenner, accepted Moshe's behavior as proof of his leadership. Brenner even helped convince those who felt that Moshe had made a mistake in talking. Moshe Carmel, however, could not be persuaded and rebuked Moshe for having revealed information to the British. If Haganah men were to be allowed to talk freely, he reasoned, there would be no way of knowing how much each individual revealed. Many would undoubtedly talk wisely and effectively, revealing nothing of vital importance; but some might be confused by the interrogators' tactics and do grave harm. According to Brenner, Carmel was alone in his criticism;

"... all the others were eventually convinced that he had acted correctly, and some even thought he saved us, since the interrogators only wanted to know whether the men belonged to the Haganah or to the Irgun."

Despite the pressure that had been brought to bear in an effort to find a quick and easy solution, and contrary to all expectations, the British Government decided to bring the Forty-three before a military court. On November 10, 1938, a year before these events, several special military courts had been established on orders from General Wavell as part of the Emergency Regulations. These courts were authorized to pass death sentences on anyone in possession of illegal firearms or caught in acts of murder or sabotage. Their decisions could not be appealed and required only the approval of the Commander in Chief of the Imperial Armed Forces in Palestine. A death sentence also had to be submitted to the High Commissioner for approval. This is another instance in which regulations passed to curb the activities of the Arab terrorists were used against the Haganah, and the application of these laws against the Yishuv eventually became official Mandatory policy emanating from the White Paper of 1939. Indeed, soon after the arrest of the Forty-three, more members of the Haganah were brought to the prison.

When it became clear that the Mandatory Government was firmly resolved to try the Forty-three before a military court, the Jewish Agency embarked on a new campaign to ensure light or even nominal sentences for the men, and Agency circles maintained their optimism and conviction that the sentences would not be severe. The trial was finally set for October 25, and the Forty-three remained in detention until then. During the daylight hours, the prisoners were taken out to the broad roof of the fortress. They were allowed to receive food parcels from outside, and a great many arrived from relatives, friends, and various Jewish institutions. They were permitted to wear their own clothes, and once a week—on Saturdays—they were allowed ten-minute visits from two relatives.

On Saturday, October 14, the first visit took place. Visiting time for the Forty-three was a mass affair. The visitors climbed a few stairs to a rampart that was separated from the detainees by a 2-meter tangle of barbed wire. The prisoners themselves stood in a sort of ditch, and the visitors, who looked down at them, could only see the men's heads and the upper part of their bodies. With prisoners' and visitors' voices raised to make themselves heard in the general uproar, the commotion was deafening.

The entire Dayan family came on this first visit and agreed that Dvorah and Ruth would go in to see Moshe. Ruth dressed nine-month-old Yael in a pale blue dress that made her look like a "little princess" and carried her in the hope that "she wouldn't be counted." As Moshe and Ruth were calling out to each other, Yael managed to get out of her mother's arms and crawl toward the barbed wire, stretching her hands out to her father. Dvorah, who was watching her son constantly, was deeply moved by the sight: " . . . He's swallowing his tears as he looks at his little girl, just as he used to do as a child." The experience was so disturbing that Ruth feared it would have an adverse effect on Moshe, and on her next visit she left Yael with her parents in Jerusalem. But his daughter's absence immediately aroused Moshe's suspicions, and Ruth had the greatest difficulty convincing him that all was well with the child. After that she brought Yael with her on every visit.

The detainees were allowed to send one letter a week, but by devious means—including bribery—they managed to send and receive many more. In his first letters, Moshe reassured his family that the warders were treating them well and the food was good, "[but] it is very dirty here." It was not the physical conditions of the imprisonment, but rather the "passivity" of the situation that was depressing, "the realization that there is nothing one can do but receive orders from an Arab policeman and carry them out promptly."

The trial was held on a British Army base, 2 kilometers north of Acre and lasted for three days. The verdicts were read on Monday, October 30, and the sentences shocked the Yishuv. All Forty-three were found guilty; one was sentenced to life imprisonment and the others to ten years each. Immediately following the trial, an intensive campaign was initiated to repeal, or at least reduce, the sentences. According to the 1936 Emergency Regulations, sentences handed down by military courts had to be approved by the military commander of Palestine, in this case General Barker, within thirty days. Consequently, Barker and his staff, as well as the Imperial General Staff in London, became the immediate targets of pressure. In America the Jewish Agency appealed, among others, to William Green, Chairman of the American Federation of Labor. Green wrote to Winston Churchill, first Lord of the Admiralty, and to Clement Atlee, the Secretary-General of the Labour Party. In London, Dr. Chaim Weizmann met with Atlee and Churchill, and Wingate promised to do what he could in Imperial GHQ circles. At a meeting with Weizmann, Field-Marshal Lord Ironside, Chief of the Imperial Staff, pronounced the sentences "barbaric and stupid." According to Ben Gurion's diary, Ironside said to Weizmann: "Fancy—they have condemned one of Wingate's lads to life imprisonment. He ought to have been given the D.S.O. instead!" The immediate consequence of this meeting was that Lord Ironside ordered General Barker to commute the sentences. The life sentence was commuted to ten years and all the rest to five.

Nonetheless, the punishments were considered severe. The Yishuv organized a public demonstration for November 28. A general strike was called; cinemas, theaters, and places of entertainment remained closed; and no Hebrew newspapers appeared on that day. The National Council and local authorities issued posters claiming that the entire Jewish community in Palestine had been tried with the Forty-three.

After the verdict, the Forty-three were transferred from the tower to the main section of the prison. Their heads were shaved and they were issued brown uniforms and sandals. They were forbidden to wear socks, receive food from outside, write more than once a month or receive more than one visit a month in place of a letter. The entire group was placed in a gloomy hall with vaulted ceilings and high, narrow, barred windows. Rag-filled mattresses and two army blankets laid out on the stone floor served as beds. They also doubled as "cupboards," for during the day the men rolled up all their personal effects inside them. Two pails stood at opposite corners of the hall— one for drinking water, the other a makeshift toilet.

The Fortress of Acre was a typical Turkish prison which the British had improved only slightly. The prisoners' day began with the ringing of a bell and a warder striking those who had difficulty waking up. First the men rolled up their mattresses. After that the first of the three daily roll calls was held. As their names were called out, the prisoners kneeled on the floor and the warders counted by tapping each of them on the head with a stick. After the initial inspection, the prisoners were left to their own devices until daylight. As soon as the sun was up, they were taken in twos for a ten-minute walk round the high walls surrounding the inner courtyard. Afterward they had breakfast, the first of the three typically Arab meals served each day. They then went to work in the prison workshops. At 3 p.m. their day was over. There was a last roll call, the mattresses were unrolled and the prisoners faced fourteen hours in the confinement of their quarters.

At the first meeting held by the Forty-three to discuss their future in the prison, Carmel announced that the commanders and instructors of the course were relinquishing their authority. He told the men that others may be better suited to organize life within the prison and that they should be elected by the group regardless of rank. The prisoners chose three men to serve as their committee: Moshe as supervisor, to represent the Forty-three in their contact with prison authorities and the outside; Ya'akov Salomon as "mukhtar," to be responsible for the prison hall itself and all the activities within; and Carmel as a manager or director, to deal with the general affairs of the group.

The prisoners also resolved to demand better conditions. From the original long list of complaints, they eventually composed six resolutions that defined their struggle's immediate aims. Moshe presented the following list of demands to the prison authorities: a cup of tea in the morning, permission to wear shoes and socks at least in the winter, light in the cell until eight o'clock in the evening (when the prisoners were supposed to go to sleep), permission to study for half the day each day; permission to use copybooks and pencils. The sixth and final resolution was "to endeavor to maintain good relations and not quarrel with the management and the warders, but to stand firm in our demands for basic rights and to defend ourselves without fear in any case of harassment or degradation." Six months after the beginning of their terms, the Forty-three were taken to work outside the prison walls and later still in the vegetable plots of the government experimental agricultural station.

Prison life for the Forty-three as described in Moshe's letters was far less gloomy than his companions—especially Moshe Carmel—would have it. Most of Moshe's letters were written in a reassuring, matter-of-fact tone. He expressed particular concern for the seemingly trivial details that could improve their conditions but might be forgotten or neglected in the course of the tremendous efforts being made to reduce their sentences or obtain a complete pardon. It is evident that Moshe was very active in matters concerning the needs of the group as a whole and more tolerant about his own personal needs. When he wrote to his family, " . . . If you could only see how joyful the Arab children are during their visit," the hint was intended to restore their good humor, for they were incapable of concealing their sorrow and tears during their meetings.

During the first few months of his confinement, Moshe came to the conclusion that imprisonment is not the most terrible disaster one can face. He discussed this with his parents in letters:

Mother writes that the pain of my imprisonment is so great that she cannot write or talk about it. I don't know how to explain to you that it is not as bad as all that. I am a prisoner and will probably have to spend an "appropriate" amount of time here. But it is not a disaster to be mourned; it is simply an imprisonment that one must bear, and then wash oneself off well and pick up where one left off.

In December 1940 he wrote to his father:

 . . . You apparently have visions of a Dostoyevskian or Turkish prison. But it is not so. The prison is not, I admit, beautiful or luxurious, but for the moment the food, clothing, cleanliness, and treatment we receive are all very good. We even managed to rid ourselves of the lice (disinfection here is very effective). We received warm, good-quality underclothes, a third blanket, etc. . . .

During the period of adjustment to prison life and trying to improve conditions there, Moshe also found time for introspection and private stock taking. His conscience troubled him about his childhood friend Nahman Betser, whom he had offended on several occasions. On December 30 he wrote to Nahman:

> . . . I remembered that a short time before I went to Yavniel I wanted to go to [Kibbutz] Ma'oz and see you. But, to tell you the truth, I was afraid that my visit would be a burden for you, that we would be as strangers . . . Since it will probably be a long time before we see each other again, and the difficulty of speaking openly as friends does not inhibit me here, I want to take this opportunity to write that I would very much like to return to the simple, frank, friendship we once enjoyed, because . . . everything that stood between us during a certain period of our lives in Shimron has passed, and all I have retained is a sense of shame for my behavior then.

This letter was an exception to the rule Moshe had adopted in his youth—never explain, never apologize. This time he asked for forgiveness and received it. His parents also weighed heavily on his conscience. Moshe felt guilty for going his own way and joining the Haganah, rather than remaining in Nahalal to help carry the burden of the farm, which now fell mainly upon his brother. Toward the end of February 1940, he wrote this letter to his parents:

> . . . Even though you do not write about it, I know and remember well the difficulties at home. Even when Aviva and Zorik were healthy and I was not stuck in this place, you had some difficult times at home, and certainly must have now! Each time I think of you—and there is a great deal of time for thinking here— I realize that I never fulfilled my obligations to my home. I should have done only simple thing—work at home; yet I went out and looked for more "interesting" things to do. Perhaps I understood this before, but then I did not have the strength to overcome the temptation . . . Who knows if things will be any different in the future? You should at least know that I am constantly aware of how difficult it is for all of you—for Zorik who began working before his time, and Aviva and Mother and Father. But what good does it do to write about these things?

In prison Moshe met not only men of the gang that killed Ya'akobi and his son ("Our personal relations with them are very good . . . I'm writing this with a pencil I borrowed from one of the members of the Kassam gang . . . "), but also Abed Abeidat from the Arab el-Mazarib tribe. This was a good opportunity to pursue his interest in the Arabs, which, he says, stemmed "from the Kassami'in." He sought to understand their motivations:

What really goes on inside the mind of an Arab who suddenly begins rioting in Jaffa? I don't think I came to any conclusions about this, but I began to understand them better, to realize that there was something there, that it was not simply a case of the good guys and the bad guys. As a result, in everyday life I felt no antagonism toward the Arabs as individuals. I was friendly with many Arabs, those I met around Nahalal as well as those I met in the prison. I said to myself: these are two nations on either side of a fence, true; but there is no personal animosity, as one might expect between a murderer and his victim. Nothing like that.

When the prisoners were finally permitted to leave the lights on until eight in the evening and were allowed to have writing materials, Moshe and the other committee members initiated studies for the Forty-three. There were lessons in English for beginners and advanced students, in Bible studies, chemistry, and other subjects. Moshe began writing to Ruth in English, and she corrected the letters and returned them together with exercises devised to help him improve his mastery of the language.

Shmuel included in his diary a letter written by Moshe February 7 (after a visit by Dvorah and Ruth) which seems to sum up the first three months of the imprisonment:

> ... Don't think for a moment that they have broken me here or that I have become an oppressed prisoner who meekly accepts everything meted out to him. Far from it! But the only way to avoid too much unpleasantness is to avoid confrontations with the prison authorities, and we do not have much contact with them. We don't ask anything of them, or try to curry favor with them; neither do we expect any favors. That's why I did not want Ruth to request anything from Grant. And I wrote to her a few times telling her not ask for anything, because she will only humiliate herself. All in all, it's not too bad ...

Six months of imprisonment, however, changed Moshe's mood, and although conditions had improved slightly, he no longer withheld complaints. The Forty-three were transferred from the Acre prison to a detention camp at Mazra'a near the experimental agricultural farm where they worked every day. There it was easier to maintain contact with the outside and to see relatives. The primary object of Moshe's complaints were the Jewish Agency representatives, who were supposed to maintain constant contact with the Haganah prisoners but, in Moshe's opinion, were not fulfilling their tasks. He also complained about the leaders of the Yishuv for not doing enough to secure the release of the Forty-three. In general, he began to show signs of increasing impatience.

A number of factors combined to produce this shift in his attitude. At the beginning of the prison term, in December 1939, he wrote that despite occasional contact with the outside and access to newspapers, "We are beginning to feel how prison life slowly replaces our previous way of life. Everything in our past is turning into memories. Our thoughts revolve upon the sandwiches we get here, and the content of our lives is growing impoverished and wretched." As time went on, the depression produced by prison routine deepened, and the lack of contact with the outside world caused the men great distress.

Another reason for the change in Moshe's attitude was the fact that from the outset the Forty-three had been led to believe they would be pardoned within a short time. When Shmuel managed to enter the prison in December 1939 disguised as an assistant to the meat supplier, he managed to see and talk to Moshe face to face. "I informed him about Ironside's decision to have the trial reviewed within six months." But six months passed and the promised review never took place. Another date the men and relatives pinned their hope on was June 6, the King's birthday. June came and went, and the King did not pardon the Forty-three.

The desire for freedom led to one of the most serious misunderstandings that Moshe experienced with his companions. When June 6 passed without a general pardon from the King, the question was raised whether it would not be preferable to seek individual pardons for each of the Forty-three. The idea was proposed by the Political Department of the Jewish Agency without consulting the Forty-three. The Jewish Agency accepted the proposal and instructed regional councils, institutions, and individuals who came into contact with the Mandatory authorities to voice "the demand of the Yishuv for the release of the men." It was believed that whereas the British Government might find it difficult to repeal the sentences, it might be prepared to consider bestowing pardons on individuals with a "clean record," that is, a record of cooperation with the British Army.

Reuven Shiloah, who headed the efforts to obtain individual pardons, belatedly wrote a note to the Forty-three informing them of the steps taken by the Political Department. The men at Acre immediately met to discuss this new development, and in the ensuing argument Moshe was the only one who came out in favor of individual pardons. The prospects of the rest of the Haganah prisoners, with neither his clean record nor family and political connections, finally weighed the scales. The prisoners' meeting decided that "Under no circumstances should individual pardons be sought—only the release of all prisoners."

A few days after the meeting, one of the prisoners inadvertently opened a letter addressed to Moshe. Ruth had written of the efforts being made in Nahalal to secure an individual pardon for Moshe and mentioned the fact that the District Commissioner in Nazareth had already signed the necessary request papers. Since Moshe had been the only one to defend the idea of individual pardons, his companions understood this letter to mean that he had disregarded the majority decision and encouraged "separatist initiative on the part of Nahalal to obtain the release of Moshe Dayan." The Forty-three had no way of knowing, of course, that despite their opposition, the Political Department of the Jewish Agency had initiated the campaign for individual pardons, and they turned their wrath against Moshe. No amount of explanation could help, although he repeatedly claimed that he knew nothing of these efforts—nor had he initiated them— and was determined to abide by the prisoners' decision. According to Zvi Brenner, "They made a whole issue out of it, and were all convinced that he was already seeing to his own release." The Forty-three lost faith in Moshe and relieved him of his duties as supervisor. In a secret ballot, Zvi Brenner was chosen to take his place. Moshe recalls that it was more a case of his resigning than being relieved of his duties. He was bitterly disappointed by his friends' lack of trust and no longer wished to represent them before the prison authorities.

The cool relations that resulted from this affair were short-lived. Moshe was very sociable—playing, wrestling, and joking with the others in their free time. Even though he was not officially reinstated as supervisor, he remained the Forty-three's representative in their contacts with the Yishuv. In this capacity he launched an attack on the leaders of the Yishuv and its institutions. Noah Dagoni points out that Moshe's letters were far more biting and aggressive than Moshe Carmel's. He called upon the leaders of the Yishuv to cease their interminable diplomatic discussions and organize public demonstrations for the release of the Haganah prisoners.

At the beginning of 1941, release seemed more remote than ever before. Then, as a direct result of Weizmann's *in camera* discussions in London, circumstances in Palestine suddenly changed radically and the British Army again required the help of the Haganah. As a result of developments in the war in the Middle East, the British Army agreed to conscript large numbers of Jewish youth in Palestine. On February 16, 1941 the Forty-three prisoners in Acre were informed that they were to be released on the following day. The men spent a sleepless night of nervous anticipation. At dawn they were given their civilian clothes, had their palms stamped with the official prison symbol, and were set free.

9 SYRIA (JUNE 1941)

When Moshe left Acre prison, the Middle East seemed in imminent danger of conquest by the Nazis. This situation stimulated renewed cooperation between the British Administration in Palestine and the Yishuv. The Jewish Agency urged Jews to volunteer for the Palestinian units of the British Army, and Dr. Chaim Weizmann drew up agreements with Admiral I. H. Godfroy, Chief of Naval Intelligence. These understandings developed into official cooperation between the Political Department of the Jewish Agency and a special joint department of the British ministries of War and Supply which was charged with preparing an underground force in Europe and Palestine.

During Moshe's imprisonment, these developments also brought about changes within the Haganah itself. In May 1941 it was decided to set up a country-wide Haganah force to defend the Jewish settlements against Arab attacks and to serve as a reserve force for the British Army. Yitzhak Sadeh was appointed special officer in charge of organizing this force. Haganah HQ had decided that it was to include the best men available, and Yigal Allon and Moshe Dayan were singled out to command the first two companies. It was originally intended that these two companies would form the nucleus of the special force. Quite unexpectedly, they were given entirely new objectives—to join the British invasion of Syria.*

When word of the planned invasion reached Moshe Sharett and his colleagues in the Political Department of the Jewish Agency, they tried to find a way to include the Haganah in the mission. They learned that Sir Henry Maitland (Jumbo) Wilson's forces required guides and sappers and quickly offered to supply them. In the memorandum Moshe wrote after the invasion, he points out that although "the British had in mind only a small group of guides who were well acquainted with the area and its roads . . . we visualized much more: participation in the conquest of Syria, an opportunity for various secondary actions, etc. Consequently, we tried to enlarge our force as much as possible. Thus, although we received only ten certificates, we managed to include thirty men."

Moshe had only a few days to recruit, train, and organize his men. He was eager for action and was undaunted by the fact that his unit

---

*Under the terms of the French Mandate, "Syria" included the territory of Lebanon.

was totally unprepared to go into action. Zalman Mart's description of his enlistment is typical of Moshe's methods of recruiting. Mart recalls that on June 6 he was passing through Nahalal when a car stopped by him. Moshe and Ruth were inside and Moshe asked, " 'Do you want to see the Australians fight?' I answered yes, and he said, 'Then get into the car.' " Mart pointed out that he was wearing his JSP uniform, to which Moshe replied that he should take off his badge. When Mart added that he was unarmed, Moshe brought him to Aviva, who gave him her pistol.

Moshe and Ruth left Yael with Dvorah and drove with Mart to Hanita, where Moshe's company was camped. On the way, Moshe brought Mart into the picture, adding that he still had to go out on a patrol that day and suggesting that Mart join him. First they drove to Haifa to pick up the Arab guide who was to accompany them and buy provisions for the company. According to Mart, "Moshe was also the supply officer of his unit."

Of the thirty men Moshe gathered in Hanita, only one could speak Arabic well, while the mission required—and the Jewish Agency had promised the British—that the entire unit would not only be fluent in Arabic, but would be able to pass as Arabs. Furthermore, only one of the men knew how to drive, though their principal function was to find negotiable routes for the invasion vehicles. Finally, as Moshe wrote in his memorandum, "We lacked the most important thing for the execution of our mission—a man who knew Syria. There was not one in the entire unit."

Moshe therefore decided that he would have to find a guide for the guides. His memorandum states:

After a prolonged search, we finally found an Arab who had at one time been the leader of a terrorist gang in that region and was well acquainted with southwest Syria and the Syrian-Palestinian border. We hesitated to approach him for obvious reasons. Once we crossed the border, he could turn us over to the French troops for a reward and then return, inventing any tale he chose. Indeed, anything might happen across the border, and who could know how he would behave? After all, he had been the leader of a terrorist gang and had accounts to settle. But since we had no one else, we contacted him. As security—or so we were told—his wife and children were brought to Haifa and held in a hotel, and he was warned that if anything untoward happened, his family would face the consequences.

Since Moshe divided his force into small units of two or three men, additional Arab guides were necessary. His directives for selecting them give a general picture of his attitude to war:

If it becomes necessary to contact an Arab for an action such as this, it is preferable to choose the leader of a gang or a murderer, rather than a simple Arab fellah or shepherd who has no feeling for this profession. The former is courageous, has an interest in this kind of game, and is good at it. The average Arab is a coward and would try to return home at the first opportunity. Thus your security would be impaired and the action jeopardized.

Between June 1 and 7, Moshe and his men, guided by the hired Arabs, made a number of reconnaissance patrols across the border. Moshe's criteria for selecting guides proved right. Upon returning from their patrols, the men drew up reports and handed them in to General Wilson's Headquarters.

The patrol mentioned by Mart gives us an insight into Moshe's eagerness for action. In his memorandum, Moshe wrote:

We made a few final arrangements in Haifa, loaded the food, and set out for Hanita. But when we came to Naharia . . . one of the Haganah liaison officers attached to the British Army stopped us and said: "We have just received word [on Friday, June 6] that there is a chance of finding a completely new route for vehicles from the south to the north. Yitzhak the Druze told us about it. He has just returned from Syria and is prepared to show us a route that can be traveled without special preparations . . . Strictly "according to the book," this may have been a mistake, because one might not return from a patrol, and this would have left my group without a commander. Then again, another commander could be found for the unit, and I had no alternative at the time. I was glad of this opportunity for action.

Our guides were in Haifa . . . and by the time we located them, it was late in the afternoon. We took some food and set out along the Acre-Safed road toward Hanita. We lacked only one thing: a driver who would remain in the car while we were on the patrol and would be able to notify the unit if we failed to return . . . In Acre we met a driver from Naharia in his delivery van, on his way back to his family for the Sabbath . . . and he agreed to join us.

To a great extent, Moshe's action in this incident forecast the kind of behavior that was to become typical of him as a commander in Zahal and as Minister of Defense. First, he was little concerned with his personal safety, assuming that a commander in the field is replaceable, but there can be no substitute for good work done. Logic, curiosity, and a spirit of adventure blended in Moshe's character and led him to the conclusion that a commander's place is always at the head of his men. Next was his desire for daring exploits. Finally, he displayed a capacity for last-minute improvisations, even twenty-four hours before an invasion. The driver of a bread-delivery van from Naharia suddenly became part of the preparations for an invasion of Syria by fifteen combat regiments. In this respect, the bread van was a precursor of the bread, milk, and citrus trucks that often transported Zahal's Reserve units into battle in later years.

Moshe Dayan at the age of five with his parents. His left eye is partially closed as a result of trachoma

above Moshe and Ruth Dayan soon after their marriage

opposite Sixteen-year-old Moshe on horseback. As a volunteer, it was one of his duties to guard the fields of Nahalal

below Moshe as commander of the armored car in the Haganah's force at Hanita in 1938

above With Yitzhak Sadeh and Yigal Allon at Hanita in 1938

below Moshe (extreme right) with his cellmates, the "Forty-three," in the Acre Fortress in 1941

Describing the patrol, Moshe's memorandum continues:

Yitzhak the Druze went first, and I followed him. For two hours we crossed one road after another along a route that could easily be traversed by even heavy vehicles . . . When we reached the Syrian road it was still early in the evening. We had completed our mission, but decided to continue the patrol and take a closer look at the town of Bint el-Jebel . . . By the time we returned, we had found the answers to a number of questions: the frequency of the night patrols along the road, their composition and strength, the number of army bases in the vicinity, how well they were guarded, and what went on inside them. We were surprised to discover that no real preparations had been made to meet a possible invasion. Everything was quiet . . . We returned before dawn thoroughly tired but with a clearly marked drawing of the route we had discovered and a report of everything we had seen. Naturally, there was no one to hand it over to. We were told that it was impossible to change anything on the night before the invasion. From a practical military point of view, all our work had been in vain. We returned to Hanita and fell into bed utterly exhausted.

When Moshe awoke on the afternoon of Saturday, June 7, Australian trucks had already begun to climb the steep road to Hanita. Moshe was introduced to the two young commanding officers of the Australian troops and they showed him a printed plan which he recognized with pride as a copy of a plan drawn by one of his patrols.

Moshe's men were given seven assignments, the principal one being to capture the sentries on the bridge north of Iskanderun. It was actually a pair of bridges on the coast road, 10 kilometers north of the Palestinian border. The Australians numbered three officers—Kippin, Allen, and Cowdrey—and seven soldiers. To these Moshe added a group of five, including himself and the Arab guide, Rashid Taher. All told there were sixteen men. The Australians had three revolvers, one Bren gun, one Tommy gun, and five Lee Enfield rifles. Moshe's men had three semi-automatic pistols of varying calibers, two Lee Enfields, one Tommy gun, and five hand grenades.

On Saturday night, before leaving on their mission, the combined force—ten Australians, five Jews, and one Arab—sat down to a festive dinner. Ya'akov Dori and Yitzhak Sadeh came to Hanita and joined the celebration. When Sadeh saw Mart, he asked what he was doing in an advance unit of the invasion. Mart replied that he was in Hanita on a private visit, but Dori and Sadeh ordered him home at once and forbade him to take part in the invasion. When Mart told Moshe, he dismissed the matter with a "never mind" and told Mart to remain there with him.

At 9:30 on Saturday night they set out on the long and strenuous march through the hilly terrain, and it was not until one o'clock in the morning that they reached the last ridge before Iskanderun and saw the village, the coast road, and their objective to the north dimly lit by the moon. They rested for a short time while Moshe and the Australians worked out their final plans for the attack on the northern bridge. Moshe thought that the bridges were guarded by French sentries and that it would be necessary to attack both of them. The unit silently approached the northernmost bridge and waited.

In his memorandum, Moshe played down his own part in the actual taking of the bridges. However, in the testimony that he gave for the Haganah Archives, Zalman Mart related what happened when they stopped at the bridges:

According to our information, there should have been a French contingent guarding the bridges. Here we expected the Australian officer to show his mettle and divide the men up into attacking forces . . . but [he] stood there waiting to hear what Rashid would say. Then Rashid said, "Well, here's the bridge that has to be taken." Of course, he had nothing to do with the tactical aspects of the operation. We therefore waited for the Australian to do something. Since he remained silent, Moshe took Rashid and went straight to the bridge, approaching it silently without being seen.

According to Mart, it was Moshe who took the initiative, and the Australian officer, Kippin, merely followed his lead.

Moshe, Rashid, and Kippin inched their way to the bridge and to their amazement found it unguarded and not prepared for demolition. Then the three men crawled to the second bridge and found an identical situation. With that, the commando unit had in fact completed its official mission. All it could do now was await the arrival of the main body of the invasion. The time was nearly 2 a.m., and by their reckoning the first British units were due in that area at approximately 4 a.m. There was a lull as they settled down to wait. Moshe, in what was to become typical behavior, went to sleep under the bridge. Mart and the others talked for a while and then tried to get some sleep, but the continuing silence made them uneasy and they soon awoke.

Moshe's memorandum relates: "One of the boys woke me at daybreak and said he thought something was wrong because no one had appeared anywhere near the bridge." In Mart's words, "The invasion never reached us." It later transpired that there was a simple reason for the French abandonment of the Iskanderun bridges: they had mined and blown up a section of the coast road further to the south, near the Palestinian border. Moshe described his reasoning thus:

It was quite clear to us that we must not abandon the bridges because they might be blown up, and we had been ordered to wait there until the invasion reached us. In the meantime, we wanted to do something. We heard that there was a French police station near Iskanderun and suggested to the Australians that we take it. We, of course, had no intention of going any further than that.

If Moshe's version is correct, then his eagerness for action and his desire to "do something" nearly cost him his life. At any rate, it is clear that the decision to attack the police station was a disastrous one for Moshe Dayan.

It was Rashid who told them about the police station. He said that it was situated 2 kilometers south of the bridges and was manned by only two or three policemen. "We left some men to guard the bridges and set out for the police station," Moshe wrote. "We walked along the road, for it never occurred to us that there was an army unit stationed in the police fort." Eleven Australians, the Jews, and the Arab proceeded south, talking and joking as they walked carelessly on either side of the road. They did not even bother to send scouts ahead. According to G. Lang:*

At approximately 5 a.m., when the unit was north of Iskanderun, they came under fire from a fortified stone emplacement. The Australians stormed the position and took it. Allen heard the shots and joined the others. A long battle ensued, and French reinforcements came to the aid of the beleaguered position. Some of Kippin's men attacked the French units in the nearby orchard, and a machine-gun emplacement was knocked out by Private Henderson, who attacked it with hand grenades.

The Australian version of the attack differs from the Haganah version in that it completely omits the part played by Moshe and Mart in overcoming the French position. Since the action in itself was unimportant and contributed nothing to the success of the invasion as a whole, a detailed military description of the events is of little interest. However, a comparison of the two versions shows certain significant aspects of Moshe's character.

According to the Haganah version, the group marched south for 2 kilometers and saw a mountain stretching east to west, an orange grove at its base, a stone wall, a road, and across the road the police station—a two-story building with a wide terrace in front and a steeply inclined hill leading down to the sea at the back. As they approached the building, some of the men remained on the road while the others made their way through the orange grove. According to Mart, they were not fired upon suddenly, as the Australian historian claimed. On the contrary, a French soldier turned and fled when he caught sight of them, and it was they who fired at him. Afterwards a "sleepy" French soldier "emerged from the house . . . shielded his eyes with his hand, and looked about him to find out

*In *Australia in the War of 1939-1945.*

what the shooting was about. A few more Frenchmen came out after him, some of them with rifles in their hands."

Exchanging fire with the French soliders, the attacking unit sought cover in the orange grove. The French in the police station placed a machine gun on the terrace and began firing long, sweeping bursts into the trees. Moshe's memorandum notes: "Our spirits were considerably dampened." The machine gun was fired at them from above and the bullets hit the upper edge of the stone wall, while the men hid behind it and counted their dwindling supply of ammunition. According to Mart:

An Australian took out a hand grenade, kissed it, and hurled it into the air, in fact missing his target. Then Moshe took a hand grenade and threw it straight onto the terrace. The explosion silenced the machine gun. This was a bull's-eye at a distance of some 23 to 25 meters. After the machine gun was knocked out, the Frenchmen continued to pour accurate fire at the top of the stone wall. Moshe turned to the officer [Kippin] and said, "You and the rest open fire and cover us. We'll run across the road and I'll throw a hand grenade into the house." The officer agreed, and that's exactly what happened. They began firing and the two of us jumped over the wall and found cover under the terrace . . . Then Moshe threw a hand grenade into the building through the upper pane of one of the doors. As it exploded, we burst into the building . . . The position was like this: an officer and a soldier lay dead on the floor . . . two men stood facing us. We fired and killed both of them. We entered the second room and found seven or eight Frenchmen sitting on the floor holding their hands over their ears, apparently from the shock of the explosion. We dealt with them as Wingate had taught us, and the prisoners received a few slaps in the face as well.

Mart's account, therefore, states that he and Moshe took the house on their own, overcoming at least twelve or fifteen French soldiers in the process.

Moshe's account of the actual capture of the house confirms Mart's in most of its details. In his first report, written before June 23, he describes the attack briefly. The memorandum written later gives a more detailed description of the events and stresses his own role in them. This is one of the few occasions in which Moshe indulged in self-praise—perhaps because he wrote the report while recuperating after the loss of an eye.

Lang states that after the police station had been captured and Henderson had knocked out the machine gun, "two of the Jewish guides [one of them was Moshe] were wounded. Kippin's men, under fire from the orchard, set up a mortar and a Hotchkiss machine gun they had captured on the roof of the fortified stone building and exchanged fire with a French column that was advancing from the north to meet the invasion. A number of trucks in this column were stopped and their soldiers taken prisoner." In the meantime, at about 7 a.m., an explosion was heard to the south. Although the commando unit did not know it at the time, the French had blown up the coast road it had been sent to keep open for the invasion. Instead, the unit was now fighting for a remote police station in an orange grove. Mart's account continues:

We all understood that we could no longer count on the invasion. On Moshe's initiative we decided to hold out inside the building. We took the Hotchkiss up to the roof. Everything we did . . . was done on Moshe's initiative and understanding . . . In the meantime, one of the Frenchmen who had surrendered told us that there was a mortar in the orange grove. We wasted no time and dashed into the grove, where we found the mortar and some ammunition. We also brought that onto the roof, but we didn't know how to operate it. Meanwhile, one of the Australians came up, said he knew how, and began firing it.

Moshe's report again corroborates Mart's version. According to the Australians, the heroes of the day were Kippin and Henderson; while according to the Jews, the credit was due to Moshe and Mart.

Nevertheless, by all accounts it was Moshe who operated the Hotchkiss on the roof, while the Australian fired the mortar. The roof provided very little cover. It had a ledge only 30 centimeters high, which barely hid them lying down. "But it was important to see what was happening around us, and this could only be done from the roof," Moshe wrote later.

On Moshe's orders, Mart climbed down from the roof and rode off with one of the Australians on a French motorcycle to see if there was any way of contacting the British Army on the border. The Frenchmen outside the building fired at the cycle, puncturing its tires and forcing the two men to return to the police station. At the same time, in Moshe's words:

I looked over the machine gun to find out how it worked and how the magazine fit in. After a few minutes, I discovered how to load it. When we began firing with the machine gun, we encountered heavy return fire. There was no real cover there, and as I was looking through a pair of field glasses, trying to locate the French positions, I was hit in the eye with a bullet. I did not lose consciousness. I was immediately given first aid. From that time on, I only heard what went on around me.

It was sometime after 7 a.m. on June 8, 1941.

Moshe had taken the field glasses from a dead French officer. The bullet hit the left side of the glasses, shattering the casing and sending fragments of glass and metal into the socket of his eye and one of his hands, severing the finger muscles. Mart, who by this time had returned from the abortive mission on the motorcycle, was hastily summoned to the roof to attend to his wounded friend. He found Moshe lying on his back, "and what a strange paradox—he had fallen right onto a French flag." According to Moshe, Mart tried to extract the casing of the field glasses from his eye. He pulled with all his strength but was unable to move the metal. Moshe finally asked him to leave it alone, in the hope that it would stem a possible hemorrhage. Mart recalls: "I said, 'Moshe what do you think?' He's the kind of man you can talk to even when he's wounded. Moshe answered, 'I've lost the eye, but if I can reach a hospital in time, I'll live.' Now, how do you get to a hospital with the French shooting at you, and the invasion's not an invasion and hasn't even reached you, and not a vehicle in sight? . . . "

Mart bandaged Moshe's face, eye, and hand with field dressings, then saw to it that he was removed from the roof. Meanwhile, the battle continued and one of the Australians was killed. Moshe ordered Mart to replace him, and the latter divided his time between the fighting and caring for his wounded friend, who lay motionless on the floor. Mart described Moshe laying quietly on the blankets all the time. "He made no requests, asked no questions, did not groan, weep, or utter a sound. He was given water without having to ask for it. He remained like that for six hours. At one o'clock in the afternoon, two Austrialians—an officer and a soldier—arrived at the police station on a motorcycle. They were the first sign we had of the invasion. Mart questioned them about the road to Haifa and, upon hearing that it was open, requested Kippin's permission to take one of the French trucks from the convoy and drive Moshe to the hospital. Kippin agreed and Mart, with the help of Rashid and an Australian driver, placed Moshe and the dead Australian on the back of the truck and set out for the border.

When the truck reached the main road it was crowded with troops and vehicles pouring northward. They made their way slowly up to the demolished bridge, but the light truck was unable to by-pass it. The Australian driver went to the headquarters of a nearby British unit and bargained successfully for the use of one of their ambulances.

Mart quickly contacted Moshe's family in Nahalal and a few of the Haganah leaders. Within a few hours a large group of relatives and friends gathered at the Hadassah Hospital in Haifa. Upon arrival, Moshe was immediately wheeled into the operating theater, but there was little the surgeons could do. His left eye was a total loss, and the only course open to them was to remove all the metal and glass fragments and to close up the empty socket. Moshe's face and hand, as well as the eye socket itself, required treatment, and in consultation with the family it was decided to send him to the Hadassah Hospital in Jerusalem.

10   OFF COURSE   (1941-1947)

The disabled often fail to grasp quickly how drastic a change their injury brings to their lives. Moshe was no exception in this respect and at first fully believed that he would still take an active part in the war. His report on the events at the police station, written in the hostipal, concludes with the following sentence: " ... On June 7 I was wounded in my hand and in my eyes [sic]. Herewith is the full report of the above events, and I wish to express the desire to continue serving to the best of my ability in the British Armed Forces." Although he was to become famous as a combat hero and was decorated by the British Army, Moshe did not return to combat duty—either in the British Army or in the Haganah—for seven years. He was relieved of the command of his company, and for a while it seemed that he would never again serve in any army. The loss of an eye is a serious handicap for a platoon leader or even a company commander. Moshe's progress from June 1941 to May 1948 was to a great extent conditioned by his injury and the fact that he was forced to remain in Jerusalem for protracted medical treatment. The same factors in turn had a far-reaching effect on his development as a public and party figure.

When he recovered from his injury, Moshe was assailed by fits of depression. "As far as the Haganah was concerned, I was an invalid, unfit for action. Personally, I too felt that I was no longer capable of military activities of any kind, and all I was good for now was work as a night watchman or something like that. It became painfully clear to me that physically I was finished, incapable of anything connected with fighting." Extracting the metal fragments from his wounds proved a drawn-out process that was accompanied by constant effusions from the eye socket which, though greatly diminished, have not ceased entirely to this day. He also suffered, and continues to suffer, from headaches. From 1941 on, Moshe was to experience constant pain, and although he learned to bear it silently, it deepened his initial despondency.

The hardest blow of all, however, was growing accustomed to his new image with its unmistakable badge—the black eye patch. As soon as the bridge of his nose had been reconstructed, it became clear that inserting a glass eye was out of the question. The bones of the eye socket had been completely shattered, and nothing was left to support a glass eye. His tireless efforts to exchange the black patch for a glass eye underscore the extent to which it distressed him.

Plastic surgeons in Jerusalem, Paris, and Johannesburg tried in vain to fill the shattered socket with sufficient fleshy tissue to support a glass eye. The last attempt was made in 1957 by Dr. Jack Penn of South Africa, one of the finest plastic surgeons in the world. As the treatment progressed and the glass eye was finally inserted, however, it turned out, in Moshe's own words, "that it looked even more sickening than without the eye." The new left eye was not in line with the right, and it looked like a glass bead stuck at an angle in the corner of his face.

Thus the black eye patch, which was to become the trademark of his image and a great asset to his political career, caused Moshe deep and prolonged agony. He became conscious of his pirate's appearance and dreaded children's fear of him. Even at the height of his fame, he was apprehensive of the curiosity of children and the questions they might ask about the patch. Whenever he was asked about it, there was a trace of anger or discomfort in his reply.

Moshe's dark moods were aggravated by the thought of his contemporaries' advancement in the Haganah. Yigal Allon, with whom he had been running neck and neck in their private race, was now leaving him far behind; in fact Moshe who had wanted "to do something great" ever since his childhood, was out of the race altogether. For a time all seemed lost, and it looked as though he would be just another member of Nahalal—without an eye. Falling back in the Haganah hierarchy in 1941, however, turned out to be the springboard for his advancement in Zahal ten years later.

Moshe refused to remain in the hospital for the duration of his treatment. He moved back to the Shwarz's house in the suburb of Rehavia and was driven to the Hadassah Hospital on Mount Scopus each day. Ruth and Yael joined him in Jerusalem, and for a while he had no interests beyond his family and himself.

Reuven Shiloah, who had been the Jewish Agency representative in the affair of the Forty-three, lived on the ground floor of the same apartment house. He was then the head of the Department for Special Affairs, a branch of the Political Department of the Jewish Agency. The new department came into being as the result of a change of policy—initiated in 1940 by the Chairman of the Jewish Agency, David Ben Gurion—suspending the struggle against the British on the background of the White Paper. Accordingly, Reuven Shiloah was able to maintain contacts with many secret and semi-secret British intelligence services and institutions.

Shiloah offered Moshe a post in his department, which solved the question of where he would work after his recuperation and also presented the possibility of an entirely new direction for his life—politics. In retrospect, the most important influence of this new position on his future was that it forced him to dwell upon the perpetuation of the Yishuv, which in Zionist ideology was but a step away from the perpetuation of the Jewish nation as a whole.

The German invasion of the USSR on June 22, 1941 and subsequent developments on the Eastern Front aroused concern in the Yishuv about the possibility of a Nazi invasion of Palestine. These fears prompted the Haganah to discuss what action the Yishuv would take in such an event. In the summer of 1941, the British authorities began preparing Palestine and Syria for a retreat. It was in this context that British Army Intelligence requested Reuven Shiloah's Department for Special Affairs to set up several small transmitting stations that would coordinate the activities of espionage rings in the event that Syria and Palestine were overrun by the Germans. Shiloah handed the matter over to Moshe and by August 15, 1941 received a detailed plan suggesting the establishment of transmitting stations in the south, Samaria, Haifa, and the Beisan area. British Intelligence approved the plan in general outline and on September 26 opened a special three-month course for twenty of Moshe's men in wireless transmitting and receiving and theories of radio and electricity.

To carry out his new duties, Moshe made his home in Jerusalem and rented a large four-room flat in the suburb of Katamon. But what became known as "Moshe Dayan's Private Network" proved narrow ground for Moshe's energy and imagination. He soon began proposing much broader fields of activity for the eventuality of conquest. On October 20, 1941 he suggested the creation of two special units whose men would be disguised as Arabs and as Germans. At first the British rejected this proposal, but in July 1942, when the circumstances of the war changed, it was accepted. The result was the establishment of the Arabic Platoon and the German Platoon within the Palmach. The project began when the British asked the Department for Special Affairs to find a man willing to parachute into Yugoslavia and serve as a wireless operator with the first British mission to Tito. Since wireless activities behind enemy lines were Moshe's department, Shiloah transferred the British request to him. Moshe chose a Nahalal boy, Peretz Rosenberg, who was dropped into Yugoslavia in May 1942. The idea appealed to Moshe, and he began asking himself why only one? Why not have an entire commando unit dropped behind enemy lines in Europe? It would serve two purposes: fighting the Germans and creating live contacts with the persecuted Jewish communities of Europe. The Political Department of the Jewish Agency submitted a detailed proposal to the British authorities, and it was accepted. Eventually, thirty-three Jewish parachutists from Palestine—most of them Palmach members—were dropped into Rumania, Bulgaria,

Italy, Austria, and Yugoslavia on guerrilla missions. Many of them never returned.

Moshe was entrusted with training the parachutists, and he employed a British officer nicknamed "Killer," a British Army major whose real name was Grant-Taylor. He was a roly-poly little man with a quick smile and a laugh made famous in an article about him in the *New York Herald Tribune,* and later in the December 1943 *Readers' Digest,* under the title "Killing is my Business." The interesting thing about Killer were the many sources of his specialized knowledge. For many years he was the small-arms expert of Scotland Yard's Special Branch, before being asked by J. Edgar Hoover to assist the FBI in its war on gangsterism in the United States. Killer spent nine years in America serving with the FBI and on the police forces of New York, Chicago, and San Francisco. By his own account, everything he had known about instinctive firing and methods of kidnapping or killing was child's play compared to what he learned from the American gangsters. To refine and improve his methods, he even consulted leading members of the American underworld.

One of the more important lessons Moshe and his men, as well as many British commandos, learned from Grant-Taylor was how to rid themselves of their reluctance to kill. "He taught us how to kill without regret," Moshe said. Killer instructed his pupils in England and America according to the following philosophy:

Unfortunately, the average American and Englishman suffers from remorse. You must learn to overcome that, or else it will slow you down at a crucial moment and cause your own death. Killing a Jerry is like swatting a fly. Keep thinking that, shoot a few, then you'll sleep like a baby after even the bloodiest shambles. Only two things will interest you: getting the job done and getting away.

Moshe remained in Jerusalem from June 1941 to September 1942. His first son, Ehud, was born there on January 31, 1942. During this period, he devoted much time to his family, and friends recall that he especially liked to play with three-year-old Yael. He would sit her down on his knee, for example, and very patiently teach her how to read. The bulk of his time, however, was devoted to affairs of state. Shiloah often told his friends that Moshe's passion for political affairs was like an insatiable passion for music. He was particularly interested in the Political Department's contacts with the Arabs.

Yoseph Harel, who often visited Moshe in Jerusalem, recalls that during this period he evinced rapid and frequently extreme changes of mood, a phenomenon that became even more pronounced in later years. He became less dependent on the company of others and increasingly sought solitude. Harel noticed the first traces of this change when Moshe, who was always sociable and gay, became more distant and "never smiled or seemed to need anyone." This was a quality Shmuel had perceived in his son from childhood. "When he emerged from a dark mood," Harel relates, "it was a pleasure just to listen to him talk; and when he laughed, you always laughed with him." In Hanita, men admired him but could not befriend him. "Everyone, of course, loved Yigal Allon, and could approach him at any time. With Moshe there was always a border-line. That was it—beyond that point you could not reach him. He never said a word about his own problems. Nevertheless, he had periods of tremendous elation. When he was happy, things were great." In Jerusalem, these periods of gaiety became increasingly rare. "He would greet you with a word, not a sentence, and with a strange smile. He was with you, technically speaking, but as far as he was concerned, you did not exist."

Another change occurred in Moshe during his stay in Jerusalem. The kinds of people who had interested him as a boy in Nahalal, a JSP Sergeant, a member of the FOSH in Hanita, and a company commander in Syria no longer attracted him. Instead, he was drawn to people concerned with politics, people who studied and contemplated the destiny of the Yishuv. From his behavior it was difficult to assess his capacity for profound political thinking. He still looked like a man of the land—his speech was sloppy, his thoughts carelessly expressed—and he bore traces of the practical joker and daring scout. Judging from appearance only, no one would have believed that the young man from Nahalal was capable of original and sophisticated thought and possessed a remarkably high intelligence. Most of his friends and military commanders thought him their equal in most things and were willing to admit his superiority only in fieldcraft and daring. They were therefore at a loss to understand his aloofness and lack of interest in them once he left military service and embarked on a life of politics.

It was Moshe's brand of charm or bonhomie that sharpened his friends' feeling of rejection. When in a good mood, Moshe could create about him an electrifying atmosphere of excitement, and his charm generated a sense of participation in the creation of this charged atmosphere. Consequently, many people who enjoyed themselves in his company also felt that real understanding and friendship had developed between them. In most cases, this impression was entirely one-sided. Many who considered themselves his friends did not suspect for a moment that their feelings were not reciprocated; and some who thought themselves his friends, or during a certain period of common interests were in fact his friends, would suddenly find themselves faced with a different, aloof and detached Moshe Dayan. As a result, those who sought his company were often deeply offended.

During this period in Jerusalem, Moshe achieved with ease the one thing that always eluded him in Nahalal: to be well-liked. He now discovered that many sought his company and his confidence and to be his friend was considered an honor. His natural tendency toward solitude forced him to protect himself from this craving. Without a doubt, the tales of his courage and daring in battle had a great deal to do with effecting this change. Among the political elite of Jerusalem, every JSP and Haganah man was said to be "brave," as naturally as he was called "a nice guy." But the participation of Jewish guides in the invasion of Syria—an event of scant significance in the annals of the Second World War—was a military event of the first order for the Yishuv. It may safely be assumed that even had he not been wounded, Moshe would have been acclaimed by the Yishuv, for of all the Jewish units that participated in the invasion, his company was responsible for the most important mission. But his injury elevated his status even more. Furthermore, the black eye patch had already begun to turn into a symbol, a focal point at which all the tales of his heroism became a single legend. Moshe rose from the limited professional circles of the military and became, as it were, the property of the entire Yishuv. From June 1941 on, his name was to become familiar to practically every young Jew interested in the public affairs of Palestine.

Fame did not affect him in any profound way. His easy-going manner, sense of humor, wit, nimble mind, indefinable charm, and love of direct contact with things, of learning from immediate experience remained unchanged. But legends fade and fame passes, as Moshe was to discover in the coming years. When the danger of a German invasion had passed, the "Private Network" was no longer needed. The German and Arab Platoons remained on as part of the Palmach, and the parachutists were removed from his control. When no official duties could be found to justify his remaining in Jerusalem, he returned with his family to Nahalal in September 1942.

But before returning to the drab routine of farm life, Moshe undertook an adventurous mission to Iraq. The British Army was preparing to transport an Indian battalion to Iraq and exchange it for a British one which would leave for Palestine a few days later. A convoy of Jewish buses was organized to make the trip, and Moshe volunteered as second driver. The Haganah took advantage of the opportunity and entrusted him with smuggling three suitcases of arms to its cell in Baghdad and helping two Persian immigrants cross the border into Palestine. The convoy reached Baghdad at the end of August, a few days before the Jewish High Holy Days. Since pogroms had broken out against Jews at that time, the British commander of the convoy forbade the Jewish drivers to enter the city. They ordered the men to remain for two days at a military base 30 kilometers from Baghdad. At dawn on the first day, Moshe slipped out of his tent, took off his trousers, and entered the sewage ditches that led out of the camp. Wading from one ditch to another, he managed to reach the main road where he joined a colorful caravan of hundreds of asses bearing fruit and vegetables to the city markets. As they neared the bridge at the entrance to the city, he noticed that guards were checking the papers of any stranger entering the city, but the Arabs were exempt from this inspection. According to Moshe, "I removed my eye patch and was no different from any local inhabitant. That's how I entered Baghdad. "Once in the city, he parted company with the caravan, put on his trousers, and—filthy as he was—entered the lobby of the elegant Omayyad Hotel to look for the Jewish Agency representative, Enzo Sereni, and complete his mission.

Returning to Nahalal, he moved his family into a hut on his parents' farm. It was only a temporary arrangement, for in 1944, with considerable help from his father-in-law , he bought a vacant farm. In order to ensure his daughter's rights, Zvi Shwarz not only contributed a large part of the cash involved in the transaction, but also put up 1,400 Palestinian pounds as a mortgage, which made the sale of the farm impossible without his prior agreement. Moshe began building up a promising farm based on dairy produce, but he was unable to sever completely his ties with the Haganah and issues of national policy and returned to work for the organization on a part-time basis. Naturally, the farm suffered as a result of this arrangement. At first he still dealt with some aspects of the parachuting project and to do so often left Nahalal. Although his role in the project rapidly diminished, he nonetheless continued to participate in a number of missions for the Haganah.

In December 1946 Moshe attended the Twenty-second Zionist Congress in Basle, where he delivered a speech as a representative of the younger generation and called for an intensification of the scope and depth of resistance to British Mandatory rule. From Basle, he continued on to Paris for treatment on his eye. The doctors began transplanting bones into his eye socket, but a violent reaction set in and he developed a high fever. His condition was critical, and both doctors and friends feared he was near death. A month later, however, he left the hospital as quickly as he could, the black patch firmly in place. His condition did not permit a sea voyage, so despite the prohibitive cost, he returned to Palestine by plane. Some time after Ya'akov Dori was appointed Chief-of-Staff of the Haganah, Moshe received the appointment of Staff Officer for Arab Affairs.

11   DEGANIA AGAIN

(November 1947 - May 1948)

The events leading up to the War of Independence and its opening clashes found Moshe far from front-line duties and the centers of power. Moreover, he did not belong to any one of the three main cliques that comprised the top echelons of the army: the Palmach, centered around Israel Galili and Yigal Allon; the Haganah and its Field Corps, led by Yigael Yadin (who became Director of Military Operations in the summer of 1947); or veterans of the British Army, represented chiefly by Chaim Laskov and Mordechai Maklef, who enjoyed the enthusiastic support of David Ben Gurion. His return to field command came about entirely by chance, for he was considered eminently suitable as Officer for Arab Affairs and it was believed that he enjoyed the position. His resumption of combat duty began with an appointment as a sector commander, followed by a promotion to the rank of major as a battalion commander. His contemporaries were already filling much higher posts. Yigal Allon, for example, was a major general, commanding units in the north and the south before receiving the command of the Southern Front.

The one advantage to Moshe's position as Officer for Arab Affairs was that it afforded him direct access to C-o-S Dori and his superiors: Israel Galili, Commander in Chief of the Haganah National Command, and David Ben Gurion, who held the Defense portfolio in the Zionist Executive. On the other hand, his work was hampered by a plethora of interested parties, all of whom dealt with Arab affairs: the Arab Department of the Jewish Agency, the Intelligence Service of the Haganah, and others. As an Officer for "Special Affairs," he was permitted to advise, but military action was taken by units not under his direct command.

Moshe had two main tasks: to recruit agents and to circumscribe the activities of the Arab gangs in Palestine and neighboring countries, particularly Syria. Throughout 1947 these gangs expanded and became steadily more violent. In fact, they constituted the only adversary in the War of Independence until May 14, 1948, the day the State of Israel was proclaimed. After the Declaration of Independence, they joined forces with the regular armies of Egypt, Jordan, Iraq, Syria, and Lebanon, which proceeded to invade Palestine.

There were others who planted agents among the Arabs, but Moshe was the only one who entrusted the search for agents to personal friends. He called them by the code name of "advisers," probably deriving the name from his own official title. Two of his most important "advisers" were his childhood friends Giora Zeid and Oded Yannai, both of whom were working as watchmen for settlements in the Nahalal region. In selecting the Arab agents, Moshe followed the same rule that had served him before the invasion of Syria: choose men who are good material for terrorist gangs.

The "advisers" initially communicated their information directly to Moshe, but as the war branched out, direct contact weakened and they began operating through the regular channels of the Haganah Intelligence Service. Moshe's network reaped its greatest successes in the north, where it was instrumental in the conquest of Haifa, Nazareth, and various other places in the Jezreel Valley and Lower Galilee. The bloodless conquest of Acre may be attributed to the contacts Moshe's "advisers" established with the Druze sheik, Salah Khnifess of Shfar'am. Moshe was bound up in this affair by more than one thread.

A Druze battalion under the command of sixty-year-old Sheik Wahab joined the newly formed "Army of Liberation," recruited in Syria by Fawzi Kaukji. Wahab joined the war against the Jews in Palestine despite the objection of Sultan el-Atrash, the leader of the Druze sect at Jebel Druze. On March 28, 1948, Wahab's battalion was given command of the Haifa District and set up its headquarters in the Druze village of Shfar'am. Wahab initiated harassing operations against Kibbutz Ramat Yohanan and the village of Kfar Ata. These actions developed into what became known as the Battle of Ramat Yohanan. Here the Druze confronted the Carmeli Brigade, in which Zohar Dayan was serving as a platoon leader. On April 12, a battle began for two villages. Four days later the Carmeli Brigade emerged the victor and, despite heavy casualties, took and held Ramat Yohanan and Kfar Ata. The official record of the battle states that the losses "were mainly among the officers, who too often endangered their lives in order to serve as an example to their men." One of the officers who led his men in battle was Zohar. On April 14 he failed to return from a mission and was reported missing in action. Only after the battle was over, on April 17, did a party go out to search for him and found his body, face down, in a field. It is not inconceivable that his brother's example later added weight to C-o-S Dayan's conviction that the proper place for a field commander was at the head of his men.

The bodies of the fallen at Ramat Yohanan remained in the field for several days and swelled beyond recognition. It became necessary for the families to identify them, and the Dayan family asked Moshe to represent them. Outwardly, there was no trace of his agony, but those close to him knew that he loved Zorik, and this was one of the rare times in his life that Moshe asked for help. Before setting out, he asked his brother-in-law, Israel Gefen, to accompany him because "I don't know if I'll be able to take it."

Before the battle of Ramat Yohanan, Giora Zeid had negotiated with the Druze battalion stationed at Shfar'am. Sheik Salah Khnifess intervened on the Jews' behalf by trying to persuade Wahab to stay out of the fighting. Two days after the battle, Giora resumed contact with them and was soon able to inform Moshe that there was a possibility of bringing the entire Druze battalion over to the Israeli side. Giora recalls being somewhat apprehensive about reporting this news to Moshe for, after all, his brother had died at their hands. "But Moshe thought for a moment—he reaches decisions quickly—then said *Yallah* [Arabic for "Let's go"]." That night some ten officers from the Druze battalion met Giora and his companions on the battlefield and drove off to dinner and a meeting with Moshe at nearby Kiryat Tivon. The Druze arrived polished and pressed, armed with pistols and rifles. When they were introduced to Moshe and told that his brother had been killed in the battle of Ramat Yohanan, they paled visibly, for according to Druze tradition blood could be atoned for only by blood. For a moment the Druze thought they had fallen into a trap, but as those present at the meeting remember, Moshe said: "Since you have come to make a pact with us, I forgive you for spilling blood of my blood." He raised a glass of wine and toasted, "To Life." Through the mediation of Salah Khnifess—who was later decorated for his participation in the establishment of the State of Israel—Wahab's battalion was persuaded to withdraw from the war, and their abstention paved the way for the conquest of Acre. It was only in December 1948 that Zahal accepted volunteers from the minority groups of Israel—mainly Druze—and established the Minorities Unit. Abed Abeidat volunteered for this unit and embarked upon a brilliant career in the army.

Moshe received his first non-advisory post after the Carmeli Brigade secured the city of Haifa on April 22, 1948. At first Mordechai Maklef, the Brigade Operations Officer, dealt with the Arab sectors of the city. On Ben Gurion's initiative, however, Haganah HQ sent Moshe to Haifa with a special assignment: to administer abandoned Arab property. It was here that he gained his first experience in military government. Later, as C-o-S after the conquest of the Gaza Strip in the Sinai Campaign and as Minister of Defense after the Six-Day War, he favored a well-regulated and liberal administration in the Administered Territories. In 1948, however, his ideas on this subject had not yet crystallized. To prevent looting, which was rife by the time he assumed the post, Moshe ordered that everything the army could use be transferred to Zahal warehouses and the rest distributed among Jewish agricultural settlements. Golda Meir, who took part in the consultations on this

issue, agreed to this policy. It was a form of reparation for the settlements that had suffered from Arab terrorism. But some felt that this
was a deplorable act of appropriation, rather than the action of a
responsible state which should keep accounts of the confiscated
enemy property and protect the rights of the individual.

Moshe's duties as Officer for Arab Affairs, which had been cur-
tailed by May 14, lost all significance with the establishment of the
state, when a proper military campaign replaced the sporadic battles
against terrorists and irregulars. Although he repeatedly expressed
the desire to be given a field command, he was not offered one and
spent much time wandering the corridors of Haganah HQ with
nothing to do. "I wandered about underfoot. I was out of a job and
felt badly about it. I wanted to join one of the units. The emphasis
was then on making war, not on directing or planning it. I wanted
to be in a fighting unit and I didn't care if I served as a brigade commander or a company commander."

Years later, in a special interview published in the daily *Haboker*
(March 6, 1964), Ben Gurion maintained that:

> Had Moshe Dayan been Chief-of-Staff of Zahal at the outbreak of the
> War of Independence, it is possible that the present borders of the state
> would have been different and we would have achieved greater military
> successes . . . It's a pity that I did not know Moshe Dayan at the beginning
> of the war. I had a feeling that efforts were being made to keep him away
> from me. Nevertheless, I managed to become acquainted with him in the
> end, and I'm glad of it, for he gave me no reason to be disappointed in him.

The question of whether Moshe deserved a higher position in 1948—
even though it arose only because of the 1960 split in the Mapai
leadership—is interesting in itself from the point of view of his
development and relations with Ben Gurion at that time. Although
Ben Gurion claimed he did not know Dayan until the state was
established—that is, May 14, 1948, or, as he put it in the *Haboker*
interview, "at the beginning of the war," meaning no earlier date than
November 29, 1947, the date of the General Assembly resolution
on the partition of Palestine—it is known that Ben Gurion met
Moshe at the Twenty-second Zionist Congress. They also maintained
contact during 1947 and at the beginning of 1948, when Moshe
served as Officer for Arab Affairs, and both Dori and Yadin testify
to Moshe's free access to Ben Gurion over their heads.

The true explanation appears to be that Ben Gurion knew
Moshe Dayan as a Haganah man involved in politics, rather than
warfare. There may have been two reasons for this. The first is an
objective one: Moshe's injury in June 1941 deferred, if not entirely
ruled out, his advancement in active military service. The second
reason was factional. There can be no doubt that the prevailing

atmosphere in the Palmach was that of a kibbutz society and that personal advancement was therefore linked to factional affiliation. Dori claims that this was true of the Haganah as well after both he and Yadin resigned and Yitzhak Sadeh and Israel Galili—both Achdut Ha'avodah leaders—were appointed C-o-S and C-in-C, respectively. Sadeh felt great affection for Moshe and regarded him as highly as he did Yigal Allon, but his personal influence in the Palmach declined steadily from 1943 on. As we shall see, when he was able to, Sadeh promptly gave Moshe a responsible position.

During the seven years Moshe was absent from active duty, new groups and individuals acquired status and valuable experience. Fitting Moshe into a command post meant disrupting routine procedures, an unhealthy practice in time of war. Added to this was the fact that everyone in GHQ believed that he was highly successful in his special duties. Yadin maintains that had he been asked to draw up a list of candidates for appointments in the Haganah, it would have resembled Galili's, in spite of the latter's political bias. In May 1948 the issue at stake was survival, and it was futile to be too meticulous in ferreting out the political implications of each military appointment.

Finally, it would seem that Moshe was a "late bloomer" and in 1948 had not achieved the maturity necessary for top-level command. Moshe himself was keenly aware of this. He still had much of the prankster of "Habibi" days in him and was endowed with daring bordering on irresponsibility. Although these traits may have been tolerable in the middle ranks of field command, they were entirely imadmissible in higher echelons.

Four days after the publication of Ben Gurion's interview in *Haboker,* Dayan sent the following letter, written in his own hand, to Ya'akov Dori:

Jerusalem, March 10, 1964

Dear Ya'akov,

With regard to Ben Gurion's statement in *Haboker,* etc.:

(a) As far as I can recall from things I heard Ben Gurion say at the time, he bore a grudge against Israel Galili for recommending and praising Achdut Ha'avodah men and detracting from the others.

(b) There is no doubt about the fact that at the time of the War of Independence, I was not mature enough either for the post of C-o-S, or even for a lesser position on the staff, and those military actions and judgments I cooked up later were based on things I learned from my elders and betters and were the fruit of extended activity and a process of gradual development.

I mention these two things to you because I have no doubt that we share the same basic attitude toward Ben Gurion, and not infrequently because of our great respect for him we are obliged to separate the wheat from the chaff and even ignore or bear quietly certain things he says and does. This time, his remarks exceeded all limits of what is permissible even in error.

Yours in friendship,

Moshe Dayan

The change in Moshe's military prospects came suddenly. The last brigade to be formed before the establishment of the state was the 8th, with Sadeh as its commander. This was the army's only armored brigade in the War of Independence and included a tank battalion and a raiding battalion. The former had only enough tanks to set up two companies, while armored vehicles still had to be found for the latter. Finding men to fill the ranks of the new brigade was no less problematical. It was decided to incorporate in the new brigade former members of Lehi,* which, like all the independent military organizations, had been disbanded with the creation of Zahal.

When Sadeh set about organizing his new unit, he was faced with a meager selection of candidates for a cadre of commanding officers. Anyone "worth anything" had already been recruited into other units. Sadeh was undoubtedly pleased to discover that Moshe was still available, for Moshe was a man after his own heart. He proposed that Moshe be given command of the 89th Battalion, which he called a "commando" battalion. Moshe was no less pleased. Yadin, who stressed the need for actions behind enemy lines because of Zahal's inability to undertake a frontal campaign, thought Moshe suitable, particularly because of his experience during the invasion of Syria in June 1941.

Yadin mentioned Moshe's name to Ben Gurion, who wrote in his diary on May 17, 1948: "Moshe Dayan has been charged with organizing a commando for the Central Front." On the following day, Ben Gurion added: "It has been decided to appoint Moshe Dayan as commander of the front in the Jordan Valley." The reason for the change was a radical turn for the worse in what was known as the "Battle for the Deganias."

On Friday, May 14, 1948, the State of Israel was established. The invasion of the Arab armies began the following day. The deployment of the defense forces in the Jordan Valley included one under-strengthed battalion of the Golani Brigade, 400 men in all, while the Zemakh-Tiberias area was held by a single company. A second company held the adjacent sector, Ashdot Ya'akov-Gesher; and a

---

* Hebrew acronym for Lohamei Herut Israel, a dissident resistance organization that split away from the Irgun.

third was tied down far to the rear of the second. One platoon and one company of Home Guards from the surrounding kibbutzim entered the village of Zemakh and took up positions in and around the police station. Meanwhile, the two forward companies of a regular Syrian infantry brigade were advancing towards Zemakh, supported by artillery, tanks, and armored cars. The brigade moved into the abandoned British Army camp and the nearby quarantine camp. Up to this point, the opposing sides had exchanged only light, exploratory fire.

The large, coordinated Syrian attack was launched at dawn on Tuesday, May 18. Its objective was to take Degania and thus gain control of the nearby dam and bridge over the Jordan. This would open up the entire Jordan Valley to the Syrian Army. The tiny force at Zemakh, lacking artillery and antitank or antiaircraft weapons, could not possible hope to hold out against two regular infantry companies, thirty tanks and armored vehicles, artillery, mortars, and planes. During its tortuous retreat over open ground, the unit was unable to gather its dead, and the wounded were left to die in the fields. The road to the two Deganias was open.

The first casualties in Degania A fell during the softening-up blows of the Syrian artillery. Word of the grave stituation at the kibbutz, and the entire Jordan Valley, reached GHQ in Tel Aviv. The C-o-S had been taken ill in February and had undergone surgery for an ulcer; he resumed his duties only at the end of May. As Director of Military Operations, Yadin therefore assumed Dori's tasks as well. Concerned about the situation in the north, Yadin was nevertheless powerless to offer reinforcements of either men or arms. This predicament is illustrated by the fact that when he wanted to send the four "Napoleonchik" cannons* to the Jordan Valley, he met opposition from Ben Gurion, who wanted them sent to the Jerusalem area. Finally, Ben Gurion agreed to send the four "Napoleonchiks" to Degania for exactly twenty-four hours, but only on condition that after that period they would be transferred immediately to Jerusalem.

On Wednesday, May 19, a three-man delegation from Degania A, Degania B, and Kinneret set out for Tel Aviv to warn the authorities of the gravity of the situation. That evening they managed to meet with Ben Gurion and informed him that Syrian tanks were approaching the fences of the two Deganias. Yoseph Baratz recalled:

Without even sitting down, we told Ben Gurion the details of the situation. We demanded cannons, planes and men. Ben Gurion did not let us go on

* French-made, model 1914, 65 mm. cannons, the first pieces of artillery used by Zahal, they were imported to Israel in April 1948 and were so nicknamed on account of their antiquity.

for long. He replied curtly, "There are none. No cannons, not enough planes, there is a shortage of men on all the fronts, the situation is very serious in the Negev, serious in Jerusalem and Upper Galilee. The front is everywhere, throughout the country. We cannot send reinforcements." Ben-Zion [Israeli, of Kinneret] interrupted him: "Ben Gurion, what are you talking about? Are we to abandon the Jordan Valley?" and burst into tears.

Ben Gurion sent the three men to Yadin, who suggested that they prepare Molotov cocktails against the tanks. Yoseph Baratz asked, "Can we take such a risk—letting them come to the very entrance to Degania?" Yadin replied, "Yes, there is no alternative. That's the only way."

Moshe's appointment as commander of the Jordan Valley sector, made before Ben Gurion and Yadin met with the three settlers, was the only consolation Yadin could offer. The three received the news with mixed feelings. In the years immediately preceding the war, Moshe had not developed the reputation of a distinguished officer. The fact that he was born in Degania and was deeply attached to it could not compensate for the lack of arms and men. Of more substantial aid were the four "Napoleonchiks" that Ben Gurion finally agreed to transfer north for twenty-four hours, on condition that they be brought to Jerusalem immediately afterward.

To return to the sequence of events, a telegram to Golani Brigade HQ was sent at 9:35 a.m. on May 18, stating that Moshe Dayan had been appointed commander—subordinate to Brigade OC—of the sector from Ein Gev to the areas north of Beisan. Before leaving for Degania, Moshe presumably discussed with Yadin the question of his authority. He was, above all, an outsider thrust upon the Golani Brigade from above. At noon on the same day Yadin dispatched a second telegram to the OC of the Brigade, ordering him to put at Dayan's disposal anything he might need to implement his task.

The acting C-o-S sent Dayan on his way with a few words of encouragement, even reminding him that he had been born in Degania. But Moshe's parting gift was more than just a pat on the back: GHQ allotted him a company from the Gadna* NCO course—sixteen- and seventeen-year-old boys without combat experience who were to relieve a battle-weary company of older men. He was also given three PIATs (antitank weapons). The Gadna company set out for Degania from its base, while Moshe loaded the three PIATs into his old, black Haganah car and raced to Degania—a one-man Salvation Army.

Moshe's only advantage, he quickly discovered, was the relatively

---

* Abbreviation for *Gedudei No'ar* (youth troops), the paramilitary framework of Zahal for youth.

large number of recruits from Nahalal serving in his sectors. There were three platoons of them, one under Uri Bar-On, apart from individuals in various roles, including his old friends Binya Zarhi and Ahya Ben-Ami. Relying directly on Nahalalites and appointing Ben-Ami as a personal assistant gained him some measure of authority over the men in the field.

Moshe arrived at his sector just before sunset on Tuesday, May 18. The massive Syrian attack began two days later, at 4:15 a.m. He therefore had only thirty hours to deploy the troops under his command. He could not make radical changes in such a short time, particularly as his fears of insufficient authority were proved justified. Although he was sector commander, the units in his sector had not been officially subordinated to his command. Moreover, he was not the commanding officer of the Barak Battalion, which was deployed in his sector, and was himself subordinate to the OC Golani Brigade.

Considering the circumstances, Moshe's need for personal friends is understandable. In addition, this was the first time he had been given a field command. He may even have feared that his orders and military terminology, rusty after seven years of disuse, would be ridiculed by the eighteen-year-olds and their officers and needed friends to bolster his self-confidence. One thing is quite clear—he did not come to Degania certain of his ability to influence men and control units.

On Wednesday he received command of his sector and ordered improvements in the entrenchments and defenses. He also issued an order which was to prove tactically significant in the ensuing battle: to take up positions in Beit Yerach and include it in the line of defense. This extension thinned out the line elsewhere, but also placed the defenders of Degania on the flank of the Syrian attack, a factor that later proved crucial.

Moshe Dayan generally tends to play down his role in the victory in the "Battle for the Deganias":

> I had no command authority. I did not save the Deganias, and without me the battle would have turned out just as it did with me there. Let's say I gave the order to advance along the road between the Deganias and Zemakh, and to take Beit Yerach so that we would be on the Syrian flank. This in itself was no great feat.

There are other accounts which describe him as an officer of considerable composure. When he toured Beit Yerach and saw the Yavnielites digging in deep, he quipped, "Stop digging—you'll strike oil," advising them to find good firing positions for the PIATs and the 20 mm. cannon instead. Chaim Levakov, also a Yavnielite, recalls that on the day of the battle the water supply ran out and the men were suffering from thirst. Moshe approached them and said, "Listen, you're here in the trenches under the trees, in the shade. If you think *you're* thirsty, just imagine how thirsty the Syrians must be, running about the open fields in the sun."

The "Battle for the Deganias" lasted approximately nine hours. From 4:15 a.m. until 1 p.m., when a surprising and decisive reversal occurred. The Syrian attacking force—an infantry brigade supported by artillery, tanks, armored cars, and two bombers—came to within a few paces of victory. It was led by the tanks that advanced to the fences of the two kibbutzim. A Syrian tank penetrated the outer fence of Degania A, crossed the antitank ditch near the road, pierced the inner fence and, was making its way through the courtyard of the settlement when the defenders leaped out of the trenches and stormed it with Molotov cocktails, setting it ablaze and killing the crew. A similar fate overtook a second tank.

At this moment of crisis, and even sometime before it, both the brigade commander and the artillery officer felt that the artillery at Poriya should be put into action immediately and a counterattack launched. Moshe, on the other hand, did not think the time was right. He felt that the artillery should be brought in only on the following day, at the most critical stage of the battle. Brigade HQ left the matter to his discretion. It was typical of Moshe to examine the situation at close hand and receive reports from the men on the spot before making a decision.

Although the main brunt of the attack was borne by Degania A, the situation at Degania B was far more serious. Preparations to defend the settlement had been carried out haphazardly and there were not enough communicating trenches. Many of the casualties were directly attributable to this fact. There was also no radio contact with the settlement. In order to get some idea of what was happening there, Moshe sent Ahya Ben-Ami from Kinneret to Uri Bar-On at Degania B. He also gave him a note which read: "Four cannons have arrived, and they're in Poriya. I want to wait and use them tomorrow. But if you say you need them now, I'll open fire." Bar-On recalls writing his reply on the back of Moshe's note: "Request that you open fire at once."

When Ben-Ami returned to Kinneret, he reported to Moshe: "I can't say for sure whether or not the Syrians have actually entered the courtyard. I heard it from someone, but I didn't see it. But I don't doubt for a moment that they *can* enter the courtyard. All they have to do is shift into gear, and there's nothing to stop them." Ben-Ami supported Bar-On's request that the cannons be put into action without delay. Moshe then sent him to instruct the artillery officer at Poriya to open fire.

In all, the three rusty guns (one broke down) fired about 500 shells, causing some damage in Zemakh and killing some thirty Syrians near the police station. None of the cannons had aiming mechanisms, and the artillery officer did not want to waste his ammunition. When he opened fire, at first he shot into the lake in order to gauge his range by the spray. This first round, as well as subsequent ones, did absolutely no damage to the Syrians; but the noise created as the shells descended the mountain spread panic among the Syrian infantry, and they simply began to flee for their lives. Moshe had counted no more than forty shells when his HQ learned that the Syrian commander had ordered his tanks back to Zemakh.

At 1 p.m. the Syrians began to flee the battlefield. The tanks turned in their tracks and the infantry actually overtook them in their haste to leave the scene of battle. All at once, as though by magic, the siege of the Deganias had lifted. By 4 p.m. total silence reigned in the area. Moshe often repeated this anecdote about the battle:

Binya told me about the attack on Degania B—how the Syrians came and how they fled. And when it was all over, an Arab suddenly got up, approached Binya—who was standing at the gate of the settlement—and said, "Open up! It's Muhammad!" It turned out that throughout the battle he had hidden in a barley field. Why should he, of all people, join an attack? He lay on the ground . . . until it grew quiet, and he was sure that his companions had taken the Deganias. So he gets up, rings the bell and announces his arrival. Binya, of course, gave him a fitting reception.

The incident remained engraved in his memory not only as an anecdote from the battlefield, but also because of his attention to seemingly insignificant details that can sometimes illuminate an important phenomenon. In this case, Moshe grasped something of the character of the Arab soldier.

At nightfall Moshe decided to find out what was happening in Zemakh. It was not clear whether the Syrians had retreated to Zemakh and were organizing their forces there or had retreated even further east, as Moshe thought likely. He gathered several of his friends from Nahalal and his staff and drove to Zemakh in his black car, accompanied by a platoon of soldiers. His friends considered it a courageous act, but Moshe's assumption about the Syrian retreat proved correct. He took a pair of Syrian field glasses as a souvenir and returned to his HQ in a Syrian communications vehicle.

From Moshe's point of view, the "Battle for the Deganias" was significant because of the Syrians' retreat from Zemakh. Their behavior was a revelation that brought about a decisive and enduring change in his attitude toward Israel's security problems.

It made an indelible impression on me, that jaunt to Zemakh at night. I saw how they dropped everything and fled. This is stamped with great vividness in my memory . . . how, after three or four shells, they got up and ran, had no idea what they were doing—they were at a total loss. With our fourth shell the entire Syrian attack collapsed. They retreated without being attacked; after all, no one attacked Zemakh, and yet by nightfall they were no longer there. I thought then that you just have to bang once on a tin and they will all scatter like birds.

A few days after the "Battle for the Deganias" Moshe returned to Tel Aviv to assume command of the 89th Battalion.

12 THE 89th BATTALION

(May-August 1948)

After Zemakh Moshe had no further doubts about his ability to command the 89th Battalion. Fired with renewed self-confidence, he told Yitzhak Sadeh, "With a few jeeps and machine guns we can take care of the Arab armies and put things in order." A series of orders was issued for the formation of the 8th Brigade. One of them, dated May 21, designated it as a GHQ reserve unit for offensive actions and counterattacks. Another, from May 31, stated that all the units of the new brigade would come under Sadeh's command no later than noon, June 1. While still sector commander in the Jordan Valley, Moshe had spoken to some of the Nahalal and Yavniel boys about transferring to his new battalion—which he told them would be a commando unit—and they were enthusiastic at the prospect of serving in a unit which bore so exciting a name.

Uri Bar-On recalls Moshe telling him that:

he had GHQ authorization to take men from other units and to select anyone he wished. He wanted me to be a company commander and asked me to round up some more of the gang. I did not return to Degania after that. On the strength of Moshe's verbal authorization, I sent word to the Nahalal boys and some others in my company. I didn't tell Meir Amit [the second-in-command of Bar-On's battalion] a thing.

Bar-On's First Company of the 89th, later known as C Company, was built around the nucleus of men Moshe had spirited away from the Golani Brigade; the Second Company (B Company) was lured away from the 43rd Battalion of the Kiryati Brigade; and the Third (A Company) came from the ranks of the disbanded Lehi.

One of the first recruits of the 89th was Yohanan Pelz, a second-generation military man. By 1935 he had already filled a string of security posts in Palestine, including service as a mounted JSP. During the Second World War he volunteered for the British Army and served as a company commander with the rank of major in the 3rd Battalion of the Jewish Brigade. He then served as the commander of the Haganah's Special Company in the Tel Aviv area during the early battles of the War of Independence. For some reason, this company became known by the English initials P.M. (for the Hebrew Plugah Meyuhedet). The unit enjoyed a high reputation and its men were known for their eagerness for action. One of its outstanding members was Akiva Sa'ar, the second-in-command. With the establishment of regular Zahal brigades, the entire company—except for Pelz—was incorporated into the 43rd Battalion of the Kiryati Brigade. Pelz was therefore between postings when Maj. Gen. Moshe Zadok, Director of Manpower Division in GHQ, summoned him on May 21 and offered him the position of second-in-command of the 89th Battalion. A while later he received notice that he was to go to Café Frack on Dizengoff Street, Tel Aviv, to meet his new commanding officer.

Pelz was of double service to the new unit. First he told Moshe about his former company and Akiva Sa'ar. If Moshe had brought a company from the Golani Brigade, Pelz would not come to the battalion empty-handed. Secondly, he explained to Moshe—and had the impression that Moshe was hearing it for the first time—that it was the practice all over the world to man commando units with volunteers. If the 89th were authorized to recruit volunteers, the commanders of other units would be powerless to prevent their choice men from requesting a transfer.

On the following day Moshe began exploiting his connections in GHQ to obtain authority to recruit volunteers, and Pelz began organizing the battalion's HQ and barracks at the Tel Hashomer army base. The new unit's first vehicles were the jeeps that Uri Bar-On and his men had driven from the Jordan Valley to Tel Hashomer.

The contrasts between Moshe and his second-in-command were evident in their very first meeting. In his book *Neguev*, Teddy Eytan described Pelz by saying " [It] seemed as though he had just come out of a British Army Officers' Mess." Compared to Pelz, Moshe looked like a member of a terrorist gang or at best a partisan—disheveled clothes, rumpled trousers far too big for him, socks sagging about his ankles. His manner of speech, although direct and very much to the point, was devoid of military terminology, and his thinking lacked discipline. Their separate areas of responsibility in the new unit were also determined at this first meeting. Moshe was not interested in administration and logistics and had no intention of trying to under-stand them. As soon as Pelz proved his worth as an organizer, Moshe gave him complete autonomy.

Pelz also began implementing his promise to bring over the men of his former company from the Kiryati Brigade. On May 28 GHQ issued an order to all brigade commanders stating that the 89th Battalion required select volunteers and every brigade was obliged to provide "a quota of forty men, including one platoon leader and four section leaders" to be approved by the 89th's representatives. The OC of the 43rd Battalion, Kiryati Brigade was unwilling to part with his best men, not to mention an entire crack company. On the other hand, neither Moshe nor Pelz were equipped with the patience necessary to have the matter resolved through regular GHQ channels.

Pelz met secretly with his former company and told the men about
Moshe Dayan's commando battalion. Akiva Sa'ar and his men
needed little persuasion. Pelz brought an empty bus to his next
meeting with the P.M. and the entire company left the 43rd.

The 43rd Battalion differed from the Golani battalion in one
important respect: its commanding officer. Like Pelz, he had been
in the Jewish Brigade, a hothouse of discipline and order. Of even
greater significance, however, was the man's name—Amos Ben
Gurion, none other than the son of the Minister of Defense. At
first he had no idea where Akiva Sa'ar and his men had vanished
to or why he was short an entire company. When he finally found
out, he was far from pleased at the appropriation methods employed
by Moshe and his deputy. Amos Ben Gurion appealed to his father,
with the result that Moshe was ordered to return Akiva Sa'ar and
his men to the 43rd. They were all confined to prison.

Moshe did not give up, however, and his efforts to get Sa'ar
and his men ended successfully. No sooner had Sa'ar returned to the
89th than he was dispatched to find volunteers in other brigades.
Armed with a copy of the GHQ order, Sa'ar presented himself
before the commanding officer of the Givati Brigade, who referred
him in turn to Zvi Zur, then commander of the 5th Battalion. Zur
told Sa'ar that he could spare no men for the 89th, but if he wished
he could take all the men in the brigade stockade. Sa'ar accepted
the offer. Other brigades refused to relinquish even their prisoners.
Thus many of the volunteers to the 89th joined it without an official
transfer and some were declared deserters by their original units. As
far as Moshe was concerned, this was the shibboleth: anyone who
disobeyed orders in order to join a combat unit was most welcome.

Moshe was surrounded by childhood friends. Nahman Betser
and Shmuel Wolf came to serve with him, as did Binya Zarhi
and Israel Gefen. Heading this personal retinue was sixty-two year
old Grandpa Havinsky, Moshe's former riding teacher, who
appointed himself Regimental Sergeant Major.

The 89th justified its reputation as a colorful and undisciplined
bunch in more ways than one. During the formative period, they
often stole civilian jeeps and drove them to the base, where they
were hastily painted khaki and provided with army license plates.
It is likely that the rapid equipping of the battalion would have
been discovered only much later—if at all—had the boys of the 89th
not laid hands on a brand-new jeep parked outside the Ritz Hotel
in Tel Aviv, which housed the Government Press Office. After the
jeep was painted khaki, had a black army license plate affixed to it,
and was fitted out with two machine guns—fore and aft—it transpired that the vehicle belonged to Arthur Koestler, who was
covering the war as a foreign correspondent.

Moshe's behavior lent a spirit of devil-may-care audacity to his battalion. Whenever he left the base in his jeep, for example, he would say to his companions, "Just watch this," and floored the accelerator as they approached the main gate. The jeep would shoot past the startled sentry, who would shout for them to halt. Moshe would bring the jeep to a stop some 30 meters from the gate and arrange his papers for the MP, who would then have to leave his post and run over to him. His escapades endeared him to his men, and he soon became their hero.

No description of the 89th would be complete without mention of Theodor ("Teddy") Eytan. Born Thadée Diffre, he was a French gentile whose arrival in Israel in 1948 and entrance into Zahal are clouded in mystery. He was one of the foreign volunteers who soon won confidence, and he proved beyond doubt that he had indeed been a captain in General Leclerc's armored formations during the Second World War. GHQ sent him to the 89th as an expert on armored warfare. The men of the battalion remember him as being rather odd, but a man of great ability who proved to be an excellent fighter. A final colorful touch was added by Akiva Sa'ar's driver, an Irish deserter from the British Mandatory Police. The battalion was fully organized and ready for action within a month, and morale was high.

As chance would have it, apart from a minor action in the village of Yehudiya, the first combat action of the 89th was not against Arabs but fellow-Jews—the Irgun. The "*Altalena* Affair" must be understood in the light of Ben Gurion's concept of statehood, his fear of the internal dissension latent in the military organizations that existed side by side with the Haganah (until the official establishment of Zahal) and his determination to set up a single, united national army. The Provisional Government regarded the independent import of arms by an independent military organization a serious violation of the laws of the State of Israel. The *Altalena* anchored off Kfar Vitkin on the night of June 20 and the unloading of cargo went on through the following day. The government decision to "prevent at all costs" the unloading of the Irgun weapons was handed over to the army for immediate execution. In their search for "loyal units" in the vicinity of Kfar Vitkin, the GHQ turned to the 8th Brigade and the Palmach.

Moshe could have refused to involve his battalion in the *Altalena* operation or found some excuse for evading it, as another battalion commander had done, but he chose to obey the orders. He set out for Kfar Vitkin with two companies from his battalion and an additional company from the 82nd Tank Battalion.

Before going into action, Moshe conferred with Israel Galili,

Acting Assistant to the Minister of Defense, who was handling the *"Altalena* Affair," and with Maj. Gen. Dan Even, OC Alexandroni Brigade, who was regional commander and therefore his immediate superior. Acting on their orders, Moshe spread his men out and surrounded the Irgun forces on the beach to prevent their breaking out with the arms and to bar other forces from joining them. Moshe's orders cautioned his men to try and avoid a clash with the Irgun. On the other hand, he explicitly instructed them to return fire if fired upon. "At first, I thought it would be sufficient merely to surround the Irgun men and say 'Enough! You're surrounded.'" As Moshe's men were taking up positions on the beach, negotiations were under way through mediators.

Toward evening on June 21, there was an exchange of fire. As generally happens in such cases, each side claimed that the other had opened fire first. Moshe's men maintained that they initially refrained from reacting to sporadic shots and opened fire only when one of their men had been killed and another three wounded.

Moshe's exact whereabouts during the battle are not quite clear. Uri Bar-On recalls that at some time during the afternoon Moshe transferred the units of the 89th to his command. When Bar-On asked why he was doing so, Moshe replied that he had just returned from a meeting with Ben Gurion and had been ordered to escort the body of Col. David Marcus to the United States. Moshe introduced Bar-On to Maj. Gen. Even and informed him that Bar-On was to be the commander of the 89th for the rest of the action (Pelz, the second-in-command, did not participate in the action). This was the last that Bar-On saw of Moshe until July 9. Although it was Moshe who issued the order to return fire if fired upon, the actual orders to open fire were given by Uri Bar-On, who states that he assumed command of the battalion "with little enthusiasm." As the plane bearing the body of Col. Marcus left for the United States only a week later, June 28, the question arises why Moshe did not remain with his men in Kfar Vitkin until the end of the battle. Could he have been eager to see the proposed trip as a way out of an unpleasant task which he had undertaken with mixed feelings? Or was it that his keen political sense forecast the public furor that the *"Altalena* Affair" would arouse? Although Moshe did not accept the task with enthusiasm, his men testify that he was energetic, aggressive, and forceful in carrying it out.

It is therefore conceivable that in leaving the scene of the action, Moshe simply was following a characteristic pattern: leaving others to complete a task they were quite capable of doing on their own. In much the same way, he had left the Deganias after the tide had turned, even though there was substantial reason to fear a Syrian attack further to the south. Moshe was with his troops at Kfar Vitkin at the crucial moment, but when the *Altalena* sailed out to sea, he considered the affair over. His behavior may well have been in line with his concept of sharply defining the limits of his personal responsibility.

The overall responsibility for the "*Altalena* Affair" rested with the Provisional Government and the High Command. Moshe had done his part by ordering his men to return fire if fired upon, after which he felt himself free to hand the affair over to others, just as it had been handed over to him by his superiors. Be this as it may, the question of why he left Kfar Vitkin before the issue was concluded remains largely unanswered. At nightfall on June 21, while fire was being exchanged between the 89th and the Irgun on the beach, Moshe was driving to Nahalal with Ruth in order to take leave of his children and parents before leaving for the United States. He was to return to the 89th only three weeks later.

Col. David Marcus, an American Jew who joined Zahal under an assumed name—Mickey Stone—was appointed Supreme Commander of the Jerusalem Front on May 28, 1948, and on June 11, a few hours before the first cease-fire came into effect, he was accidentally killed by a Zahal sentry. In his will, Col. Marcus asked to be buried at the West Point Military Academy, where he had been a cadet. It was Alex Braude, a former lodger in Moshe's flat in Jerusalem in 1942 and Marcus' A.D.C., who recommended that Moshe and Yoseph Harel, accompanied by Ruth and Mrs. Braude, be escorts on behalf of Zahal.

The government had chartered a cargo plane for the flight, and Col. Marcus' coffin was tied to rings on the floor, as were the fuel tanks beside it. The four passengers had plenty of room to move about, but no seats, and they were forced to improvise seats and beds for the long flight. After trying every possible combination, they found that the most comfortable surface for both sitting and sleeping was the coffin itself. The women could not bring themselves to rest on top of the body, but Moshe and Yoseph Harel spread blankets over the coffin and used it as a seat and sofa. Legend has it that during the night the two men woke in terror, after hearing noises from inside the coffin. Like the legend of the cask of brandy in which Lord Nelson's body was kept and which made creaking noises thought to be his voice, so Moshe and Harel thought Marcus was alive and addressing them. Moshe maintains that the differences in temperature did cause the coffin to make loud creaking noises, but neither he nor Harel thought for a moment that they were witnessing a resurrection.

On June 29, a telegram from Ben Gurion caught up with Moshe in Paris. It read: "DO NOT CONTINUE TO NEW YORK STOP RETURN HOME

IMMEDIATELY STOP CABLE." This sudden change in plans occurred on the background of Ben Gurion's determination to relieve Maj. Gen. David Shaltiel of his post as Commander of the Jerusalem Area and appoint Moshe in his stead. Moshe was caught up in the excitement of the trip to the United States, however, and did not reply to Ben Gurion's cable.

The most important event of Moshe's week-long stay in New York was a chance meeting with a man named Abraham J. Baum, who was employed on a voluntary basis by the Haganah mission in the United States. It was his task to interview American volunteers for the Haganah and later for Zahal. Moshe met Baum as he sat in the cocktail lounge of Hotel 14, which housed both offices and staff of the Haganah mission. During the preliminary small talk, Moshe learned that Abe Baum was one of the most daring, decorated, and scarred veterans of the U.S. Army in the Second World War.

What Baum had to say was exactly what the commander of the 89th Raiding Battalion wanted to hear. He had been the operations officer of an armored infantry battalion belonging to Combat Command B of Col. Creighton W. Abrams when he was given a special mission: to organize a task force, break through the German lines, and rescue American POWs from a camp near Hammelburg on the Saale River. Hammelburg lay some 60 miles behind the German lines, to the rear of two German divisions. It was the size and composition of Task Force Baum, as it was called, that attracted Moshe, for they were similar to the 89th. To undertake a large-scale mission with a small but daring force was not only his personal ideal, but the central military concept of Zahal.

At 2:30 p.m. on March 27, 1945, the force crossed the Saale River, and half an hour later it broke into the POW camp near Hammelburg. But by this time it had been spotted by a German reconnaissance plane and had lost half of its men and vehicles. Even if he could have made it back to his own lines, Baum by now had no vehicles to transport the 1,291 prisoners he had come to rescue. Task Force Baum was wiped out on its way back, its men all killed, wounded, or—like Baum himself—taken prisoner. Ten days after their mission, on April 6, the POW camp at Hammelburg was liberated by a large force of the American Army.

In the bar of Hotel 14, Moshe thirstily absorbed Baum's stories and committed to memory the essence of his theories on mechanized warfare: (1) if there is a road, make use of it; (2) attack with a man's force to do a boy's job and make every effort to have it appear much larger than it is; (3) penetrate in narrow formations, preferably in single-line columns; (4) use your fire power more as a psychological factor than a weapon of death; (5) keep moving—once you stop, your advantage as an armored force is lost; (6) forget about reserve

above With men of the 89th Raiding Battalion in 1948

below Lt. Col. Dayan, Commander of the Israeli Sector of Jerusalem, with Col. Abdullah el-Tel, his Jordanian counterpart, in 1948

above, left Chief-of-Staff Dayan
demonstrates throwing a grenade

above With officers of the Paratroop
Brigade following a reprisal action in
1955. Standing from left, Lt. Meir Har-
Zion and Maj. Ariel Sharon; at extreme
right, Col. Assaf Simhoni

Resting during an army maneuver in the south with Maj. Gen. Chaim Laskov

troops—use them all and let the enemy think there are more; (7) bring in infantry to occupy; (8) keep your armor mobile for counter-attacks.

Returning to Israel on Saturday night, July 9, a few hours before the expiry of the first cease-fire, Moshe hurried directly from the airport to his battalion, which was in the midst of preparations for "Operation Danny." The objects of the operation were to push the Arab Legion back from its positions near Tel Aviv, liberate the road leading to Jerusalem and the city itself from the pressure of the Arab Legion and irregulars; afford Zahal a new, more tenable line of defense, and capture the two important centers of transportation—the airport and the railroad station at Lydda.

On his way to change clothes, Moshe had time to reflect on the battle plans prepared by Pelz and reached the conclusion that he had the perfect opportunity to put into practice all he had learned from Abe Baum. In his excitement, and with his peculiar charm, he swept the men up in his enthusiasm. After his lecture on the tactics the battalion would adopt—delivered while Pelz was getting some well-deserved sleep—Moshe overruled Pelz's learned and detailed plan, which called for separate routes of approach and lines of fire for each unit, and decided that the entire battalion would move in a single column—jeeps, half-tracks, armored cars, and mortars. Undoubtedly he aspired to something similar to Task Force Baum.

When Pelz arrived on the scene, Moshe explained that he had canceled his plan because it was "a good plan for fighting against a European Regular Army. But we are fighting Arabs, not Germans." Judging by what he had seen at Zemakh, he doubted that there would be a battle at Kulla or that he would have to set up his mortars, as Pelz had planned. He still thought that "You just have to bang once on a tin and they all scatter like birds." In Pelz's opinion, as far as military training was concerned, Moshe was at best at the level of an untried platoon leader. But he won the men over "with his fantastic courage. He was simply nerveless."

At the break of dawn on Saturday, June 10, after swiftly taking Muzira and a few other villages, the entire battalion moved in a single column with Moshe in the lead and Pelz with the mortar platoon on two armored cars in the rear. The assault on Kulla began. But the battle did not develop as Moshe had anticipated. It was not enough merely to "bang once on a tin" for the Arabs to flee the town. Chroniclers of the War of Independence agree that the battle at Kulla was a "hard" one. Moshe was forced to call in Pelz—who had judged correctly that mortars would be needed before the assault for a softening-up barrage—and ask him to set up the mortars and begin covering fire so that Akiva Sa'ar's B Company could break into Kulla. Without detailed fire or approach plans, however, Pelz did not know exactly where the men of the battalion were positioned and was afraid the mortar fire might hit his own men. Nevertheless, with great presence of mind and not inconsiderable courage, he managed to set up the mortars and bombard the town.

The column halted and the drivers of the half-tracks, experiencing driving under fire for the first time, began reversing in an attempt to find cover. Moshe jumped down from his open, thinly armored scout car and decided to deviate slightly from the original brigade battle plan by leading the attack personally. This change of plans afforded the battalion an easy victory, but the second attack on Kulla, though successful, met stiff opposition, and victory was achieved only after fierce fighting. Moshe did not remain on the battlefield until the battle ended. At ten o'clock he was summoned to Ben Gurion's office in Tel Aviv.

When Moshe failed to reply to the cable he received in Paris on June 29, Ben Gurion sent another cable to New York instructing him to report immediately upon his return. When Ben Gurion learned that Moshe had returned and gone straight to his battalion without coming to see him first, he sent out an explicit order that he present himself at his office without delay, regardless of where he happened to be or what he was doing. Afterward, as he entered Ben Gurion's office in field dress, grimy and dusty, Moshe learned for the first time the reason for the summons: Ben Gurion's intention of appointing him Commander of the Jerusalem Area. Ben Gurion was determined to return the Old City to Jewish Jerusalem, and sought an aggressive officer. Moshe's success in Degania qualified him for this weighty task in Ben Gurion's eyes. Moshe balked at the notion of parting with his battalion in the midst of battle. Neither was he very enthusiastic about the appointment, although it entitled him to the rank of lieutenant colonel. Above all, he wanted to serve in a combat unit. He related: "I managed to delay the edict by pointing out that I was in the middle of an action. Ben Gurion did not relinquish the idea, but agreed to postpone the discussion of my appointment to a later date."

Meanwhile, in his absence something had happened to change the brigade's plans radically. The 89th was ordered to take the village of Dir Tarif after the 82nd Tank Battalion failed to do so and was forced to retreat. As the casualties of the company began to mount, its ability to withstand additional attacks diminished. From Moshe's departure until midnight, Pelz commanded the battalion, and to do so he had to cover considerable distances at a run. At midnight he was still busy issuing orders for the following day, and at 1 a.m. he finally spread a blanket under an olive tree at Tira and told the sentry to wake him at 4:30. At 3:30 he felt himself being shaken and opened his eyes to find Moshe leaning over him, asking him repeatedly what had happened in his absence. Still groggy from sleep, Pelz tried to give as coherent a report as possible Finally he said, "If you don't mind, I only have another hour to sleep," to which Moshe replied, "All right," and left.

When Pelz awoke it was seven o'clock in the morning and a bright summer sun was shining over the mountains. He looked around and to his astonishment found himself alone. The battalion had vanished without a trace. He was the only person in Tira. He again set off at a run along the road to Dir Tarif. On his way he met a jeep that had lost its way and ordered the driver to take him in the direction of the battalion. Afterward he was told that Moshe had moved the battalion out before dawn. According to one account, Moshe had said to his men, "Yohanan's tired. Let him sleep."

As Moshe had not slept since leaving New York and had certainly not rested since rejoining the battalion on June 9, he must certainly have regarded his deputy's sleeping habits with a mixture of anger and ridicule. His inherent objection to collective responsibility absolved him, as it were, of the duty to wake Pelz. This macabre prank may also have been occasioned by the sense of strangeness that the self-styled partisan fighter felt toward the proper, strait-laced model of a British Army officer. It is possible that these factors far outweighed any desire on his part to circumscribe a rival, as Pelz and some others suspected.

On Sunday, July 11, Moshe appeared at Dir Tarif in a jeep and discovered a Jordanian armored car that had overturned on the battlefield. Lacking a turreted armored car, Moshe desperately wanted the vehicle and initially tried to extricate it personally, despite heavy Jordanian machine-gun fire. After Sa'ar pleaded with him not to endanger his life, he agreed that Sa'ar's men would free the car with cables; but the Jordanians began bombarding the area with mortars to prevent them from salvaging it. "Despite the fascination of this game, we had to stop wasting time," Moshe wrote in his report. "The Dir Tarif positions were completely in our hands now, and the question was—what next?"

Moshe did not wait for further orders from Brigade HQ. He sought a suitable objective for his battalion in the area before him:

In the west, Lydda could just be glimpsed beyond the orange groves. Between Lydda and ourselves there was a flat plain. For a moment it seemed that the best move would be to let the Jordanians engage a small part of our troops here and for us to leave and attack Lydda. It was unlikely that Lydda would be fortified and properly defended on its eastern side—the one nearest us—since this was the connecting corridor between the city and the Legionnaires in the Lydda- Beit Naballa- Ramallah area.

Be that as it may, if a breakthrough had to be made, it would best be done when Lydda did not expect it.

Lydda was not included in the 89th's objectives. According to "Operation Danny" plans, the town was to have been taken by the Palmach Yiftach Brigade, supported by the 82nd Tank Battalion. Disregarding this point, Moshe rapidly calculated how many of his men were fit for action and estimated the battalion's ability to mount an attack.

As he was inspecting his units, he was called to the wireless by his signals officer. Mulla Cohen, OC Yiftach Brigade, was trying to contact the commander of the 82nd Tank Battalion. Moshe was aware of the fact that he was talking to the OC of Yiftach. "He came directly to the point. One of the units had gone out to Lydda but had encountered strong opposition and was now in the citrus groves on the southwestern outskirts of the city. Could we come to give them support?" Moshe replied in the affirmative.

It was therefore not solely because of an error in communications that Moshe began preparing his battalion for a new objective. He felt that extricating the armored car was taking too long and was delaying the sortie to Lydda. "With an armored car, we'll be kings," he later wrote, describing his eagerness to gain possession of the vehicle. Moshe himself climbed into the half-track Sa'ar's men had been using, asked one of the mechanics to accompany him, and—ignoring the Jordanian fire—pulled the armored car out of the ditch. Within an hour it was ready for action. The men dubbed it "The Terrible Tiger," and as soon as one of the soldiers had learned how to fire its cannon, it was jubilantly welcomed into the battalion as the most modern and effective weapon at their disposal. The 89th had already taken Dir Tarif, which was to have been captured by the 82nd, and was now on its way to Lydda in its stead.

Before the 89th left Dir Tarif, Moshe gathered his officers and described the method of action they were to employ. His orders were: "There is to be no stopping. If you come up against an obstacle, heavy fire, or the devil knows what, the scouting jeeps move aside and the armored car and half-tracks break through. If one of our vehicles is hit, no one should stop to repair it or hold up those behind. Pass it and continue advancing. No one except myself is allowed to hold up the column. Keep moving at all costs. Shoot, run over, and keep moving." Thus without having received orders or notifying 8th Brigade HQ, most of the battalion drove to "Operation Danny" HQ in Ben Shemen.

The raid on Lydda was considered a brilliant military victory. For the Zahal of 1948 it was an innovation and a preview of the future.

In his book *Battles of the Palmach,* Yigal Allon wrote that the 89th "charged with great daring into Lydda." Ben Gurion claimed, "I became acquainted with Moshe from Lydda-Ramle, which was the greatest of our conquests."

The plan Moshe chose was extremely simple and took no more than five minutes to explain. According to Akiva Sa'ar: "Moshe holds up a map of Lydda and points with his finger: 'We're going to attack Lydda. We'll enter from here, drive through the city and leave from there. Clear?'" Once the battalion had passed the first line of defense, it was to split. One company was to turn north along the main street, the other to head south. After looping through the city, firing continuously, the two companies were to meet at the crossroads. Moshe's plan was to stun the enemy, cause havoc, and "bring about a capitulation."

Before the charge into Lydda, the effective fighting force of the Raiding Battalion stood at 367 men, 150 of whom were to take part in the actual attack. At their disposal were eight half-tracks, nine scout cars, one turreted armored car (the "Terrible Tiger"), with its 2-pounder cannon, and twenty jeeps with mounted machine guns. Facing them were an unknown number of Arab irregulars, reinforced by two regular companies of the Arab Legion equipped with cannon-bearing armored cars and artillery.

The Yiftach units launched the attack on the southeastern quarter of Lydda at twelve. The Raiding Battalion began its charge into the city at 6:20 p.m., and it lasted forty-seven minutes by Moshe's watch. Moshe was in the first company of half-tracks that led the way behind the "Terrible Tiger." This was one of the rare instances in 1948 that a battalion commander headed his unit in an assault. The battalion deployed in a single column and moved out along the road. It was met by heavy fire and halted at an antitank ditch. Moshe left his scout car and moved from one half-track to another, ordering their drivers personally and not relying on the wireless to spur on the advance. The men inside the armored car asked him, "What if the road is mined?" "Then you'll be blown sky high," was his reply.

Only after the men began moving again did he return to his own car. The battalion slowly gathered speed and soon the entire unit entered the city along its main street, drawing fire from every possible direction. The heaviest fire issued from the fortress-like police station. The "Tiger" returned the fire and the column continued on its way past the police station. Up to this point everything went more or less according to plan. When the column reached the main intersection of the town, however, the "Tiger" turned right as Moshe had ordered, but the two half-track companies did not split up as planned. Thus the entire force, except the "Tiger," moved through the town in a single column from north to south. The "Tiger"

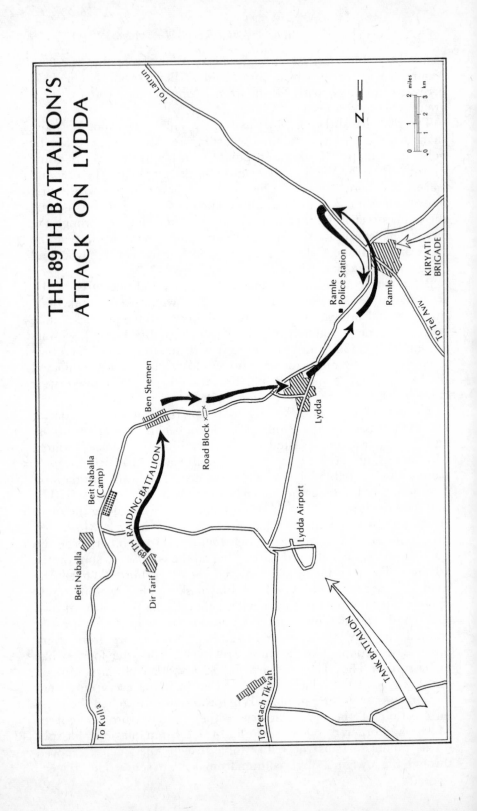

THE 89TH BATTALION'S
ATTACK ON LYDDA

To Latrun

Ramle
Police Station

Ramle

KIRYATI
BRIGADE

To Tel Aviv

N

Ben Shemen

Road Block

Lydda

Beit Naballa
(Camp)

89TH RAIDING BATTALION

Beit Naballa

Dir Tarif

Lydda Airport

To Kull'a

To Petach Tik'ah

TANK BATTALION

0   1   2 miles
0   1   2   3 km

fought its own private battle, advancing and firing until it reached the city square. There it turned around, bestowed three well-aimed shells on the water tower, engaged the police station in a duel, and remained there, courageous and alone, until the battalion returned through the town.

The battalion's initial momentum carried it right through the town of Lydda, and the vehicles did not stop until they reached the Teggart police fortress on the Lydda - Ramle road, where a company of Legionnaires had taken positions. Its sudden entrance caused panic and even the beginnings of mass flight of both civilians and armed men. The first company of half-tracks managed to pass the building safely before the Legionnaires realized what was happening. The second company, however, came under heavy fire from the machine-gun emplacements in the station tower and the firing hatches in its walls. One jeep was hit and caught fire, while soldiers in the other jeeps were wounded, some of them falling from the vehicles. The Jordanians flung hand grenades at the half-tracks from the tower and managed to score a direct hit on one of the vehicles, wounding all the men inside.

Moshe tried to stop the half-tracks of the first company as they went roaring on south, but his wireless set had ceased functioning and he could not make contact. His voice hoarse from shouting, he gathered the men of the second company at the police station and urged them on after the first. It was only in Ramle, after the column had turned eastward on the road to Jerusalem, that Moshe managed to catch up with his first company and learned the reason for its wild dash. The brakes on the lead half-track had failed, and the driver had been unable to stop at the intersection. All the other vehicles in the column had dutifully followed like ducklings in a row.

When the battalion halted near the Ramle railroad station, Moshe counted the casualties. The vehicles were in a sorry state: most of the tires had been punctured, radiators had fallen off, and brakes had ceased functioning. A number of men had fallen from the jeeps near the police station. According to Moshe, "morale started to sag."

At about the same time, mortars set up in the police station began bombarding the battalion. "Things became 'hot' and uncomfortable," Moshe related, "and the men began to get nervous." He made up his mind to break through Lydda once again, this time northward to Ben Shemen. The wounded were loaded on the half-tracks and the wireless set repaired. Bullets from the Jordanian armored cars were already whistling past their heads as Moshe finished organizing his men to move again.

Although the battalion looked beaten when it entered Lydda for the second time (Moshe's car was traveling in first gear with two flat tires and a boiling radiator), the men's fighting spirit was undaunted. And this was the sole advantage they enjoyed as they slowly made their way back along the Lydda-Ramle road and engaged in their fiercest battle of the day. Now the Arabs were ready and waiting. Moshe told his men that their only hope of escaping the curtain of fire was their own accurate return fire. To make things worse, a few of the wounded found shelter in a ditch opposite the Jordanian stronghold. Stopping to pick them up, the 89th would be a sitting duck. Nevertheless, Moshe ordered his men to collect the wounded and dead. Pistol in hand, under a hail of bullets, he personally helped gather the casualties.

Slowly, painfully, and suffering casualties on the way, the column moved out of range of the police station, and Moshe stopped to take a count and make sure none of the dead or wounded had been left behind. Moving out again, the jeeps took the lead and a half-track pushed Moshe's scout car from behind, as by now it had only one good tire. Half-tracks pushed half-tracks and jeeps pushed jeeps. Near the police station in town, they met the "Terrible Tiger," which had been fighting a solo battle with the Jordanians all this time. The armored car now joined the column at the rear, and the vehicles moved on. The "Tiger" and one half-track were the only vehicles that could still move under their own power; all the others were pushed. The machine guns on the forward riding jeeps swept the streets and houses lining the main road, and the rest of the battalion followed slowly behind, bearing nine dead and seventeen wounded.

The last streaks of daylight could still be seen in the west when the battalion reached Ben Shemen and began reorganizing, changing tires, refueling and replenishing its ammunition supply. At eight that evening, Maj. Gen. Yigal Allon, the commander of all "Operation Danny" forces, compiled the first report on the actions of the 89th:

> As the men of Yiftach captured the southern outskirts of the city, the raiders charged into the city, swept along the main street and then returned to Ben Shemen. They suffered losses in men and vehicles. The Arabs of Lydda were astounded by the quantity of fire and the daring breakthrough tactics of the raid, but immediately recovered and intensified their opposition. At this moment, our men are in possession of the city mosque and a fierce battle is in progress for the police station nearby. We shall gain control of as much of the city as we can tonight and finish tomorrow morning.

Indeed, the only source of Arab opposition at that time was the police station, and by midnight it too was abandoned, as the last of the Arab Legionnaires left the city. On the morning of July 12, Lydda and Ramle surrendered.

In a report compiled on July 12, Moshe summed up the achievement of the 89th's breakthrough into Lydda: "Destruction of all positions and barricades along the main streets of Lydda and Ramle, except the Lydda police station; sowing confusion and [causing] a panicked flight from both cities that disrupted the defensive network of Lydda and Ramle and was the main factor in their surrender." Thus, while Maj. Gen. Allon spoke of a coordinated action against the two cities, Moshe considered the 89th's action "the main factor" in the surrender.

The oral and written traditions of Zahal generally tend to ascribe the fall of Lydda and Ramle to the 89th's raid. The attack was considered particularly daring as it was carried out in full daylight. In fact, it was one of the few actions carried out by the 89th that was not under cover of darkness. Immediately after the assault on Lydda, Moshe ordered his battalion to return to its base at Tel Hashomer without either coordinating the move with "Operation Danny" HQ or receiving orders to that effect from the Brigade Commander, Yitzhak Sadeh. The only possible justification for his action was his faulty communication with Brigade HQ. However, a more disciplined officer could have made personal contact with his Brigade Commander to receive distinct orders.

While "Operation Danny" was in action on the Central Front, the battle which became known as "The Ten Days" was already at its height. Fighting began on the eve of the expiry of the first cease-fire July 8, 1948, and ended ten days later, when the second cease-fire came into effect. The day after the 89th returned to its base, Moshe was summoned to GHQ to receive orders for his part in "Operation Death to the Invaders," whose aim was to open up the way to the Negev.

Signs of fatigue were evident in Moshe during the meeting which took place on July 13, and he emphasized the weakness of his battalion. He asked Yadin not to give the men a fresh mission, fearing that it would wear the battalion down completely. After consultation with Ben Gurion, however, Yadin told Moshe, "Even if it means breaking the battalion, it is essential to break a way through to the Negev. Make that breakthrough. After that there'll be a truce and we'll set up a new battalion."

On July 15, in the midst of his preparations for battle, Moshe was once again summoned to Ben Gurion's office. He told Ben Gurion about the Lydda action and the losses the battalion had suffered. Ben Gurion was impressed and entered the details of the action in his diary. He did not, however, accept Moshe's suggestion that the battle of Lydda be used as a model for future actions. According to Yadin, the Lydda raid strengthened Ben Gurion's impression of Moshe as a "partisan fighter." The real reason for this meeting, however, was Ben Gurion's insistance that Moshe assume the post of Commander of the Jerusalem area. As he had done five days earlier, Moshe again asked for deferment, but Ben Gurion's mind was made up. As soon as the second cease-fire came into effect, the appointment would be made.

Shimon Avidan, OC Givati Brigade, was appointed commander of "Operation Death to the Invaders." The main object of the operation was to drive a wedge into the Egyptian lines by capturing two Egyptian army bases north of the Majdal-Faluja road (Beit Affa and Hatta) and one south of the road (Karatiya). From there the Givati forces were to join up with the besieged Jewish forces in the Negev. According to the plan, units from the Negev Brigade were to come up from the south and capture Bir Abu-Jabber and the vantage points at Kaukaba and Huleikat.

The importance of the 89th in "Operation Death to the Invaders" was the "capture of Karatiya, which was considered the most important objective of the entire operation ... [and] required deep penetration into enemy territory. Therefore, the brigade decided to entrust the mission to the commando battalion—a mobile, armored unit with great firepower."

In the Orders Group that took place on July 15, Moshe cited one of the drawbacks of his tactics in the breakthrough at Lydda, namely the absence of infantry units to move with the armor, take advantage of the enemy's initial shock, and establish positions within his territory before he recovered. In order to avoid making the same mistake in Karatiya, Avidan added to the 89th an infantry company from the 3rd Battalion of the Givati Brigade.

During the three days before the operation began, Moshe carried out reconnaissance patrols with his officers, but he was unable to reach the Faluja-Karatiya road and was therefore unaware of the most serious obstacle the battalion would encounter: the deep ravine of Wadi Mufared. On the map, it seemed negotiable for vehicles and was therefore included in the approach route; but it was actually much deeper than the map indicated, with high, steep banks on either side.

On the eve of the operation, the ranks of the 89th were seriously depleted. Yohanan Pelz, who had been wounded on July 12 as B Company was making its way from Dir Tarif to Tel Hashomer, was still in the hospital, as were two of the best company commanders— Uri Bar-On and Akiva Sa'ar. The fighting strength of the battalion stood at 221 men (compared to 367 before "Operation Danny"). The battalion's heavy weapon remained the turreted armored car with the 2-pounder—the "Terrible Tiger." The addition of six half-tracks brought the total number of vehicles to what it had been before "Operation Danny": twelve jeeps, eight half-tracks, four open scout cars, and two improvised armored cars, known as "tin cans" (regular trucks covered with armor fashioned from wood sandwiched between steel plates). Only the "Tiger" bore armor that could withstand heavy fire; the "tin cans" could at best stand up to small-arms fire.

Moshe repeated the instructions he had given on the drive to Ben Shemen and the Lydda raid: should one of the vehicles be hit, the others were to pass it and continue the assault. The battalion moved out as planned at 10 p.m. on July 17. At the same time, Geva's infantry company set out by a different route for the rendezvous in Wadi Mufared. The 89th moved toward the Faluja airfield with two jeeps scouting ahead, followed by the "Tiger," the half-tracks, and the rest of the jeeps bringing up the rear. Moshe rode in the second half-track after the "Tiger," in other words, in the fifth vehicle of the column.

The Egyptians brought down withering cannon, mortar and machine-gun fire on the battalion as it gained the road leading from the Faluja airfield to the Faluja-Karatiya road. The heavy fire accompanied the battalion for a kilometer, until Moshe ordered the vehicles off the road. On the steep bank leading down into the field, one of the "tin cans" overturned. But the other vehicles overtook it, as Moshe had instructed, and continued south through the fields without further mishap, until they reached the dirt road connecting Faluja and Karatiya. Upon reaching Wadi Mufared, however, only 500 meters from Karatiya, they discovered that it was all but impassable. Four jeeps managed to cross to the other side and took up positions facing south to protect the battalion in the wadi. While the battalion was struggling to get the vehicles across, the men heard the sound of troops fleeing the village. They opened fire on the Egyptians and even managed to capture two. If Moshe had entertained any hopes of exploiting the element of surprise under cover of darkness, he was now forced to abandon them.

The battalion was due to have begun its assault on Karatiya at 2 a.m. on July 18, but Wadi Mufared proved far more stubborn an enemy than the Egyptians. The "Tiger" managed to cross to the other side, but a half-track that followed it overturned. There was no choice but to take out picks and shovels and dig out easier inclines on either side of the wadi. At first Moshe tried to organize the work himself, but the chaos and commotion grew steadily. It then occurred to him that there must be someone in the battalion better qualified to organize this aspect of the operation. He spotted a platoon leader from Yavniel who had come to the operation directly from Officers' Training Course and "was not as tired as the rest." Moshe transferred the command of all operations in the wadi to him. To demonstrate his own peace of mind and complete indifference to the Egyptian mortar fire, he lay down near the bank of the wadi and promptly fell asleep. The sight of their commanding officer in complete repose was a definite sign to the men that he had no intention of canceling the mission. On the contrary, he was simply gathering strength for the coming battle. Moshe thus managed to restore their calm and confidence in the outcome of the battle. "When I awoke, about an hour later, I was glad not only that I had rested and handed over the job of making a passable route to the right man, but also that I had not rushed into a decision in a state of fatigue and exhaustion."

The decision that formed in Moshe's mind was to wait another half hour at most, then attack Karatiya at 4 a.m. with whatever vehicles had crossed the wadi by then. The men transferred the weapons and ammunition from two half-tracks and four "tin cans," that were stuck in the wadi to the attacking vehicles, and at four o'clock the attack began. The "Tiger" led the way, followed by five half-tracks and eleven jeeps. The men were ordered to hold fire, and only when they were some 200 meters from Karatiya did Moshe spread the half-tracks out, send the jeeps to the flanks, and place the "Tiger" in the lead. At a distance of 150 meters from the village, he gave the order to fire with all weapons. But the opposition was minor and Karatiya was taken easily without a single casualty. The infantry company followed the half-tracks into the village and began securing it and setting up positions.

As was his custom by now, Moshe decided that "the commando had done its job" and was now free to leave. Two hours after the attack, at 6 a.m., Moshe's battalion moved out of Karatiya and returned to its base. Therefore, when the Egyptians began bombarding Karatiya with 25-pounders and mortars at 8:30 the same morning, in preparation for a counterattack, the 89th was already far to the north on its way to Masmiye. The only force left in the village was the infantry company.

Avidan regarded the 89th's prompt evacuation of Karatiya as a serious breach of discipline on Moshe's part and brought it to the attention of the GHQ. On July 20, Yadin instructed the Military Attorney General to arraign Moshe Dayan for insubordination; but after he was questioned and some of his claims were justified, the case was dismissed.

13   JERUSALEM

(August 1948 - October 1949)

Moshe's appointment as OC Jerusalem-stationed Etzioni Brigade
was the threshold of his career in Zahal. Were it not for this post,
it is doubtful whether he would have been mentioned in the annals
of the War of Independence as anything more than a daring, though
undisciplined, battalion commander. The appointment carried
another advantage. It brought to light Moshe's political faculty,
which might well have gone unnoticed had he remained a field
commander. In Jerusalem he became involved in negotiating the
Armistice Agreements, had contact with the UN truce-keeping
apparatus, and became known to the public at large as a soldier-
statesman. As a result of his rise in status and change of image, he
also began to be referred to by his surname, rather than on the less
formal first-name basis appropriate for a "partisan fighter." It is
therefore significant to note that Dayan was posted to Jerusalem
only at the stubborn insistence of Ben Gurion.

On August 1, Dayan took up his new duties in Jerusalem surrounded by a large retinue of admirers and loyal friends. They lent him the
appearance of a sheik. At Degania he needed the support of fellow-
Nahalalites and close friends to bolster his self-confidence and
facilitate his control over the units; in setting up the 89th he needed
them to form the nucleus of an effective unit; but in Jerusalem, all
his friends—or so it seemed to some of the men in the Etzioni Brigade—were the adjuncts of his success and the first step toward the
creation of a court. The impression is worth noting, for Jerusalem was
the last time Dayan appeared in company of an entourage. From
then on he went to each new posting alone, very much the lone wolf—
so much so, in fact, that a time came when his capacity for teamwork
was doubted. As Uri Bar-On recalls, one of the reasons Dayan
brought men of the 89th with him was his desire to instill a fighting
spirit in the Jerusalem Brigade. The soldiers and citizens of the city
had experienced many failures and disappointments. Jerusalem had
been under a protracted siege and suffered incessant street battles,
artillery barrages and sniping. The Jewish Quarter of the Old City
had been lost, as had a string of settlements on the outskirts of the
western city. Many fighters were killed or taken captive at the Etzion
Bloc*, and the threat of Jordanian conquest still hovered over
several suburbs.

---

* Four agricultural settlements south of Jerusalem on the Bethlehem - Hebron road.

The Etzioni Brigade, which Dayan now took over, was never shaped into a proper brigade and had never operated in the field in units higher than a company. It was highly fragmented and mutual criticism was rife. Only one thing united the men—their desire to have Maj. Gen. Shaltiel replaced.

This state of affairs became quite clear to Dayan on his first patrol to Kibbutz Ramat Rachel. The kibbutz, which is in fact a southern suburb of Jerusalem overlooking Bethlehem, changed hands several times during the war. Throughout the patrol, Dayan discovered a feeling of holding on to ground according to an established code of do's and don't's. The apathy and indifference of the brigade is illuminated by the fact that the very act of taking officers on a patrol to Ramat Rachel was considered highly exceptional and remained imprinted on the memory of those who participated in it.

During the same patrol, an incident occurred which was indicative of the mood in the brigade and of Dayan's own qualities of leadership. The road connecting Ramat Rachel to Jerusalem was under constant observation by the Arab Legion and was traveled only in armored cars—the "tin cans." There was also a footpath which, in its exposed sections, became a trench stretching for a few kilometers until it reached dead ground again. Dayan wanted to study the situation at first hand and was reluctant to waste time waiting for the armored car. He struck out to Ramat Rachel on foot, accompanied by five officers, and the armored car was sent to take them back to Jerusalem. As they walked through the trench, they could hear the shots being fired at the armored car on the road. After the patrol, they approached the waiting car and found the driver wounded. He told them that machine-gun bullets had penetrated the "tin can" through the joints of the welded steel plates and spattered steel fragments into his face and shoulder. Upon hearing the driver's description of the ride, one of the officers said to Dayan: "Listen, it's dangerous to travel in this armored car. Let's go back on foot through the trench." According to Uri Bar-On, Dayan turned on the officer and said: "Aren't you ashamed? This soldier drove here just to take us back. He was wounded on the way. And now do you really think we're going to send him back along the road while we walk back safely in the trench? Go ahead, if you want to—walk back through the trench. I'm going in the car!"

This departure from convention raised the soldiers' spirits somewhat. As a rule, though, a military unit's character is forged only in action. But although Dayan constantly sued for action—Ben Gurion's choice was clearly justified in this respect—and continually pressed GHQ to authorize local operations, political considerations placed restrictions on military actions in the Jerusalem sector. In fact, by the time Ben Gurion sent Dayan to Jerusalem, it was already too late. Though no one suspected it at the time, Shaltiel's abortive efforts to break into the Old City between July 9 and 19 proved to be the last opportunity for large-scale actions in the Jerusalem sector. The debates in the UN General Assembly and Security Council, the steadily growing efficiency of the UN Observation Force in Jerusalem, and the renewal of Count Folke Bernadotte's efforts to reach a lasting settlement—all occurring a short time before Dayan's assumption of duties in Jerusalem—precluded the possibility of any large-scale offensive in the sector. It was only by virtue of his personality and connections that he managed to win approval for the two offensive operations that were carried out, and even they ended in failure. In Jerusalem, the cease-fire arranged by the UN was reinforced by local agreements, negotiated by Count Bernadotte. Despite minor infringements, these agreements generally held. According to the terms of Bernadotte's agreements, Mount Scopus was a demilitarized zone guarded by a force of Israeli policemen. Government House was similarly demilitarized and became the HQ of the UN Truce Supervision Organization. Two areas of vital importance to Jewish Jerusalem were therefore eliminated from the game.

After the Arab Legion violated the neutrality of Government House Hill, Dayan was eager to exploit the opportunity and attack in a night action to gain control of the area. GHQ approved his proposal for an action that was to take place on the night of August 17. Ben Gurion stipulated two restrictions: a twenty-four hour time limit on the operation and an explicit prohibition against taking the UN-occupied Government House or even penetrating its fenced-off grounds.

While preparing the operation, Dayan met with two former officers of the Jewish Brigade: Hillel Fefferman, the brigade's new operations officer, and Meir Zorea ("Zaro"), OC Beit Horon Battalion, which was slated to carry out the operation. Fefferman and Zaro had served together for six years and had become close friends. They both left the Jewish Brigade with the rank of captain.

On a reconnaissance patrol of the area of the proposed action, the two were greeted by Jordanian small-arms fire soon joined by 2-pounders and mortars. In Fefferman's opinion the enemy fire was accurate—the work of a well-trained, alert army. They discovered that the Jordanians had dug a row of positions on the southeast slope of the hill. When they moved over to the southern—Egyptian-held—side, they encountered no fire, and therefore assumed that this would be the easier side to penetrate.

Upon their return Fefferman reported that it would be impossible to gain control of the hill and hold it without taking the crest, that is, Government House itself. Admittedly, a night action might temporarily succeed without it—but at dawn the soldiers would be helplessly exposed to enemy fire on the bare slopes of the hill. As

Zaro was of the same opinion, he proposed an alternative plan: should his men run into serious difficulties, they would be given permission to take the crest of the ridge and the roof of Government House. Dayan rejected the idea for he had explicitly promised Yadin that he would not take Government House. This was probably the first expression of Dayan's obedience to higher echelons when he bore sole responsibility for an action or an area. When the supreme authority was in the hands of others, he allowed himself a degree of freedom that bordered on insubordination. But in Jerusalem, the responsibility was his alone. His stand did not stem only from considerations of loyalty, however. The memory of the Syrian retreat from Zemakh, the stunning raid into Lydda, and the easy conquest of Karatiya reinforced his self-confidence and trust in his own good judgement and sharpened his reservations about the pedigreed veterans of the British Army. Fefferman urged Zaro to disobey the order, but Zaro resigned himself to carrying out the operation because "an order is an order."

At nightfall on August 17, two companies of Zaro's battalion, each comprising only two platoons, moved out in a pincer movement to encircle Government House. Zaro controlled them by wireless from a command post in the nearby suburb of Talpiot. The force's initial gains were soon nullified as the Arab irregulars, paying no heed to political limitations, quickly took the top of the hill and gained control of the vital ground, leaving Zaro's unit exposed to vicious cross fire. As casualties began to mount, Zaro began pressuring Brigade HQ for permission to take Government House. The operations officer tried for an entire hour to contact Dayan without success. In the OC's absence Fefferman refused to give Zaro permission to take Government House Hill and when it became clear to him that the irregulars controlled the crest and Zaro's battalion would be in an untenable position at daybreak, he ordered Zaro to retreat. When Dayan returned to Brigade HQ, he approved Fefferman's order. In the meantime, Zaro was having difficulty contacting his men, and their retreat became disorderly. Far from raising morale in the battalion and the brigade, the operation brought spirits plummeting down to a new low.

At daybreak, Dayan summoned the men of the Beit Horon Battalion and gave them a severe tongue-lashing, saying they had fought like idlers and were a disgrace to their weapons. He may have done so to rally volunteers for a renewed assault with armored cars. Fefferman dismissed his talk as pure rhetoric, for the GHQ injunction against taking the hill was still in effect. But Dayan's words aroused only rancor in the battalion and were especially painful to Zaro, who felt his men had fought courageously and did not deserve the OC's wrath.

Bitter exchanges followed in the brigade summation session, which took place immediately afterward. Although Dayan did not doubt Zaro's personal courage, he took the battalion commander to task for not leading his men in battle. Dayan believed that Zaro's presence in the battlefield might have turned the tide in his favor. Zaro countered that at night the physical presence of the battalion commander could have no effect on the men, with the possibile exception of those in his immediate vicinity. He felt it was preferable to have remained in the command post, where he could communicate with and control the entire force. Zaro centered his criticism on the missing hour of communication with Dayan. Fefferman was so bitter about the entire affair that he demonstratively walked out of the meeting. He was so furious at the unprofessional way in which Dayan had prepared for the action that he even tried to persuade Zaro to join him in prevailing upon Yadin to remove Dayan from Jerusalem. Zaro, a model of inbred discipline, rejected the idea.

Ill feeling pervaded the Etzioni Brigade for a time. Fefferman was relieved of his post as operations officer and given command of the brigade armored-car battalion. In the following months, Dayan invested all his energy in the reorganization and training of the brigade. He had two infantry battalions and a new battalion of armored cars, in which Akiva Sa'ar and Uri Bar-On served as company commanders.

After two months of persistent demands for large-scale actions, an opportunity finally presented itself. From the outset, Dayan had requested permission to carry out operations in the south, toward Bethlehem. On October 15, when "Operation Yoav" was launched on the Southern Front to defeat the Egyptian Army and gain control of the Negev, Dayan renewed his pressure on Ben Gurion. The line south of Jerusalem was held by units of the Egyptian Army, which controlled the Hebron area. From a military standpoint, the need for action in this area concurrent with "Operation Yoav" was obvious. Yadin, as Chief of G Branch in GHQ, supported Dayan's request to deploy his brigade in the southern sector of Jerusalem and carry out an operational plan known by the code name "Operation Wine Press." Yadin relates that because of political considerations, Ben Gurion would not hear of it, but Dayan finally prevailed on the Prime Minister. "Operation Wine Press" was allotted only twenty-four hours, from nightfall on October 21 to dawn of the 22nd, for on October 19 the UN Security Council had resolved to impose another cease-fire—effective from October 22—and to order either side that violated it back to its previous positions.

While the battles of "Operation Yoav" were being waged in the Negev, Central Front HQ launched "Operation Mountain" with the two-fold aim of engaging the Egyptian Army in the Hebron area, and preventing it from interfering in the Negev battles, and widening out southward the corridor between Jerusalem and the Coastal Plain.

This operation was carried out by the Palmach Harel Brigade with considerable success. For four days the brigade advanced south from the Jerusalem-Lydda railroad, and on the final night of "Operation Mountain" Dayan was allowed to carry out "Operation Wine Press."

Breaking into Bethlehem—the last barrier on the way to Hebron—via the main road from Jerusalem, which was held by the Arab Legion seemed beyond the strength of the Etzioni Brigade. Dayan therefore planned to enter "through the back door," via the high mountain on which the village of Beit Jalla is situated. The mountain was regarded as a natural barrier and was therefore held by only a small contingent of Egyptian troops, about the strength of one company. Dayan reasoned that if his units were able to overcome the topographical difficulties, they could easily overcome the Egyptian soldiers, who were inferior to the Jordanians of the Arab Legion, and achieve a neat surprise by attacking from an unexpected direction. By taking Beit Jalla, the Etzioni Brigade could by-pass the Jordanian troops on the Jerusalem-Bethlehem road.

There were those who doubted the brigade's ability to overcome the difficulties posed by the terrain. Fefferman, a native Jerusalemite, claimed that of all the mountains around Jerusalem, "the mountain of Beit Jalla is the wildest." Dayan's plan called for finding a way down the steep slope of one mountain and then climbing the even steeper incline of the one opposite. He assumed that once Beit Jalla was taken, Bethlehem would fall like so much ripe fruit and the way to Hebron would be clear. The most arduous task—scaling the mountain and capturing its crest—was assigned to Zalman Mart's Moriah Battalion. The other two battalions were to guard its flanks, Beit Horon (under Zaro's command) to the left and the 64th Armored Car Battalion (under Fefferman) to the right.

Either because of his persistent belief in the lesson he had learned in Zemakh or because of his implicit trust in Mart's ability, Dayan did not make his customary reconnaissance patrol along the route the Moriah Battalion was to take, and Mart contented himself with sending out a scouting section on a night patrol of the route. The scouts claimed that they discovered a path which the battalion could use to descend the mountain to the railroad tracks. They also marked what they considered a more or less easy place to cross the wadi and begin the ascent to Beit Jalla. No patrol was carried out to find a route for the subsequent climb up the mountain side.

Even the most cursory of patrols would have sufficed to indicate the difficulties of the terrain. One of the brigade staff officers maintained that even on a mild day, and carrying a light pack, it would be extremely difficult to cover the route in the given time. How much more so, then, at night, with full battle gear, and under battle conditions. There were terraces 5 meters high on the slopes leading down to the wadi. It was therefore unlikely that Mart's battalion would be able to overcome the topographical difficulties, let alone engage in battle. But Dayan believed that if the Arabs "get hit, they'll start running."

Dayan set up his command post in the quarry near the suburb of Bayit Vegan. It was a high vantage point that afforded good wireless contact with the battalions. The brigade moved out at 8 p.m. The two flanking arms achieved their objectives successfully and continued their advance according to plan. But Mart's battalion, which stood at six companies, moved extremely slowly and lost valuable time, until it was stopped altogether. Recounting three of Mart's errors will suffice to explain his failure. First, the battalion moved out in single file, like a long, undulating snake extended over several kilometers. A witness remarked that the battalion looked like a nursery-school excursion halted at a crosswalk. As a result of the inordinate length of the column, the last men in line were still at the starting point several hours after the operation had begun. The second error was that for reasons of his own and because of the heavy artillery support he had been promised, Mart turned the support company into a regular rifle company and put it at the point, leading the column. But a support company's training and its function within an infantry battalion make its men ineffective as assault troops.

Either because the scouts could not find the track they had chosen earlier or because it was badly chosen to begin with, the battalion soon found itself without any clearly defined path at all. When the point company finally approached the wadi, it ran into an ambush—or so it seemed to Mart. It was actually a single machine-gun position which managed to put the entire point company out of action, for after one man was killed the rest could not get up the courage to carry on.

Mart's third—and fatal—error was his failure to order a small force to deal with the machine gun so that the rest of his battalion, which was vast in comparison to the machine-gun emplacement, could by-pass it. Mart himself was with the third company, still on the slopes leading down to the wadi and some 200 meters behind the point. He contacted the point company by wireless, and its commander managed to persuade him that "there's nothing to be done. It's impossible to overcome the ambush." At that moment light riffle fire was opened up on the long, winding column, and Mart was totally at a loss. When Dayan contacted him on the wireless to ask what was happening, he replied, "There's such confusion here that I don't know how we'll find our way out of it! They're firing from here, firing from there, and the point company has been stoppped."

Mart concluded that even if he replaced the point company and overcame the Egyptian machine-gun position—he later claimed that this could easily have been achieved by two or three soldiers—he would not have enough time left to complete the mission. He therefore requested permission to turn back, and Dayan replied: "You know how important this action is. I don't have to explain it to you. But if you say you can't go on, you're the commander on the spot, and you must decide what is to be done." The upshot was that a single machine-gun position blocked the advance of the Moriah Battalion and, consequently, the entire brigade. The only ground gained by "Operation Wine Press" was the capture of Woulaja, an Arab village west of Jerusalem opposite the ancient village of Batir. While this in itself was later to prove of importance in the demarcation of the armistice lines, it was the only positive aspect of an otherwise total fiasco.

The lesson of Zemakh, reinforced by the successes of Lydda and Karatiya, was to some extent the cause of Dayan's failures at Government House Hill and Beit Jalla. In retrospect, it seems that he was only a step away from victory in the Jerusalem sector as well and his guiding principle—that with daring and ingenuity, a small force can defeat numerically superior Arab forces—was correct. In fact, had it not been so, it is doubtful whether the War of Independence could have ended in an Israeli victory. Dayan correctly assessed the enemy's weaknesses, but he failed to perceive his own or those of Zahal. His experiences in Jerusalem taught him the difference between a group of partisan fighters and a regular army unit. Furthermore, as he later admitted, he himself lacked sufficient professional knowledge. Later on, as Chief of G Branch and C-o-S, Dayan fused the daring and élan of a partisan with the training and experience of a professional to mold the character of Zahal. But at the time, the failure at Beit Jalla became something of a byword in the army and rather damaged the reputation he had acquired after Lydda and Karatiya. He was labeled a "partisan" and was considered a "rash" and "dangerous" commander who did not devote sufficient thought to the planning of military operations.

Dayan never once expressed a single recriminatory word against Mart. Although he was most disturbed by the events at Beit Jalla, he did not treat Mart as he had Zaro and his battalion. On the face of it, it appeared that he was discriminating in favor of Mart, a close friend to whom he owed his life. But Dayan simply believed that Mart had "tried to do the best he could. It's not like telling someone to attack and then discovering that he didn't attack, didn't assault, didn't even move. Mart tried. He told me: 'My time is up and I haven't been able to get any further.' One can criticize his operative ability, but not his personal efforts." Indeed, Dayan drew his private conclusions about his friend's ability to command in the field; but on a personal level he remained a loyal friend, and when Mart was injured in an accident, he sat by his bedside in the hospital and did whatever he could to help. As for his military career, as far as Dayan was concerned Mart's fate was sealed at Beit Jalla. He filled several other posts in Zahal until his release in 1968, at the age of fifty-one. But his rank upon retirement was lieutenant colonel—the rank of a battalion commander and the same one he held in 1948.

In November 1948, C-o-S Dori appointed a committee of three, headed by Maj. Gen. Chaim Laskov, to review the chain of command in the Jerusalem area. Acting on the recommendations of the Laskov committee, GHQ appointed Dayan Commander of Jerusalem, while he continued to serve as OC Etzioni Brigade. His special status as Commander of Jerusalem both expanded his responsibilities for the sector and intensified his insubordination to Central Command. Maj. Gen. Zvi Ayalon, OC Central Command, displayed considerable patience in dealing with his subordinate, even when Dayan arrived late for staff meetings—sometimes because he had stopped on the way to pick fruit just as the meeting was scheduled to begin. On one occasion, however, Ayalon felt Dayan had gone too far.

On February 14, 1949, Tu Bishvat (a Jewish festival celebrated by the planting of trees), new forests were planted in memory of the dead of the War of Independence. The central ceremony took place at Sha'ar Hagai—where the road to Jerusalem enters the hills and begins the ascent to the capital—in the presence of bereaved parents, the Prime Minister, Cabinet members and members of the Knesset. To protect them from possible attack, Ayalon ordered every formation in his command to send a guard unit. Dayan thought Ayalon was being overcautious, and in an unclassified telegram informed his superior that he would not send a platoon of guards for the ceremony. Ayalon reiterated the order in an open telegram to Dayan, and Dayan repeated his refusal. A public argument by telegram erupted, and the upshot was that Dayan did not send a platoon as ordered. The tree-planting ceremony went without a hitch as Dayan had foreseen, but Ayalon could not forgive him and demanded that Lt. Col. Dayan be court-martialed for disobeying orders. Ayalon remained OC Central Command until after Dayan became Chief of G Branch and C-o-S and was thus in the unique position of being his superior officer and subordinate in the space of a few years. It was he who coined the phrase "It's much easier to serve under Moshe than to have him serve under you."

A military court found that although Dayan had several substantially defensible arguments, he was guilty of disobeying orders. The problem was to find a suitable punishment, and here the judges were at a loss. Zahal had yet to complete a code of military law, so they had neither precedents nor any other standards to go by. To complicate matters even further, at that time—February 27, 1949—Dayan was appointed a member of the Israeli delegation to the armistice talks with Jordan, which were to take place on the Island of Rhodes. The court was therefore forced to seek a sentence that would be adequate punishment for the offence but not bar Dayan from joining the Rhodes delegation. Finally Dayan himself came up with a solution: temporary demotion from lieutenant colonel to major. His suggestion was accepted and the demotion duly effected. This punishment was reminiscent of the tale of Brer Rabbit, who begged not to be thrown into the briar patch. Hardly anyone learned of the demotion, and Dayan was not even required to change the rank insignia on his uniform, as at the same time he was accorded a temporary rank of lieutenant colonel to equal the rank of his Jordanian counterpart at the peace table. Thus "Major" Dayan traveled to Rhodes in his usual uniform.

The position of Commander of Jerusalem carried with it the right to maintain contact with the press. In fact, apart from Dori and Yadin, Dayan was the only officer in Zahal permitted to speak to the press in his own name. His press relations were excellent, though more intricate than one would have thought. Jerusalem was a source of world-wide, Israeli, and Arab interest, and Dayan's statements received extensive coverage all over the world, often appearing on the front pages of leading newspapers. His manner of speech nonetheless remained straightforward, though colored by swift repartee, charm, and a sense of humor.

Among his other duties on Dayan's staff, Captain Alex Braude dealt with promoting a soldier-statesman image for Dayan. One of Braude's more spectacular achievements was "selling" Dayan to *Life* Magazine as a future Prime Minister of Israel. The July 18, 1949 issue ran a pictorial feature entitled "New Israel" in which a picture of Dayan figured prominently. He was the only Zahal officer mentioned in the entire article.

In Mapai circles, the *Life* article was regarded as a huge joke. Ben Gurion was at the height of his political power; his prestige was immense and his national fame at its peak. And in the second line of Mapai functionaries, no one dreamed of making way for Moshe Dayan. He was still part of the nebulous mass known in party circles as "the youngsters."

Dayan's diplomatic-political activities began a few days after his failure at Government House Hill. At the end of August 1949, the Commander in Chief of the UNTSO, Maj. Gen. William Riley, summoned representatives of the Egyptian, Jordanian, and Israeli armies to the Assyrian monastery near the Jaffa Gate to discuss the situaion in the area surrounding Government House, where UNTSO HQ were situated. The UN wanted the hill around Government House to be demilitarized. The meeting ended in an impasse, and it seemed as though the second meeting, scheduled for September 5, would end similarly. But Dayan took an unprecedented step. "When things came to a standstill and the mediation of the UN observers . . . proved not to be the best way of settling issues, I suggested to Abdullah el-Tel that the two of us leave the distinguished company for a few moments and talk privately in the next room." The two men soon established rapport. After a quarter of an hour in the adjoining room, they returned and informed the other participants that they had agreed to set up a direct telephone line between the Israeli and the Jordanian commanders of Jerusalem.

The meeting between el-Tel and Dayan was the first to be held between representatives of Israel and Jordan without the participation of a third party—the UN—since the outbreak of the war. Its principal importance lay in the effect it produced upon Dayan's political thinking. As early as September 5, 1948, he sought direct contact with the opposite side in war or peace.

From the outset, Dayan brought to his political activities great personal charm, intelligence, a rapid grasp of essentials, and a frank, open personality that inspired confidence. All of these qualities combined to persuade el-Tel of the wisdom of a practical arrangement upon which Dayan—and later others—based the concept of direct negotiations with the Arabs or nothing at all. The direct telephone line was also the first expression of a conviction that was to crystallize when Dayan served as C-o-S, namely that the UN was a buffer between Israel and the Arab states, rather than an instrument of rapprochement. Accordingly, the frequency of Dayan's meetings with el-Tel increased until they became a regular feature in Jerusalem and received routine press coverage.

Dayan and el-Tel reached agreement on many arrangements made necessary by the very existence of cease-fire lines, such as safe passage for workers to the university buildings in the Israeli enclave on Mount Scopus, demilitarization of areas, exchange of prisoners, permission for pilgrims to cross the border to the holy places, and the demarcation of no-man's land. The success of direct contact produced an official agreement between the two local commanders. On June 29, 1949, when Dayan was appointed head of all the Israeli delegations to the Mixed Armistice Commissions, he tried to promote similar arrangements between the local commanders of both sides in all the sectors.

Dayan soon became a regular participant in all the top-level discussions concerning the formulation of cease-fire policies and to some extent subsequent state policies. Following a meeting between the two Jerusalem commanders on 12 December, Lt. Col. Moshe Dayan was quoted as saying that due to the complete implementation of the cease-fire in the Jerusalem sector, he saw no need to convene

further meetings unless they dealt directly with the "translation of
the cease-fire into an armistice that will bring in its wake a lasting
peace." According to the official press release, Col. el-Tel replied that
he would have to consult his government on this issue. This was the
first overt intimation of the beginnings of direct, secret talks betwen
Israel and Jordan, in which Dayan played a role described by Ben
Gurion as "important."

In September 1948, Eliyahu Sasson renewed contacts with representatives of the Hashemite Kingdom of Jordan and met with Jordanian diplomats in Paris. On December 10, 1949, Dayan handed el-
Tel a message from Sasson to King Abdullah which asked that the
King dispatch to Jerusalem a man he trusted "for a meeting and
talks." The King agreed, and at the end of December Sasson and
Dayan met several times with el-Tel and Dr. Shaukat Sati. The four
men prepared the ground for a series of meetings with the King.

On January 4, Prime Minister David Ben Gurion and Foreign
Minister Moshe Sharett empowered Reuven Shiloah and Eliyahu
Sasson of the Foreign Office and Lt. Col. Moshe Dayan to act on behalf of the state, granting them full authority "to negotiate and sign
an agreement with His Majesty the King . . . in order to put an end to
hostilities and establish peaceful relations" between Israel and the
Hashemite Kingdom of Jordan. The first meetings with King Abdullah
(on January 16 and 30, 1950) appear to have left a deep impression on
Dayan. They were conducted in the strictest secrecy. Sasson and
Dayan, wearing foreign uniforms, crossed the lines as soon as night fell,
entered el-Tel's car, and were driven directly to the palace at El-Shuneh.
In order to clear the way, el-Tel often called out from a distance, "It's
Colonel Abdullah el-Tel." As an added precaution, Dayan removed his
eye patch and wore dark glasses. The second of these meetings lasted
long into the night and as the car wound its way through the hills near
Jerusalem, el-Tel told his Israeli passengers to lie down on the floor
of the car and he covered them with a *keffiyeh*.*

To ensure that good spirits prevailed at the meetings, the King would
begin by serving a festive meal. "Afterward he would open the meeting
by stating the issue and suggesting to all present that it be discussed in a
congenial atmosphere. He adorned his speech with Bedouin aphorisms
and explained that we were like a heavily laden rider, and in order to
reach our destination we would have to remove our bundles of problems one by one." Dayan's impatience with the slow circumspect
Bedouin style of negotiation and the two Israelis' differing interpretations of the meeting with the King typify some of the differences of approach that had begun to crop up between the Zahal officers—
the younger generation of Israel—and the Foreign Office officials—the

*Traditional Arab headdress.

veterans, including all the original members of the Political Department of the Jewish Agency. While the thirty-four year old Dayan was brisk and practical, Sasson, a veteran diplomat with the Political Department since 1934, believed that warm, human contact and a courteous manner can solve international problems.

The armistice talks between Jordan and Israel were held on two levels: the ceremonial, external negotiations that took place in the Roses Hotel in Rhodes, and the secret, decisive discussions in the royal palace at El-Shuneh. Walter Eytan, the Director-General of the Foreign Office and head of the Israeli delegation to the armistice talks, maintained that the King deliberately sent "unimpressive" representatives to Rhodes to enable him to direct the talks himself at his palace, with the aid of his closest advisers. Thus a few days after the start of talks with Jordan in Rhodes, the key members of the Israeli delegation returned to Israel to participate in the secret talks with the King and his advisers.

Dayan kept up a running criticism—which he confided to some of his staff officers in the Etzioni Brigade—on the manner in which the representatives from the Foreign Office were handling the talks. Even Ben Gurion was not exempt from this criticism. From the outset, Dayan's respect for Ben Gurion was not that of a convert to the teachings and vision of a master, but the outcome of daily tests in practical affairs. The attitude toward the UNTSO, questions of the truce in Jerusalem, obedience to or violation of the cease-fire agreements, and the negotiations with the Hashemite Kingdom and their military implications were all issues on which there was a constant polarity of views between Ben Gurion, on one hand, and Moshe Sharett, on the other. The two men clashed daily over matters on the general agenda and particularly on matters specifically in Sharett's charge. Although the gap between their respective view-points was not constant, it was never bridged.

Dayan often drove to meetings with Ben Gurion in a machine-gun-mounted jeep, as though he believed that troublesome political problems could be solved with the aid of such armament. It was natural for him to be attracted to Ben Gurion, the activist, rather than to Sharett, "who always weighed things against their immediate difficulties." But when he came to know Ben Gurion better, he discerned the meticulous deliberations underlying his seemingly unhesitant activism. Sharett always expressed fears of how the English would react, and what the Americans would do, or what the French would say and was most reluctant to take risks, while Ben Gurion's analyses and assessments of developments generally proved to be more accurate.

Dayan was also greatly impressed by Ben Gurion's manner of taking action. He first posed the question, "What, in fact, do you really want to achieve?" Only then did he decide what was important and what secondary and marked out objectives and a plan for attaining them.

One trait in particular won Dayan's admiration: "He never reacts as though he were offended or angry. He has a point toward which he strives, and to reach it he must take action, be stubborn, or even take risks. As for the unimportant things, there is no need for stubbornness, risk, or effort, and others can handle them." Ben Gurion always concentrated his strength and energy on the main effort. In later years, Dayan began to resemble him in this respect, focusing on the main endeavor and delegating to others anything that seemed of secondary importance.

The comparison that Dayan drew between Ben Gurion and Sharett was wholly favorable to Ben Gurion. Sharett's mode of speech was discursive, characterized by rhetoric and neatly wrought phrases, rather than practical, purposeful clarifications. Though Sharett was undoubtedly the more eloquent of the two, it was Ben Gurion's speech that generated "tremendous voltage." Ben Gurion never made public the rules of his game. His secrets were revealed only to the astute, who discovered them on their own by inference and analogy. Dayan learned these secrets as though he were a sorcerer's apprentice, eager and quick to learn. His admiration for Ben Gurion went very deep, and he chose to regard Ben Gurion as a teacher. On the copy of the *Diary of the Sinai Campaign* Dayan gave to Ben Gurion, he wrote, "To Ben Gurion, teacher and leader."

Ben Gurion's habit of regarding everything in the light of an all-encompassing philosophy won Dayan's admiration when it was applied to major developments, but provoked criticism or a smile when it was applied to technical details, people, or events. Dayan first discerned this weakness when he reported on his meetings with King Abdullah and commented on what he thought the King would or would not be willing to agree to. Sometimes Ben Gurion would reject his conclusions and proceed to explain what the King had in fact meant when he said such and such and what he would not agree to when he said otherwise. Dayan quietly bore these explanations until one day his patience ran out and he challenged the elder statesman:

You haven't met King Abdullah even once, while I've sat with him many times. I say he will agree to this, and you say he will not—he will agree to this and not to that. And why? Because you explain to me what the Egyptians agreed to, and what people used to do in China, and how things happen in history. But King Abdullah doesn't know all these things, and he'll agree to one thing and not another according to what he thinks. You haven't met him, haven't even set eyes on him, while I go back and forth from him to you. Yet before I can say a word, you have already told me what he will agree to and what not. That's not the way it is at all!

The difference between the young army officer who saw things in the present only, without reference to their historical background, and the seasoned statesman who tread a path of concepts in the broad avenue of an historical outlook frequently gave rise to mutual barbs. While looking at the setting sun through the window of Ben Gurion's office, Dayan once mused: "When I look out of the window and see the sun setting, I understand it to mean that the sun is setting and evening is coming on. But you? The fact that the sun is setting right now is unimportant. You see the stars move and the cosmos turn on its axis, and the entire world in flux. You're incapable of considering a single detail as a separate entity, an episode." In some respects, however, the admiration was mutual. Ben Gurion was impressed by Dayan's political-diplomatic aptitude and tended to attribute Israel's achievements in the negotiations with Abdullah to him.

On January 7, 1949 the fighting in Palestine ended in an Israeli victory, and on January 13 talks began in Rhodes on an Armistice Agreement between Israel and Egypt. By that time King Abdullah no longer enjoyed the advantage he had before May 14, for whether the Arab Legion intervened in the fighting ceased to be relevant to Israel. Zahal was no longer concerned with the Egyptian Army, and if necessary it could now turn all its attention to the Legion and trounce it. But Ben Gurion wanted to make political capital from Abdullah's position, for while the other Arab governments were at most prepared to sign an Armistice Agreement, there seemed a chance that Abdullah would be willing to sign a peace treaty. In return, Israel would have to abide by part of an agreement that Golda Meir and Eliyahu Sasson had proposed to the King, which stipulated partial annexation of the West Bank by Jordan. The Israeli Government was inclined to recognize the annexation—as in fact it later did—but was unwilling to allow the King control over Lydda and Ramle or to accept Jordanian control of the southern Negev, including Eilat. As for Jerusalem, the Israeli representatives concurred with the King in opposing the internationalization of the city and favoring its division into Israeli and Jordanian sectors; but they did not agree to the partition lines he suggested.

The Jordanian-Israeli negotiations became complicated in December 1948, when Iraq, in direct contravention of the Security Council resolution of November 16, announced its refusal to hold armistice talks with Israel. The Iraqi Army had invaded Palestine at the outbreak of hostilities and spread out along the foothills of the Samarian Mountains, cutting off the Jezreel Valley from the southern part of the coastal plain and leaving Israel with a long, thin waistline which could easily be severed. Although there was talk of the Jordanian Government representing the Iraqi Government at the armistice talks, when negotiations between Israel and Jordan opened at Rhodes, Iraq let it be known that she was not interested in an armistice of any kind. She intended merely to evacuate her troops from Palestine and allow the Arab Legion to take their place. Israel, of course, could not agree to such an arrangement. Had the Arab Legion entered the sectors held by the Iraqi Army in the face of Israeli opposition, a new war would have broken out. The dire consequences of such a confrontation were obvious to King Abdullah.

As the chances of reaching a proper peace treaty with the King seemed so good, the Israeli representatives at Rhodes adopted a moderate stance. The King, who feared defeat in battle, showed willingness to forgo some of the territories in the Iraqi sector, which he would lose in any case should the war be renewed. The negotiations with the King were the responsibility of Yigael Yadin and it was he, together with Walter Eytan of the Foreign Office, who met the King or his representatives in Jerusalem and El-Shuneh for preliminary talks. Dayan returned from Rhodes in order to direct the negotiation for the partition of the Iraqi-held sector between Israel and Jordan. The King referred to him as "one-eye" and on one occasion wrote that he would like to add him to "the list of his friends in Israel."

According to Major Yehoshafat Harkabi, who accompanied Dayan to El-Shuneh on March 19, "Moshe was excellent in his talks with the King. He produced a clever formula: 'With the Iraqis we were there as enemies. With you we shall be there as friends. Therefore we need the first line of hills.'" Dayan's contribution to these talks was his insistence, in the face of Yadin's skepticism, on including the Jerusalem-Lydda railroad line in Israeli territory, even though it was difficult to defend. Thus Dayan achieved across the negotiating table at least part of what his brigade had been unable to achieve in its abortive attack on Beit Jalla.

In his capacity as Commander of Jerusalem, Dayan and his opposite number, el-Tel, were charged with allocating responsibility for areas of no-man's land between the two sides. Here he proved a hard and shrewd bargainer. The formula that guided him was "ask for a mountain so as to gain a molehill." When these talks came to a satisfactory conclusion, appropriate instructions were sent to the delegation in Rhodes, and on April 3 the Israel-Jordan Armistice Agreement was duly signed.

Nothing ever came of the peace talks with King Abdullah, except the King's own death. He was assassinated as a traitor on Friday July 22, 1951, as he made his way to prayers in the el-Aksa Mosque. Of all the arrangements agreed upon between Jordan and Israel, only one materialized: the right of Israel to change guards on the Mount Scopus enclave. The "Green Line"—as the armistice line became known—which should have become "a place where friends are," became instead a barrier separating enemies.

"He was a King," Dayan wrote of Abdullah, "but he was unable to achieve what he wished to achieve." The time of royal courtesy, pomp, and Oriental custom, in which Israeli diplomats had seen a ray of hope, had passed. In Jordan, though to a lesser extent than in other Arab countries, revolutionary and fanatical forces began to emerge and demanded a military solution to the Palestine problem. At the same time, the politicians of the old Political Department school began to lose their exclusive control of Israeli policy, as Israel was faced with a growing need to defend its very existence with the aid of its army. Young officers began to figure far more prominently in developments on both sides of Israel's borders.

Dayan, too, awoke from the fleeting dream of peace that he may have entertained. From here on, the field commander within him again gained over the diplomat. In a letter to Ben Gurion dated September 22, 1949, just before leaving his post in Jerusalem, he no longer suggested negotiating with Jordan to implement the clauses of the armistice agreement concerning free access to the holy places, passage through Latrun, and the normalization of life on Mount Scopus. He now proposed the planning of a military operation to take Mount Scopus by force. His main concern was that with the passage of time the armistice lines would harden into established borders without the attainment of a peace settlement.

14 FRONT COMMANDER

(October 1949 - December 1952)

On July 20, 1949, the War of Independence came to an end with the signing of the last Armistice Agreement (with Syria). The stated purpose of the four armistice agreements was to facilitate the transition from a truce to a lasting peace, and the parties undertook to cease employing threats or force as means to solving the Palestine problem.

The feeling that peace was within reach spread through Israel and prompted a growing sense of antimilitarism. Within a short time Zahal changed from a large popular army, which had attracted the cream of Israel's youth, to a small army composed of a permanent command framework and conscripted soldiers. The latter were now the first representatives of the mass immigration of Jews mostly from Arab-speaking countries—undereducated, ignorant of Hebrew, strangers to the newly formed traditions of Zahal. In many ways, they resembled natives serving in a remote colonial army. The attempts of GHQ to persuade the outstanding young officers of the War of Independence to choose a military career met with little success.

Dayan was also beset by doubts about the Regular Army. He confided to his friend Ahiya Ben-Ami, who visited him in Jerusalem in the autumn of 1949, that he wanted to leave the army, where he could not "envision his future," and his ambition was to engage in politics. Apart from the influence of the general antimilitaristic mood of the country, Dayan may also have felt his own lack of the military education necessary for a career soldier. "My military education is nil," he told his friends. He was therefore faced with the choice to "Either study army work or leave it." His inclination to acquire a military education was slight, but he was fascinated by politics.

It was Ben Gurion who prevailed upon Dayan to remain in the Regular Army and accept the appointment of OC Southern Command. Ben Gurion listened to Dayan's objections. For example, "If I go to Beersheba [the HQ of Southern Command] I'll get bogged down in problems of development and won't be any good as a soldier." But the Prime Minister persisted, promising Dayan that he would be given the opportunity to complete his military education. On October 25, he was appointed CO Southern Command, four days after he had been promoted to the rank of major general. Ben Gurion's influence had again shaped the course of Dayan's life: within four years he was to become C-o-S.

On November 9 Yigael Yadin received the flag of C-o-S from Lt. Gen. Dori. This marked the beginning of an era that was dominated by the first generation of officers reared in Zahal. The senior officers of the Haganah gradually began to disappear. Dayan was thirty-four years old at the time, and since the age of twenty-one he had been engaged in national service, during a period fraught with strife and war, which had left him little time for the pleasures of life. The prospects for the future were no brighter, for it was now clear to him that the struggle would endure and that his life would be structured around it. And if he were to accept all the injunctions of discipline and professional etiquette that apply to a military man, he would have to forgo many of his natural inclinations and desires.

His pleasures were simple. The men of Southern Command soon discovered that their new commander was not a stickler for order or discipline in dress. Zahal had just begun to enforce stricter standards of military discipline and etiquette, for Yadin's major goal was to create a regular, well-disciplined army out of the partisan, popular army of 1948. But it never occurred to Dayan to spoil his sense of well-being by wearing ties, shining his shoes, or saluting merely because he was a general. Once, when Dayan arrived at a General Staff meeting with his shirt pocket unbuttoned, Yadin ordered him to leave the room and return properly dressed. It also never occurred to him to deprive himself of fruit straight from the tree, just because he was OC of a command. His sociable, straightforward, and egalitarian approach made a deep impression on his subordinates.

Familiarizing himself with the territory under his command— nearly half the area of the State of Israel—was a task he shared with his men on adventure-filled expeditions. He studied all the sectors thoroughly, even driving through areas that had not yet been cleared of mines. These patrols-cum-excursions into the desert were Dayan's greatest pleasure during his first few months at Southern Command. Captain Rehavam Ze'evi ("Ghandi"), the newly appointed Intelligence Officer of Southern Command, recalls that while he was in the process of acquainting himself with the Negev Mountains, Dayan accompanied him on several occasions. They would penetrate deep into the wild desert in a jeep, often disappearing from Command HQ for days at a time. Provisions and fuel were brought to them in the field by land or air.

Dayan once took out a patrol in six vehicles to seek a route to Kadesh Barnea and Kusseima, near the Israeli border with the Sinai peninsula. Zahal did not yet have detailed sector maps or aerial photographs, and Dayan and "Ghandi" used outdated 1:100,000 British maps. As the convoy drove on, they suddenly noticed a commotion on the hills facing them. They immediately realized that they had crossed the border into Egyptian territory and anticipated an unpleasant confrontation. Dayan ordered the patrol to deploy and awaited developments. After recovering from his initial astonishment, the Egyptian commander in the area sent an officer across to inform the Israelis that they had crossed the border and that they were to turn about and leave. Dayan thought this was a good opportunity for a little fun and proceeded to argue with the Egyptian officer, trying to prove, with the aid of a 1:250,000 map, that the opposite was the case. Drawing lines and dots on the map, Dayan claimed that it was the Egyptian force that had crossed the border. They would now have to evacuate their buildings and installations and return to Egypt, Totally bewildered, the officer returned to report the results of his talk to his commander. Apparently a bitter argument ensued between the two, which gave Dayan and his men ample time to withdraw into Israeli territory.

Dayan brought along his eleven-year-old daughter Yael on a long drive to the Kuntilla area. Her most vivid memory of the day is of the stray sheep that the men caught, slaughtered, and roasted. The soldiers of Southern Command remember their commander as frank, friendly, and funded with jokes and anecdotes. They were impressed by his love of the country and intimate knowledge of the Bible, always drawing comparisons and images from it.

At about that time, Dayan read a newspaper account of an American who made necklaces from lions' claws and sharks' teeth. Following a newspaper report of the appearance of some sharks off the shores of Eilat, he flew down there and acquired a shark's head, which he cooked in a pressure cooker for days—unperturbed by the awful smell. He later took the teeth to an army dental clinic, where a dentist broke a few drills until he managed to pierce the teeth as requested. Dayan strung them on a silver thread and created a necklace, which he kept for a special occasion.

The difference between Dayan and the new C-o-S of the Command, Col. Zvi Zur, soon made itself felt in Southern Command. Of his first period of work with Dayan, Zur said, "The contrast between us stemmed from differences in our approach and style of work. I felt that as command C-o-S I should see to it that there was order, a framework, and a system. I was not built to work any differently. Moshe's methods were entirely different." Dayan sought to invest all his energies in a major effort and considered compulsory order and formal methods bonds that must be severed. He would reach decisions and finalize actions while in the field, on any level he saw fit—even the lowest—without coordinating with or even informing his C-o-S. He certainly lacked the patience to wait until orders went down the chain of command to the operative unit, so he simply jumped on a jeep, went out to the unit, and gave the relevant instructions on the spot.

One of the differences of opinion between Dayan and Zur centered on the question of cultivating Israeli lands along the armistice lines. Jewish settlement in the south was sparse, and the border kibbutzim—an indispensable part of Israel's defenses—were few and far between. This enabled Arabs from across two borders—from the Gaza Strip and Hebron—to cultivate areas on the Israeli side of the "Green Line." Dayan regarded this situation as a danger to Israel's borders, fearing that the Arab farmers would push back the borders and succeed where their armies had failed. He traveled throughout the south, urging the members of kibbutzim and moshavim to sow and harvest in the uncultivated lands along the borders and promising the full assistance of the Southern Command. For a starter, he offered to put at their disposal as many army vehicles as they required. Zur, with a characteristic sense of order, felt it was wrong "to take vehicles belonging to the nation, military vehicles, and give them to some farm so that it can harvest wheat for itself, not even to achieve a common aim." If the government considered it sufficiently impor-tant, he argued, it had the means to ensure agricultural cultivation along the borders, and if the Minister of Defense so wished, he could provide such means by issuing orders through regular channels. Zur maintained that the functions of the command should be restricted to military duties alone.

To Dayan's way of thinking, a firm delimitation of the armistice lines was paramount, and he realized that agriculture could achieve this better than Zahal. Moreover, there was no fighting going on during that period, and the men and vehicles of the command had no tasks that could not be postponed. Rather than leave the vehicles parked in neat rows at the bases, greased, fueled and equipped for action—of which there was no sign—he preferred to violate the good but impractical order of things and mobilize them for an important task, without waiting for government machinery to arrive at decisions that were likely to come too late—or not at all.

In time, Zur acknowledged that Dayan had been right, but in 1950 he rebelled. After seven months of endless misunderstandings and unsuccessful attempts to accustom himself to his commanding officer's way of working, Zur's patience snapped. Maklef, then Deputy C-o-S, recalls that Zur appealed to him in desperation, "I can't work with Moshe any longer." Maklef transferred him to GHQ to become Assistant Director of Military Operations. As director of Manpower Branch in GHQ, however, Zur was to grow very close to Dayan, and in 1967 he was prepared to leave a presti-gious post as Director-General of the Mekorot Water Company, among the largest economic organizations in Israel, to serve in what seemed a temporary post—Assistant to the Minister of Defense, Moshe Dayan.

Nineteen-fifty was an uneventful year. Southern Command was involved in the exchange of the Arab populations in Ashkelon and with the problems created by the Bedouin Azazma tribe, which penetrated the Negev from the Sinai peninsula. Dayan even found time in December to take a vacation with Ruth in Turkey. By that time he had attained a certain measure of international fame, for a number of newsmen linked his trip to Turkey with Ben Gurion's concurrent visit to Greece, as though Israel had intentions of signing military treaties with both of these countries. In fact, Ben Gurion had only made a short stop in Greece before continuing on to London, where he intended to investigate the possibility of Israeli ties with the British Commonwealth.

Dayan was recalled urgently from Turkey because of an incident that became known as the "78th Kilometer," a border dispute with Jordan in the Arava desert which many feared might develop into a war. Dayan took immediate steps to concentrate as many troops as possible around the contested area, in order to deter the Arab Legion from taking action. To provide the Jordanians with an honorable way out, he devised a unique solution. He ordered his soldiers simply to set back the milestones which marked the 78th kilometer of the Eilat road, and the incident ended with the confirmation of Israel's sovereignty over the disputed area.

The relative quiet of 1950 enabled the GHQ to build up the Reserve Army of Zahal and consolidate a cadre of Regular Army officers through an intensive training effort. In 1949, Maj. Gen. Laskov established the first school for battalion commanders. His aim was to impart the lessons of the War of Independence and educate his students in the professional subjects they would require in their duties. Zahal officers learned for the first time what battle procedure was and how to draw up a fire plan, a warning order, and an operation order. It was here that all the military concepts of Zahal from the Palmach, the Jewish Brigade, and the Field Corps were fused into a single, Zahal, school of military thought.

When all the battalion commanders in the army completed the course, there remained the problem of the brigade and area commanders. Their subordinates were now better educated in military matters than they and spoke a new language—"Zahalese"—which was foreign to them. It was therefore decided to have the front and brigade commanders take the battalion commanders' course and then go on to a more advanced stage. Ben Gurion's promise to fill in the gaps in Dayan's military education began to be realized. For a total of nine months, in 1950 and 1951, Dayan became a pupil again.

Dayan surprised everyone in the Battalion Commanders' School. From the C-o-S Yadin, down to the last instructor, they all expected a disorderly, wild and rebellious student. Instead they found that Dayan took his studies extremely seriously. As is often the case with those who begin their organized studies late in life, he had accumulated a thirst for knowledge which was not to be quenched by two years of military studies; so much so, that he registered at the Tel Aviv School of Law and Economics for evening classes and nearly completed his studies in law. Students and instructors alike were impressed by his ability. Yadin asked the instructors to report on their generals-cadets, but demanded that the reports be made verbally. Of Dayan, they said: superlative tactical skill, a diligent student, critical of anything that he does not agree with, and impatient of technical details. For example, he never remembered—or wanted to remember—the compositon of the point unit in a brigade march.

The school's basic didactic approach was a universal one. School solutions to tactical problems were therefore equally applicable to the armies of Ceylon, India, France, and Israel. All the students accepted the school solution to the brigade defense problem—except Dayan. As far as he was concerned, the answer to questions such as "Grandmother gave you two candies, and mother gave you two candies—how many candies do you have?" was "But Grandmother gave me a cake."

For the purposes of one exercise, the school looked for a topographical area that would suit the problem at hand, regardless of the existing settlements. An appropriate location was finally found in the vicinity of the main crossroads leading out of the Gaza Strip— one east to Iraq-Suweidan and the other north along the coast road. The question put to the students was: "Where would the brigade deploy in a defensive formation facing south?" According to the school solution, the logical place to set up positions, from a purely tactical point of view, was around the two crossroads. But this "universal" defense plan left Kibbutz Yad Mordechai and other border settlements in the area outside the defended locality. If anyone understood this to be a defense plan against an Egyptian attack from the Gaza Strip, then these settlements were left defenseless somewhere between the brigade line of emplacements and the jumping-off line of the enemy.

All the students willingly accepted the school solution; Dayan tore it to pieces. "You may be able to teach a defense plan at West Point, but not in Israel," was the gist of what he said to his instructors. "Do you mean to say you're going to set up positions on the crossroads and leave Yad Mordechai outside? And what about all the new settlements in the south? Who's going to defend them? Are we going to give them up to the Arabs? Out of the question! The defense must be set up right on the border of the Gaza Strip!" The instructors explained that according to military theory the defended locality should be set up on two crossroads. They repeatedly told him to disregard the specific area that had been chosen solely for the purposes of a theoretical exercise. Again and again the instructors repeated, "Moshe Dayan, get Yad Mordechai out of your head! Try to see it all as a theoretical problem. Let's say it's just an empty area, without settlements. Try to regard it as just that—an empty area." But Dayan countered, "In that case, everything is permissible," and refused to be swayed. No amount of arguing could make him change his mind.

According to his team instructor, Uzi Narkiss:

This was a blow to the school. It was a very basic issue. The instructors had prepared the school solution according to military doctrines, while Moshe Dayan also saw the political and educational aspects of the problem. It didn't interest him in the least which crossroads were to be held, as long as there were settlements left undefended. We, the instructors, were in an uncomfortable position and had no choice but to change the exercise and the solution to include Yad Mordechai and the other new settlements in the line of defence.

Dayan likened himself to a fox, which was the emblem of Southern Command (derived from the biblical story of the foxes' tails Samson set alight to burn the Philistines' crops). The emblem of Zahal Training Division was an owl. At the party celebrating the end of Stage A, Dayan read out a rhyme he had composed called "The Owl and the Fox," in which he described himself as a lean and hungry fox who begs the owl to let him enter his school and to feed him with his wisdom. At the end of the poem, he mentions the brigade defense exercise and dwells upon the difference between the practical wisdom of the fox and the abstract theories of the owl, who—even when the entire country is overrun—still continues to behave by the book:

> So, suitably armed with pencil and paper,
> Take down the relevant exercise data:
> Tel Aviv's conquered, Haifa's a shambles,
> Through Negev and Galilee the enemy ambles.
> Jerusalem's in flames like so many candles.
> You're the commander, with fifty-five aides
> You're to move out, deploy, finalize raids,
> To wrap around, mechanize, foil, and outflank,
> The target, objectives, positions of tank.
> . . . .
> In local localities, on this side or that,
> To fire trajectories high, low, and flat
> Infilade, defilade, reporting-line too,
> Knock out the enemy with the famous one-two.

Five months later, at the party celebrating the end of the Advanced Course, he wrote a sequel to the poem entitled "The Fox's Swan Song." Generally reserved, almost never in need of a friend, and known as a man who had no use for confidants, Dayan suddenly exposed himself in this poem. He confessed that he would never succeed as a man of uniform and order, obedient to directives and regulations, and hinted at an inner conflict similar to the contradiction between the chains of office and love of life. In his swan song, the fox said:

> The course did little good for me,
> Be it God's work or destiny,
> A general I'll never be.
> I've planned and projected in vain,
> I've criticized, argued, debated,
> North, south, east, west again,
> And countered everything stated.
> So Gentlemen, if I may,
> I'll confess with an ego in tatters,
> Though I've already three kids at home,
> It's love, love alone men, that matters.
> For I love without any shame,
> And I suffer without demur,
> I love when they call me "Moishe,"
> And suffer when they call me Sir.
> To stroll with my hands in my pockets,
> Cracking sunflower seeds with my teeth,
> To walk 'round in sandals in summer,
> With a dunam-wide patch back beneath.
> I love steaming corn and felafel*
> And to lick ice cream cones to a peak,
> And I sting from the constant improvements
> Of Lt. Col. Hodorovsky each week.
> These are flaws in my nature—I know it,
> For a flag cannot fly without staff,
> But since childhood days in the barnyard,
> I've been no less the lover and daff.

Dayan came away from the course with his instructor, Lt. Col. Uzi Narkiss, who became his Director of Operations in Southern Command. Within a short time the two men became an effective, smoothly functioning team that proved its mettle in the large-scale Zahal maneuver of August 1951, a few weeks after the conclusion of

---

* Oriental dish made of mashed chick peas rolled into balls, fried and sandwiched in flat Arab bread.

the Advanced Course. Maneuver B, as it was called, not only gave a surprising foretaste of the tactics Dayan was to employ five years later as C-o-S during the Sinai Campaign, but was also an expression of his criticism of Zahal as it had been consolidated under Yadin. Indeed, at the end of the maneuver there was an outright clash between Dayan and Yadin.

One of the vital tasks facing Yadin upon his appointment as C-o-S was to arrest the process of the army's disintegration after the War of Independence and to create something new in its stead. His answer to this challenge was to create a small standing army with a high capacity for mobilizing reserves, which could grow within a short time into a full-strength, battle-ready force capable of shifting the scene of action onto enemy territory.

This plan met opposition in economic quarters. The loss of so many working hours, at a time when everyone felt the heady sense of an approaching peace, led economists and businessmen to consider the Reserves as the games of children in uniform. Yadin claimed that the only way to test his system was to try it out in practice. He therefore requested that Zahal be allowed to carry out at least one maneuver involving 100,000 men, in other words almost the full complement of troops Israel would have at her disposal in case of war. The Minister of Finance and other ministers involved in the country's economy objected to the maneuver, claiming that it would ruin the country. Yadin's answer was: that is exactly what we must find out.

Three of Yadin's maneuvers were approved: A (in 1950), designed to examine the method of calling up Reserves; B and C (in 1951), tactical maneuvers in which Yadin wished to test the Reserves against two strategic and tactical hypotheses: that the enemy had launched a surprise attack on Israel, and that Israel had undertaken a preemptive attack on one of her enemies.

In Maneuver B, Southern Command played the role of the enemy (the Green State) and was to launch a surprise attack on Central Command, playing Israel (the Blue State). Moshe Dayan was the commander of the enemy troops and Zvi Ayalon the commander of the Israeli Army. The game was divided into three stages: (1) initial Green success, (2) arresting of the Green advance by the Blues, (3) a Blue counterattack. The task of Maneuver HQ, headed by Maj. Gen. Zadok, was to ensure that the situations which GHQ wished to test did in fact materialize. He did so by attaching umpires to the two forces. The high cost of the maneuver—which involved practically a complete call-up of the Reserves—obliged all the participants to adhere closely to the rules of the game, down to the smallest details.

The war game began on August 29, 1951, and on the very first day it looked as though Maj. Gen. Dayan, commander of the "enemy" troops, was going to reduce the complex and carefully planned maneuvers to utter chaos. The battle procedure of Maneuver B was scheduled to last thirty-six hours. Ayalon's Blue Force could therefore expect to have at least twenty-four hours before the Green Force launched its attack. But Dayan, who correctly read his opponents' reasoning, seemed to be asking himself, what would happen if the battle procedure were shorter than the prescribed time or were not followed at all?

He decided to go into action at once. No sooner had Maneuver HQ given the signal for the game to begin than Dayan climbed into the command vehicle of the OC 7th Armored Brigade, and ordered him to move out. The umpires were not informed of this change of plans, and the 7th Brigade surprised the Blue Force in the preliminary stages of its battle procedure, penetrating deep into its rear. In fact, the game was over before it began. To a great extent this move was a large-scale variation on Dayan's penetration of the Haganah camp at Ju'ara in 1937. When he heard the protest "You can't do that! It's not fair," he replied, "It's very fair indeed."

The director of the exercise immediately reported to Yadin that the Green Force was not abiding by the rules of the game. Furthermore, it was quite clear GHQ would not be able to test the tactical situations it had chosen, for the required conditions no longer existed and the Blues had been deprived of the stage in which they were to arrest the Green advance. As Maneuver B had involved so much cost and effort, however, it was decided to continue and try to save whatever was still left of the plan.

Dayan did not accept Narkiss's insistence that they leave the war game in retaliation for the twenty-four-hour penalty the Greens had received. He continued the game and even instructed his men to play fair. But his drive to win nonetheless got the better of him, and sometimes he and his units would slip away from the umpires attached to them.

The summing-up of Maneuver B was a stormy session. In the presence of the senior commanders of Zahal, the director of the exercise, Maj. Gen. Zadok, accused Dayan and his Green Force of placing their ambition to win and deceive the other side above all else. Yadin accused the Green Force of disobeying Maneuver orders. The Greens had regarded the umpires—not the Blues—as their principal enemy and tried to exploit their objective limitations, even though they had been told in advance what the umpires' duties would be, what the purpose of the maneuver was, and that the tactical and operative orders would not always be to their liking. He did not mention names, and the sharp criticism he aimed at Dayan was couched in general terms. The Greens' behavior, he claimed, indicated rank immaturity. But before he finished, he could not refrain from loosing one dart directly at Dayan by relating the following anecdote. Four pirates sat playing poker quietly, until one of them rose and said, angrily, "I don't want to mention names, but if someone here doesn't stop cheating I'll put his other eye out!"

Yadin, in his own words, was drawn to Dayan by his charm and sense of humor, and had it not been for Yadin's attraction to his subordinate, the relationship between the two might have become severely strained. Yadin was fond of recalling the following incident. In 1952 GHQ launched a special road-safety campaign. He instructed the Military Police to deal severely with anyone caught driving at speeds higher than 70 kilometers an hour, regardless of rank, position, or mission. One day the Commander of the Military Police reported to Yadin that his men had caught Maj. Gen. Moshe Dayan, driving at speeds higher than 120 kilometers an hour. Yadin ordered the Military Police to court-martial him like any other soldier. But the Commander of the Military Police had not completed his report. When the MP stopped Dayan and said, "Sir, didn't you notice that you were driving at 120 kilometers an hour?" Dayan returned, "Excuse me, I have only one eye. What do you want me to look at, the speedometer or the road?" Yadin told the commander, "For that reply, let him go."

Yadin nonetheless felt that Dayan was immature, and had little patience for his constant insubordination. His main flaw, in Yadin's estimation, was his disregard for staff work.

At the end of 1951 Dayan was sent to the British Army's Senior Officers' School in Devizes, England. Although he had been skeptical about the ex-British Army officers serving in Zahal, Dayan found the course at Devizes valuable. He corresponded with Yadin. His letters related how he "found great interest in the course," that he was "studying extremely well," and that armor was the main topic of the course. His craving for formal military instruction had grown so that he requested permission from Yadin to take additional courses, even at a lower level. Yadin did not approve the request but noted that Dayan was among those self-taught men, or men who have a sense of their own strength, who are generally reluctant to admit that they have anything more to learn. After being broken once, however, and discovering the scope of their ignorance, they are intoxicated by studies and develop an unquenchable thirst for knowledge.

When Dayan returned from England, Yadin invited him to his office and offered him the post of Deputy C-o-S, placing him in line to be next, or after next, C-o-S. But Dayan claimed that he did not believe in deputies. To be a deputy meant to identify with the views of another, or at least to express such identification, which was something he could not bring himself to do. Yadin was one person; he another. According to Dayan, they had always been on friendly terms, but to the same extent they had also maintained separate and often contradictory views. As a deputy, if he voiced his reservations he would be disloyal; if he kept silent, he would be untrue to himself.

When Yadin was certain that Dayan would not be his second-in-command, he called on Maklef to return from London (where he had begun studying business administration) and resume his post as deputy. On May 26, 1952 Maklef returned to his post as Deputy C-o-S, and Dayan was appointed OC Northern Command.

In the six months Dayan served as OC Northern Command, he dealt extensively with training and field exercises. He was not unlike a first-year university student who wishes to share his new and fascinating discoveries with all the freshmen. Chaim Bar-Lev, who was appointed C-o-S of the command, was an officer of the line and an experienced instructor. The first task Dayan charged him with was preparing a war game in which he could stage the assault of a fortified objective using the methods he had learned in England.

One of the men who observed Dayan's first steps as OC Northern Command with interest was the Command Intelligence Officer, a young major named Ariel Sharon, the man who was later to create the crack paratroop force of Zahal and assist C-o-S Dayan in raising the spirit and fighting ability of the army. Sharon recalls that, much to his surprise, Dayan instilled a new spirit in the command. His first act was to gather all the officers in the canteen and talk to them about their service in the Regular Army. Many of the officers gave the distinct impression that they were doing the nation a favor. In an attempt to counter this phenomenon, GHQ developed a method of persuasion composed of high-flown rhetoric about national duty, promises of material benefits, and a large proportion of plain begging. Moshe's approach was entirely different. His appeal to his officers was: You're here, and so am I, and there is no need to explain what we're doing here. Whoever wants to stay on and serve is welcome. I'll be glad to work with him. Anyone who doesn't want to, who feels as though he's being forced into something, or thinks he is doing the people of Israel a personal favor is free to get up and leave. I don't ask anyone here to serve in the army against his will. That's it. And good luck to you all. In the circumstances of the times this "don't-do-us-any-favors" approach was nothing short of revolutionary. It was greeted with approval and some relief by those officers for whom the army was both a national service and a personal ambition. They borrowed Dayan's approach and applied it to their own commands.

In effect, Northern Command may be regarded as the starting point of Dayan's leadership in Zahal. It was here that he began developing an army in which soldiers were proud to serve. Almost everything he did from then on was completely original and often revolutionary. The change of mood in the command was instantaneous. Since operative actions were few and far between, he immediately instituted an extensive training program of tactical exercises, with and without troops, and two-sided maneuvers. He would sum up these exercises out in the open, generally to the accompaniment of munching on fruit. Their heads deep in red slices of dripping watermelon, his officers would listen to summaries or to a lecture on defense or attack. He once concluded a two-sided exercise by saying that neither side had won, because Zahal cannot defeat Zahal. Yadin winced when he heard of this. Once again Dayan proved how different he could be when given command, when he himself directed an exercise.

His leadership in combat also began to crystallize in Northern Command. One of his guiding principles emerged from a two-sided exercise. When one of the brigade commanders informed Exercise HQ that his own headquarters were surrounded, Dayan asked why he thought so. The officer told him that the opposing force had cut off his HQ from the main body of the brigade. Dayan replied in a few sentences that were to become famous throughout Zahal: "In that case, perhaps your opponent is surrounded? Being surrounded is a matter of perspective, of feeling, not a physical thing. From my point of view, you are not surrounded—your opponent is surrounded. Act accordingly."

15   CHIEF OF OPERATIONS
(1952-1953)

Lt. Gen. Yadin's term of office as C-o-S spanned the years of the mass immigration to Israel. In the first years of Israel's existence (1948-52), the Jewish population of the state was doubled by the arrival of 700,000 immigrants, and 580,000 of these entered the country over a period of three years (1949-51). Transition camps, an austerity economy, unemployment, and a shortage of vital services all generated bitterness and a wave of harsh criticism against government agencies, which were floundering under the burden of immigrant abosrption. In the face of the government's helplessness, Yadin responded by ordering Zahal to come to its assistance. Instead of spending their time only in military training, soldiers assisted in setting up transition camps, administering them, and providing the immigrants with education, food, and even instruction in methods of agriculture. Furthermore, the army succeeded where the civilian authorities had failed.

Members of Mapai—by now Israel's largest party—pointed out to Ben Gurion that public opinion of this sort would provide fertile ground for a military takeover—a "Putsch," as they called it. Some also tried to incite Ben Gurion with a petty equation: the public gives all the credit to Zahal—that is, its commander, Lt. Gen. Yadin—and vents all its displeasures on the government and the largest party—that is, Ben Gurion. But the envy of Mapai functionaries and the fear of a "Putsch" would have been insignificant were it not for an affair, on the same background, which crossed paths with this attitude and ultimately determined the course of events.

In the middle of 1952, financial difficulties, particularly a shortage of foreign currency, brought about a government decision to cut Zahal's budget by IL 10 million, a considerable slice out of its total budget of IL 50 million. Moreover, Ben Gurion gave Yadin clear instructions on how the cut should be implemented, namely, by effecting the discharge of 6,000 military and civilian personnel. This order was to become a bone of contention between the two men. Yadin insisted that he be given leave to achieve the savings in his own way, by reducing the size of some of the units, while Ben Gurion demanded that he completely disband certain Zahal frameworks and discharge their personnel.

Yadin felt that if Ben Gurion did not accept his proposals, the only possible conclusion was that he had lost faith in him. On November 22, 1952 he wrote four separate letters to Ben Gurion and sent them off together. One letter was a request to be released from his post;

the second explained the first; the third was a continuation of their correspondence about the correct way of effecting the savings; and the fourth was a personal letter. Ben Gurion was astounded by Yadin's reaction and in an uncharacteristic move asked him to withdraw his resignation. But Yadin was firmly resolved.

At this point, Ben Gurion took an unprecedented step: he offered Yadin the post of Minister of Defense; that is, he proposed that Yadin leave the army and enter the government as a Cabinet minister, thus becoming free to carry out the military-budget cuts as he saw fit. But Yadin rejected this suggestion as well, for he considered it vital that the Prime Minister also hold the Defense portfolio. He retired from the army and returned to the study of archaeology at the Hebrew University, Jerusalem.

Ben Gurion parted from Yadin with a heavy heart and wrote him a unique letter of farewell, studded with superlatives. He continued to value Yadin highly as a man of the finest virtues, the most gifted of the entire younger generation of the War of Independence, and the man best suited to fulfill important national functions. Eventually, he offered Yadin the post of Minister of Education and in 1963, with his final resignation from the government, the position of Prime Minister.

Before his appointment as C-o-S, Mordechai Maklef requested Ben Gurion's approval for the appointment of Yitzhak Rabin as Deputy C-o-S and Chief of G Branch. But when his personal choice was vetoed, Maklef agreed to Ben Gurion's candidate, Maj. Gen. Moshe Dayan. Dayan, however, still retained his objection to serving as a deputy and expressed the wish to be appointed Chief of G Branch only. In this position, he felt, he would be free to express his own views and would not be obliged to identify in all things with his chief. On December 7, 1952 both men assumed their new posts. The two agreed that since Dayan had refused to become a deputy, as Chief of G Branch he would be the senior head of a branch in GHQ and acting C-o-S in Maklef's absence. Dayan would thus enjoy the privileges of a deputy without any of the obligations.

In Nahalal, Dayan's appointment evoked surprise that bordered on amazement, as did his subsequent appointment as C-o-S. It was generally agreed that he was a daring and valiant fighter and a good battalion and even brigade commander. But the post of Front Commander already seemed beyond his powers, and Chief of G Branch and later C-o-S—with all the logistics and administration they entailed— seemed impossible to the men of Nahalal. His appointment one year later as C-o-S was not only regarded as strange to some of his childhood acquaintances, but a downright irresponsible act on the part of Ben Gurion.

To a great extent, opinion in Nahalal was indicative of a much wider range of public opinion, both military and civilian. Dayan's image at this stage was still that of an unruly, insubordinate troublemaker. Even Ben Gurion—his principal, consistent, and perhaps lone supporter—was not altogether certain that his choice was wise. These doubts were occasioned mainly by Dayan's behavior, but no less by the fact that he was a man unto himself—a lone wolf, as he had begun to be known. In contrast to others of equal rank, he did not have a solid bloc of supporters, either in military circles or in the Mapai leadership, and certainly not in the other political parties. His opinions, thoughts, reflections, and plans were known only to himself. Dayan was an unknown quantity, and therefore suspect.

Maklef described him as a "tough customer," primarily because he was forever unpredictable. Not that Dayan's reasoning was defective; Maklef considered it excellent. But conclusions reached in GHQ were never final. "We would think we had finalized something, and then he would come in the next day with something new." Lacking patience, Dayan also gave instructions that frequently appeared to contradict his own previous orders or those issued by the C-o-S. Thus, although not motivated by disloyalty, his actions were often interpreted as such. Further difficulties were created by the differences of opinion between the two on matters of discipline. Maklef was a stickler for order, while Dayan never bothered to check if a soldier's shoes were laced, if he was wearing a hat, or if the hat was perched on his head at the appropriate angle. Maklef believed that Dayan had so tempestuous a nature "that . . . he could never have been [Zahal's] Number Two."

From the beginning of his term of office, it was clear that Dayan did not understand the functions of orderly staff work and had no inclination whatsoever for administrative matters. This characteristic remained unchanged as C-o-S. His first chief aide, Shlomo Gazit, described these qualities with an illustration from parade drill. When a column is marching in a line and is given the order for a right turn, the first man in the line turns on the spot, while the rest have to travel successively longer distances to cover the ground and keep the line. The same phenomemon in matters of administration was beyond Dayan's comprehension. As far as he was concerned, the entire column turned on the spot like the first soldier in the line. The fact that the others had to run meant nothing to him. He believed that juggling things about had its positive side in that change for its own sake is a good thing. Zahal seemed to him a cumbersome machine, and he considered it important to be jarred from time to time, being forced to move, decide, change, so that things would not stultify.

In Yadin's time a system evolved whereby the C-o-S was the Commander of the Army (Israeli law does not stipulate who is the commander of the army) while the Deputy C-o-S or Chief of G Branch served as Chief of Staff to the C-o-S. Maklef's main difficulty was that Moshe Dayan did not fulfill the function of his Chief-of-Staff, coordinating the staff divisions and running the army according to his orders. Dayan was also not part of a group, a man who would execute the C-o-S's orders by working as one of a team. He dealt exclusively with issues that interested him and delineated his own area of responsibility. He tried—with complete success—not to interfere in the work of the other branches, which were his direct responsibility, at least in theory. Maklef was therefore forced to serve as his own Chief-of-Staff.

The relations between Maklef and Dayan may best be described as a classic example of a lack of communication. Maklef commented that Dayan "doesn't quarrel with people, he simply breaks off communications with them." He soon learned that "Maj. Gen. Dayan cannot be tamed," that it was impossible "to get him to toe the line," that he had "exceptional combat cunning," radiated "charismatic leadership to soldiers and people in general," and that he did not understand—or did not wish to understand—the mechanism of staff work. Dayan simply delegated all the coordination duties and contacts to his assistant, Col. Meir Amit. Much as it vexed Maklef, he had to admit that Dayan's way of working left him leisure to think. A situation therefore developed in which the C-o-S was overburdened with details of staff work, issues of logistics, and personnel, while his deputy enjoyed free time for reflection and reviewing military issues in broad perspective. Relations between the two became increasingly strained, and in August Dayan asked Ben Gurion for study leave. Ben Gurion agreed in principle but postponed Dayan's leave until the following year.

In addition to troubles with his senior staff officer, less than six months after taking office Maklef began to encounter difficulties with his superior, Acting Minister of Defense Pinhas Lavon. As Ben Gurion had planned to retire for two or three years, he asked the Cabinet for a two-month leave in order to study the country's security problems and leave his successor a clearly structured line to follow. (Foreign Minister Moshe Sharett became Acting Prime Minister.) Ben Gurion's leave came to an end on October 17. On the 19th and 20th, the government heard and unanimously approved his eighteen proposals on army and general security issues, and on the 20th he announced his wish to retire from office immediately. While he retained his two posts for a short time to enable his successor as Prime Minister to form his own coalition, Ben Gurion intervened little in the routine work of the Ministry of Defense and came in only on matters of major importance, leaving more and more of the routine work to Pinhas Lavon. On December 7 he resigned and on December 14 he moved with his wife, Paula, to the Negev kibbutz of Sde Boker.

Lavon served as Acting Minister of Defense throughout the latter half of 1953. He will probably remain a mystery. Thin, stooped, his hair prematurely grey, bibulous, learned, nimble-witted and sharp-tongued, intellectually head and shoulders above the majority of Mapai leaders, Lavon had risen through the ranks of the Histadrut. The transition from a labor union to the national platform, and particularly to the Ministry of Defense, produced contrasts of which no one had suspected him capable. According to his followers, he was "an anti-activist, one of the most consistent . . . who was opposed to a policy of force which might jeopardize what had already been achieved." Yet upon entering the post of Minister of Defense, Lavon underwent a transformation from sworn pacifist to extreme activist; from a scholar delving into the teachings of the Socialist vision to a compulsive action-seeker and advocate of change; from a preacher of the fraternity of nations to an Arab-scorning nationalist; from a prophet of social justice and champion of the general good to an egoist who would turn the world inside out to seek redress for what he considered a personal injustice. Lavon, as Ben Gurion later described him, was "a mistake." And the first person who tried—in vain—to warn Ben Gurion of the extent of the mistake was Maklef.

Lavon and Maklef were at loggerheads from the start, initially because Maklef sensed that Lavon was privately contemptuous of the army and regarded officers as "bureaucrats in uniform."

The lack of mutual respect between Maklef and Lavon served as the background—though not the direct cause—of a crisis in their relations over the issue of the structure of the General Staff and the Ministry of Defense. Maklef was opposed to what he called a duplication of functions, that is, maintaining manpower and supply divisions both in GHQ and in the Ministry of Defense. He wished to apply the American system, whereby the Minister of Defense would appoint personal assistants to deal with issues of manpower, material, and supply. The special assistants would issue directives to be executed by the corresponding GHQ branches. This would mean a smaller Ministry of Defense, which would now become a guiding political and economic body, while General Staff would have the administrative apparatus and the manpower to execute its directives. In the course of this dispute, Lavon, Dayan, and Shimon Peres (then Acting Director-General of the Ministry of Defense) formed an anti-Maklef alliance. Dayan welcomed Lavon's appointment as Ben Gurion's replacement for he also felt that Zahal should not be saddled with anything that did not serve its sole purpose—making war. This stand further aggravated the tension between Dayan and his commanding officer.

The weakness of Maklef's position stemmed partially from the fact that he had to effect his desired changes alone, while his opponents' purpose was served by the prevailing circumstances. Maklef interpreted opposition to his reform as an effort to restrict his authority. He feared that Lavon and Peres were conspiring to create a strong Ministry of Defense which would circumscribe his powers as C-o-S. Why did Dayan support them? Perhaps to weaken Maklef and hasten his retirement, so that he could become C-o-S. In a last effort to save his position, Maklef demanded—in what amounted to an ultimatum— that Dayan, Peres, and a few others be dismissed. His struggle was doomed from the outset, and at its conclusion he found himself weaker and more isolated than ever.

This conflict occurred as Ben Gurion's retirement became a certainty. He did not consider removing Dayan, as Maklef had demanded; on the contrary, he wanted Dayan for C-o-S. Consequently, on December 6, 1952, a day before Ben Gurion tendered his resignation to the President, Maklef carried out one of the conditions he had stipulated upon taking office and handed in his resignation. In fact, on the morning of the 6th Ben Gurion appointed Dayan C-o-S, effective from 4 p.m., and then drove from Tel Aviv to Jerusalem to hand in his resignation. When Ben Gurion parted from the nation in his radio broadcast, Dayan was already the new C-o-S.

Despite the short time he served as C-o-S, Maklef made important advances toward shaping Zahal into a fighting force, a task which Dayan carried on with increased momentum. In reducing the number of Regular Army officers and civilians working for Zahal, as Ben Gurion had instructed him, Maklef saw a rare opportunity to rid the army of older and unsuitable personnel, men who might otherwise stand in the way of younger, more talented officers. As Chief of G Branch, Dayan became involved in these reductions of manpower, and as C-o-S he accelerated the process even without explicit orders to cut costs. Dayan took the revolutionary step of cutting down on personnel and investing the money saved in the acquisition of combat equipment under the slogan "better bayonets than stoves." At one of the Senior Commanders' Conferences, officers complained of a shortage of shirts in their units, to which Dayan replied, "I won't be bothered with shirts. What concerns me is whether there are enough rifles." And in a conversation with soldiers who complained about the sorry condition of their mess hall, he replied with some heat, "Garibaldi and his men didn't have a mess hall at all."

A more important trend begun by Maklef was assigning first-rate, better educated recruits to combat units. During his own term of office, Dayan energetically continued this process as well. Another beginning which was to gain crucial importance was Maklef's decision to form Unit 101, a group of hand-picked, daring fighters, out of which Dayan later built the paratroop unit of Zahal. Thus steps initiated by Maklef became an integral part of Dayan's achievements, and the path he was to follow as C-o-S actually began during the time he served as Chief of G Branch. It is therefore reasonable to regard Dayan's terms as Chief of G Branch and as C-o-S as a single entity.

By employing shock tactics, Dayan created an immediate awareness of his presence as "Number Two" in Zahal. To begin with, he ate in the regular GHQ officers' mess, which catered mostly to officers up to the rank of lieutenant colonel and rarely to full colonels. Moreover, when Dayan first took a seat at the long table, he rolled a slice of bread into a ball and threw it at the waiter to attract his attention. At the time, GHQ was situated on a hill in Ramat Gan, and the offices of the Chief of G Branch were on a slightly higher level, virtually a second story. December 1952 was a rainy month, and whenever the skies cleared a bit Dayan would leave his office and warm himself in the sun, dictating to his secretary, holding meetings with his aides, or chatting with visitors on the steps or on one of the stones lining the path. One of his first visits as Chief of G Branch was to an artillery unit. On the way he told his driver to stop near one of the orange groves along the road. Dayan got out of the car, climbed through the fence, and picked an armful of oranges, which he and his escorts ate on the way. When they arrived at the base, there were still two left. A guard of honor received them, and as the sergeant-major raised his hand to salute, Dayan shouted "Catch!" and threw him an orange.

Shimon Peres recalls that one day some of his aides rushed into his office in the Ministry of Defense—which was also on the hill in Ramat Gan—and shouted "The Chief of G Branch has gone completely mad. Do something!" Peres went outside and saw Maj. Gen. Dayan standing on the porch, shotgun in hand, coolly firing away. Dayan explained that he was shooting wild pigeons, which abound on the hill. He had invited some friends to dinner and had promised Ruth he would see to the meat. His secretary, Lt. Neora Matalon, also recalls an unusual meeting that was called for a Saturday. She arrived with Shlomo Gazit at the appointed hour and opened the office. Then they saw the general approaching, "sloppily dressed and in sandals," shotgun in hand. He had come to tell them that the meeting was canceled and that he was going hunting—dinner again, this time for twenty-five guests. He began firing in Bnei Brak, a strictly religious suburb of Tel Aviv, and stopped only after Neora cried "You must be crazy! This is Bnei Brak!" This was typical of their informal relationship. According to Neora, "He restrained himself until Mikve Yisrael" (an agricultural school west of Tel Aviv), where he drove the car straight into the fields. One of the wheels sank in a pothole and they were unable to move until a taxi driver who caught sight of them from the main road helped them extricate the car. The catch at Mikve Yisrael was meager, so they drove on until Dayan stopped the car in the middle of the road and disappeared into an orange grove. Drivers found their way blocked, began sounding their horns, and were alarmed by the sound of gunfire issuing from the grove. Only after he had bagged fifty wild pigeons did Dayan call it a day and return home.

His style of dress made it quite evident that etiquette and regulations were of little concern to him. Though he was particular about his personal cleanliness and in the summer often showered several times a day, he did not find it necessary to wear polished shoes or pressed uniforms. Neora described him as "a terrible *shlumper*" (Yiddish for sloppy dresser). He was capable of arriving at a passing-out parade of officers after sleeping in the back seat of his car. He would walk along the parade ground with pants bagging at the knees and socks falling about his ankles. His staff decided to force him to alter his appearance by keeping sets of freshly pressed uniforms in the office and persuading him to change uniforms and dress properly for parades, public appearances, or meetings.

Within a short time everyone in GHQ, and many people outside it, knew that there was a new Chief of G Branch. For several weeks after he assumed office, Dayan was the central topic of conversation. Once he felt he had achieved the aim of asserting his presence and setting himself apart from the common run of General Staff officers, his pranks ceased. When he was appointed C-o-S, however, he again took steps to emphasize dramatically that he was now "Number One." He rearranged the offices in the C-o-S's suite, taking for himself the smallest room, which had previously served his predecessor's chief aide. Yadin and Maklef's long, luxurious room, in which a visitor had to traverse a considerable distance before reaching the C-o-S, now became a regular conference room. He also canceled the post of the C-o-S's adjutant, a position that had been imported into Zahal from the British Army, for he considered it foreign, unnecessary, and against the grain of Zahal field officers. He also lacked patience for pomp and ceremony.

The act that most impressed Zahal was replacing the imposing, horseshoe-shaped desk Yadin had ordered with a regulation field table covered by an army blanket. The small room, in which no more than four people could sit comfortably, now acquired the intimate, companiable atmosphere of a HQ tent in the field. When GHQ moved from Ramat Gan to its new offices in Tel Aviv, Dayan's aides took the opportunity to change the rough field table for a well-finished field-style table ordered from a Tel Aviv carpenter. Later they also covered the table with a glass top. Yet even in the new building, Dayan refused to use air conditioning to demonstrate his solidarity with the combat units in the field.

Dayan's choice of aides was unconventional, and they enjoyed the same broad delegation of power that he practiced with his staff officers in the two commands. When he came to GHQ as Chief of G Branch, he brought no loyal supporters, old friends, or even aides from previous posts. He "inherited" Lt. Col. Shlomo Gazit, who had been Maklef's chief aide. As it was accepted practice for senior officers to bring their own aides, Gazit understood that his days with Dayan were numbered. Nonetheless, Dayan retained Gazit as his chief aide, though he would sometimes check up to make sure he was carrying out his duties faithfully. On the one hand, Gazit felt as though he was on his way out; but on the other he was struck by the fact that Dayan increasingly brought him in on the inner workings of G Branch and entrusted him with entirely new areas of responsibility. The ice was finally broken during a meeting when Dayan passed Gazit a note in which he asked a question in rhyme, and Gazit replied with a limerick.

Red-headed Neora Matalon was responsible for Dayan's daily schedule, which was not especially complicated. One day each week was devoted to visiting units and solving problems on the spot, instead of referring them to GHQ; another was reserved for personal meetings with heads of branches and corps; a third was taken up by the weekly meeting and conference with the Minister of Defense; and Friday, at Dayan's request, was left free whenever possible so that he could pursue his new hobby, digging for antiquities. Since, in Neora's words, "he likes his free time," the only instruction she received was to leave him as much free time as possible. As a result, meetings with Dayan did not have to be set three weeks in advance, and two or three meetings could be arranged for the same or the following day. Dayan still arranges his daily schedule in this fashion.

An unwritten but important task fell to Dayan's aides as a result of the fatigue of his one eye: to hand in only short memoranda, and when longer ones arrived to draw up brief summaries. He did not, however, request newspaper clippings and went through papers himself. In his free time, he and his staff would sit like a group of old friends in the anteroom or the typists' office. Often he would read out the draft of an Order of the Day or a speech, recite poems by Natan Alterman, or even relate some of his personal experiences. He was extremely sensitive to public opinion and would prepare his statements very carefully, the small group in his office serving as a preview audience.

In the winter of 1954, Dayan was "overcome quite suddenly" by a passion for archaeology. His interest was aroused accidentally. One Saturday he went hunting wild pigeons with his thirteen-year-old son Ehud. They wandered in the fields southeast of Masmiye and reached Tel el-Zafi. To his amazement, Dayan saw jars standing upright in the wadi. At first he thought that local Arabs had left them there, but when he drew closer he found that heavy rains had washed away the earth covering them. He took one of the jars and on a subsequent trip to Jerusalem showed it to Yigael Yadin, by now a well-known archaeologist. Yadin estimated that the jar was approximately 3,000 years old and belonged to the Israelite period. Dayan was thrilled and at the first opportunity returned to the tel (archaeological mound) which had been a settlement during the Canaanite and Israelite periods. He began scooping out the earth and suddenly, "as I began digging, a whole room opened up. The jars stood here, the lamps there; here was the floor, the place of ritual. It was as if I had entered the days of King David." From then on, digging for, uncovering, and reconstructing antiquities was to become a central preoccupation in his life and the cause, on more than one occasion, for breaking the law. He once said that if he were given the choice of digging for antiquities half of his life and spending the other half in jail, or not digging at all and remaining a free man, he would choose the former.

Since 1954 Dayan has amassed a collection of antiquities unrivaled by any private collector. The unique aspect of the collection is the fact that Dayan himself uncovered and reconstructed most of the pieces. He has made the repair of ancient pottery a high form of art. Recently he laid out a garden of antiquities which in the dark looks like a legendary country stretching back to the distant past. It is as though Dayan has enlarged his world in time and space. The precious relics in the garden, as well as in his house, have made ancient Israel, Egypt, Mesopotamia, and the Mediterranean islands an inseparable part of his daily thoughts. Public opinion, however, censured Dayan for his disregard for convention and the laws of the state. Lawlessness became another element of his image, lending a somber, somewhat frightening, and even repellent overtone to his natural leadership.

(1953-1954)

Zahal's inadequacy was epitomized for Dayan by two incidents that occurred in the first month of his term as Chief of G Branch. The first occurred on the night of December 14, 1952, when a group of soldiers tried to bring ammunition to the guards on Mount Scopus, the Israeli enclave in Jordanian-held Jerusalem. After one or two shots were fired in their direction by the Jordanian guard, they turned tail and ran, abandoning their packs and a few hats with their names and indentification numbers on them. According to Commander Hutchinson, the chairman of the Israel-Jordan Mixed Armistice Commission, the Israelis tried to retrieve the equipment that night but were repulsed.

The second incident was far more serious. On the night of January 22, 1953, a company of Israeli soldiers crossed the armistice lines to blow up several houses in the village of Falama, near Kibya, as a retaliatory action. When the unit reached the outskirts of the village, the local militia opened fire, killing one of the attacking force and wounding five others. The unit then retreated to Israeli territory without carrying out its mission. The casualties it had suffered were considered proof of the enemy's superiority and sufficient justification for a retreat. For Dayan, however, the failure at Falama was a clear indication that Zahal was incapable of implementing the policy of retaliation initiated in 1950, when it became clear beyond all doubt that the Armistice Agreements would not achieve their stated aim of bringing peace. Arab infiltration into Israeli territory increased steadily. It was easy to penetrate the unfortified border and attack the new immigrant settlements hastily set up along the armistice lines and in the wide, empty Negev desert. But what had begun as spontaneous and haphazard acts of infiltration gradually came under the official wing first of Jordan and then of Egypt.

During 1952-4, the infiltrators reaped success. Transport to and from the settlements became hazardous and sometimes ceased completely for fear of ambushes, mines, and mortar attacks. Inhabitants of the large cities were afraid to venture outside the city limits, and youth groups refrained from going out on excursions. The public looked to Zahal, but it was incapable of imposing order on the borders and more remote areas of the country. The Knesset and the press leveled bitter criticism at the army for its ineffectiveness. Zahal attempted to reciprocate an eye for an eye, and every so often small units were sent across the border to blow up a house or a well in retaliation. Falama was only one example of the failure of such combat units between 1951 and October 1953.

There were reasons and excuses for these failures. Zahal was still in the process of reorganization after the war. The entire army was undergoing a transition from the partisan army of 1948 to the Regular Army of a sovereign state. The majority of the soldiers in combat units were new immigrants who had not yet been integrated into the country. The senior officers did not trust their soldiers and did not rely on their junior officers. Training did not effectively prepare the men for aggressive warfare, and units spent part of their training time in tasks concerned with immigrant absorption—"growing tomatoes." as it was called. Training methods and equipment were still mostly borrowed from foreign armies and were unsuited to the conditions and needs of Israel.

It was Dayan who drove Zahal to deal with routine security as its principal undertaking and considered the small actions an inseparable part of the army's ability to undertake large-scale ones. The principal difference between him and other officers was that while others were willing to accept a variety of excuses, Dayan flatly rejected them all; others blamed lower echelons of command, or unsuitable equipment, or lack of correct guidance, while Dayan blamed everyone from GHQ down for the failure. What particularly annoyed him at the GHQ level was that failures were regarded as the result of objective circumstances. He admitted that it "drove me mad . . . when they accepted the excuse that it was genuinely impossible, that their inability to penetrate Falama was all right, that the operative turn of events made it impossible to carry out the mission. After Falama I moaned . . . 'They can't even reach a house or a well? What's going on here?'"

Dayan's drive to raise the combat fitness and fighting spirit of Zahal began at this point. His first step was to make Falama a byword, the shameful symbol of all Zahal's failures. He intimidated the officers with the fear of being branded with the stigma "Falama" and did something that was a unique expression of his personality: he arbitrarily ruled that "any officer in Zahal who shrinks from fulfilling his mission before the majority of his soldiers, or at least half of them, have been hit will be dismissed from his post." This significant—and highly effective—statement was made without the foreknowledge of C-o-S Maklef. Although he shared Dayan's view that Zahal must become a more effective fighting force, Maklef said, "I would not have expressed it the way he did."

The outline of what was to become Dayan's doctrine crystallized slowly and in stages, and it was only in the autumn of 1955, two and a half years after Falama, that he delivered a lecture to Zahal officers on "Military Actions in Peacetime," which was his own thesis set out under sixteen headings. In 1953, however, he was still guided by intuition.

Dayan stood alone in his view that the success of a mission should be measured against the achievement of its goal. While his colleagues accepted with equanimity actions that ended without the aim having been fulfilled and without casualties, Dayan was outraged; and while they criticized actions that achieved their purpose but were costly in casualties, he felt that the end justified the losses. A case in point was the Tel Mutilla action in May 1951, which drove the Syrians back from positions they had taken on the Israeli side of the Jordan River's entrance into Lake Kinneret at the cost of twenty-seven Zahal soldiers. Even before the GHQ survey, Dayan (who was then still OC Southern Command) came to the area and asked Meir Amit and Rehav'am Ze'evi ("Ghandi")—the brigade commander and battalion commander, respectively—for a description of the action. He later inspected the area a second time with the General Staff. In the summing up, the brigade and battalion commanders were harshly criticized, and the action was pronounced a complete failure because of the high number of casualties. Dayan was the only one who felt otherwise, maintaining that the importance of the Tel Mutilla action lay in the perseverance displayed by the officers and the soldiers.

Before Dayan became Chief of G Branch, units would sometimes return from an action without having fulfilled their mission, and the commanders would invariably offer the excuse that there had been four or five casualties. As Chief of G Branch, Dayan was not prepared to accept this explanation. After the Falama action, he met the battalion commander near the border and asked him point-blank how many men had been killed. From the officer's reply, he concluded that his losses had not justified a retreat before the completion of the mission.

Dayan's demand that missions continue until casualties amounted to at least 50% was contrary to the attitude prevalent in the country. Israel, with its small Jewish population, and the Jewish nation as a whole, in the wake of the Nazi holocaust, were gripped by the sense of being a diminishing tribe. Life was dearer than all else, sometimes even national security. This sensitivity to the value of an individual's life was a guiding factor in the planning and execution of actions. On certain occasions it bordered on the ridiculous: concern for soldiers' health might well interrupt training in rain or bad weather. Dayan believed that it was in the interests of national security to overcome the sensitivity concerning losses. In contrast to his contemporaries, his strength lay in the ability to overcome his own sensitivity and compassion and accept responsibility for mangled limbs and lost lives.

Nevertheless, the choice of 50% as a justifiable minimum was a random one. Initially Dayan tried a method of persuasion, though in his own original way. He brought together G Branch personnel from all sectors of the army at conferences devoted to the issue of fighting spirit and emphasized that the most important thing is the will to act. When this factor exists, every aspect of the mission is exhausted, even when the order is not entirely clear and in the absence of charts or precise operation plans; but when the will is lacking, nothing can help, not even the clearest orders, the most accurate diagrams, or the most brilliant plans. The key phrase in Dayan's address was "exhausting the mission."

At that stage in the development of his outlook, Dayan believed the fault in Zahal's behavior in battle lay in the distance of the commanding officers from the action itself. The order "Follow me!" was to become a sacred tenet of his doctrine only after his 1955 lecture on "Military Actions in Peacetime," when he stated: "The commander is not 'the most valuable man in the unit,' who must be protected from injury. The most valuable thing for a unit is the enemy objective . . . Controlling a unit does not mean a wordy communication given personally or in writing . . . The chief means is leadership: the order 'Follow me!'"

Maj. Gen. Laskov viewed the Falama-style failures differently. He believed they occurred because of inadequate training. But Dayan was convinced that if officers led their troops, everything would function smoothly. He also wanted only one man to bear the responsibility for a mission. His outlook eventually raised the question of why Zahal fared so well in the 1948 war.

The War of Independence was a war of heroism. Dayan did not dispute this. But unlike his colleagues, he added an important qualification, namely, that it was in the main a defensive war, and the heroism of men and units was motivated by the fact that they were defending their homes. A defensive war is also one of no alternative, and the self-sacrifice it occasions is totally unlike that demanded in an aggressive war, where the soldier in the field does have an alternative. In the latter case, sacrifice is made for comrades, or the commander, or what is known as the "honor of the unit." Dayan perceived this difference at the beginning of 1953 and later incorporated it into his doctrine as the tenth paragraph of his 1955 address: " . . . The soldiers and officers now being trained in the army are tested not in defensive battles but in attack, and stories of the wondrous deeds of the War of Independence and promises that we will fight likewise in the next war are simply not enough." Ben Gurion and Yadin had already established the principle that the next war would not be fought on Israeli territory. Even in the event of a surprise Arab attack, the fighting was to be shifted onto enemy ground. In practical terms this meant preparing Zahal for an offensive war. When Dayan became Chief of G Branch, Zahal was incapable of carrying out even minor attacks across the border. It was he who first trained Zahal to follow the cardinal rule of Israel's security: defense through attack.

For this purpose, Dayan gathered ten of his men and instructed them to prepare tactical exercises without troops in order to practice breaking through a fortified line. The unique aspect of this exercise was Dayan's directive that no solutions involving sophisticated flanking, surprise, or attack deep in the rear would be acceptable. He ordered an exercise that would "be devoid of Jewish cleverness. The way of exhausting the mission will be by frontal attack, fighting hard on the objective, and paying for it with lives."

This directive surprised his men. Yuval Ne'eman (Head of Planning Division) recalls that it "disturbed" him: "I had just returned from the École de Guerre, where I was taught solutions such as the one Moshe wanted, and yet I always found a 'Jewish way,' the kind that finds a substitute for hard fighting on the objective. But here Moshe, of all people—the master of stratagems—demanded the kind of solution accepted abroad, a 'non-Jewish' solution." Dayan explained to the planners how deeply he had been affected by the failure at Falama and that the habit of always trying a round-about way with a minimum of losses was liable to produce serious failures and higher casualties if the soldiers were not able and willing to launch a full frontal assault when necessary.

A pass in the Negev Mountains was chosen for the exercise and approximately one hundred officers were invited to take part. As expected, every single one of them initially tried to devise "crafty" solutions, by flanking or a similar action which had been encouraged in Zahal until then. But Exercise HQ directed the exercise so that no solution was possible other than a frontal attack and hard fighting on the objectives. At the end of the exercise, Dayan gave a lecture. The essence of his statement was: "Exhausting the mission must not be affected by losses." One of the participants asked, "How many losses? What is the limit?" And Dayan replied, "Twenty, thirty, even fifty per cent losses." Thus, his directive, which was never issued as a formal order, began to take shape. The same tactical exercise was repeated, with minor modifications and for other officers, throughout the country. It became part of Dayan's campaign to accustom Zahal's officers to the dictum that in war, when there is no other alternative, "You must kill, be killed, and not go round-about."

The concept of exhausting the mission and accepting inevitable losses in the process crystallized as Dayan went from one command to another, gathering all the officers from company commander up and reading them an unequivocal instruction: "Any officer in Zahal who shrinks from carrying out his mission before most of his soldiers—or at least half of them—have been hit will be dismissed from his post." The threat of sanctions emphasized what had already been explained verbally and visually. But an army—as Dayan himself said—is not led on the strength of orders, but by personal example. On this count he was in for several disappointments at the start of his campaign. The most bitter of all was the paratroop battalion, which should have been the crowning glory of Zahal's combat units. Returning from one of their actions in August 1953, the paratroopers reported complete execution of their mission. Dayan was so pleased that he drove to the border to meet them with a bottle of brandy and drank a toast to their success. On the following day, however, when the report of the UN observers on the Jordanian side came through, it transpired that the mission had not been "exhausted" at all, and what the paratroopers thought to be enemy dead were nothing but an ass and two cows.

Many of the border incidents occurred in the area of the Jerusalem Reserve Brigade, which was commanded by Col. Mishael Shaham. Shaham believed that most of the acts of violence against Israel originated in the village of Nebi Samuel, the home of an Arab terrorist who had vowed to kill one hundred Jews. He thought it would be fitting to retaliate by blowing up the man's house. Since there was no unit in his brigade capable of crossing the border, penetrating an Arab village, and blowing up a specific house, and considering the fact that even Regular Army units had failed on such missions, he decided to organize a "team" of outstanding fighters of the 1948 war. He chose one of his own battalion commanders, Ariel Sharon, to lead the mission.

Sharon quickly gathered seven friends, all civilians like himself, and on the night of August 11 they crossed the armistice line and made their way up the mountain to Nebi Samuel. Dressed in civilian clothes, each carrying a heavy load of explosives and arms, they penetrated the village without incident. But they failed to identify the proper house and then put down too few explosives, causing only slight damage. The explosion woke the villagers and Legionnaires in the area, but followed by a hail of bullets, the eight men made it safely back to Jerusalem.

The action proved to Shaham and Sharon that it was possible for a unit to penetrate behind enemy lines and that their mistakes could be corrected by proper training. Shaham dispatched a letter to Maklef proposing the creation of a regular, secret unit that would specialize in guerrilla actions across the border and be administratively attached to the Jerusalem Reserve Brigade. He suggested that Maj. Ariel Sharon be appointed commander of the unit.

When Maklef raised the idea of a special unit at a staff meeting

Dayan opposed it strenuously, claiming that all of Zahal should be on the level of a commando unit. He regarded reprisal raids as the best possible training for the army and feared that being relieved of this responsibility would lower the general ability and fighting spirit even further. In August 1953 Dayan believed that establishing a commando unit to shoulder the entire burden of the retaliatory actions would undermine his own efforts to imbue Zahal with a new spirit and prepare it for an offensive war. Overriding these objections, Maklef issued the necessary orders for the rapid establishment of Unit 101 to be trained and led by twenty-five year old Ariel Sharon, who rejoined the Regular Army.

Unit 101 was to carry out in practice everything Dayan preached in theory. Although he was opposed to its establishment, Dayan was drawn to its men and its commander, particularly to Meir Har-Zion. Even at the peak of its activity, 101 numbered no more than forty men and was more of a partisan gang than a Regular Army unit. Its men dressed as they pleased, in short pants, white or colored shirts, multicolored *keffiyot,* peaked caps, berets, and beards; they were armed with Tommy guns (rather than regulation Zahal arms), Molotov cocktails and commando knives; and they wore no rank insignia. The total disregard for etiquette, spit and polish, inspection, and military hierachy must certainly have endeared the men of 101 to Dayan.

It is doubtful whether Sharon's daring and innovations would have been realized in action had it not been for Meir Har-Zion, a young man with a rare gift for fieldcraft and combat and a genius of individual warfare. Eighteen-year-old Har-Zion (known to his friends as "Har") was born in Kibbutz Ein Harod and resembled the young Moshe Dayan in more ways than one. It is likely that Dayan was aware of this similarity from their first meeting, for he remembered it clearly enough fourteen years later to recount it in great detail.

The unit's baptism by fire came in September 1953, when it was given the task of driving out the Azazma tribe—armed Bedouin carrying Egyptian identification cards who crossed the southern border at will, relaying information to Egyptian Intelligence and often firing on Zahal patrols. The entire tribe, numbering a few hundred men, was driven back into Sinai by sixteen members of 101 on jeeps and command cars. Dayan made a special trip to the southern border to congratulate the men on their success. As he was talking to them, he spotted a large black bird perched on the carcass of a camel, one of the victims of the recent battle. He knelt down quickly and aimed his rifle at the bird. A tall, bushy haired boy in short pants pulled his arm and cried angrily, "What are you doing? That's an eagle! There are only thirty pairs of them left in the country." At first Dayan was enraged by the corporal's audacity, but then admiration for his boldness took him over.

Years later, Dayan called Har-Zion "our greatest warrior since Bar Kokhba," and mentioned him in his article on Zahal's spirit as an exemplary Israeli soldier: "What sets Har-Zion apart is . . . that he is a combination of a daring, tough fighter (capable of enjoying the battle itself) and a farmer who finds fulfillment in hard, routine work." He considered Har-Zion "an amazing fighter and model combat leader."

It is likely that certain qualities they had in common also drew Dayan to the younger man. Har-Zion wrote a lyrical, poetic hiking journal and preferred to hike alone or with a single companion, usually his younger sister, Shoshana. But his expeditions were far more daring and adventurous than any Dayan ever undertook. The main resemblance between them, however, was their inner sensitivity. Like Dayan, Har-Zion did not hate the Arabs and more than once suffered pangs of guilt over the fact that he was forced to fight them. After the rout of the Azazma tribe, he wrote in his diary: "Once again I am beset by this strong feeling of discord. Is this the enemy? Is all this justified? I have yet to experience . . . the feel of battle, the will to victory, the hatred toward one who wishes to take from you what is most precious of all—your life. These first victories have been too easy." Just as Dayan needed to be taught by Wingate and "Killer" to be able to "kill without remorse," Har-Zion was taught in 101 and afterward in the paratroop unit.

One may well describe Har-Zion as the embodiment of Dayan's entire military doctrine. The men of 101, the paratroopers, and later all of Zahal were inspired by him. Dayan gave him a field commission without first sending him to Officers' Training Course: "What would he do in OTC except teach?" Captain Har-Zion served in the army for only three years. He was critically wounded in his throat and arm on September 12, 1956 in Rahawa, during one of the last retaliation raids before the Sinai Campaign. An army doctor saved his life by performing a tracheotomy on the battlefield. Dayan, then C-o-S, waited at the border about 2 kilometers from the objective. Dayan remained near the border only a few moments more. Unable to contain his emotions, he raced his car after the ambulance, waited until they brought Har-Zion out of the operating theater, and stood motionless by his bed for a long time, until the injured man opened his eyes, smiled, and closed them again. His chief aide recalls: "I've never seen such a look on his face. He stood by the bed like a father; you could sense his deep pain. He stood there . . . not to cheer him— there was no one to cheer. He stood there only because of an emotional bond."

Unit 101 proved its battle fitness and fighting spirit for the first time in a retaliatory raid against the village of Kibya. From a military point of view, the Kibya action was the diametric opposite of Falama. If the latter was indicative of a downward trend, Kibya marked the beginning of a surge upward. On the night of October 12, 1953, Arab infiltrators from Jordan penetrated the village of Kfar Yahud and threw a hand grenade into a house dimly lit by a kerosene lamp. In the explosion, a mother and two of her children were killed. Until then infiltrators had killed 124 Israeli citizens, but the triple murder in Kfar Yahud enraged public opinion in Israel as no previous incident had. Reaction was strong on the other side of the border as well. The commander of the Arab Legion personally supervised the inspection of the tracks leading from Kfar Yahud into Jordan and even conveyed a request that the Israeli Government refrain from retaliation, as the Jordan Government itself intended to punish the assassins. This request reached the C-o-S and the Minister of Defense too late, as they were both away from their offices.

At the time a large maneuver was being carried out in the north, in the presence of Ben Gurion (still on leave), Acting Minister of Defense Pinhas Lavon, Maklef and Dayan. Maklef recalls that on the morning of October 13, after hearing the news of the Yahud murders, the four held an impromptu meeting and agreed that a stern reaction was called for. As Zahal knew that the village of Kibya, facing Kfar Yahud across the border, served as a base and refuge for infiltrators, it was decided to attack and destroy about fifty houses. Apparently there was mention of instructing the army not to be deterred if Jordanian civilians were killed in the course of the operation. There is reason to believe that there was talk of ten to twelve Jordanian losses—soldiers and civilians. Dayan was sent to GHQ while the others remained in the north to watch the maneuver.

In accordance with the directives, Dayan drew up an operation order which included an attack on three Jordanian villages—Shukba, Nihilin, and Kibya. Blocking and deception actions were required for the first two, while a large number of houses were to be blown up in the third. The plan was that in the absence of the commander of the 890th Paratroop Battalion, the second-in-command would assume responsibility and take command of all the units participating in the action. The paratroopers were to carry out the principal mission in Kibya, while 101 was assigned supporting actions of blocking and raiding Nihilin and Shukba. During the meeting, however, the second-in-command of the 890th expressed doubts about the ability of the paratroop company to carry out its mission, claiming that it was not fully consolidated as a combat unit. Sharon, the lowest ranking officer present at the meeting, intervened and offered to lead the "unconsolidated" company. The situation was thus reversed, and Sharon became the commander of the operation with both the paratroop company and 101 under his leadership. He drew up his plans and was then called to Dayan's office in GHQ. Sharon received an order to blow up as many houses as possible in Kibya; the number fifty was mentioned. Dayan felt this was an inordinately large number. Dayan feared too many Zahal casualties and counseled Sharon, "Don't insist. If you see that it's very hard going, blow up a few houses and come back." According to Sharon, "I heard what he said and decided to do it all." Dayan then returned north to take part in the maneuver, and Sharon returned to prepare his units for the operation which was to begin that night, October 14.

Participants in the Kibya action later testified that Sharon was aware that the success of the mission would have considerable bearing on the future of his unit, and he was determined not to fail. Before going into battle, he visited his units and told the men, "We don't come back unless we complete the mission," a paraphrase of what Dayan said at the Commanders' Conference. It was clear to Sharon that he would not be deviating from his orders if ten to twelve Jordanians would be killed in the execution of the mission.

One of the daring elements in Sharon's plan was ordering his men to hold their fire until the last possible moment. The raid began at night. The paratroopers and the men of 101 who were spotted by the Jordanian Home Guard did not return the fire that was rained down on them. The lack of any reaction on the part of the raiders astounded the Jordanians, and they laid down their arms in confusion and fled to the darkened fields. When the raiders did open fire, the Jordanian commander and his second-in-command were killed, creating even greater havoc in the ranks of the fleeing Legionnaires. But the raiding force had lost the element of surprise and was now pressed for time. Since the Jordanian reinforcements could be expected to arrive shortly, they had to complete the demolition work quickly.

One hundred and three Zahal soldiers took part in the raid, eighty of whom entered Kibya. The streets of the village were deserted. It looked as though all the inhabitants had fled in the tracks of the retreating Jordanian soldiers. The section commanders marked out forty-five houses, and the soldiers, heavily laden with a total of 700 kg. of dynamite, prepared them for demolition. Sharon and his men were convinced that not a soul remained in the houses. They testified that after the short battle the only sound in the village was the music issuing from a radio left blaring in a deserted café. The houses were blown up one by one. At 3:30 on the morning of October 15, four and a half hours after it began, the Kibya action was over. On his return, Sharon reported that his force had suffered no losses and that there were ten to twelve Jordanian casualties, all of whom had been killed outside the houses. In return, he received a note from Dayan: "There's no one like you!"

In the course of that day, an unsuspected horror came to light. Sixty-nine Jordanians—half of them women and children—had been killed, most of them within the demolished houses. Fearing the raiding Israeli soldiers, they hid and went unnoticed by the men who were laying the explosives around their homes. The Israeli Government, together with the public in Israel, Jordan, and around the world, was profoundly shocked. The direct responsibility for this action remains contested, to this day, between Ben Gurion and Lavon. At any rate Ben Gurion accepted the idea that the public be told that the action was an act of revenge on the part of the inhabitants of border settlements, who bore the brunt of the infiltrators' attacks. Ben Gurion felt that a lie in the interest of the state was pardonable. Moshe Sharett agreed, and it was he who made a few corrections in the draft of Ben Gurion's broadcast to the nation defending the action as a natural desire for revenge.

On October 19, one day after resuming his posts of Prime Minister and Minister of Defense, Ben Gurion broadcast the statement, in which he said: "We have examined the matter most carefully and have discovered that not a single unit, even the smallest, was absent from its base on the night of the Kibya action." He attributed the tragic raid to the settlers on Israel's borders, "the majority of whom are Jewish refugees from Arab countries or the survivors of Nazi concentration camps who for years have borne murderous assaults with great self-restraint."

It would appear that shame added a touch of absurdity to this statement. Although the paratroop company did contain some refugees from Arab countries and the Nazi holocaust, the men of 101, who sparked the entire operation, were without exception native-born Israelis, most of them from veteran agricultural settlements. All had been raised on the values of justice and the brotherhood of man. They did not hate the Arabs but willingly carried out their task because they believed that the existence of Israel depended on it. The troops who carried out the action in Kibya later claimed that "No one said anything explicit about not harming women or children. It was taken for granted that we wouldn't." In the wake of the action, attacking units were ordered to ensure that no one is left in houses about to be blown up. Dayan, first as Chief of G Branch and then as C-o-S, insisted that even at the risk of their lives, soldiers must enter houses and ascertain that they are empty. Furthermore, he issued explicit orders forbidding Zahal to fire on civilians. In GHQ operational orders, units carrying out retaliatory raids were proscribed the use of artillery, mortars, and in some cases even hand grenades for fear of injuring civilians. When he became C-o-S, Dayan made a radical change in the policy of retaliation by selecting military objectives only, and during his term of office there were no further Zahal actions against villages and their inhabitants. This was therefore Zahal's first Kibya and its last.

Dayan was one of the few top-ranking men in the country—if not the only one—who was not mortified by the unexpected results of the Kibya raid. Although he was upset by the deaths of the defenseless civilians, he regarded the incident as one of the accidents of war. He knew very well that the casualties were so high only because the soldiers were convinced they were blowing up empty houses, and he gave 101 and the paratroop unit his full backing. Leadership, particularly in combat, is not acquired through detailed and theoretical analysis or apt slogans. It is achieved through firm backing and the assumption of responsibility for the bloodshed of war. His reactions to Kibya can therefore be viewed as the cornerstone of Dayan's combat leadership.

On October 19 Dayan flew to Lake Success to join the Israeli delegation to the UN General Assembly and advise it on the Jordanian complaint to the Security Council. Israel was unanimously condemned for the Kibya action, but world public opinion did not diminish Dayan's belief in the essential justice of retaliatory raids and did not change his views on Kibya. On December 8, a few weeks after returning from Lake Success, he told the OTC graduates in his first public address as C-o-S:

You will come face to face with the Arabs of Palestine, who bear in their hearts the memory of the defeat of the War of Independence and the hope of a second round. The Government [of Jordan] is helping them reorganize and turn their villages into bases [for actions against Israel] . . . When [world public opinion] sees fit to condemn the action at Kibya and the State of Israel, there are many who take up the cause; but when the time comes to defend the capital of Israel and the Knesset, which is situated only a few hundred meters from the border, you alone will bear this responsibility.

As Chief of G Branch, Dayan considered the Kibya action a success. It was the first action since Tel-Mutilla, in May 1951, in which the mission was "exhausted," as he put it. This fact, by all accounts, changed his opinion of the special unit, an important instance of Dayan's ability to change his mind to correspond with new circumstances. Yadin considered the fact that he did not affect the selfish complacence of those who said "I told you so" to be one of Dayan's most valuable qualities. Up to then he had been opposed to a select "team" in the belief that all Zahal should be an elite force; but the idea now occurred to him that 101 might spread its spirit throughout the army. To begin the process, he ordered the merger of 101 and the paratroops into a single unit. His aim was to match the originality, daring, and fighting spirit of the "gang-style" 101 with the organization, discipline, and training methods of the paratroop battalion, whose commanding officer, like the cadre of instructors, had been trained in the British Army. So great was British influence in the battalion that until the merger the training program was written in English. There was a chain reaction built into Dayan's plan: 101 would influence the paratroops, and they in turn would influence the entire army.

In 1948 a new nickname was coined for Dayan: "Arabber" (Yiddish for Arab). It apparently had two sources. The first was the fact that he had been the Haganah Officer for Arab Affairs, a position known colloquially as *"Arabische Gescheften"* (Arab business). The second was the assumption that his constant involvement in Arab affairs lent him something of what was commonly considered Arab characteristics, or at least Arab mannerisms. The nickname "Arabber" is generally applied to someone who does not always say exactly what he thinks. The way in which the merger of 101 and the paratroop battalion was carried out illustrated for many why the nickname was so apt.

The merger itself took place on January 6, 1954, a month after Dayan was appointed C-o-S. However, he made up his mind about it a few days after the Kibya raid and did not keep his views secret. Yet in the ten weeks from the end of October 1953 until the end of the first week of January 1954, each of the two candidates for the post of commander, Lt. Col. Yehudah Harari and Maj. Ariel Sharon, was certain that Dayan had promised it to him. Or, to put it more accurately, the commander of the paratroop battalion, Yehudah Harari, was not the only one who thought he was going to be given the command of the new elite unit. As a lieutenant colonel, he was senior to Maj. Sharon, and he was also the older of the two. Moreover, he enjoyed the backing of Training Division and its head, Meir Zorea. Convinced that Dayan shared his opinion, Zorea made the necessary preparations for the merger, not doubting for a moment that Harari would be the commander of the new unit.

Yet in the strictest confidence, without the knowledge of GHQ or Zorea, Dayan informed Sharon that he would command the new unit. Zorea, who went about things in the correct way, summoned Sharon in November and informed him of the plan to merge the two units, adding that Harari was to be appointed commander and that Sharon would command one of the units. Nor was this all. Harari summoned Sharon to a meeting and showed him the plans of the new unit's structure. When Harari was summoned to Dayan's office, he was certain that he was about to receive his official appointment as commander of the special unit. To his amazement, he heard otherwise. Dayan informed him that Maj. Ariel Sharon would be appointed commander of the new force, which was to be called Unit 202.

Why did Dayan keep his candidate for top post in Unit 202 a secret for so long and cause Harari such unnecessary pain? Part of the answer lies in the fact that both units—101 and the paratroopers—were opposed to the merger. The former did not want to become military puppets, and the latter did not want to stoop to the partisan style of 101. Indeed, when the merger took place many paratroopers and 101 men left the new unit. It is quite probable, then, that Dayan was trying to limit the initial loss of men that would follow a premature announcement of the commander's name. This was not all, however. It would appear that Dayan wanted to leave his options open up to the last possible minute. It is also possible that the practical joker in him was tempted to deceive Harari, for here was a man certain beyond a shadow of doubt that he was walking on a firm path to an important post and a promotion, while all the time he was treading on thin air. In retrospect, there is no doubt that Dayan's choice was justified. Drill, order, and discipline can be taught by many officers, but very few can impart resourcefulness and daring. In appointing Sharon as commander of the new unit, Dayan made 101 the backbone of Unit 202 and transmitted its fighting spirit to the entire army.

From the early stages of 202's activities, Sharon established a new relationship between GHQ and the operative unit, for he interpreted orders in his own way and passed his own interpretation on to his soldiers. Though Dayan as Chief of G Branch demanded the "exhausting of the mission," with even 50% losses, operative orders in Zahal remained "If you can, do it." Dayan considered the units capable of a good deal more than his colleagues did, for they gave a moderate interpretation to the stipulation "If you can." Sharon took the opposite track and made Dayan's maximum his minimum, and he always strove for more. Just before Kibya, Dayan relented and told Sharon that should he run into difficulties, he could blow up a few houses and withdraw. But Sharon was determined to do it all—forty-five houses—as ordered. In his opinion the only way to extract the maximum performance from low-ranking officers was the order "Follow me!" and not "If you can, do it." Everything Dayan had preached as Chief of G Branch, all he had painstakingly explained in lectures, conventions, and tactical exercises suddenly found a natural, gifted, and daring champion in the new unit. For the paratroopers of 202, "exhausting the mission" and the commander's cry "Follow me!" were second nature.

Within a short time, the paratroopers (the Red Berets) became the cream of Zahal's units. Given the added status of parachutists, they served as the model to which all of Zahal aspired. However, after a trip to the United States with Yitzhak Rabin in July 1954, Dayan decided to adapt a system employed in several American military units and have all Zahal officers undertake a parachuting course. Pinhas Lavon was somewhat apprehensive about the idea, fearing the possible loss or disablement of vitally needed officers. He strenuously objected to Dayan's personal request to take the course and wrote to him, "You may not realize your own importance." Dayan returned the note to Lavon, adding in his own hand, "My self has importance only as long as I remain myself and am not a puppet on a string." He successfully passed the course, and toward the end of 1954 Sharon pinned paratrooper's wings on his uniform.

With the development of 202, the combat performance of Zahal began to rise noticeably, a fact which reversed Dayan's attitude toward the front-line units of the army. Whereas he had previously been forced to encourage and even flatter them with bottles of brandy, he now found that the men of 202 needed a restraining hand. Sharon's frequent demands for new actions were ultimately balanced by Dayan's increasingly restrictive influence. For two years, until December 1955, Dayan gave all of Zahal's combat actions to the paratroopers of 202. The unit therefore became a "hothouse for heroes," as Ben Gurion put it, and inspired warriors with the spirit of the Maccabees. Dayan authorized their actions, gave them backing, encouraged them with demonstrations of affection, awarded them citations, and knew them all by name. He was also trying—success-fully, as it turned out—to arouse the envy of the commanders and men of other units.

This atmosphere provided a perfect setting for motivating all of Zahal to adopt 202's spirit and standards in battle. The goal was achieved by attaching observers from the General Staff, commanders of other units, to paratroop actions or by attaching to the raiding unit extra officers who would later return to their units and pass on what they had learned. Eventually, officers of 202 were trans-ferred to other units and brought into Training Division. Within two years Zahal's doctrine of infantry warfare had taken shape.

By December 1955 Dayan was satisfied that his system had borne fruit and the paratroopers had instilled their singular spirit throughout Zahal. He now began giving other units the opportunity to carry out combat operations, such as those at Sabha and Kinneret and "Operation Yarkon." By October 1956 and the opening of the Sinai Campaign, Zahal was a new army.

A unique aspect of Zahal that became ingrained during the first few months of Dayan's term as C-o-S and served as a major factor in consolidating the fighting spirit of the army was the principle that no dead or wounded were to be left in enemy territory. As far back as the 1948 war, soldiers had made special efforts not to leave their wounded behind. The reason was simple: on a number of occasions Arabs committed atrocities upon the wounded who fell into their hands. There were instances when the wounded were taken to hospitals and given proper treatment, but the fate of wounded men who fell into enemy hands was never predictable. Moreover, the treatment which prisoners of war received in the Arab countries, particularly Syria, was notoriously inhumane, and in some cases death was considered preferable to captivity.

Initially, the rule never to leave wounded behind was not second nature to the men of 101 or 202. In 1954, in retaliation for the murder of a Jew in Ra'anana, seven 202 men carried out a daring raid on the Arab Legion camp in Azun, killing three soldiers. The march to Azun was a hard 30 kilometers there and back. During the fighting, Sergeant Yitzhak Jibli, one of the first 101 men, was wounded. His companions carried him for the greater part of the trek back to Israeli territory, but there was a danger that dawn would expose them to a large-scale attack by the Jordanian Army. During a short break, the men discussed their predicament. It was 2:30 a.m., there were two hours of darkness left and they were 13 kilometers from the border. Meir Har-Zion wrote in his diary: "The only alternative creeps into my consciousness, paralyzing me with terror. Jibli must be left behind, must die. The man, the fighter, the companion, lying here helpless. I can't do it. I can't leave him here. Thankfully, I'm not alone here; Davidi is here. Davidi, there's no choice, Jibli must be left behind. We look at each other, both refusing to reconcile ourselves to the thought." Jibli himself asked the men to go on without him. The commander of the operation kissed him on the forehead, and the six ran almost all the way back to Israeli territory.

A few days later, information was received that Jibli had been taken alive by the Arab Legion. According to these reports, he had been severely tortured but had not broken down during the interrogation. The paratroops now requested GHQ to take action to secure his release. Dayan, who realized the importance of not deserting wounded comrades and knew from his own experience the bitterness of captivity, approved a series of extraordinary operations in which men of 202 were to capture hostages from the Jordanian Army and then offer their release in exchange for Jibli. A unit led by Meir Har-Zion entered Jenin and brought back one Jordanian soldier, and in two further actions, on August 13 and 18, four more hostages were taken. Zahal now had five Jordanians, and Dayan took steps to initiate negotiations for Jibli's release.

On August 19, at his first meeting with Lt. Gen. E.L.M. Burns, then chief of UNTSO, Dayan said (according to Burns) "that he did not believe in wasting too much time on preliminaries before getting down to business." Burns then asked that the five Jordanian captives be returned unconditionally. Did he think, Dayan asked, the Jordanians would be similarly generous and return Sergeant

Jibli, whom they had been holding since July 28? Burns remarked that Dayan's offer seemed to him both outrageous and insolent for, after all, Jibli had been captured in Jordanian territory after he and his companions had killed several Jordanians, while the five Jordanian captives had been kidnapped by Zahal in Jordan. Nevertheless, he mediated between the two sides, and the exchange was effected. When Jibli returned to Israel safe and sound, his friends and the C-o-S gave him a jubilant welcome. Dayan later awarded him a citation.

Jibli was the first and last soldier that the paratroopers, and subsequently all of Zahal, abandoned on the battlefield. From then on, every operation order carried the explicit injunction that "Wounded men are not to be left in the battle area." This principle became a tenet of Zahal, sanctified by the blood of soldiers who paid with their lives trying to rescue wounded comrades. Its ultimate significance was that members of a unit would prefer death to leaving a wounded comrade in the field. This feeling generated a unique faternity of fighters that may well be unequaled in any other army in the world.

17   THE YOUNG ARMY

(1954)

Heavy rain fell on December 7, 1953, Dayan's first day as C-o-S. Nevertheless, he did not cancel the OTC passing-out parade scheduled for that day. With wind and rain beating on the faces of the cadets and guests, Dayan made his first address as C-o-S. He stressed that the new officers must prepare themselves for a situation in which they—and not the UN, world opinion, friends, or allies—would bear the responsibility for the continued existence of the State of Israel.

There was something symbolic in that dismal winter's day. After meeting the young officers at OTC, Dayan returned to his office in GHQ for a series of meetings with senior and older officers. He felt that many of them had outlived their usefulness in Zahal and the time had come for them to retire. It is quite clear that one of Dayan's primary aims as the new C-o-S was to build up a young army, or, in the parlance of those days, "to inject new blood." As a result of the stormy weather, there was a power failure in Tel Aviv and candles were lit in GHQ. It was as though the heavens had intervened to lend a gloomy setting to the painful interviews. Dayan remained in his office until late in the evening, receiving a long line of officers. Neora recalls her impression that "everyone who went in came out with tears in his eyes, and I didn't know if it was only the reflection of the candlelight or real tears."

It is generally thought that as soon as Dayan assumed office, heads began to roll and his first act as C-o-S was "dismissals." This impression stuck and gave him—in the eyes of at least part of the public—the reputation of an "operator," one who cared nothing for the feelings and privileges of men who, in his opinion, did not promote the central aim of "exhausting the mission." At that time, the name "operator" had the ring of a hangman, particularly in Mapai and Histadrut circles. They followed Dayan's actions intently and carefully noted that he would constitute a danger should he choose a political career after retiring from the army. Party functionaries considered him "a dangerous man" even before he was appointed C-o-S. Moshe Sharett, then Foreign Minister, was outraged by the appointment. He despatched a letter to Ben Gurion voicing his objection and claiming that Dayan was too much the partisan and lacked a sense of political responsibility. Sharett was presumably venting on Dayan part of his anger at Lavon for having authorized retaliatory actions of which the Foreign Minister had no prior knowledge or which had consequences far beyond anything he could have expected on the basis of the data received beforehand. Fear of Dayan and the label "a dangerous man" was occasioned no less by the fact that he came to his post alone, without a loyal group of friends, aides, or assistants. Political circles in Israel knew something of his childhood friends' attitude toward Dayan, but he was feared most of all because he kept his thoughts to himself. Party members and statesmen were never certain they could rely on him as an ally for any length of time or that it was possible to coordinate a plan of political action with him. Dayan was a mystery which intensified with the development of his ability to change direction in accordance with circumstance or the glimmerings of new solutions.

The general mood of suspicion and the candlelight flickering late into the night in GHQ gave birth to the legend of a "Bartholomew's Night" on Dayan's first day as C-o-S. Actually, he implemented the policy of creating a young army slowly and gradually. It was Ben Gurion who fathered this policy by appointing the thirty-two year old Yadin as C-o-S, passing over an entire generation of veteran Haganah men. In military circles, this process was called "disposing of the generation of the wilderness." Ben Gurion began it, and Dayan completed it within three years after becoming C-o-S. In the words of Zvi Zur, who was then Chief of Manpower Branch, "he did it slowly, but systematically; gently, but firmly. Many of the top-ranking veterans of the Haganah left the army during his term of office." The older officers who left their posts were not actually dismissed. They left of their own accord, since no positions corresponding to their rank and seniority were found for them. Lt. Col. Yehudah Harari, who (legend has it) was the first to be dismissed, was not "fanned," as it was known, but was told that 202 was being turned over to a lower-ranking officer.

Thus an important process of limiting the cadre of Regular Army officers was initiated in Zahal. Among the reasons for it were continuing pressures on the army to cut costs and Dayan's desire to save as much as possible of the reduced budget for purchase of arms and equipment. But above all was Dayan's unflagging efforts to rid the army of ineffective personnel, to discard the surpluses that did not serve the central aims of the army, and to create an alert, compact Zahal that would be all lean, combat muscle. As part of this program, he disbanded units for which he saw no future combat activity, such as the cavalry and the carrier-pigeon units. Dayan regarded the Ministry of Finance pressures an ally, and even doubled these pressures by demanding cuts in salaries in order to finance equipment and arms, thereby creating a powerful momentum for the achievement of his aims.

Dayan's initial "head rolling" and his new appointments presaged

a more comprehensive plan aimed at perpetuating Zahal's youthful-
ness. The details of the plan crystallized only at the end of his first
year as C-o-S, and it was indeed original, revolutionary, and
instrinsically age-defeating. If it is true to say that Dayan brought
the guillotine down on the heads of the "generation of the wilderness,"
then one must add that he made the guillotine a permanent institution. With characteristic impatience, he did not wait until his
intentions were crystal clear to the general military public. According
to Meir Amit, then Assistant Chief of G Branch, "he began holding
meetings at his house. I never understood whom he invited or why.
He gathered people with no apparent system, just men he liked and
whose opinions he respected." Rank and position played no part
in his choice. Apparently there were some twenty or thirty army
people at his home for the first meeting, when he elaborated on what
he called the "double life" or "second sphere of life." His basic idea
was extremely simple: a good army is a young army. The stratum
of officers who grow old in their posts leads to a cumbersome,
inefficient army, the withering of new ideas, and the rejection of
young, enterprising officers. It results in marking time and the
dissolution that results from fringe benefits and egoism. Accordingly,
Zahal must institute compulsory retirement at an early age. He
suggested forty for staff officers and even less for field officers. Anyone
making the army his career should know that he must prepare himself for a second—civilian—sphere of life.

Hearing these views for the first time, many of the assembled
guests did not immediately grasp Dayan's intention, and those
who accepted his plan in principle disagreed with some of its details
and the proposed method of implementing it. The only vocal
opposition heard that night came from Chaim Bar-Lev, then
thirty-one years old. "Dayan's idea was initially greeted with
considerable criticism and opposition. Even officers in my age group
opposed it. We agreed among ourselves and told him that while it
is true that forty is old, you're not dead yet. At any rate, he carried
out his plan by force." Dan Tolkowsky, then Commander of the
Air Force, related, "The way he presented the plan created the
impression . . . that he was too impulsive. Suddenly he gets up [and]
fires a lecture at us on how to throw out men over forty. The people
there were appalled. His premise was right, but did he have to
develop the theory like that?" Indeed, many found it difficult to
imagine an army whose senior officers were all under forty. Zvi
Zur, who was charged with working out the plan in detail, said,
"The double life concept was a Dayan invention. No one understood
it, and we had many reservations." Searching questions were asked.
Is it good for the army? Is it good for the army man? What will he
do after forty? Will he end up unwanted, wandering from one civilian

job to another until he dies? And how will he support his family?

Once the plan was formulated in detail by Manpower Branch, it became clearer, and the axiom that a career officer would not serve in the army for the entire span of his active life gained widespread support. Manpower Branch drew up the Military Pensions Act to facilitate the retirement of army officers at the age of forty. In time, however, this concept was modified, and after Dayan's term the army began to grow older.

Dayan's concept had a far-reaching influence on Israeli society. His "double life" plan let loose into civilian life forty-year-old ex-officers—talented, ambitious, vital men at the height of their powers. The economy began wooing these youthful pensioners with offers of top-level positions, so much so that the profile of Israeli society assumed an increasingly military aspect. While Zahal approved the "double life" policy for the sake of a better army, party functionaries feared it might be applied on a wider scale and consequently marked Dayan as one who discards the old for the young. Naturally they asked whether he would not translate his ideas into civilian life, should he be voted into public office, and draw up a new plan for a "double life" which would squeeze out any functionary forty or even fifty years old. It appears that Mapai functionaries did note the nonmilitary ramifications of Dayan's policy, a fact that is essential to the proper understanding of the older Mapai members' hostility toward those they called the "Youngsters" within their party.

To sharpen the army's alertness, Dayan began a series of surprise visits. He generally traveled to the bases alone and at night, inspecting duty officers. If he found anything lacking in the duty procedures, he went into details of the problem on the spot, conferring with junior officers or even sergeants. The duty officers who were not where they should have been were summarily dismissed from the army. Fear of these surprise visits soon spread throughout Zahal.

During one such visit he spoke to soldiers who had just returned from night exercises. They complained that whenever they returned from the strenuous exercises at night, the kitchen was closed and they were forced to go to bed on empty stomachs. It seemed manifestly unjust to Dayan that while combat soldiers exerted themselves at night, rear-echelon soldiers followed a regular daily routine and enjoyed a good night's sleep every night. He immediately issued a GHQ order entitling combat soldiers to a hot meal after a night exercise or action. To ensure that his order was being carried out, he added the mess halls to his tour of surprise inspections. In matters he considered vital, he trusted no one but himself. Late one night he came to an armored unit and found that while hot tea had been prepared for the men, there was no sugar. He was told that the regular sugar rations were not sufficient for an additional night meal. He phoned the Chief of the Quartermaster Branch at his home, woke him up, and demanded that he personally, or one of his senior aides, bring three sacks of sugar to the unit that night. Moreover, he demanded that whoever carried out the order report to his office first thing the following morning with a signed receipt for the sugar. Neora remembers the Q Branch officer waiting for Dayan early in the morning with a note from the commander of the tank unit saying, "Received, items: three sacks of sugar."

Although this method afforded Dayan intimate contact with army life at the soldiers' level, as well as first-hand acquaintance with the men and their problems, its fault lay in the difficulties of coordination and follow-up at GHQ. Chiefs of GHQ branches often learned of the C-o-S's orders only after they had been given to the units he visited. Staff branches were then forced to readjust their plans and alter schedules to accomodate the new orders issued without their prior knowledge. Their inconvenience bothered Dayan very little, for he gave first priority to the fitness and welfare of combat units. He explicitly told his Chief of G Branch, Meir Amit, "All these logistics don't interest me in the least. I say this is what should be done. Now let them work it out for themselves."

Jolts in structure or procedure—such as the decision in November 1954 to disband Southern Command as an entity and subordinate it to Central Command, only to reinstate it a year later—added to the general impression that Dayan was like a ping-pong ball: precipitate, hasty, and careless. Those who worked in close contact with him, who observed the way he reached decisions and how he reasoned, knew that this was a mistaken impression. Appearances to the contrary, Dayan always planned his steps carefully. According to Amit, "No one can possibly imagine just how cautious Dayan is, particularly when it comes to obtaining approval from his superiors. I do not recall a single instance when he made a move without first receiving the approval of the higher authority."

This quality surprised even Ben Gurion. On the night of October 10, 1956, during the Kalkilya retaliatory action, the raiding unit encountered serious difficulties. Losses mounted from minute to minute and there was reason to fear that the blocking unit would be surrounded and wiped out. Dayan wanted to bring in artillery and even considered the possibility of using the Air Force to extricate the imperiled unit. Ben Gurion was amazed that Dayan did not act on his own and appealed to him to lift the Minister of Defense's injunction. In his parting letter to Dayan as C-o-S, Ben Gurion wrote: "You displayed two basic—and seemingly contradictory—qualities that made you one of the finest soldiers of the Israel Defense

Forces: an almost reckless daring, balanced by profound tactical and strategic reasoning."

Whatever Dayan lacked in patience and in understanding of staff work, he more than made up for with his keen, intuitive understanding of people. In matters of fighting spirit and fitness for battle, he went into the minutest details. He knew many of the soldiers personally, and in appointing commanders for combat units he used a single rule of thumb: "Tigers only." Anyone lacking daring, courage, ingenuity in battle, and the willingness to lead his men was neither appointed nor advanced, be he the best administrator or instructor. The soldiers he befriended were those who displayed the greatest courage. For staff and rear-echelon duties he chose men whom he felt to be effective and capable of understanding his hints, for he lacked the patience to go into the fine details of issues which were not part of the main endeavor. He sought out men who would understand what he considered important and then carry out the task on their own.

To get results, Dayan relied more on the right people in the right places than on elaborate doctrines. By October 1956, at the time of the Sinai Campaign, most of the appointments in Zahal were his own and he enjoyed the admiration and respect of the entire army. Nevertheless, a distance remained between him and his men. Under different circumstances—of proper staff work, ceremony, and etiquette—this would have been a natural phenomenon. But Dayan created a free-and-easy, even nonchalant, atmosphere about him. He accorded the same respect to privates and generals alike. Israel Tal, Commander of OTC at the time, noted that when Dayan addressed the cadets, he would talk as though he were one of them or—more accurately—they were all like himself. He made jokes at his own expense and generated a sense of informality. It may have been in contrast to this behavior that his unbending aloofness stood out as an extraordinary phenomenon.

The status of his office undoubtedly contributed a great deal toward his subordinates' awe. An army is a body that naturally creates hierarchy, distance, and prestige. It sometimes seems that even a C-o-S with a wooden head would be accorded the outward tokens of respect and awe, not through the stupidity of his subordinates but through their apprehension of the fact that a person's standing in the eyes of those below him rises in direct proportion to the elevated status of his own superiors. Although Dayan himself cared little for ceremony or spit and polish, his aides and secretaries did their best to ensure that he appeared in full military regalia; and although the C-o-S received his officers in his modest office, those who came to see him entered the room as though it were the drawing room of a king. There were some who claimed that the people around

Dayan feared him because he had the authority to decide the fate of any officer, and he never hesitated to dismiss anyone.

Nevertheless, it was not only his status that produced self-effacement. In his presence one felt the awe inspired by a great artist or powerful personality. This feeling apparently stemmed from two of his personal characteristics. The first was the fact that he never allowed anyone to develop a close, intimate friendship with him; on the contrary, he became increasingly introverted. People who worked with him had to guess whether there were hidden meanings in his statements and actions, and if so what they were. Dayan, like Ben Gurion, never elaborated upon the thoughts and feelings on which his decisions were founded. The need to divine his intentions and the fear of misreading them clearly served to emphasize his aloofness.

The second characteristic was his swift change of moods, which became increasingly marked. He would generally start the day in a gloomy mood that gradually brightened as the day wore on. There were self-styled "Dayan experts" who claimed to be able to divine when he was "in a mood," in which case they postponed presenting vital issues until he had regained his spirits. Anyone who began a discussion when he was in a bad mood discovered that he did not let them finish their sentences and, in army parlance, "climbed all over them" even before he knew whether or not they were in the right. In general, his rule was "Never explain, never apologize." His apologies were in fact few and far between and occurred mostly after he had left the army and entered politics. The victims of his temperament had one consolation: he never drew far-reaching conclusions from a chance statement, for his opinions of people were generally formed on the basis of their actions.

Dayan's attitude toward people, superficially direct and uncomplicated, became increasingly complex over the years. He remarked that he did not like the company of others, that people bored him. According to the "experts," the cornerstone of his attitude is not love or hate, but respect. His attitude is therefore as impersonal as he can make it. In Amit's view, Dayan respects only two kinds of people: the courageous and the wise. "I wouldn't say he loathes fools or faint-hearted people; he simply discounts them. With the courageous he is willing to discuss even the most trivial issues—how and why something happened, down to the minutest detail—and he always remembers their names. With the wise he loves to discuss questions of interest to him, from professional military affairs to archaeology and literature. He is willing to learn from both kinds of people and is a patient, interested listener."

The choice of people he liked and his impatience with others created an impression of arrogance. It was clear to party men that

Dayan was not cut out to be a politician. Dayan himself found both these assessments correct, and these very traits constituted an important aspect of the development of his character into what might be called a "sovereign personality," that is, one who does exclusively as he wishes and associates only with people of his own choosing. Dayan successfully managed to avoid having circumstances or the positions he filled force him into actions, conduct, or company not strictly to his liking.

It would seem that he is a man born to be an artist upon whom the military man and later the statesman have been grafted. Many facets of his personality recall those of a true artist: his desire to do things with his own hands, without intermediaries, and without a set formula. Like a painter he adds and removes colors as the work progresses, as his moods change, or in sudden flashes of inspiration. His interest in minute details is also reminiscent of the artist, who delves deep into the subject of his creation. Inspiration and originality are an integral part of his character, and they grow out of associations and circumstances, rather than the scholarly study of military doctrines or history. Dayan has never read military literature or the memoirs of military men or statesmen. Poetry and literature have occupied his time and thought. Insofar as the creation of a resourceful, daring, and highly motivated army may be considered a work of art, Dayan is to be regarded as an inspired creator.

It is clear that the Mapai veterans' resistance to Dayan as an eventual candidate for party leadership began to harden during the first period of his work with Lavon. Top-ranking party members like Levi Eshkol and Golda Meir informed Ben Gurion of their disapproval of Pinhas Lavon as Acting Minister and then Minister of Defense and even warned of the potentially harmful consequences of the appointment. As Acting Minister of Defense, Lavon in turn opposed Dayan's appointment as C-o-S. He was inclined to favor a candidate with fewer political aspirations.

Despite Lavon's attitude toward Dayan, there was no discord during the first stages of their work together. Lavon took an activist stand, quite the opposite of Sharett's. Dayan claims that it was for precisely this reason that he welcomed Lavon's appointment. Dayan's initial support for Lavon may have been based on other considerations, such as the intense opposition that developed between Lavon and Maklef and which was likely to hasten his own appointment as C-o-S. Be that as it may, the two worked together in harmony until June 1954. Dayan considered Lavon an "intelligent man, sharp, bright, and above all the antithesis of Sharett's military and political thinking." Whatever Sharett proposed, Lavon opposed, in Dayan's opinion quite rightly. Even later, when the rift between them grew, Dayan continued to believe that Lavon's line was not far from his own. Lavon developed an independent stand and did not consult Prime Minister Sharett, even on major issues. Sharett, however, felt that the differences between Lavon and himself went beyond an internal Cabinet or party controversy and that Lavon had been trying to undermine his position. He made no secret of his suspicions and reprimanded Lavon in two letters.

It was clear that taking Ben Gurion's place during his extended leave of absence was but a dress rehearsal for Ben Gurion's forthcoming retirement. Sharett suspected Lavon of wanting to discredit him not only as Acting Prime Minister but also as incumbent Prime Minister. But Lavon was not the only one suspected of attempting to topple Sharett. Veteran Mapai leaders regarded Lavon, Dayan, and Peres as a trio conspiring against Sharett and his fellow anti-activists. The trio was suspected of being united by one common purpose: hastening Ben Gurion's return from Sde Boker.

Deep-seated suspiciousness was second nature to many Mapai veterans, and whereas in Yadin's time the army's efficiency in purely civilian matters had kindled their jealousy and fear, now that Dayan restricted Zahal to solely military activities, these same emotions burned even more intensely. The veterans feared that the young Zahal—trained now only for war, capable of carrying out retaliatory raids that involved great loss of life on both sides, with units that could kill "without remorse" and carry out orders with great courage—might, in the absence of strong social values, also direct its strength against the civil rule of the state. Even Ben Gurion was not without his apprehensions about the possibility that the soldiers of 101—and afterward the paratroopers of 202—would turn the destruction they had mastered against civilian sectors of Israel. He even went so far to ask Ariel Sharon, the commander of 202, if he too thought this was a possibility.

In fact, this fear of Zahal and its officers was totally without foundation at any time. The Mapai veterans were not fully attuned to the nature of Israeli youth, and some of their fears undoubtedly stemmed from this unfamiliarity. On the other hand, the suspicions which attended Zahal from its early years had the constructive effect of reinforcing the army's self-restraint and its total subordination to the civilian authorities. The first period of Dayan's work with Lavon, therefore, prepared the ground for the Mapai veterans' hostility and their fear of him as a "dangerous man."

Relations between Lavon and Dayan slowly cooled, and by the summer of 1954 there was talk of a complete break between them. The dispute centered on whether the Minister of Defence had the right to maintain direct contact with army units and personnel, as Lavon believed should be the case, or everything should be conducted through the regular channels—in other words, the C-o-S's office—as Dayan believed and as had been Ben Gurion's practice. The dispute seems to have been motivated by distrust. Lavon charged in 1954 and in 1960 that "the C-o-S frequently misled him about [military] actions . . . He would considerably enlarge the scope of actions during their execution, going beyond the original order approved by the Minister of Defense. Actions of a specific, limited scope would be approved, and afterward, when the exact circumstances and data on what took place came to light, it would be too late." According to Dayan, Lavon's accusations were the fruit of his innate distrust and were never borne out by the facts. Shimon Peres, whose relations with Lavon began deteriorating at about the same time, supported Dayan's claim. Indeed, stories circulated in the army that officers were invited to the Minister of Defense's office to be questioned behind Dayan's back.

There is evidence that Lavon was not satisfied with his right merely to receive direct reports, and he tried to extend it to issuing direct instructions to GHQ branches. His directives to a certain officer, labeled by the censors the "Senior Officer," resulted in what later became known as the "unfortunate business," which in turn gave birth to the "Lavon Affair" that shook Israel in the early 1960s. It is generally agreed that Lavon met privately with the "Senior Officer" and gave him planning instructions for the "unfortunate" operation. But Lavon and his supporters, as well as their opponents, disagree vehemently about whether or not he gave the officer operative instructions as well. There is no disagreement about two other important points. The first is that as C-o-S, Dayan opposed every stage of the "unfortunate" operation. The second is that at the time of the events, including the meeting between Lavon and the "Senior Officer," Dayan himself was away on a visit to the United States.

Foreign newspapers linked the "unfortunate business" to certain acts of sabotage in Egypt. On December 11, 1954, eleven Jews were brought to trial before the High Military Court in Cairo for allegedly belonging to a "Zionist espionage and sabotage ring." Newspapers in Israel and abroad carried accounts of the prosecution's charge that in July 1954 the members of this ring placed incendiary bombs in a post office, cinemas, and USIS offices in Alexandria and Cairo at the time when Anglo-Egyptian negotiations over the Suez Canal were in progress and the United States was beginning to replace Britain as the influential power in Egypt. The prosecution claimed that the defendants acted in the guise of a so-called "popular resistance group," but in fact meant to disrupt the strengthening of ties between Egypt and the United States. Some of the accused confessed to the sabotage but denied having any connection with espionage activities. In January 1955, the Egyptian court handed down severe sentences: two of the defendants were sentenced to death and six to terms of imprisonment from seven years to life. Only two were acquitted, and one of the eleven committed suicide in his cell before sentence was passed.

The harsh sentences aroused a public outcry throughout the world and threw Israel into a turmoil. People began to ask whether the government had any effective control over the Ministry of Defense and its undercover activities. On February 11, 1955 the poet Natan Alterman devoted his weekly newspaper column to the Cairo defendants and wrote: "We shall ask not only *how* but *why* heroes fell."

In January 1955, Prime Minister Moshe Sharett, who had no inkling of the "unfortunate business," appointed Lt. Gen. Ya'akov Dori, a former C-o-S, and Yitzhak Olshan, the President of the Supreme Court, as a commission of inquiry to try to determine whether Lavon had issued the order for the "unfortunate business' or whether the action was carried out on the initiative of the "Senior Officer." Dori and Olshan did not, in effect, discover the truth. Their findings stated: "In the final analysis, we regret that we have been unable to answer the questions put to us by the Prime Minister. We can only say that we were not convinced beyond any reasonable doubt that [the "Senior Officer"] did not receive orders from the Minister of Defense. We are equally uncertain that the Minister of Defense did in fact give the orders attributed to him." In other words, a draw.

While the Mapai leadership—Sharett, Eshkol, Golda Meir, and others—felt that following the Olshan-Dori findings Lavon must resign, Dayan displayed compassion towards Lavon in his downfall and even repeated to Lavon the essence of his testimony before the Olshan-Dori committee. On January 25, Dayan told Ben Gurion that "if Pinhas Lavon remains in his post another six months, [we] will be able to establish a proper relationship."

Throughout the developments of the "unfortunate business" and the subsequent "Lavon Affair," Dayan maintained that Lavon and the "Senior Officer" shared the responsibility for the abortive operation equally, although formally he held Lavon responsible. He persisted in this view even when Ben Gurion's political career hung in the balance. His instincts told him that it was in his own interests to be as far as possible from direct involvement in what was then a dispute between Lavon and his colleagues in Mapai, and he refused to take any part in it.

On February 2, 1955 Lavon handed Sharett his letter of resignation. The entire Mapai leadership felt it should be accepted. Sharett sent a messenger to Ben Gurion at Sde Boker and asked him to serve as Minister of Defense. Mapai needed Ben Gurion in the Cabinet as it approached the general elections to the Third Knesset. On February 21, 1955, nearly fifteen months after he retired, Ben Gurion returned to assume the post of Minister of Defense. On August 18, after the general elections, he formed a coalition Cabinet and again became Prime Minister and Minister of Defense. The "unfortunate business" receded into the background, but only temporarily, for it was a time bomb which was due to explode in 1960 and result in Ben Gurion's final retirement in the spring of 1963.

18 PRELUDE TO SINAI

(1955 - 1956)

It was only in February 1955, with Ben Gurion's return to the government as Minister of Defense, that he developed a close working relationship with Dayan. Although outwardly Ben Gurion made no secret of his favorable attitude toward Dayan, privately he continued to test him. Ben Gurion is not one to reveal his true feelings. His unique status in Israel gave him the power to get what he wanted even without making his wishes explicit. No one could make him say what he chose not to say. At conferences, when asked questions which he was not inclined to answer, he would listen, make no comment, and pass on to something else. Upon receiving a document, telegram, or plan from Dayan, he would study it without saying a word. Meetings with him were over when he began writing and took no further notice of the people in the room. Those who came into daily contact with him soon learned to read the signs. One of Dayan's first tests, therefore, was whether he could read Ben Gurion's thoughts correctly and interpret one silence as agreement and another as refusal.

Contrary to popular belief, Dayan and Ben Gurion did not fall into each other's arms at their first meeting as C-o-S and Minister of Defense. In fact Dayan often wondered about Ben Gurion's real attitude toward him. At about the time of the last large-scale retaliatory raids before the Sinai Campaign, he sensed that Ben Gurion was finally convinced of his ability. He later won Ben Gurion over completely with the Sinai Campaign itself. Nevertheless, Dayan was not completely sure of Ben Gurion's feelings until he read the Prime Minister's farewell letter to him, in which Ben Gurion called him "one of Zahal's finest soldiers."

Ben Gurion had the disconcerting habit of asking "What are you doing here?" He would put the question to his staff officers as they entered the weekly meeting with him. Peres would generally explain that this was his way of saying "How are you?" One of Dayan's stories sheds some light on the guesswork involved in his relation with Ben Gurion:

During the first period of my work with him, whenever I came into his office Ben Gurion would ask, "What are you doing here?" And I would reply, "Ben Gurion, I'm the C-o-S." Ben Gurion would say, "What, not Yigael Yadin?" And I would say, "No, he's left. I'm the C-o-S." I took this to mean that I hadn't yet reached Yadin's level and must aspire to higher things. After some time, he started asking me again, "What are you doing here?" When I said that I was the C-o-S and he asked "What, not Laskov?" I understood that the party was over, that I had to go.'

This story, Dayan admits, is "just this side" of the truth, for he adds:

There can be no doubt that he was deeply attached to Yigael Yadin, respected him, and parted with him reluctantly. For a long time he found it difficult to accept me. He had to change many of his ideas before he could see me as a good C-o-S. But he considered Yigael an excellent C-o-S. Afterward he was crazy about Laskov, he really loved him deeply. He wanted him to be my deputy, but I didn't want him. It was not as though for four years Ben Gurion really forgot that I was C-o-S. His question "What are you doing here?" was intended as a jibe. He never hesitated to resort to mockery and used it to good effect on a number of occasions.

It is possible that Ben Gurion's initial attitude was affected by the charge that Dayan misled Lavon by enlarging missions beyond the scope that had been authorized. Indeed, at a staff meeting in 1955, Ben Gurion made a joking remark that cast doubt on the reliability of Dayan's reports. After the meeting Dayan sent him an indignant note, to which Ben Gurion replied: "I received your note concerning my remarks about your relaying information. I am pleased to note that I consider your reports reliable and I regret what I said half-jokingly. I would be grateful to you if you would show this note to all those who heard my remark this morning." Ben Gurion was to condemn in the Knesset public statements that preached morality to the officers of Zahal, claiming that Zahal and its officers did not need such lectures. The four Chiefs-of-Staff differed from one another, but all shared an "unqualified loyalty to the authorized institutions of the state." Further-more, he added, "Moshe Dayan would not lie. I do not think he is capable of lying." Whereas Lavon's deep-seated distrust led him to see Dayan's actions as deliberately misleading, Ben Gurion's confi-dence in himself and his men led him to view them as the outcome of circumstances.

Proof of this attitude may be found in what became known as the "Kinneret Action." From its fortified positions on the slopes of the Golan Heights, the Syrian Army made a habit of firing on Israeli patrol and fishing vessels on Lake Kinneret. On December 10, 1955 the Syrians attacked Israeli boats on the lake with cannon fire. On the following day the Paratroop Brigade and a company of the Golani (infantry) Brigade destroyed all the Syrian positions along the lake shore. Fifty Syrian soldiers were killed and thirty taken prisoner. Israeli casualties were six dead and twelve wounded.

The scope of the action, its ferocity, and the numerous Syrian losses had widespread repercussions. Although the action was carried out only after Syria had been repeatedly asked by UN representatives to put an end to their attacks on Israeli vessels, and despite the fact that the Chief-of-Staff of UNTSO, General Bennike, ruled that on the basis of the Armistice Agreement Lake Kinneret was sovereign Israeli territory, the UN Security Council condemned Israel by a considerable majority. The scope of the action came under fire in Israeli circles as well. Moshe Sharett, then Foreign Minister, was in Washington for talks with American Secretary of State John Foster Dulles on the acquisition of American arms. Sharett charged that the "Kinneret Action" ruined good chances of persuading the American Government to sell arms to Israel in order to offset the flow of Soviet arms into Egypt that had begun that year. He believed that Ben Gurion's timing in authorizing so large and unpopular an action at such a delicate moment in the negotiations with Dulles was ill-chosen, to say the least.

It was generally believed that Ben Gurion had actually authorized a smaller operation. He had spoken in terms of a local reprisal raid, and on the following day it transpired that a regional battle had been fought. Dayan was again blamed for enlarging the scope of the action. The truth was that at the last moment he requested and received Ben Gurion's permission to include two additional Syrian positions in the attack.

The mistaken impression was partly due to differences of opinion between Ben Gurion and Sharett on the policy of retaliation. Earlier, in November 1955, after a retaliatory action near Nitzana on the Sinai border, Sharett claimed that the raid would in effect serve Egyptian interests by furnishing palpable evidence of Israeli aggression and hence justification for the Egyptian-Czech arms deal. Sharett also feared that large-scale reprisals would antagonize public opinion in the West. After the "Kinneret Action," the controversy flared up again, this time between Sharett and Dayan. The first claimed that the Israeli overreaction ultimately defeated his efforts to acquire arms from the United States. Dayan felt that it was a waste of time and effort to obtain arms by Foreign Ministry means, that is, by nurturing public opinion and convincing the foreign offices of other countries. He felt that negotiations should be held with those bodies directly interested in selling arms, such as arms industries or military officials. Peres, the Director-General of the Ministry of Defense, adopted this line of thinking and later refined it in practice. Sharett told Ben Gurion that he was opposed to Dayan's concept of arms purchases, but Ben Gurion gave his C-o-S full backing, telling Sharett, "In my humble opinion, the Chief-of-Staff's line of thought is logical." Thus in 1956 the signs were unmistakable: Sharett realized that his days as Foreign Minister were numbered.

Dayan claimed that the size and scope of military actions were not always predictable. He believed that the unexpected results of the "Kinneret Action" were the outcome of the paratroopers' combat ability, which had been underestimated, for in fact Dayan's request had not been for additional troops but additional objectives to be attacked by the force originally agreed upon. Before the action Ben Gurion expressed the view that this force would, in any case, be incapable of carrying out the entire mission, and this may have been the reason he authorized the added objectives. Dayan recalls, "I was certain that the entire action could be carried out by the same force, but Ben Gurion didn't believe for a moment that it could be done. I knew that the paratroopers would carry out the mission from beginning to end. Only after the action did Ben Gurion realize that the results were beyond anything he had believed possible, and he told me that he had not thought it would be so large an action, involving so many enemy casualties and such widespread destruction to their positions. He did not believe that the paratroopers could rout the entire Syrian force in the area. He was not sorry, just surprised." After the "Kinneret Action" Ben Gurion laid down limits for the size of raiding units and their targets. Dayan was required to submit a completely detailed account of the scope and depth of any action, even if it was to be carried out by a small unit.

During the period they worked together, there was no overt tension between Ben Gurion and Dayan, though personal differences rankled beneath the surface. Ben Gurion took note of complaints about Dayan's toughness in dealing with people. He told Dayan of these complaints and asked, "Why are you so hard?" To which Dayan replied, "They said of the sons of Zeriah that they were 'hard,' yet they helped King David conquer the realm," a clear appeal to Ben Gurion's love of biblical history, as well as a hint of the role Dayan had chosen for himself.

Nevertheless, beneath the untroubled exterior, both men felt free to manipulate one another. A case in point was the appointment of Laskov as Deputy C-o-S. Dayan, who refused to serve as a deputy, was equally opposed to having one of his own. He also wanted as aides men of his own choosing. As far as possible, he worked directly with Amit and Uzi Narkiss, virtually ignoring his "Number Two," Maj. Gen. Yoseph Avidar, the Chief of G Branch and a Ben Gurion appointment. In October 1955, when Avidar retired from the army and was appointed Israeli Ambassador to the USSR, they parted as friends, and Dayan even presented Avidar's wife with the shark's tooth necklace. Ben Gurion, who believed that the "Number Two" should be the temperamental opposite of the C-o-S, appointed Laskov as Chief of G Branch and Deputy C-o-S. This was clearly a maneuver on his part, for he was fully aware of Dayan's objection to Laskov.

Dayan did not fight Laskov's appointment, and although he was sure they would not get on, he accepted Ben Gurion's decision. At GHQ, however, he treated Laskov as though he simply did not exist. In the summer of 1956, he appointed Laskov Commander of the Armored Corps, offering the explanation—flattering in itself—that the corps needed a commander of his caliber. Dayan thus managed to complete his term of office without a deputy. At his suggestion, Meir Amit was appointed Chief of G Branch, so he effectively rid himself of the checks Ben Gurion had sought to impose upon him.

Familiarity with Ben Gurion and his methods taught Dayan how to gain his support without resorting to undue pressure. The "Old Man" made it a rule to protect the status of the C-o-S and the front, branch, and corps commanders. On the one hand he did not interfere in differences of opinion that arose between them; but on the other he made every effort to ensure that these differences did not result in loss of prestige or status. Dayan was adept at predicting the outcome of disputes submitted to Ben Gurion's arbitration, a maneuver army men called "the Ben Gurion gambit." This was not an entirely appropriate name for the practice of bringing contested issues before Ben Gurion, for it was as much a democratic procedure based on fair play as an exercise in manipulation.

A well-known example of the "gambit" centered on the differences of opinion between Dayan and Laskov on the employment of armor. To resolve the issue, Dayan suggested holding a discussion with Ben Gurion. On September 1, 1956 he gathered over forty officers, all of whom he thought might have useful ideas on armored warfare. Ben Gurion listened intently to the handful of Laskov supporters and the large number of his opponents. During the discussion, which continued throughout the day, Ben Gurion did not express his own opinion on any of the subjects raised and only asked a few questions. After the discussion, however, he summoned Laskov and told him that he must "bow to the decision" and act in accordance with the C-o-S's directives. Some of the officers regarded the discussion on armored warfare in so large a forum as a transparent ploy on Dayan's part to place Laskov at a disadvantage in Ben Gurion's presence and expose him as a minority voice that lacked convincing arguments. Laskov himself thought otherwise and, despite his rivalry with Dayan, said, "Dayan was not afraid to submit differences to Ben Gurion's arbitration. He knew that he was fully authorized to force me to accept his opinion without a discussion and that Ben Gurion would give him full backing. In spite of this, he saw fit to bring these disputes to Ben Gurion's attention." Laskov's only complaint against Dayan was that he had "packed" the discussion in his own favor.

Ben Gurion and Dayan were in complete accord on the need for an aggressive security policy. It is not inconceivable that Ben Gurion was actually the more aggressive of the two: Dayan himself remarked, "Deep down, Ben Gurion is a great fighter, but he always tries to check his impulses for fear of dragging Israel into a rash venture just because something had made his blood boil." Ben Gurion's inner restraint and ability to divorce his analytical powers from his volatile emotions were sometimes even to produce situations misinterpreted as hesitancy.

The years 1953 - 6 provided many incidents that incensed both Ben Gurion and Dayan. They were the result of three principal developments in the area: acts of terror and sabotage perpetrated by Arabs against Israeli settlements and citizens, the Egyptian blockage of Israeli shipping in the Suez Canal and the Straits of Tiran, and Egyptian preparations for an all-out war against Israel. Israel's reactions developed accordingly from retaliatory actions to a pre-emptive war in October 1956.

As far back as 1951, Arab terror was the main cause of unrest along the borders. In that year Arab infiltrators carried out 1,665 acts of plunder, sabotage, and armed attack on civilians. In 1952 the number of incidents rose to 1,751. The terror, at first carried out by individuals, was encouraged by the Arab governments' refusal to implement the Armistice Agreements (that is, to replace them with peace settlements) and by incessant declarations of their intention to attack and destroy Israel. Initially, the Government of Israel regarded these acts as the last sparks from the cinders of 1948. According to Dayan, "In the second half of 1954, however, the anti-Israel terrorism intensified. In the succeeding months it became clear to the Israeli Government that these were not isolated incidents prompted by individual whim, but an organized operation carried out with the full knowledge of the Arab governments and on the initiative and responsibility of Egypt." It would seem that Dayan helped consolidate this opinion in the Israeli Government. The number of citizens killed and wounded by Arab infiltrators rose steadily: in 1950, nineteen killed and thirty-one wounded; in 1951, forty-eight and forty-nine; in 1952, forty-two and fifty-six; and in 1953, forty-four and sixty-six, respectively. The total for the four years was 153 civilians killed and 202 wounded. Extensive damage was caused to property, and life in the border settlements was repeatedly disrupted. There were times when transportation at night was prohibited or permitted only in convoys.

At first Israel displayed forbearance and appealed to the Arab governments to abide by the Armistice Agreements. When these measures had no effect, the first retaliatory actions were carried out, on the principle of "an eye for an eye." If Arab citizens took the law into their own hands and crossed the border to kill and destroy, Israeli citizens would do likewise. Small detachments of two or three soldiers would cross the border at night, carry out an attack, and return. Even when larger forces were used, the principle remained the same: if Arabs stole sheep from Israelis, Israelis smuggled sheep out of Jordan; if Arabs burned threshing floors in Israel, Israelis burned threshing floors in Jordan; if one side fired upon an Israeli settlement, the other blew up a well or the house of a *mukhtar*. As the Israeli Government did not yet hold the Arab governments responsible for the terror, but only appealed to them to take preventive steps, Israel did not admit to all the retaliatory actions she carried out and—to avoid a military confrontation—tried as far as possible to conceal the fact that they were carried out by Israeli soldiers. The government held the view that the terror and the retaliation should not be allowed to go beyond what could be interpreted as a dispute between civilians. It was only after the Kibya action that the Israeli Government began ascribing the execution of retaliatory actions directly to Zahal.

Dayan's attitude toward reprisal passed through two stages. Until the Egyptian blockade of the Straits of Tiran in September 1955, he believed that even if hard-hitting attacks on military objectives would not completely end the infiltration, murder, and plunder, they would at least drastically reduce them. In an address to Zahal officers published in September 1955, he stated:

We cannot safeguard every water pipe and every tree; we cannot prevent the murder of workers in orchards or families asleep in their beds. But we can put a high price on our blood; too heavy a price for an Arab settlement, an Arab army, or an Arab government to pay. The Arab army will be able to fight infiltration and explain its actions to the people only if it knows that stealing a cow from [a kibbutz] jeopardizes [the city of] Kalkilya and the murder of a Jew [on a moshav] endangers the population of Gaza.

Dayan revolutionized the reprisal policy by directing actions solely against military objectives, so as to avoid another Kibya and place the responsibility for the infiltration upon the Arab authorities. In an article entitled "From Falama to Sinai," he wrote: "The object of the retaliatory actions was not to exact revenge or mete out punishment, but to serve as a deterrent. Their aim was to bring home to the Arab rulers that terror against Israel would do them more harm than good."

Subsequent events were to bear him out. In his first year as C-o-S, it looked as though the Arab governments and armies—especially those of Egypt and Jordan—took note of the increasing severity of the retaliatory actions and tried to restrict infiltration into Israel. In 1954 the number of Israeli citizens killed by terrorists went down to thirty-three, (the number of wounded rose to seventy-seven), and in 1955 it went down even further to twenty-four killed (and sixty-nine wounded). Then in 1956, apart from the losses of the Sinai Campaign, the number of civilian casualties again rose steeply and stood at fifty-four killed and 129 wounded. After the Sinai Campaign this number dropped steadily, and from 1959 until 1967 the number of Israeli civilians killed each year as a result of Arab attacks was less than ten and in some years even less than five.

In 1955, however, as opposed to the steady drop in the number of civilian casualties, there was a sharp rise in military casualties: fifty in that year and sixty-three, apart from Sinai, in 1956. The high rate of Israeli casualties, civilian and military, over this period seemed to indicate that the larger retaliatory actions were not in fact achieving their aim. But it was at this point that the second stage of Dayan's approach to these actions began to take shape. Its essence was the concept of fortifying Israel's security by developing Zahal's deterrent power. Dayan achieved this not by increasing the number and frequency of retaliatory actions—as popular belief held. On the contrary, he launched fewer attacks, but intensified their scope and daring. In his September 1955 address quoted above, Dayan said that after a hard-hitting raid, the Arab country that was attacked generally restrained itself for a time and did not allow forces to cross the border to carry out actions in Israel. This restraint "was interpreted by the citizens of that country as weakness and the inability to confront Israel in battle." Accordingly, from September 1955 onward, the loss of soldiers' lives should be regarded as an inevitability shared between routine security and the building-up of a deterrent capacity.

In the four years before Dayan's term of office as C-o-S, 143 soldiers were killed as a result of enemy actions. In the four years of his term (1954-7), excluding the Sinai Campaign, the same number of soldiers fell. Had the situation been allowed to develop unchecked, this number would probably have grown much greater. After the Sinai Campaign the borders were quiet, and in Dayan's last year as C-o-S and for two years after his retirement, Israel did not carry out a single action. In these important aspects, Dayan's policy fully justified itself.

Both Ben Gurion and Dayan were highly sensitive to the loss of soldiers' lives. Some of Ben Gurion's aides believe that his torment over the losses reflected in his face and constituted a major part of the fatigue that led to his temporary retirement in 1953. Dayan betrayed his feelings less. Nevertheless, one of the aides with him throughout the Kalkilya action, in which eighteen soldiers were killed and eighty-eight wounded, noticed a change come over his face. Dayan apparently sensed this expression and felt that his sorrow would do little to encourage the commander and his men, for he left the command group and went to GHQ, returning only at dawn to meet the soldiers returning from the action.

Unlike Ben Gurion, Dayan was sensitive to the fate of the other side as well. Despite his part in the struggle to establish and secure the State of Israel, he was not blind to the injustice dealt the country's Arabs, and his loyalty to Israel was not attended by self-righteousness. He expressed something of his feelings in a manner that surprised and even shocked many Israelis over the open grave of Ro'i Rotberg, a member of Kibbutz Nahal Oz near the Gaza Strip. Rotberg was attacked by a group of Arabs as he sat on his horse talking to them and was dragged across the border, where he was tortured to death. At the graveside on May 1, 1956, Dayan said:

Yesterday morning, Ro'i was killed. The quiet of the spring morning blinded him and he did not see the murderers lying in wait for him along the furrow. Today, let us not condemn the murderers. What do we know of their fierce hate for us? For eight years they have been living in refugee camps in Gaza, while before their eyes we are making the lands and villages they and their ancestors lived in our land. We should demand his blood not of the Arabs of Gaza, but of ourselves ... Let us make our reckoning today. We are a generation of settlers, and without a helmet or a gun barrel we shall not be able to plant a tree or build a house ...

In the public debate on the best way to achieve peace with the Arabs—by diplomatic efforts and moderate military reactions, as Sharett and his supporters proposed, or by a powerful military force which would prove to the Arabs that they could not annihilate Israel, as Ben Gurion insisted—Dayan was entirely in favor of the latter. He referred to this debate in his eulogy for the murdered boy, for Ro'i Rotberg believed he had come upon Arabs who wished to talk to him in friendship, and they deceived and murdered him:

Beyond the furrow that marks the border is a sea of hate and the desire for revenge, hate that is lying in wait for the day when the calm will dull our readiness. Ro'i's blood cries out to us, and only to us. For we have vowed that our blood shall not be shed in vain, and yesterday once again we were deceived, we listened and we believed ... Let us not be afraid to see the enmity that consumes the lives of hundreds of thousands of Arabs around us. Let us not avert our gaze, for it will weaken our hand. This is the fate of our generation. The only choice we have is to be armed, strong, and resolute, or else our sword will fall from our hands and the thread of our lives be severed. The light in [Ro'i's] heart blinded him, and he did not see the slaughterer's knife. The longing for peace deafened him, and he did not hear the sound of murder.

Although he understood the injustice dealt the Arabs and their hatred for the Jewish settlers, Dayan believed that the governments of Egypt and Jordan could be deterred from backing the *fedayeen* actions and launching a military attack only if they knew for certain that they stood no chance in a war against Israel. In his September 1955 address to Zahal officers, he said: "The Arabs will oppose military involvement with Israel only if they have reason to believe that this course will be met with harsh reactions and will drag us into *a dispute* in which *they will be the losers*" (italics in the original).

The second stage of Dayan's approach to the retaliation policy stipulated not only "an eye for an eye" and a high price to be exacted for every attack on Israeli lives or property, but the proof of Israel's military superiority. Continuing the address, he stated: "Our victories and losses in small battles along the border and across it are vital for their effect on routine security, on the Arabs' assessment of Israel's strength, and on Israel's belief in her own strength . . . Indirectly, the retaliatory actions serve as a demonstration of the Israel-Arab balance of power as viewed by the Arab governments."

In the past, apart from the Tel-Mutilla, Falama, and Kibya actions, the raids had generally been carried out by very small units. Initially, Dayan employed small forces—four on a raid on Hebron and seven to the Legionnaires' camp at Azun. The change came on the night of February 28, 1955, a week after Lavon left the government and Ben Gurion returned to the Ministry of Defense. Two paratroop platoons raided an Egyptian Army base near the Gaza railroad station, while a smaller force laid down an ambush for the Egyptian reinforcements expected there.

The background for the Gaza action was a series of border incidents instigated by the Egyptian Army, particularly the infiltration of a sabotage squad sent by Egyptian Intelligence to ambush civilians and cause damage to property. But the results of the Gaza action seemed to indicate that it had a far more significant, long-range aim than a mere reprisal, namely, to prove Israeli superiority and serve as a deterrent. Thirty-six Egyptian soldiers were killed in the action, and two civilians and thirty-one soldiers were wounded. In addition, several houses and a well inside the Egyptian base were blown up. These results strengthened the impression that the paratroopers, who lost eight men, were in complete control of the Egyptian base throughout the action. After this action, the units implementing the policy of retaliation were to grow steadily larger.

The Gaza action was linked to Ben Gurion's return and his determination to implement a hard-line defense policy. But it would be more correct to view the success as the result of effective training, fighting methods, and the high standard of the Paratroop Brigade. It would appear that this unit's excellence in battle had more to do with shaping the policy of retaliation than any other single factor. Dayan noted that the policy of retaliation developed through the actions themselves: "The way actions were carried out was to a great extent the product of earlier experiences that taught us what could and could not be done."

The policy of reprisal was founded on several levels, however. First there was Ben Gurion's decision that forays across the border into Arab villages sheltering terrorists, the killing of inhabitants, and the destruction of houses was completely justified. Then, in the light of the Kibya tragedy and on Dayan's initiative, came the decision to attack only military objectives and personnel. On the second level were Dayan's operative concepts, the revolutionary shift to military objectives, the choice of the objectives themselves, the composition of the attacking forces, and the methods they were to employ. The third level was the actual execution of the actions, and in this respect the Paratroop Brigade proved that it was capable of doing what had previously been considered impossible.

For a long time the true size of the forces taking part in the much-publicized reprisal actions was unknown outside Israel. UN observers, for example, estimated that 500 soldiers took part in the Kibya action, while in actual fact there were only 103. Likewise, it was estimated that an entire brigade was involved in the "Kinneret Action." These exaggerations defeated Dayan's intentions. Instead of intimidating Egypt into curbing the activities of the *fedayeen*, fear of Israel's superiority spurred Nasser's government to equip and prepare for a war of annihilation, which in turn brought about a third stage in the policy of retaliation: recognition of the need for a preemptive war, or at least an anticipatory strike.

Whether events would have taken a different course if there had been another C-o-S at the time can only be surmised. A less dynamic, political, or daring C-o-S might have served as a restraining factor, whereas Dayan's success in raising morale and the fighting spirit of the army, his political orientation, and his daring were undoubtedly an escalating factor. After the Egyptians concluded an arms deal with Czechoslovakia in September 1955, Dayan, more than Ben Gurion, pressed for the intensification of the border clashes through hard-hitting retaliatory actions in order to precipitate a war in which he believed Israel's victory—with only small losses—was assured. Ben Gurion, on the other hand, for political reasons as well as fear of numerous casualties, was apprehensive of undertaking a full-scale war or any steps that might precipitate it.

Although Dayan was in favor of escalating the struggle, he did not deliberately instigate incidents, as some Israeli critics claimed at the time. His loyalty and obedience to Ben Gurion were exemplary, but he knew Ben Gurion could be persuaded. He therefore continued to hope for a strong Egyptian reaction to a retaliatory raid that would force Israel into an even stronger action, thus initiating a chain of action and retaliation that would provide a convenient background for seizing the Gaza Strip. During one period when the border was "hot," a brigade commander ordered his units to dig defensive positions. When Dayan visited the brigade, the commander proudly showed him around the excellent fortifications, confident of the C-o-S's approval. Far from praising him, Dayan was furious. "What did you dig in for? If anything serious happens, we want to attack, not defend!" He ordered the brigade to fill in all the trenches and dismantle the fortified positions. In fact, he forbade the digging of defensive networks anywhere along Israel's borders.

The month of September 1955 saw the blockading of the Straits of Tiran and the signing of the Egyptian-Czech arms deal. All shipping from the Red Sea to Eilat was halted, and El Al flights to South Africa, which traversed Egyptian air space, were suspended. The arms deal simultaneously accelerated the build-up of Soviet weapons in the Egyptian Army. Furthermore, in April 1955 Egyptian GHQ, concluding that terror and sabotage provided an effective way of waging war against Israel, established a special unit called *fedayeen* or "self-sacrificers," who carried out raids against Israel from Egyptian, Syrian, Lebanese, and Jordanian territory. In September Egyptian HQ stepped up *fedayeen* activities, and Dayan expressed the opinion then that "now more than ever before, Israel must confront the Arabs with an ultimatum: to preserve the peace or slide into war."

Dayan feared that if Israel did not strike first, she would be attacked by Egypt, have less of a chance of victory, and suffer greater damage. His fears were well founded. On September 29 word leaked out that ships bearing heavy weapons (tanks, cannons, and planes), as well as Soviet submarines, were entering Egyptian harbors, and Radio Cairo declared, "The day of Israel's defeat is at hand. There will be no peace on the borders, for we demand revenge, and revenge means death to Israel." As soon as the Egyptians closed the Straits of Tiran, Dayan suggested to Ben Gurion that Zahal reopen them by force. Ben Gurion (still Minister of Defence in Sharett's Cabinet) did not consent, however.

On October 19, 1955 Dayan flew to Paris for a month-long vacation, but on the 22nd Ben Gurion recalled him. On the following day he met Ben Gurion, who was recuperating from influenza. Dayan was understandably eager to know why he had been recalled so urgently, but Ben Gurion entered into a general conversation, asking Dayan for a review of the security situation and current problems. It was only as Dayan was leaving that Ben Gurion gave him various instructions, one of which was "to prepare to capture the Straits of Tiran—Sharm e-Sheikh, Ras Nasrani, and the islands Tiran and Sanapir—to ensure free Israeli shipping through the Gulf of Aqaba and the Red Sea."

On November 2, after the general elections, Ben Gurion again became Prime Minister and Minister of Defense. In presenting his coalition Cabinet to the Knesset, he hinted at his readiness for war:

... The Egyptian representatives to the UN have declared openly that a protracted state of war exists between Israel and Egypt. The Egyptian Government has violated a basic international law governing the freedom of shipping through the Suez, on which there was a specific resolution of the Security Council. Thus Egypt is now seeking to block the way of Israeli vessels in the Red Sea, contrary to the international principle of freedom of the seas. This one-sided war will have to end, for it cannot remain one-sided indefinitely.

. . . If our rights are violated by acts of violence on land or sea, we shall reserve freedom of action to defend those rights in the most effective manner. We seek peace, but not suicide . . .

Dayan knew in advance what Ben Gurion intended to say to the Knesset. He immediately set about implementing the Prime Minister's instructions to prepare for the capture of the Straits of Tiran and ordered the formation of a special task force—paratroopers and infantry units under the command of Col. Chaim Bar-Lev. A reconnaissance patrol was sent out to check the possibility of moving vehicles down to the straits by land.

The Sinai Campaign was an expression of the tragic duality circumstances had forced upon Israel: being vulnerable, she was forced to be strong; her desire to defend herself forced her to attack; and her wish for peace compelled her to wage war. There can be little doubt that had Israel been an expansive country with a large population and a strong economy, things would have developed differently and the dispute would not have gone beyond a certain point. But being small—literally tiny—in comparison with the Arab countries, Israel seemed an easy target. Her refusal to fall prey to the larger Arab countries compelled her to be strong; her very vulnerability fostered her strength.

In Israel, and to some extent abroad, even the fiercest of the retaliatory actions were regarded as defensive acts. The disadvantage of the retaliation policy was that no single action—or even two or three, for that matter—could deter the Arabs definitely or even ensure a lull in the present. On the other hand, too many actions provoked counteractions, which in turn necessitated renewed retaliation, and so on in a never-ending cycle. The momentum generated by this process led to a gradual escalation on all fronts and, of necessity, to war. By September of 1956 Dayan was completely convinced of the inevitability of all-out war.

In one month, Zahal carried out four retaliatory raids which inflicted increasingly higher casualties on both sides. On September 11 at Rahawa, nine Israeli soldiers were wounded and twenty Legionnaires killed; on September 13 at Garandal, Zahal suffered thirteen casualties and the Arab Legion twenty-two; on September 25 at Husan there were twenty-six Zahal casualties and fifty-one Jordanian; and on October 10 at Kalkilya, Israel suffered more casualties than in any single action since the War of Independence—eighteen killed and eighty-eight wounded, while the Arab Legion lost eighty-eight soldiers and fourteen others were wounded.

To Israelis, the number of casualties has always been the most important gauge of a military action. In 1956 the total number of casualties rose to the point where the Israeli public began doubting the usefulness of the reprisals. The outstanding feature of the retaliatory raids was the fact that they were carried out without any intention of conquest. Immediately after an action, Zahal would evacuate the area of the battle and return to Israeli territory. But the question arose: if repeated raids failed to put an end to Arab aggression, what purpose was served by the increasing loss of soldiers' lives? In September 1955, when he still believed in the effectiveness of the retaliation policy, Dayan maintained that what he called "routine security incidents" (attacks by Arab infiltrators on Israeli citizens) must be "considered not as transient episodes but as a condition that will last for some time—ten, twenty years."

A year later, the fourth year of the retaliation raids, Dayan realized that the policy had outlived its usefulness. In a General Staff meeting on October 15 devoted to the Kalkilya action, "the main topic was . . . the whole problem of the retaliatory actions. There was general agreement that the present system needs revision," Dayan wrote in his *Diary of the Sinai Campaign*. In his opinion, the reason for this situation was the prolonged use of the same formula of retaliation: "[If] at first it was the standard experience that our actions against the Egyptians and the Jordanians took them by surprise . . . now after every murder committed in Israel by the *fedayeen*, the Arabs know that they can expect an attack on a military installation, so that when our units go into action . . . they find the enemy well prepared and well organized for defense." This, he felt, was the reason for the ever-growing number of Zahal casualties.

After the Kalkilya action, Dayan met with newspaper editors and presented the problem as follows: "We are a small army, and after every action like this we put our best men in the hospitals . . . The question is where do we go from here?" He did not think in terms of nonmilitary actions. His doubts about the reprisals were aroused only by the growing number of casualties. He had no doubt whatsoever about their effect on the enemy: "I do not think Jordan can remain indifferent after what happened last night [in Kalkilya]. If a hundred of their soldiers and policemen are killed in retaliation for the murder of two Israelis, they must reassess the value of sending *fedayeen,* and it is doubtful that they will continue sending them once they know that a price will be paid for every action. I believe that if we pursue this method, we will force the Jordanians to stop sending *fedayeen.* But the question we must ask ourselves is, if *we* can continue this method." He seemed to be hinting quite clearly that his answer to both questions was a preemptive war.

When Ben Gurion proposed opening the Straits of Tiran by force, he encountered stiff opposition in the Cabinet, which decided that the time was not ripe for such an action and that Israel should act "at a time and place she deems appropriate." Dayan was deeply disappointed when Ben Gurion told him of the Cabinet decision. It was this reaction, among other things, that gave rise to the description of Dayan as "optimistic about the Arabs and pessimistic about the Jews." In other words, he believed that the Arabs would force Israel to fight before the Israelis would make up their own minds to do so.

In a letter to Ben Gurion written on December 5, 1955, Dayan reacted strongly to the Cabinet decision. The formula that Israel would act "at a time and place she deems appropriate" seemed pompous and hollow to him, for it was not backed by a concrete plan for opening the straits. He claimed that the policy chosen by the government was "incorrect and will, in effect, lead to the loss of our naval and aerial freedom through the Straits of Tiran. Eilat will thereby become a coastal strip along a closed lake, exit from which will be conditional on Egyptian agreement." The government's failure to act following the closing of the straits constituted "a *de facto* surrender of our freedom of shipping and flight through the Straits of Tiran." He expressed the view that Israel must "undertake as soon as possible (within one month) the capture of the Straits of Tiran." His opinion was overruled, and the task force he had established under Bar-Lev's command was disbanded. Dayan's criticism of Ben Gurion is implied between the lines, for he reminded the Prime Minister that Israel lost free access to Mount Scopus and the use of the Latrun road (as stipulated in the Armistice Agreements) "owing to the Jordanians' refusal, on the one hand, and our failure to implement [our rights] by force, on the other." Dayan had suggested implementing both of these rights before leaving Jerusalem in 1949. He also wrote that Ben Gurion had committed himself to military action in several unequivocal declarations and had "made known to the Prime Minister of Egypt, through General Burns, the policy of the government, which holds that Israel will not agree to a one-sided adherence to the Armistice Agreements." Dayan was suggesting here that Ben Gurion was endangering his credibility.

Although the tone of Dayan's letter is critical of Ben Gurion, in his *Diary of the Sinai Campaign* he lays the blame elsewhere: "Although my letter was addressed to Ben Gurion, it should not have been directed to him, for after all, he was the one who was anxious to instruct the army to break the blockade, and it was the Cabinet that decided that the time to do it had not yet come." Strictly speaking, this was true; but Dayan knew that Ben Gurion was capable of pushing through the Cabinet any decision he considered vital. Being in the minority had never stopped him from fighting for his views. On the contrary, in such cases he would persevere until he had his way. Dayan believed that Ben Gurion's status within the Cabinet, particularly in matters of security, was such that if he was convinced that the only way to open the Straits of Tiran was by military force, he would be capable of bringing the other ministers round to his opinion. Sometimes Ben Gurion simply found it expedient to appear as a minority hamstrung by the majority.

Their approach to security matters had an identical source—the dread of shedding Jewish blood. But whereas Ben Gurion feared wholesale slaughter and a new holocaust should Israel succumb to Egypt, Dayan was more concerned about the possibility that too low a price would be set on Jewish blood. Born in Poland, Ben Gurion could perhaps visualize far more vividly the horror of the East European pogroms and the Nazi holocaust. Dayan, the soldier, fully confident in Zahal's renewed fighting ability and recalling the sight of "Arabs scattering like birds at one bang on a tin," could not easily conceive of the slaughter of the Jews of Israel. Years later he referred even to the Six-Day War as an expression of the nation's yearning for the land of its forefathers, rather than a war of survival.

The differences in their approach to war were even more pronounced. In presenting his Cabinet on November 2, Ben Gurion stated: "We do not covet one inch of foreign soil. Yet as long as we live, no one will taken an inch of our land from us. We do not see any real reason for the dispute between ourselves and Egypt; on the contrary, we see fertile ground for cooperation between the two nations, and there is no lack of good will on our part." Indeed, it was in order to maintain peace on the borders that he opposed using force to gain access to Mount Scopus and transit through the Latrun area or to expel the Syrian Army from the positions it had taken up inside the Israeli demilitarized zone in the north. Dayan came close to suspecting that Ben Gurion was prepared to forgo free shipping in the Straits of Tiran to avoid war.

In cases where territory was at stake, Dayan was the more extreme of the two. Ben Gurion opposed seizing the Gaza Strip not because he disagreed with Dayan that the Egyptian Army should be driven out and the saboteurs' bases destroyed, but because he predicted an entire complex of problems in the densely populated area. As far as Dayan was concerned, territory outweighed potential problems. He had previously expressed his reluctance to forfeit "one inch" during the demarcation of no-man's land in the Jerusalem area. To Dayan, shipping rights constituted territory, and the prevention of free shipping was tantamount to shrinking Israel's borders.

The principal difference between the two men lay in their outlook on the war and its consequences. Ben Gurion, more than Dayan, envisaged a bitter war with many casualties and was more sensitive to world public opinion, particularly that of the Great Powers. He was also mindful of the strengthening of Egypt's army with the aid of Soviet arms. In a review of the security situation in the Knesset on January 2, 1956, he said: "Throughout the years, since the end of hostilities seven years ago, all the Arab armies, even Egypt alone, enjoyed quantitative superiority of weapons in all its military branches—on land, sea, and in the air. This, without taking into consideration their tremendous advantage in manpower." In general, Ben Gurion, like many others, believed that Zahal made up in quality for what it lacked in quantity and thus counterbalanced any inferiority in arms and equipment. But following the Czech arms deal, the USSR not only poured into Egypt unprecedented quantities of arms, but included modern weapons, the likes of which had never before been seen in the Middle East. According to Ben Gurion, "The Czech deal has, in the past few months, reversed the situation in a most serious and dangerous manner."

Dayan was less disturbed than Ben Gurion by the quantitative military superiority of the Arab countries. Although he considered the Soviet build-up of Egypt serious, he did not consider the Czech arms deal an immediate danger. In March 1956 he said, "Israeli youth can furnish more pilots and tank crews than all the Arab countries put together. Our enemies have Migs, Stalins [heavy tanks], and Centurions, but all these require educated and capable pilots and operators." He was certain that an Egyptian attack on Israel would result in the aggressor's defeat and believed in Zahal's ultimate victory "because of Israel's high technical potential, its internal network of defensive lines, and the high morale of Zahal." These words marked the beginning of his calm, reassuring leadership in times of stress. It may well have been from this point that his military leadership began to radiate beyond the army to the public at large.

Ben Gurion's deep concern over the possibility of aerial bombardments on Israeli population centers was at the heart of his conviction that Israel should not go to war without a strong ally. Dayan, on the other hand, told the Israeli public that it might be impossible "to prevent fatal aerial bombardments on our settlements, and perhaps even the capture of small areas," but he promised ultimate victory. He felt that Israel could manage without an ally, and his words carried a hint of his belief that a preemptive war—before the Egyptian Army had time to familiarize itself with the new Soviet arms—would to a great extent improve Israel's security position.

Ben Gurion was troubled by the possibly damaging consequences of a preemptive war. An Arab defeat would certainly not endear Israel to her neighbors or bring peace any closer; the rift between the nations would widen and the barrier of hatred grow. A preemptive war would also give Israel the image of an aggressor, rather than a nation seeking peace, and further weaken the already faltering support of world public opinion. There was also the political aspect. Jordan and Egypt had mutual defense treaties with England, and Egypt had begun strengthening its ties with the Soviet Union. Israel was isolated in a world that was rapidly consolidating into blocs. Her gains on the battlefield would probably be wrested from her by the Arabs' allies. The need for a powerful ally seemed so vital to Ben Gurion that at one time he thought Israel should join the British Commonwealth and tried to suggest as much to the British Government. Later his aides explored the possibility of Israel joining NATO. Both of these attempts came to naught, and without allies Ben Gurion felt that Israel would gain little or nothing from war with the Arabs.

Finally, Ben Gurion may have had a further objection to a preemptive war. He told Shimon Peres, "Any state that is in danger, even if it is under great pressure, must not disregard the historical dimension that invokes the judgment of future generations, who will be in a position to evaluate objectively the spirit, content, logic, and morality of decisions reached under the duress of circumstances."

The sum of all these considerations prevented Ben Gurion from pressuring the government into approving a military action at the end of 1955. According to Peres, Ben Gurion regarded war as the outcome of necessity, rather than an opportunity to be seized. He was prepared to undertake a preemptive war only in a "no alternative" situation in which any delay would mean suicide. Dayan felt that it was unwise to wait until the last minute, until Israel had been maneuvered into a corner. He believed there was a right moment for launching a war and was afraid to miss it. In his December 5 letter to Ben Gurion demanding the opening of the blockade on the straits within a month, he wrote, "As to time, it does not seem to me that the moment for action will be more favorable a few months hence. With the strengthening of the Egyptian forces, particularly in the air, our prospect of succeeding in such an operation will be weakened." Ben Gurion knew, however, that history generally abounds with "opportunities." Indeed, within a few months a new chance appeared on the horizon.

The military situation in 1956 deteriorated steadily. Egyptian spokesmen declared with increasing frequency their country's intention and ability to destroy Israel. The details of the Czech arms deal began to leak out to the public: in return for Egyptian cotton, and at less than half price, Egypt was to receive "530 armored vehicles . . . some 500 cannons of various types; almost 200 fighter aircraft, bombers and transport planes; and a number of warships . . ." This deal, in Dayan's words, "wiped out in a flash the shaky arms balance" in the Middle East. Prior to the Czech deal, Egypt had eighty jet planes to Israel's fifty. The new deal increased the number of Egypt's jet planes to 200, ultramodern fighters and bombers. The balance of air power, now heavily weighted in Egypt's favor, was the weakest link in Israel's defenses. The situation was not much brighter regarding armor or artillery.

The intensification of the *fedayeen* raids was regarded as only part of the preparations for an all-out Egyptian attack. To complete the picture, Egypt set up joint military commands, first in September 1956 with Syria and then in October with Jordan. On October 24 a tripartite military agreement was signed between Egypt, Syria, and Jordan, tightening the noose around Israel. The gravity of Israel's situation was relieved somewhat by rapid developments in her relations with France. Military ties with France had been established at the end of 1954, when Shimon Peres flew to Paris equipped with a personal letter from Ben Gurion to General Pierre Koenig, then Minister of Defense, who agreed to supply arms to Israel. In August of that year, before Peres' trip, Dayan was awarded the French Legion of Honor for his part in the invasion of Syria in June 1941, and during his stay in Paris he held talks with Generals Koenig, Guillaume, Zeller and Admiral Noamey. Nevertheless, Peres summed up 1955 "with some satisfaction mixed with disappointment: direct contact with many French politicians was established, the ice was broken on the question of arms, we have already acquired tanks and cannons, but as for planes, apart from a few Mosquitoes, we have not been able to over-come the obstacles." It was Peres, Director-General of the Ministry of Defense and only thirty-two years old, who saw in France the ally that Ben Gurion was seeking. At the very least, he felt that France could be a "more regular" or "political" source of modern arms, partic-ularly planes.

It was only at the beginning of 1956, after the general elections in France and the establishment of Guy Mollet's Socialist government—with Christian Pineau as Foreign Minister and Bourges-Maunonry as Minister of Defense, that Peres could write, "At last, the harvest . . . The obstacles—real and formal—that barred our way have been removed, and arms supply has begun on a political scale." In March 1956, the first French Mystère 4 jet planes touched down in Israel. The "French arms deal" began to cancel out the military advantages of the Czech one.

The possibility of a concerted Israeli-Anglo-French action against Egypt was mooted only after Nasser nationalized the Suez Canal on July 26. According to Peres, the most authoritative source on this issue, the idea was raised by France. At the time, Peres was in Paris and met with Bourges-Maunonry, who suddenly asked him, "How much time do you think would it take for your army to cross the Sinai peninsula and reach the Suez?" Peres replied that "the accepted estimate in Israel was five to seven days . . . Bourges-Maunonry then asked if Israel had any intention of taking action along its southern borders, and if so, where? I replied that our Suez is Eilat; we would never agree to its being closed off, and this could be the reason for an Israeli action."

These may well have been merely hypothetical questions at the time with no immediate implications. But it was only three months later that, as Peres relates, "We returned to the subject seriously . . . again in a conversation with Bourges-Maunonry, in September 1956. He told us of the hesitations and arguments in London over the Suez affair and added with a smile: 'Perhaps the British timing [for an Anglo-French action against Egypt]—which has not been set—is closer to the Israeli timing [for opening the Straits of Tiran by force, for which no date had been set either] than to the French timing." Peres cabled Ben Gurion and received the following reply: "If the timing is all you are discussing, then we are closer to Paris than to London." Peres conveyed the essence of Ben Gurion's cable to the French Minister of Defense. France, Bourges-Maunonry replied, was interested in launching a war against Egypt "before the end of the year, before the winter, before the resignation of the present Cabinet." The latter part of 1956 seemed propitious because riots in Poland had drawn the attention of the Kremlin from the Middle East to Eastern Europe, and America was preoccupied with presidential elections.

Dayan wrote in his *Diary* that on September 1, during a meeting of the full General Staff, a cable arrived from the military attaché in Paris "with information on the Anglo-French plan to seize the Suez Canal—'Operation Musketeer.' " During the lunch break, a brief consultation was held and it was agreed that "in any event, we had to prepare for the possibility of war in our area." Dayan ordered his secretary to cut down the meetings scheduled for him over the next two weeks and used the time to visit operational units. In his entry for September 25, he relates a discussion that took place between Ben Gurion, Peres, and himself as they were driving up to Jerusalem. At first they discussed a possible target for a retaliatory action and later "reviewed the results of Peres' visit to France." Presumably it was only then that Israeli participation in an Anglo-French action against Egypt was seriously discussed.

It appears that initially only Ben Gurion, Peres, and Dayan were party to these secret developments. Ben Gurion widened the circle of informed people when he brought in Levi Eshkol, the Minister of Finance, who would bear the burden of mobilization and equipping the army, and Golda Meir, who in June of that year replaced Sharett as Foreign Minister. Dayan secretly flew to France a number of times to discuss arms purchases. On October 21, 1956 Ben Gurion flew to France for four days of talks with representatives of France and Britain. On October 24, his last day in France and only five days before the commencement of the Sinai Campaign, he signed the minutes of what was known as the Sèvres Conference, committing Israel to a joint action in the Suez area with Britain and France. Ben Gurion brought the issue before the Cabinet on Friday, October 26, and informed the opposition only on the 28th, the day before the Campaign began. The single-minded way in which Ben Gurion pushed the decision through the Cabinet strengthened Dayan's conviction that had Ben Gurion wished, he could have done likewise in December 1955.

It seems that from July to the beginning of October, Dayan and Peres were instrumental in the deliberation and major steps that resulted in Israel's participation in the Suez War (the overall name for the joint action, in which Israel's part was called "Operation Kadesh" or the Sinai Campaign). As we shall see, Dayan and Peres also played an important part at the last moment of Ben Gurion's decision.

Dayan opens his *Diary of the Sinai Campaign* with subtle criticism of Ben Gurion: "The Sinai Campaign was the product jointly of a sharpening of the political-security conflict between Israel and her neighboring Arab states, and of the Anglo-French decision to establish control of the Suez Canal zone by force. If it were not for the Anglo-French action, it is doubtful whether Israel could have launched the campaign; and if she had, its character, both military and political, would have been different." In Dayan's opinion, Ben Gurion should have launched the campaign to open the straits without any reference to the nationalization of the Suez Canal. He therefore draws a distinction between the capture of the Straits of Tiran, which he proposed in the autumn of 1955, and the Sinai Campaign of October-November 1956. The first was to have been an independent Israeli action, while the second, although also based on Israeli interests, was dependent upon France and Britain. It appears from this criticism that he would have preferred an independent action in 1955, which might have averted the complex and disappointing Sinai Campaign.

Of the three, Dayan and Peres were far more eager for war than Ben Gurion. Dayan claims that until the last moment, he doubted whether Ben Gurion would finally opt for war. According to Peres, "Ben Gurion revealed to no one, not even to us, what his final position would be." In the political debate in the Knesset on October 15, only two weeks before the opening of the campaign, he still spoke against preemptive war. Arguing with members of the opposition who demanded an Israeli-initiated war, Ben Gurion said: "The members of the Cabinet and I do not accept this view. We favor self-defense, and if we are attacked we shall fight with all the strength at our disposal until victory is achieved. But we know the horrors of war, its destruction of human lives and property, and we do not believe that wars solve historical problems; they certainly do not achieve lasting solutions. For these reasons we are not eager for war."

Ben Gurion's first move which could be interpreted as favoring the action came on October 17, when he received a telegram from Guy

Mollet inviting him to Paris for secret talks with British and French representatives. When Peres entered Ben Gurion's office with the telegram, he found Levi Eshkol, Golda Meir, and Dayan sitting there, tense and impatient. According to Peres, there were no basic differences of opinion in the consultation that ensued. "Golda was skeptical," he claims; Eshkol was in favor of the trip; while "Dayan could hardly contain his enthusiasm." Needless to say, Peres was no less enthusiastic. At the time, Peres "went about with the feeling that a great historical moment in Franco-Israeli relations was in the offing, but if it were not exploited wisely, this too would be lost forever."

The question remains: to what extent did Dayan and Peres influence Ben Gurion's decision on the Sinai Campaign or the escalation of the retaliatory actions that preceded it? One thing is clear: from the very first day of negotiations with the French on a joint military action, Ben Gurion adopted a perplexing and apparently contradictory stand. While he remained critical of all the proposals and telegrams being exchanged, he did not prevent, and in fact encouraged, the moves that ultimately brought about the Sinai Campaign. In this way, he achieved the freedom to withhold his final decision until the last possible moment. The large quantity of arms Israel purchased from France might have been an indication of an underlying intention to go to war, but this was only an impression. Equipment was needed to defend Israel against a possible Egyptian attack, and Ben Gurion had no scruples about the arguments used to persuade France to sell his government arms. Likewise, the fact that what might be termed joint Franco-Israeli planning took place was not in itself proof of his approval. At the last moment, he could always decide against a preemptive war and relegate the plans to the obscurity of the archives.

Peres' influence on Ben Gurion stemmed from his demonstration that France could serve as an ally and a source of arms in case of war. Dayan's influence was more fundamental, for he had made Zahal into an army whose ultimate victory was assured. This was the real significance of the increasing scale of the retaliatory actions, which Dayan regarded not as acts of revenge but as warnings that should the Arab countries fail to control their citizens and prevent them from attacking Israel, "Israeli forces would wreak havoc in their country."

Had it not been for the retaliatory actions and the proof they furnished of Zahal's ability, the French Government would not have agreed to equip Israel with modern arms. This is borne out by a statement made by General Koenig: "Israel must be given more arms for her excellent soldiers to use." According to Dayan, it was clear "from the very first contacts with the French representatives . . . that we were not only requesting arms as a deterrent, but that we envisaged the possibility of using them to fight the Arab terror." Had Zahal's string of Falama-like defeats continued, it is doubtful whether France would have agreed to supply it with arms. Under Dayan, Zahal became a new and influential factor in France's—and later Britain's—political deliberations, despite the traditional pro-Arab policies of both these countries.

Ben Gurion, Dayan, and Peres arrived in Paris on October 21. Ben Gurion stayed at the villa in Sèvres, while his retinue was put up at the Reynolds Hotel in Paris, where they registered under assumed names. Though he wore dark glasses to conceal his identity, Dayan apparently found it difficult to discard his true identity and signed the register as "Mosh Dya," a transparent variation on his own name.

Dayan was influential in another respect. The actual negotiations with the British and French representatives at the Villa Sèvres were in danger of breaking down over the form the joint action was to take. The British were concerned with satisfying public opinion about their reasons for attacking Egypt. They strongly suggested that Israel attack Egypt first. With the fighting at its height, Britain and France would issue a cease-fire ultimatum and then send troops to intervene and seize the canal zone in the guise of international peace-keepers. Ben Gurion's answer to this suggestion was a vehement no. He was certainly not prepared to agree to an arrangement whereby Israel would appear as the aggressor and Britain and France the righteous guardians of the peace. He also feared the effect of Egyptian aerial bombardments on Israeli cities and towns during the first week (from the opening of the battle until the intervention of Britain and France). Furthermore, he was deeply suspicious of Britain and considered her capable of withdrawing from the entire plan at the last moment. Ben Gurion considered the British position a prime instance of Albion's perfidy and even an attempt to destroy the friendship and cooperation between Israel and France under a clever disguise of a tripartite action. He also had a positive motive—stronger than any of his negative considerations—for rejecting the British proposal, namely, his determination to ensure full cooperation between Israel and the two European powers. The acquisition of powerful allies was in itself a political aim. It may be said that Ben Gurion was prepared to pay for allies with war. But the British position precluded full cooperation and assumed an independent Israeli action on the one hand and Anglo-French intervention—against both Egypt and Israel—on the other.

For Dayan, the most important aim was to repulse the Egyptians. The excuse, that is, the political formula and the form it was to take, were secondary issues in his eyes. He was not quite as suspicious of the British, nor as concerned about the fate of Israel's cities in case of aerial bombardment. As far back as November 17, 1955, Maj. Gen. Dan Tolkowsky had submitted a document to Dayan detailing his reasons for the immediate launching of a preemptive war.

He asserted that the Israeli Air Force could attain superiority in the air within two or three days. Dayan had asked Tolkowsky to convey the document directly to Ben Gurion. A short time before the Sinai Campaign, Dayan asked Tolkowsky for a renewed assessment of the situation and was again told that the Air Force "is not afraid of confronting the Egyptians on its own." What worried Dayan was the possibility that Israel would let another opportunity slip. If anything, circumstances were now even more favorable because of the Hungarian Revolt. On September 7 he wrote in his diary that Israel must "not be caught in a position in which we would have to pass up favorable political opportunities to strike at Egypt."

An ingeniously simple formula, proposed by Dayan, saved the Sèvres talks, helped the three sides reach a satisfactory compromise, and must certainly have influenced Ben Gurion's final decision. The British sought to justify their intervention by citing certain clauses in their 1954 treaty with Egypt, which allowed for military intervention in case of war. Dayan therefore suggested that instead of launching a full-scale war against Egypt, Israel would undertake an enlarged retaliatory action. In this way he satisfied the British and eased Ben Gurion's fears, for an enlarged retaliatory action would be acceptable to local public opinion as well as to the Cabinet and Israel would not be labeled an aggressor and would not provoke Egyptian aerial bombardments, Ben Gurion's major concern. As for world public opinion, a retaliatory action could be explained as an act of self-defense intended to secure the lives and property of Israel's citizens.

The main advantage in Dayan's proposal was the fact that a retaliatory action would be an independent Israeli effort. On September 17, 1956, he wrote in his diary: "The operation which is likely to be launched will have been prompted by the abrogation of the international status of the Suez Canal. This is not a specific Israeli problem, and even though it is naturally of close concern to us, we have no aspirations to reach the Suez or become an involved party in this dispute." This was apparently his basic approach at the Sèvres talks. He favored an independent Israeli action, according to Israeli calculations. Should there be a possibility of carrying out the campaign in conjunction or coordination with others, he would have no objections. But unlike Ben Gurion, he did not feel that full cooperation of a major power was absolutely necessary.

In translating his suggestion into operative terms, Dayan, according to all the participants of the Sèvres talks, displayed great talent. For the initial Israeli move had to appear both as a retaliatory action and—to satisfy the British—a warlike act that would call for Britain's intervention in the area. The solution he devised was to begin the war from the end, as it were. In operative terms, this meant dropping a paratroop battalion at one end of the Mitla Pass—near the

Parker Memorial—not far from the Suez Canal and in the vicinity of Zahal's final objective. Should Ben Gurion's fears prove correct and Britain renege on its promise of intervention, the paratroop unit's retreat would be assured by a second paratroop unit that would break through the Egyptian lines and link up with the first at Mitla. The action would then be over and could be regarded as no more than a large reprisal raid. Should Britain and France carry out their part of the agreement, the drop near Suez could be construed as an act of war in the Suez Canal zone and fully justify their armed intervention.

Britain agreed that the campaign should begin with a raid and that France would provide air cover for Israel's cities and a naval bombardment of the Egyptian bases along the Sinai coast. This would satisfy Ben Gurion's request for an unequivocal sign of Anglo-French participation in the Israeli action. From this point the plan began to take shape and a timetable was drawn up.

Dayan's plan was no momentary flash of inspiration. At GHQ the operative concept of starting a war from the end had been studied before the Sèvres Conference. In the *Diary of the Sinai Campaign,* he wrote: "In my view, we should open the campaign with a paratroop drop in the vicinity of our final objectives, to seal the routes against Egyptian reinforcements and to capture dominant positions of tactical importance. The paratroopers will have to hold their ground until our main forces catch up with them—which I estimate should be not much more than 48 hours later."

Even after Dayan's proposals were accepted by the British and French, Ben Gurion gave no indication of whether or not he had made up his mind. A few hours before the signing of the Sèvres protocols, he sat in the garden with Dayan, Peres, and their aides. After meditating silently for quite a while, he turned to Dayan and asked, "And what do you think?" Dayan replied, "I think we should go ahead." Ben Gurion said nothing. Only when he signed the agreement was it clear that he had finally made up his mind. A few days later, Dayan wrote in his diary: "The moment when I finally knew that doubts had been resolved and the decision taken to launch the campaign . . . occurred on the 25th, four days ago."

On the surface, Ben Gurion was wary, circumspect, and a stickler for detail, yet secretly he had to suppress a volcanic and far-reaching vision. Dayan discovered at the very beginning of their acquaintance that Ben Gurion tackled every issue against the background of an all-embracing world view. He likewise considered the Sinai Campaign in the light of a total reorganization of the map of the Middle East, which would bring peace between a secure Israel and her Arab neighbors on the one hand, and renew British and French influence in the area on the other. He believed that France had erred in expanding the borders of Lebanon, for the additional area brought into the country's borders a large Moslem population that threatened the Christian majority and consequently weakened the prospect of another pro-French country in the Middle East. Ben Gurion felt that this mistake could be rectified by taking the Litani area from Lebanon and annexing it to Israel. A much more ambitious "rectification" of this kind was his proposal to divide the strife-torn, politically unstable Kingdom of Jordan between Israel and Iraq, thereby completely eliminating Nasserist influence in Syria and bolstering Britain's influence in the Middle East. In the south he envisaged Israeli sovereignty over the Gulf of Aqaba and an internationally controlled Suez Canal.

Ben Gurion expressed something of his vision of the post-Sinai Middle East on November 7, two days after the end of "Operation Kadesh," while the Suez War was still raging, when he announced in the Knesset "a new revelation at Sinai" and spoke of "freeing" the Bay of Shlomo—the biblical name for the bay at Sharm e-Sheikh—which, according to Procopius, a sixth-century Greek philosopher he quoted, had been settled by Jews. In fact, Ben Gurion proclaimed a new kingdom of Israel stretching from Dan in the north to the Isle of Yotvat in the south (Yotvat, according to Procopius, was the Hebrew name for Tiran, one of the two islands in the neck of the Straits of Tiran). As far as Ben Gurion was concerned, the aims of the Sinai Campaign went far beyond merely opening the straits to Israeli shipping and destroying the *fedayeen* bases in Sinai. If he was prepared to pay the heavy price of war, he wanted the maximum in return. Peres was also fired by a far-reaching political vision. He imagined the genius of the Jewish people functioning as a high-powered engine, propelling the Middle East toward economic, industrial, and political prominence in the world. He too considered Sinai a beginning, not an end.

Although Dayan could hardly contain his excitement at the prospect of going to war and was afraid the opportunity would again be lost, he was nevertheless the most realistic of the three. Prophetic political visions, new maps of the Middle East, or the creation of favorable political alliances were castles in the air for him. He was far more concerned with immediate problems: ending the terror, eliminating the possibility of an Arab attack, and opening sea and air traffic to and from Eilat. The territorial adjustments he sought were based solely on concern for Israel's well-being, rather than the status of France or Britain in the Middle East. Dayan felt that Israel needed the Gaza Strip in order to remove the threat of the Egyptian Army and *fedayeen* from Israel's cities.

He was therefore more impervious than Ben Gurion or Peres to the political developments that followed the campaign. Thirty-six hours after Ben Gurion proclaimed an Israel reaching to the Isle of

Yotvat, he returned to the Knesset and, under pressure from the Soviet Union and the United States, announced the conditions under which Israel would agree to withdraw from its conquests. Instead of a new political constellation in the Middle East, things remained exactly as they had been before, with some unpleasant additions. Soviet penetration into the area gained added momentum, Anthony Eden's government fell, and its successor was far from enthusiastic about the idea of the Suez War. After the campaign, Ben Gurion set less presumptuous objectives for the war and said that its first aim had been to bolster Israel's security and break Nasser's military power—Dayan's aims from the outset. Ben Gurion's achievements were the suspension of the Egyptian threat of war for a few years, in fact until 1967, and the political entrenchment of Israel in the consciousness of the nations of the world.

On June 3, 1956 the doctors made their final diagnosis—Dvorah Dayan had cancer of the liver and lungs which was spreading rapidly. She died at noon on July 28, 1956. Dayan was digging for antiquities near the Gaza Strip, and GHQ sent out a Piper plane to find him and inform him of his mother's death.

19   THE SINAI CAMPAIGN

(October - November 1956)

Speed and daring, the two battle-tried virtues of the commander of the Raider Battalion in 1948, became the keys to Dayan's success in the Sinai Campaign of 1956. Dropping a paratroop battalion behind Egyptian lines, 150 kilometers west of the Israeli border on the road leading to Port Taufiq at the southern tip of the Suez Canal, involved a very serious risk. Large Egyptian forces blocked all routes to the battalion, and there were powerful reinforcements only 60 kilometers away on the other side of the canal. Furthermore, the paratroopers could expect scant air cover, for the drop zone was at the edge of the range of Israeli jets and they would not be able to engage in prolonged dog fights over the area. The Egyptians, on the other hand, had airfields in Sinai itself and could send up fighters and bombers, as they did, inflicting some casualties on the paratroop battalion.

The battalion was to hold out in this hazardous position for twenty-four hours, until the second unit, moving on land through 200 kilometers of enemy territory, could reach it. In fact, because of the terrain and the difficult going, there was reason to believe that the paratroop battalion would remain alone in the middle of Sinai for more than twenty-four hours, and Dayan estimated it might take up to forty-eight. During this time, the superior Egyptian forces could cut it to ribbons.

In the *Diary*, Dayan explained the reasoning behind his decision:

I know that this approach may not be appropriate for every campaign, but to my mind it is correct and feasible in the present circumstances when the objective is the Sinai Peninsula and the enemy is the Egyptian army. It also suits the character of our army and of our officers. To a commander of an Israeli unit I can point on a map to the Suez Canal and say, "There's your target and this is the axis of advance. Don't signal me during the fighting for more men, arms or vehicles. All that we could allocate you've already got, and there isn't any more. Keep signaling your advances. You must reach Suez in 48 hours."

This confidence enabled him to drop a paratroop battalion far from Israeli lines and order the second battalion to join up with it in less than forty-eight hours.

Starting the battle from its final objective and dropping a single battalion into the heart of the Egyptian defenses in Sinai were part of the agreement reached at Sèvres on the basis of Dayan's proposal. In Lt. Gen. Bar-Lev's words, "At every stage of the Sinai Campaign,

Dayan wanted to be in a position where he could stop or turn back according to developments and say that Zahal had only carried out a raid. It was because of this consideration that he did not want to launch the war at full strength in all the sectors, but preferred to make one move and then wait before deciding on the next. Professionally speaking, this was contrary to Zahal's basic concepts of warfare." The Egyptians thought likewise, for they could not imagine that the drop of a single battalion deep in their territory signified the outbreak of war.

On October 29, at 4:59 p.m., one minute before schedule, the battalion jumped near the eastern entrance to the Mitla Pass. At the same time, relatively small Israeli forces crossed the border at two points—Ras el-Nakeb and Kuntilla. Within a short time, these movements turned into deep penetrations, one aimed at joining up with the paratroop battalion and the other at capturing Sharm e-Sheikh. On the night of the 29th, however, these three moves still looked like part of a large retaliatory action. Their limited scope made it possible to release an official statement which, according to Dayan, was to be "firm and threatening, but must reveal nothing of our true intentions." He personally wrote the statement issued by the Army Spokesman, which was broadcast on the 9 p.m. news bulletin:

The Army Spokesman announces that Zahal entered and engaged *fedayeen* units in Ras el-Nakeb and Kuntilla and seized positions west of the Nakhl crossroads in the vicinity of the Suez Canal. This action follows the Egyptian military assaults on Israeli transport on land and sea, designed to cause destruction and the denial of peaceful life to Israel's citizens.

To compound the Egyptians' misinterpretation of the Israeli "reprisal" action and to conceal as far as possible that it was actually a war, GHQ used a simple but effective ploy. For three months before the Sinai Campaign, Zahal concentrated all its activities on the Jordanian border and maintained strict quiet along the Egyptian one. While four large retaliatory actions were carried out against Jordan in September and October, Zahal did not react to Egyptian provocations on the southern border. Relations between Israel and Egypt at this time seemed "routine" or even "good," compared to the tense period of 1955.

While activity against Jordan was stepped up, Dayan made certain that Zahal's real target—Sinai—remained secret. Zahal generals not directly connected with the campaign, such as OC Northern Command Yitzhak Rabin, were not invited to staff meetings devoted to planning it. The Sinai Campaign achieved its aim of total surprise, and Egypt was not the only country completely taken in. The U.S. Government, for example, woke up to the developments only a few days before the outbreak of hostilities.

The element of surprise afforded the paratroop battalion at Nakhl temporary safety and time to dig in. The Egyptian Army's Eastern Command reacted to the parachute drop exactly as Dayan had predicted. Instead of declaring a state of emergency and immediate war alert, it operated according to its standing orders. A few hours after the drop, the 2nd Egyptian Brigade was sent to hold the Mitla Pass and begin moving toward its eastern entrance, where they waited without advancing for two days, until the battle for the pass on October 31. This slow, localized reaction left Zahal complete freedom of action in all sectors.

Another daring move was sending the 9th Brigade by land to Sharm e-Sheikh. The brigade first sent a small unit across the border to capture Ras el-Nakeb. From there, two days later, it was to begin a drive of over 400 kilometers through wadis and trackless sand dunes down to Sharm e-Sheikh. The last 150 kilometers were the hardest: scores of vehicles sank in the sand and often had to be extricated by hand. In some places the way was blocked by rocks and cliffs. At one point it looked as though the entire brigade would grind to a halt in the middle of the desert.

The speed Dayan demanded from his units was partially a political expedient. The longer the action lasted, "the greater will be the political complications: pressure from the United States, the despatch of 'volunteers' [from the Communist bloc] to aid Egypt, and so on. It must take no longer than two weeks." Basically, though, speed was an operative factor: "Rapidity in advance is of supreme importance to us, for it will enable us to profit fully from our basic advantage over the Egyptians." In much the same way as his understanding of the Egyptian mentality allowed him to risk dropping a paratroop battalion near the Mitla Pass, so Dayan was prepared to bear the risks of speed. "The Egyptians are what I would call schematic and their Command Headquarters are in the rear, far from the front. Any change they wish to make in the disposition of their units— such as forming a new defense line, switching the targets of attack, moving forces not in accordance with the original plans—takes them time to think, time to receive reports through all the channels of command, time to secure a decision from Supreme Headquarters, after due consideration, time for the orders to filter down from the rear to the fighting fronts." By comparison, Zahal was flexible, swift, and unhampered by military routine.

Despite criticism from doctrinaire officers, Dayan played his game according to the enemy and not according to the book. Just as he had reminded Pelz, his second-in-command in 1948, that they were not fighting the German Army, in 1956 he repeated this view to Pelz's teacher, Maj. Gen. Chaim Laskov, the OC Armored Corps and one of Dayan's chief critics. "We must avoid analogies whereby

Egyptian units would be expected to behave as European armies would in similar circumstances."

The argument was about the priorities that Dayan laid down in order to achieve maximum speed of action: "First, paratroop drops or landings; second, advance through the enemy positions; third, breakthrough." Dayan's instructions were explicit:

If at all possible, it is preferable to capture objectives deep inside enemy territory right away by landings and Paratroop drops than to reach them by frontal, gradual advance after head-on attacks on every Egyptian position starting from the Israeli border to Suez. By the same token our infantry and armored forces should try to advance wherever they can by going round the enemy emplacements, leaving them in the rear and pressing on. They should resort to assault and breakthrough of enemy posts only where there is no way to bypass them, or at a later stage in the campaign, when these posts are isolated and cut off from their bases in Egypt.

Thus Zahal units had to push on until they completed their missions, carrying with them all the supplies they would need. Dayan's order meant run as far forward as your legs will carry you. His critics claimed that the method and priorities he proposed would make it very easy for Egyptian units left intact in Zahal's rear to mount counterattacks and cut off the forward units' supply lines. Dayan agreed that a European army might indeed do just that, but not the Egyptians.

As for the proposed parachute drop of a battalion deep in enemy territory, he was criticized for the logistic problems it would entail. His plan did not take into account the chance of anything going wrong, and no war is without its contretemps. Once again, Dayan relied not on doctrines but on the enemy's mentality. The Egyptians, he felt, would not attempt to wipe out the paratroop battalion. They would be as shocked, confused, and prone to defeat in the Mitla area as they would be in other sectors.

The principal argument about Dayan's methods involved Laskov, the OC Armored Corps. It began at the discussion on the employment of armor on September 1 in a meeting of the full General Staff together with Ben Gurion. Dayan expressed himself in terms that would make any self-respecting armor commander blanch. He presented a concept of armor as supporting weapons for infantry, or, as he put it, in war "we must regard the following as a characteristic formation: infantry battalion, plus tank company, plus artillery support . . . The armor must be built into formations trained to fight as combat teams that breach the enemy lines and penetrate through to their rear . . . it must include a minimum of close support . . . its target will not necessarily be enemy armor."

Laskov and Zorea repeated what every tank commander in the world since Guderian had said, namely, "The crucial weapon of the land forces is armor, not infantry . . . Employing tanks against tanks is the key to turning armor into the decisive force on land . . . Armor must be employed in concentrated formations . . . Armored units must not be a pool from which tanks are 'issued' to the infantry units . . . Splitting up the armored forces precludes the possibility of employing armor for a concentrated offensive." To Dayan, all these statements sounded as though they belonged to a different region and another war. He could not visualize the Egyptians eagerly engaging in tank battles as though they were Patton's or Rommel's troops. The developments of the campaign bore him out, for the only tank battle in the Sinai Campaign was fought inadvertently between two Israeli units.

Bearing in mind the logistic complexity of armored units, Dayan visualized the tanks moving slowly and ponderously, sinking in the soft sands of the desert. Compared with the light, mobile infantry borne on command cars or half-tracks, the tanks seemed like gigantic, cumbersome, and superfluous machines. After the meeting, in which Dayan stated that highly mobile battle teams of "infantry riding on command cars and half-tracks" would drive westward and "reach the Suez in a minimum of time," Laskov asked Dayan, "What will the tanks do?" and Dayan replied decisively that the tanks "would only encumber [the infantry] and would not make it." He apparently still remembered the tanks of the 82nd Battalion at Dir Tarif in June 1948 and even more clearly the Armored Corps exercise in 1955, in which most of the tanks went out of action because of technical breakdowns and never reached their objectives. He therefore proposed a plan that made the tank officers' hair stand on end: driving the tanks to Suez on their transporters, with the crews riding behind in buses. And even at the canal, he said, they would be used only to assert Israeli presence, rather than for making war.

Dayan felt that a few daring actions by highly mobile, fast-moving forces would be enough to disrupt all the plans of the Egyptian Army and cause its collapse. He did not need ponderous tank formations and European doctrines for this. It was only a short time before the campaign that he understood the folly of this notion. Without changing any of the written orders, he approved new instructions that allowed the concentrated deployment of tanks. Dayan's ability to change his mind without regret or fear of losing face thus enabled him to replace misguided theory with correct practice.

Another disputed point between Dayan and Laskov and Zorea was what Dayan termed "the collapse" and described at length in his *Diary*. His operative order of October 25 included the aim "to confound the organization of the Egyptian forces in Sinai and bring about their collapse." In the debate on the employment of armor, he said, "Our units will capture localities on their rear-axis routes . . . and their deployment will collapse . . . the enemy's armor will collapse together with the rest of the enemy forces, to the extent that its entire deployment will collapse . . . "

Dayan rejected the commonly accepted war aim of "destroying the enemy forces" because he felt "we should try and capture what we can of the enemy's weapons and equipment, but we have no interest in killing a maximum number of [Egypt's] troops. Even if she suffered thousands of casualties, she could replace them fairly quickly. Manpower for the forces is not a problem either to Nasser or to the other Arab rulers." He was reluctant to intensify the hatred between the two nations by large-scale killing and stated, "It is better that as little blood as possible should be shed." He therefore proposed a different formula: "To confound the organization of the Egyptian forces and bring about their collapse. In other words we should seize crossroads and key military positions that will afford us control of the area and force their surrender." Dayan's aim was to incapacitate the enemy, but not through bloodshed.

Laskov and Zorea were of the opinion that a collapse such as Dayan envisaged would not come about of its own accord; nor would the capture of crossroads and key positions cause the enemy to surrender. They felt that the Egyptian Army would continue to fight in the positions that were bypassed, and only "very heavy fire and much lead" would cause its "collapse." They visualized prolonged tank battles over every locality and felt that Dayan's plan for the employment and composition of the armored forces was seriously misguided. Yet Dayan proved right on both counts. Although he displayed an apparent ignorance of armor, he actually grasped the essence of modern warfare, which sets the swift collapse of enemy forces as its primary aim. Though he based this approach on the mentality of the Egyptian soldier, it was very much a development of the German's swift penetration tactics during the Second World War, when wide sections of enemy deployment were ignored in order to capture vital areas, key crossroads, and important routes.

The Sinai Campaign turned out as Dayan envisaged it, thanks to brilliant planning, intensive training, speed, aggressiveness, precise (though hasty) preparations, and faithful, flexible execution of orders. Forty-eight hours after the beginning of the war, the key points of Sinai were in Zahal's hands. Only the capture of Sharm e-Sheikh took longer, and the 9th Brigade rolled into the southernmost point of the peninsula almost without a fight on November 5, after an arduous trek. There was at least one point in the fighting which seemed to bear out Laskov and Zorea's objections. The defensive positions of Um Katef and Um Shihan, which were bypassed by the Israeli advance, held out tenaciously, forcing

Zahal into prolonged battles. Yet it was precisely here that Dayan's strategy found its most telling defense, for Zahal's assaults on these positions failed, and the Egyptians ultimately abandoned them only because they were surrounded and cut off in an area entirely under Zahal's control.

Thorough knowledge of the enemy was the key component in Dayan's doctrine of warfare and turned his recklessness into calculated risk. Understanding the Arab mentality made it possible for him to see through the trimmings—modern weapons, Soviet instructors, tanks, and planes—and gauge the Egyptians' real strength. He was not greatly concerned by the size of the Egyptian Air Force, for he knew that the number of planes had no bearing on operative performance. Its array of hardware did impress the RAF units assigned to the Suez War, for they decided that they did not have enough planes to destroy the Egyptian air bases. The British naval units assigned to the Suez War felt likewise about their targets, as did, in fact, all the forces at the disposal of the Supreme Commander, General Stockwell. The sheer quantity of weapons at Egypt's disposal led the British to delay the opening of their campaign, draw out their battles on the canal, and ultimately fail to fulfill their part in the Suez War.

Once the battles had begun, Dayan left GHQ and joined the soldiers in the field. He returned to GHQ only two or three times throughout the war. His *Diary* relates: "I returned to GHQ command post each night, but of course my non-appearance during the day makes things difficult and upsets the orderly organization of the work. In the field there is a radio transmitter with me all the time and I am in constant contact with GHQ, but my staff officers complain that this is not enough. They may be right, but I am unable, or unwilling, to behave otherwise." He left the administration of the war to his assistant, Meir Amit.

In his *Diary*, Dayan expressed his belief in the need to be present on the scene of a retaliatory action: "During such engagements I like to be at the forward command post of the fighting unit; battle, even on a limited scale, is after all the army's basic business. I do not know if the unit commander 'enjoys' finding me at his elbow, but I prefer, whenever possible, to follow the action—and if necessary, even intervene in its direction close to the scene and while it is happening, rather than to read about it in a dispatch the following morning and reveal the wisdom of hindsight." There was another reason for his presence on the battlefield, however. A man like Dayan would never miss a war and sit quietly in the tedium of GHQ, away from the action and the dangers of the battlefield.

The timetable of the campaign enabled him to be present at the important events in several sectors. In his directives for the operational order, he divided the battle into three phases. The first was on the night of October 29-30: the parachute drop at Mitla Pass, the capture of Nakhl and the routes to it from Kusseima, Kuntilla and Ras el-Nakeb. Phase Two was on the night of October 30-31: the capture of Kusseima and the advance of the 9th Brigade from Ras el-Nakeb southward toward Sharm e-Sheikh. Phase Three was on the night of October 31-November 1: the capture of Rafah, Abu Ageila, El Arish, and other targets in the vicinity.

Dayan drove around the battlefield in a jeep followed by a signals jeep, which did not always manage to keep up with him. He took only one officer with him—Lt. Col. Mordechai Bar-On, his chief aide, who was responsible, among other things, for keeping the diary. On the morning of October 30, Dayan arrived in the Kusseima area and was astounded to hear that in spite of explicit orders stating that armored forces were not to be employed until the 31st, OC Southern Command, Col. Assaf Simhoni, had sent the 7th Armored Brigade into battle, and it had already crushed the opposition along its axis. Simhoni and the other officers had been told that the decision was based on political-military considerations, namely the desire to retain the character of a retaliatory action until the 31st, when France was to intervene with a naval bombardment on the Rafah area. Until it was absolutely certain that Britain and France would keep their word, Ben Gurion and Dayan wished to avoid any clear acts of war, such as a full-scale penetration by an armored brigade.

A heated argument developed between the two, in which Simhoni merely declared that he was not prepared "to rely on the possibility that 'someone else' [that is, the Anglo-French forces] might go into action, and he therefore found no justification for holding up the main attack for forty-eight hours. He felt that GHQ orders on this matter were a political and military mistake." To some extent Dayan was reaping what he had sown. The excellent fitness and morale of the army, its eagerness for battle, the readiness of its officers to lead the assault, its speed and daring, as well as the breach of discipline by a Front Commander, were the results of his leadership. But Dayan was doubly infuriated by Simhoni. First of all, moving an armored brigade twenty-four hours before the appointed time would reveal Zahal's intention to the Egyptians. If up to that point they thought that Zahal's action was just another retaliatory raid, it would now be clear that it was war. Secondly, it would seriously endanger the lives of the 395 paratroopers in the Mitla Pass. His reaction to this breach of discipline became evident during the next twenty-four hours. Parting angrily from OC Southern Command, he raced after the 7th Armored Brigade for 20 kilometers, trying to decide how he should react to Simhoni's disobedience. It is clear

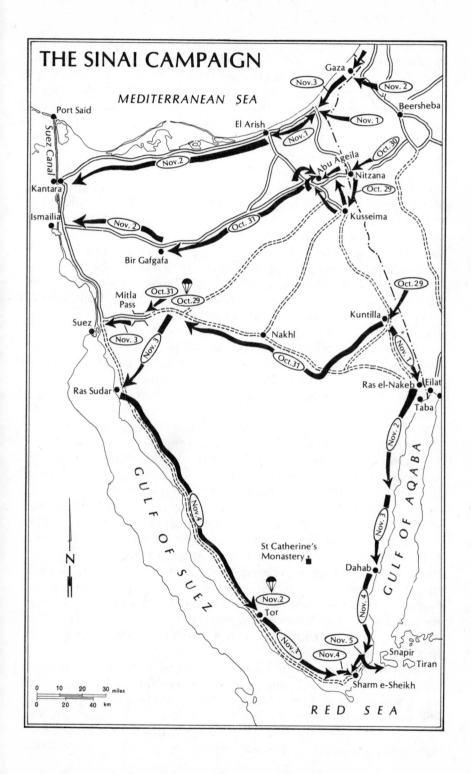

THE SINAI CAMPAIGN

MEDITERRANEAN SEA

Port Said

Suez Canal

El Arish

Nov.2

Gaza

Nov.3

Nov.2

Beersheba

Nov.1

Nov.1

Oct.30

Abu Ageila

Nitzana

Kantara

Oct.29

Nov.2

Oct.31

Kusseima

Ismailia

Bir Gafgafa

Oct.31

Mitla
Pass

Oct.29

Oct.29

Suez

Nov.3

Nov.3

Nakhl

Kuntilla

Nov.1

Oct.31

Ras el-Nakeb

Eilat

Ras Sudar

Taba

Nov.2

Nov.4

GULF OF SUEZ

St Catherine's
Monastery

Nov.3

GULF OF AQABA

Dahab

N

Nov.2

Tor

Nov.5

Snapir

Nov.3

Nov.4

Tiran

10   20   30 miles

20   40   km

Sharm e-Sheikh

RED SEA

from his *Diary* that he intended to give orders directly to the commander on the spot, over the heads of GHQ Operations Branch, the Front Commander, and Division HQ. There was no doubt in his mind that the order required at that point was to turn the brigade around and have it retract its steps: "... From the point of view of discipline and good order, there is no question that this would be the correct course; but was it also correct in terms of advancing the success of the campaign?"

Seven hours elapsed from the time Simhoni gave the 7th Brigade its orders to the time Dayan caught up with its commander. In the meantime, the brigade had launched an attack on Um Katef in the defended locality of Abu Ageila, even though Simhoni had maintained Dayan's directives and ordered the 7th only to take up positions facing Um Katef. It was now the brigade commander's turn to comprehend the strategy of the battle better than his commanding general. This seems to have been Dayan's impression when he wrote in his *Diary*, "But, as may happen in such cases, 'communications were faulty' and an armored battalion team opened up on Um Katef."

Dayan understood that events could not be reversed: it was impossible to recall a brigade that had already engaged the enemy. He therefore decided to extract the maximum from the brigade's move and advanced its timetable, ordering its commander "to begin immediately to execute its assignment in 'Operation Kadesh,'" which it was to have done only in Phase Three. Dayan ordered Ben-Ari to leave Um Katef, bypass it, and continue westward toward the Suez Canal along two parallel axes. His reasoning was that "it is unlikely that all the Egyptian positions will put up strong opposition. There are bound to be weak spots; and when the entire front opens up and the more resistant enemy posts find themselves surrounded and cut off, it will be less difficult to subdue them." This statement reiterates his concept of collapse, which was to prove entirely accurate. From this point on, the 7th penetrated deep into Sinai without stopping. The early employment of the 7th Brigade necessitated advancing all the other actions planned for that front. Dayan therefore ordered the 10th Brigade to put forward its assignment by twenty-four hours and to proceed that night (October 30/31) to capture the forward Egyptian positions in the Nitzana area, which had remained an enclave.

From the 7th near Um Katef he returned to Kusseima to spur on the forces advancing along the Kusseima-Nakhl axis. As he was doing so, he followed the tank tracks that furrowed a hillock nearby and discovered a heap of flint chips, blades, and other ancient artifacts. He forgot the war for a moment, dug into the sand and was amply rewarded: "This was apparently the site, between 8,000

and 6,000 years ago, of a workshop manufacturing flint implements . . . Who knows what wild tribe suddenly descended on this
community thousands of years ago, scaring them into such panic that
they left behind their implements, workshop, and raw materials?"

Late on the night of the 30th, he visited Ben Gurion, who had come
down with influenza. Here he heard that the Anglo-French forces
had postponed their attack on the Egyptian air bases by twenty-five
hours. Until then the Egyptian Air Force would be able to operate
freely, and Ben Gurion, who was worried about the paratroopers in
the Mitla Pass, requested that they be brought back to Israel that
night. Dayan cheered him with the confident prediction that even
without the Anglo-French invasion, Zahal could successfully complete "Operation Kadesh." Dayan spared Ben Gurion the unpleasant
news of Simhoni's breach of discipline and the premature entry of
the 7th Brigade into battle without a proper operative plan. He
apparently did so out of a desire not to provoke Ben Gurion (he told
the Prime Minister the details only three days later), but also because
secretly he sympathized with commanders like Simhoni, who were so
like himself. He commented in his *Diary*, "Better to be engaged in
restraining the noble horse than in prodding the reluctant mule."

Leaving Ben Gurion, Dayan returned to Sinai and found that he
had indeed to deal with "reluctant mules." In the *Diary*, he describes
a "stiff contretemps" with the OC 10th Brigade, who had been
ordered to attack and take Um Katef, a defended locality situated
on the only asphalt road which could serve as a convenient supply
route for the 7th Brigade and other units that had penetrated Sinai.
Dayan felt he had not adequately impressed upon the men of the
10th the need for an urgent, all-out effort: "I was impatient with
them. I had no ear for the complaints, problems, difficulties raised
by the brigade command. The men are tired, supplies do not reach
them on time, the nights are cold, the days are hot, their dust-clogged
rifles do not fire, their vehicles get stuck in the sand. I know that all
this is true, but I have no solutions to such problems. The Negev
I cannot change, and the new axis *must* be opened."

Compared to the 4th Brigade, the 10th put up a very poor show.
The 4th captured Kusseima and then, on orders received directly
from Dayan, continued towards Nakhl to assure Israeli control
over the axis to be used by the paratroop battalion to link up with
the unit dropped at the Mitla Pass. Dayan was impressed by the
ability displayed by this Reserve brigade. Within less than forty-eight
hours, brigade command had managed to mobilize, equip, and
arm 90% of its men. From the brigade staging area, they drove 200
kilometers to their deployment area and then another 20 kilometers
through treacherous sand dunes to Kusseima. At various stages of
this journey, men who had not arrived at the initial call-up managed

to catch up with their units. To keep to its timetable, the brigade moved out of its staging area before receiving all the vehicles it had been allocated, leaving behind some of the ammunition. Since the difficulty of the brigade's route made it impossible to bring up ammunition, on the morning of October 29 the OC ordered that the ammunition of one battalion be divided up between all three. His sole concern was to keep moving, to "exhaust the mission," which the 4th did even before the units had received all their supplies and equipment.

The 10th Brigade fared very badly by comparison. The attacks it mounted on the night of the 31st, together with a unit from the 37th Armored Brigade, failed. "That they failed is certain. Less certain is whether the actions can be called attacks," Dayan commented in his *Diary*. In fact, the 10th's moves were hampered by Dayan's method of working, for the brigade command received a series of conflicting orders. After successfully capturing the first positions across the border, it had been ordered not to carry out unnecessary attacks and to await further instructions. At that time the OC learned at Division HQ that his brigade was not assigned to attack Um Katef. Yet at 2 p.m. on the 31st, Dayan visited 10th Brigade HQ and, without the knowledge of either the Front Command or the Division, gave a direct order to advance and attack Um Katef that night. The brigade began a hasty battle procedure in preparation for the attack, but at 6 p.m. OC Division arrived at 10th Brigade HQ and demanded that the attack plans be changed. At midnight two battalions went out across 15 kilometers of sand dunes to reach their targets. An hour later it transpired that a unit from the 37th Armored Brigade had entered the sector without first coordinating with the 10th. The 37th had been moved up from its base in Israel by Col. Uzi Narkiss, the Director of Operations Branch in GHQ, without Dayan's knowledge, for he had been unable to locate the C-o-S. Simhoni, OC Southern Command, sent the 37th into battle without waiting for all its units to form up. As a result, the Brigade Command rode with the first assaulting company. The command half-track struck a mine, killing the Brigade Commander and wounding his entire staff. Dayan commented on this in the *Diary*:

There is no doubt that the manner in which the 37th Brigade command carried out its action was incorrect and ill-considered. To undertake a motorized attack at night, over mined and unknown terrain; to leave without waiting for tanks due to arrive shortly; and to crowd all the officers of the command into the same half-track—for this there was no military justification. But it was not only mistaken judgment that led the command to act as it did. There were two other factors. One was faulty intelligence. For some reason, the information in the hands of the GOC Southern Command indicated that the Egyptian force at Um Katef was crumbling, its men in flight, and it would therefore be enough for our unit simply to approach and open fire for them to give up. The second factor was the pressure of the GOC Southern Command—following my pressure on him—to hasten the opening of the Um Katef—Abu Ageila axis. The southern commander told the brigade commander he had promised me the axis would be opened by first light.

There were therefore extenuating circumstances for what Dayan felt was the 10th's unnecessary hesitancy. Whereas Dayan did not punish the "noble horse" who defied orders but completed its mission, those "reluctant mules" who followed orders to the letter but failed to achieve their missions were punished severely: the OC 10th Brigade was relieved of his command. A few days later the brigade commander appealed the decision, claiming that events beyond his control had caused the brigade's failure. On November 4, 1956 Dayan replied, "I am certain that there are details unknown to me that can explain the course of events. I am equally certain that I am capable of erring in my judgment. Nonetheless, I must act on what I believe best for the army . . . " In this way, Dayan let it be known that it was better to be reprimanded for doing too much than for doing too little.

The bloodiest battle of the Sinai Campaign, in which thirty-eight Israeli soldiers were killed and 120 wounded (more than the total casualties of all the breakthrough battles) was, in Dayan's opinion, unessential and the consequence of a breach of orders. There was an explicit GHQ order forbidding Ariel Sharon, commander of the 202nd Paratroop Brigade, to capture the Mitla Pass and the battle that took place followed Sharon's decision to take the pass anyway.

The second paratroop battalion linked up with the one dropped at Mitla late on the night of October 30. In the early hours of October 31, Sharon wanted to advance into the Mitla Pass to improve his tactical position. He had good reason not to be satisfied with the position he held. The topographical features of his position did not provide a secure tactical base, particularly in the event of an Egyptian armored attack. At 11 a.m. the C-o-S of Southern Command, Rehav'am Ze'evi ("Gandhi"), flew to 202 HQ with an explicit order from Dayan not to enter the pass or get involved in skirmishes. Even before Ze'evi arrived, Sharon had received similar orders by radio from GHQ and Southern Command. The reports he heard from Ze'evi about the advances and successes in other sectors could conceivably have aroused his envy. In *The Paratroopers* (a book devoted to the paratroop brigade's battles), there is a suggestion of this attitude: "They wanted to fight, these old war horses, battle-hungry men of arms. They had gone out now on a real battle for the first time since the War of Independence, and all of Zahal was fighting: armor, infantry, motorized infantry, air. They too wanted to fight, to break through and be the first to reach the Canal." Sharon requested permission to send out a patrol to the pass, and Ze'evi agreed on condition that only a reconnaissance force be sent in and that it would avoid becoming involved in battle.

Even before his plane took off, Ze'evi saw a large force deploying for movement, too large a force for a mere patrol: half-tracks, light tanks, gun carriers and jeeps. This column entered the Mitla Pass and drove straight into a trap prepared by the Egyptian Army, which had taken up positions in caves and niches lining the wadi. As soon as the battle began, the entire brigade had to be brought in to extricate the trapped column. For seven hours the paratroopers fought for their lives in fierce hand-to-hand combat. Egyptian losses totaled 200. It was undoubtedly the unit's finest, most heroic battle.

Once again, Dayan was forced to pass judgment on excessive action following a breach of orders. In the *Diary* he wrote, "In analyzing the action at Mitla, we should distinguish between the faults or errors and the breach of orders. I am angered by their decision to attack in defiance of orders, but I can understand them. It is only eight years since our War of Independence when I was in charge of a jeep commando battalion, and I can imagine a situation where I would decide to seize a tactical position to give a secure base to my unit even if my action were contrary to GHQ orders." In order to leave no doubts as to his stand in this matter, he added, "As for the breach of my orders and my forgiving attitude, the truth is that I regard the problem as grave when the unit fails to fulfill its battle task, not when it goes beyond the bounds of duty and does more than is demanded of it."

Two questions arose as a result of the Mitla battle. If it was clear that Sharon had disobeyed GHQ orders and was consequently responsible for the death of thirty-eight of Zahal's best soldiers in an unnecessary action, why did Dayan not relieve him of his command and court-martial him? In fact, Dayan did appoint an Investigating Officer, Maj. Gen. Chaim Laskov. In his testimony to Laskov, Sharon stated, "Had the enemy armor not retreated toward the canal that night, I'm not sure our losses wouldn't have been higher." As the commander on the spot, he decided to reconnoiter a tactically superior area. He claimed that he too ordered the patrol force "under no circumstances to engage in battle," but the patrol fell into a trap and the battle for the Mitla Pass became a battle for men's lives. For this reason, Sharon claimed, "The casualties of the Mitla were not in vain. The only way to abide by the order not to engage in battle would have been to abandon dead or wounded comrades. The battle, from a humane point of view, was essential."

Dayan brought Sharon and the conclusions of Laskov's inquiry to Ben Gurion for arbitration, an extraordinary move made possible only by Ben Gurion's warm personal relationship with Sharon. In reply to Ben Gurion's question whether the Mitla Pass battle was essential, Sharon replied: "Sitting here with you today, in a room, on a comfortable chair, drinking tea, I am prepared to agree— knowing now what I did not know then—that it was not an essential move. But on the basis of the information I had in the field, cut off, with faulty communications ... with no instructions, with intelligence and everything in the field my responsibility, my judgment then was different." Dayan then presented his version of the events leading up to the battle, and finally Ben Gurion declared that he could not arbitrate in differences of opinion between two officers. Sharon was therefore "acquitted." Why did Dayan choose such an odd course? The answer is to be found partly in his admiration for those "noble horses" whose only offense was their doing too much.

The second question is, after the clarification session with Ben Gurion and after his declaration that under similar circumstances he might have done the same, why did Dayan condemn the battle in the *Diary*, declaring that it was "not essential" and suggesting that soldiers had lost their lives in vain? Why did he disregard the feelings of widows, orphans, and bereaved parents whose loved ones fought and died at Mitla? The question was asked by many who read the *Diary*. Neora, to whom he gave a draft of the *Diary* before its publication, asked him about it directly. Dayan replied, "Because in my opinion, it's still the truth." This passion for the truth is shaped to a large extent by one of Dayan's basic character traits: marking out his area of responsibility. By revealing the truth and making it common knowledge, he feels less beholden to the public. Dayan seems to be proclaiming at every opportunity: this is what I am, these are my virtues, these my faults; these are my achievements, these my shortcomings; this I have done and here I have erred. If, after all this, you the public want me, trust me, elect me, then you do so on your own responsibility. No one can blame me afterward for having taken on, or been elected to, a position on false pretences.

On the morning of November 1, Dayan watched the battle for Rafah from close quarters and discovered one of the errors in the planning of the Sinai Campaign. To avoid heavy casualties and in line with his theory of collapse, he postponed the capture of Rafah until the day Britain and France were to launch their campaign. France had undertaken to bombard the Rafah positions from the sea, and in his mind's eye Dayan visualized a heavy coastal bombardment, such as those he had seen in American war films. "I myself hoped— and I said so to the officers in charge of the Rafah operations—that the naval action would bring about the collapse of the Egyptian defenses, and the follow-up assault of our infantry would meet with weakish opposition."

In fact, the French naval bombardment was, as Dayan himself put it, "a complete flop . . . the leviathan gave forth a sprat." All together the French destroyers fired 150 rounds of 155 mm. shells, much less than the number a land-based artillery unit would have laid down for such an attack. Moreover, some of the shells fired from the sea fell on or about the command post of Maj. Gen. Laskov, the OC of the division group mounting the assault on Rafah, and Laskov repeatedly requested by radio that the useless bombardment be stopped.

Anticipating a collapse after the French naval bombardment, and for political reasons, Dayan had not included the attack on Rafah in Phase One of the campaign, when Zahal still had the advantage of surprise. By November 1 surprise was out of the question. On the battlefield, Dayan changed the OC Southern Command's orders, instructing him to assault Rafah from the north instead of from the south, so that as much armor as possible could be employed at an early stage. Zahal thus mounted a frontal assault at precisely those places where the Egyptian Army was best arrayed for defense. After the 7th Brigade provided brilliant proof of the effectiveness of armor, Dayan had become a disciple of tank warfare. He himself joined the units of the 27th Armored Brigade under Col. Chaim Bar-Lev and intended to remain with them until the capture of El Arish.

He witnessed the capture of the Rafah crossroads, and after a battle that lasted a few hours the Egyptian front line was breached at 10:30 a.m. on November 1. The second stage then began, with the 27th Armored Brigade beginning its advance on El Arish. Dayan and his escorts rode in a six-wheel command car escorted by another with signals equipment. Dayan dubbed these two vehicles the "Chief-of-Staff's Unit" and positioned it among the vehicles of the Brigade Command, immediately behind the point— an armored battalion team that included a seven-jeep reconnaissance unit, a section of engineers, an infantry company on half-tracks, six light AMX 13 tanks and a troop of four self-propelled 105 mm. guns. Following Dayan and the Brigade Command were the rest of the forward units, two additional armored battalion teams.

For twenty-four hours, until November 2, the C-o-S advanced with the 27th Brigade like a company—or, at most, battalion— commander. There were times when the "Chief-of-Staff's Unit" moved ahead of the Battalion Commander and drove right behind the point company. The only attempt the Egyptians made to stop the Zahal advance was at the Jeradi Pass where anti-tank fire was aimed at the "Chief-of-Staff's Unit" as well. Dayan watched with fascination as an Egyptian gunner fired at his two vehicles and later wrote in his *Diary* that for some reason "he had not fled—there are exceptions in every group." Dayan and his aides were forced to jump out of the vehicles and lie low in the ditch on the side of the road. He observed the Egyptian gunner from afar until the emplacement was destroyed.

He watched the assault of the lead unit on the Jeradi position and was greatly impressed by the ingenuity of the unit commander, so much so that he asked his name and, when he discovered that he was an officer whose promotion he had held up, promoted him on the spot. Toward evening the point units stopped some 6 kilometers from El Arish, refueled, took on ammunition and rested, while Dayan began replying to a batch of signals sent from GHQ during the day. Afterward he found a comfortable spot in the sand and, to the surprise of the soldiers, wrapped himself in a blanket and lay down to sleep. He did not sleep long, for an Egyptian artillery bombardment began zeroing in on them. Ze'evi claimed that a shell fell next to the C-o-S, who emerged smiling from a black cloud of smoke and went to look for another, more comfortable place to sleep.

At dawn the 27th entered El Arish as the Egyptian Army retreated from the city. Dayan was immediately surrounded by soldiers who asked him to autograph maps, identity cards, bandages, cigarette packets, and pictures of Nasser. He then informed Bar-Lev of his intention to tour the city. He refused the offer of a half-track, but soon discovered that not all the Egyptian soldiers had fled the city. At one point, as they were looking through the open window of a building, Dayan's signalman, who was standing next to him, was killed by a burst of automatic fire. At that the C-o-S returned to Brigade Command and requested a half-track for the rest of the tour.

Laden with dates and ancient jars, he continued his tour and then sat down to compose directives for the commander of the infantry battalion that followed the 27th into the city. He appointed him Military Governor of El Arish and gave him instructions on how to deal with the civilian population. The preparations for "Operation Kadesh" had not included directives on military rule, and Dayan now set about improvising a policy. At 11:30 he took off in a Piper for Tel Aviv and miraculously escaped being shot down by Zahal soldiers who mistook it for an enemy plane.

The Gaza Strip, with its hundreds of thousands of Arab inhabitants, fell to Zahal on November 2; but Dayan began to implement the main points of his concept of military rule in smaller concentrations, first at El Arish and then at Tor. He flew to this small village on the southern shores of the Sinai peninsula with his Chief of G Branch, Meir Amit, whose assistant, Uzi Narkiss, was left to run the war at GHQ. Dayan's visit to Tor came at the point when he felt the political time of the campaign was running out and international pressures were beginning to mount. He therefore wanted to speed the paratroopers toward Sharm e-Sheikh to ensure that one of the campaign's principal targets would not slip through their fingers. The village of Tor numbered some 5,000 inhabitants and once served as a station for pilgrims to Mecca. It had a tiny port, a dilapidated hotel, a quarantine camp, and a lepers' hospital. Fishing was the villagers' main source of income.

Dayan immediately ordered that the curfew be lifted and in the same breath instructed the paratroopers to "help the inhabitants return to normal life." He allowed the Arabs to return to their work in the orchards and to fish near the shore. As Minister of Defense, eleven years later, he would apply the same principles in the territories occupied by Zahal in June 1967. On his way back from Tor, he landed in El Arish. Here, too, he ordered that civilian life be restored to normal and implemented one of his most important concepts of military rule (which was to find full expression in 1967)—the employment of existing civilian bodies to run the affairs of the town with minimal Israeli intervention. His general directive—a very light hand on the local inhabitants and refraining as far as possible from causing the Arabs unnecessary suffering—prompted them to cooperate. The City Council and dignitaries unanimously elected the Military Governor as Mayor. The Council also offered to provide what the army lacked in vegetables and eggs (the offer was politely refused).

After the fall of Rafah and El Arish, the remaining Egyptian troops put up very little resistance, and the entire Gaza Strip fell on November 3. Dayan's "collapse" theory proved completely accurate in this case. The decision to enter Gaza was the last stage of a long dispute between Dayan and Ben Gurion. In 1948 the strip was under the authority of the Egyptian Minister of War and Minister of the Navy, who did not annex it to Egypt and considered it strictly a part of the future Arab Palestine. In 1956, the population of the Gaza Strip included 60,000 native inhabitants and 200,000 Palestine refugees. The concentration of so large an Arab population in so small an area was at the root of Ben Gurion's objection to annexing of the strip to Israel in any way. With Gaza as part of the State of Israel, it was not difficult to envisage a day in the not too distant future when the Arabs would constitute the majority in the country.

Dayan, on the other hand, considered the Gaza Strip "a bridgehead on the other side of the Sinai desert for [an Egyptian] military attack on Israel, and in time of 'peace' a base for terrorist and sabotage actions." One of Dayan's aides claims that he viewed the strip as "an Egyptian finger poking into Israel's ribs." Ben Gurion regarded the strip as a demographic threat to the Jewish character of Israel, while Dayan was concerned with the military threat posed by an Egyptian base only 60 kilometers from Tel Aviv. Now, however, he realized just how complex and unwieldy this area was, demographically speaking. An apparently simple solution was to drive away the refugees and prepare the strip for an uncomplicated annexation to Israel. But neither Ben Gurion nor Dayan was prepared to accept that solution, and neither of them could come up with another. Dayan was in favor of preserving the status quo in the Gaza Strip, that is, continuing to control it by military rule. This would certainly make the security picture look brighter, and time would take care of the rest.

By the time he arrived in Gaza, an outline of Dayan's principles of military rule were already clear in his mind. His childhood relations with the Arab el-Mazarib tribe and other Arabs must certainly have contributed—consciously or unconsciously—to the shaping of a liberal policy free of hate or vengefulness. The military rule imposed on certain areas with a high concentration of Arab inhabitants in the State of Israel after 1948 had also given him food for thought in the periods he served in Southern and Northern Command, as Chief of G Branch, and as C-o-S. He frequently proposed abolishing what he regarded as an unnecessary precaution, but encountered the opposition of Ben Gurion and his advisers on Arab affairs. One of the interesting aspects of a comparison between Ben Gurion and Dayan is the difference in their attitudes toward military rule. Dayan, who had advocated war, claimed that military rule should be as humane and liberal as possible, even to the extent of canceling some of its more important functions. He constantly sought to relax control by extending the validity of the travel permits required by all Arabs under Israeli military rule. On the other hand, Ben Gurion, who had been so hesitant to launch the war and had feared its outcome, insisted on the necessity for a hard line and full military control.

The attempt to mesh a stringent security policy with a liberal approach toward the Arabs met with remarkable success in the Galilee in what was known as "Fire Area 9." Dayan, who was generally opposed to the expropriation of Arab lands, agreed that a certain area be taken over by the army for training purposes. But he refused to use military excuses to evict Arabs from their lands and insisted that arrangements be made for the Arabs to continue living on and cultivating their lands within the fire area.

Arriving in Gaza on November 4, 1956, Dayan saw "a sorry and unnecessary sight." He was displeased with the curfew that had been imposed and ordered that life be restored to normal and arrangements be made for the United Nations Relief and Works

Agency to continue caring for the refugees. In further talks with the Military Governor and the Prime Minister's Adviser on Arab Affairs, he proposed a policy which would guarantee Israel's security and yet not harm the Arabs unnecessarily. He repeatedly explained that these orders were designed "so that we will be able to live together again." This was to become the concept underlying his instructions to Zahal's military governors in the territories conquered in the Six-Day War. Dayan was afraid that the security aspect of military rule would be willfully misinterpreted and used as an excuse for oppressing the Arabs of the Gaza Strip. Since he regarded them as permanent neighbors—whatever the final solution for the strip—he wished to make good neighborly relations the foundation and aim of his policy. One expression of this attitude was granting Gaza fishermen permission to return to their work at sea, even though he knew they often used the fishing grounds to contact Egyptian Intelligence. In his opinion, restoring life to normal and protecting civilians from harm were more important than the possible security risk.

A major principle Dayan applied from the outset was that military governors were not to employ collaborators. He ordered that the municipal departments elected or appointed by the Egyptians should return to their normal routine. Dayan personally loathed collaborators and was highly skeptical of their usefulness, but it seems that the most important reason behind this order was his concept of noninterference in the normal conduct of the Arabs' lives as long as they did not endanger the security of Israel or Zahal. Hence, the composition of the Municipality in Gaza—except for the Mayor—remained exactly as it had been under Egyptian rule. Dayan appointed Rushdi el-Shawa to replace Munir el-Ra'is, formerly a senior official in the Municipality who was appointed Mayor by the Egyptians. El-Shawa was a Gaza notable, generally acceptable to the townsmen. In Dayan's meeting with the notables of the city, he demanded only one thing: that they resume their normal business. He did not ask for their political allegiance, nor did he expect them to love Israel; they could think and feel as they pleased, as long as they did not cause Zahal any harm. The military rule in Gaza was short-lived, but it served to crystallize the concept that Dayan as Minister of Defense in 1967 introduced in the territories captured in the Six-Day War.

After discussing the military rule in the city, he went up to Tel Ali Muntar, an elongated mound that was traditionally the key to the capture of Gaza. As he inspected the fortifications there, his attention was drawn to the earth in the trenches cut by the Egyptians, and before long he was digging and had uncovered a Canaanite grave of about 1300 BC with a jug and plate containing a meal

Dayan searching for archaeological finds in the desert

above With troops after the victory in the Sinai Campaign, 1956

below Meeting with General Burns, Chief-of-Staff of the United Nations Truce Supervision Organization, during negotiations about Zahal's withdrawal from Sinai in 1957

above With Minister of Defense Pinhas Lavon

below Dayan with Rafi leaders David Ben Gurion and Shimon Peres

War correspondent Dayan with American troops in Vietnam

offering to the deceased. The abundance of antiquities to be found in the Gaza Strip and the Sinai peninsula drew him southward many times until the final withdrawal. He undertook long excursions to ancient sites, dug for antiquities, and bought them or accepted them as gifts. A miniature cannon presented to him by the monks of St. Catherine's Monastery at the foot of Mount Sinai graces the lawn of his home in Zahala to this day. He was accorded great respect on his visit to this monastery. One of the monks opened the guest book to the signatures of General Leclerc, who signed on behalf of Napoleon, Czar Nicholas I, and Isma'il Pasha and asked Dayan to add his own.

He developed an effective exchange system with the Bedouin in the vicinity of Sheikh Zuweid, near the site of ancient Anteidon and its port on the Mediterranean Sea. On a special patrol with a command car and two half-tracks, Dayan arrived at the Egyptian experimental station there and was shocked to find date seedlings being grown in ancient jugs, which had apparently been part of the granary stores in the port and now served the Bedouin as cheap containers for the seedlings. His chief aide remembers Dayan recoiling at the sight. He later drove over to the village, but the inhabitants all fled at the sight of the army vehicles. On a return visit to Sheikh Zuweid he asked the Bedouin where they had found the jugs and on the spot made a deal with them, promising to buy anything they found. At first Dayan came down personally every Friday to the prearranged meeting place, which began to resemble an Indian trading post. In exchange for some money and great quantities of coffee and tea, he would be given all the jugs and coins they had found. Afterward he began sending his chief aide, and finally his driver would come alone and carry out the transaction.

Dayan's last foray during the Sinai Campaign was perhaps the most typical of his way of directing the war. On November 4 he found himself unable to sit quietly in Tel Aviv because of the conflicting reports received on the whereabouts of the 9th Brigade. Two reports that it had captured Sharm e-Sheikh were later contradicted, and he felt that "even an army commander more long-suffering than I would have lost his patience." He therefore decided to go out personally, find the 9th, and ensure that Sharm e-Sheikh be taken that same day.

At 8 a.m. on November 5, he left Tel Aviv with the Assistant Chief of G Branch, Uzi Narkiss. After a two-hour flight in a Dakota transport plane, they landed at Tor. A Piper should have been waiting there to take them down to the 9th Brigade, but it had not yet arrived. Dayan did not want to abandon his plan and decided to catch up with the paratroop battalion that had left Tor at 3:30 that morning to attack Sharm e-Sheikh from the north.

He asked Narkiss to find some vehicles and in the meantime haggled with a local Arab over the price of an ancient jug.

An hour later Narkiss returned with three vehicles: an army command car and two civilian vans, which Dayan considered "doubtful." Escorted by a few soldiers from the Reserve battalion holding Tor, Dayan, Narkiss, and the ancient jug set out for Sharm e-Sheikh. They covered 50 kilometers without incident. Suddenly they sighted hundreds of Egyptian soldiers walking singly and in groups—most of them armed—coming in their direction. These were the troops that had fled Sharm e-Sheikh after its capture at 9 a.m., while Dayan was still in the air. The closer the convoy got to Sharm e-Sheikh, the more soldiers they met retreating from it. Narkiss recalls being quite frightened. The armed soldiers could easily have vented their frustration and perhaps vindicated the shame of their defeat by attacking Dayan and his small company of soldiers. Dayan, again the platoon leader, took command and ordered his escort not to fire back at isolated shots. "The last thing I wanted was to get stuck that day between Tor and Sharm e-Sheikh and to become involved in skirmishes with fleeing Egyptian soldiers." He also feared that the Egyptians would tear his group to pieces should a fight develop. The Egyptians, however, remained indifferent to the sight of the small convoy. They passed by Dayan apparently without noticing him. "There is no doubt that they knew we were Israeli soldiers, but they neither fired at us nor did they seek to hide from us. They simply let us pass by, their faces a study in feebleness and exhaustion. The wounded among them dragged one foot after another with difficulty and some who were on the road did not even bother to move aside to let our vehicles pass."

After the visit to Sharm e-Sheikh, Dayan flew back to Tel Aviv and informed Ben Gurion that Sharm e-Sheikh had been captured and the campaign was over. Ben Gurion replied half-jokingly, "And I suppose you can't bear that, can you?" Recounting this in his *Diary*, Dayan wrote, "I said nothing. He knows well that what disturbs me is not the end of the fighting but my apprehension about our capacity to hold our own in the political campaign which now begins." Perhaps he also feared that the political campaign ahead would cause a rift between him and the "Old Man."

20 STORMING THE PARTY

(1958-1959)

On November 14, 1956 the Knesset approved the Cabinet decision to withdraw from the territories captured in the Sinai Campaign, pending a satisfactory arrangement with the United Nations Emergency Force constituted by the Security Council. The wording of the UN resolution allowed Israel some room for maneuvering, stalling, or even leaving troops in areas where no satisfactory settlement had been reached. Dayan did his best to delay the withdrawal as long as possible in the hope that something would turn up to avert it entirely, but to no avail. Zahal retreated from Sinai step by step until the withdrawal was complete.

Dayan's main argument against withdrawal, particularly from the Gaza Strip, was that the UNEF and the weight of the Security Council resolution would be unable to prevent the Egyptian Army from returning to Sinai and the strip and again turning them into a convenient base for hostile infiltration. He voiced these objections during discussion with Ben Gurion on the cabled situation reports sent by Abba Eban, Ambassador to the UN and the United States. Dayan did not share Eban's conviction that in the face of opinion at the UN and American and Soviet pressure, Israel had no choice but to carry out a complete withdrawal. Ben Gurion made no secret of the C-o-S's objections. With his permission, Dayan addressed the Mapai Knesset members in a closed session before the debate in the House.

The public got a true hint of Dayan's feeling on the day Zahal evacuated Sharm e-Sheikh. The C-o-S gathered all the soldiers and officers before they were exposed to the scores of newsmen and said, "Just smile. Let's not make it a tragedy, and don't let them think we're upset." On another occasion, he was even more candid. On January 15, 1957, after saluting the lowering of the Israeli flag from the Military Governor's house in El Arish, he told newsmen, "Officers have to eat army rations, the sweet as well as the bitter ones." The controversy over the issue of withdrawal was to erupt again after the Six-Day War. In return for a true and lasting peace, Ben Gurion supported withdrawal to the borders of June 4 (with the exception of Jerusalem), while Dayan maintained that there must be no withdrawal from Sharm e-Sheikh, the Gaza Strip, or other captured territories.

With the completion of Zahal's withdrawal in the spring of 1957, Dayan went on an extended vacation and on several trips abroad. In September he arrived in Johannesburg, where he was admitted to the private clinic of Dr. Jack Penn, a plastic surgeon. Apparently even after sixteen years he had not become reconciled to his appearance. He certainly did not think, as many others did, that the black patch would be an advantage to him in politics. He only wanted to look normal again. But his eye socket could not be fitted with a glass eye. In January 1958 he again traveled abroad, this time to Burma and Thailand and then to London and Paris, where he was awarded a high rank in the French Legion of Honor. Upon his return he handed Ben Gurion a request to be relieved of his duties as C-o-S.

At this point Dayan began his approach to politics, which he formally entered only in 1959 before the elections to the Fourth Knesset. His moves seemed to have been cautious and calculated and in many ways were a game of hide-and-seek with Ben Gurion. Although Dayan was certainly interested in entering the second sphere of his "double life" and pursuing a political career, his public stance never revealed his intentions, for he assumed the posture of one who must be courted, if not actually coerced, into accepting a state position. He did not want to continue serving as C-o-S, but should pressure be placed on him he would stay on; he did not want to embark on civilian life— which for him certainly meant a life in politics—and was therefore prepared to stay on in the army and be demoted to the rank of major general (he even suggested that Ben Gurion appoint him commander of OTC), but if this were not acceptable he would like to study; should he be denied study leave, he would remain in the army; and quite apart from all these alternatives, there might still be "others."

It is likely that his apparent tractability concealed shrewd calculations, the most important of which was that a direct statement of his intentions would be interpreted as "pushing," and "pushers" are not welcomed in Israeli politics. The accepted rules of the game obliged aspirants to be modest and display unwillingness to accept a position unless invited, begged, or pressganged. Then there was the question of the ministry he could expect, since the one that attracted him most— Defense—was held by Ben Gurion himself. All things considered, it seemed preferable that he declare his political aspirations only after he had a firm promise from Ben Gurion.

In these games of pretence, however, Ben Gurion was a past master. It is not unlikely that he saw through all of Dayan's hints and, playing along, chose to accept them at face value. If Dayan did not want to remain in Zahal unless he was pressured, Ben Gurion obliged by bringing pressure to bear. In his letter of parting from Dayan he did so explicitly: "For several months I deliberated and hesitated about accepting your request to be relieved of your duties as Chief-of-Staff in Zahal." Did Dayan want to study? "I have finally agreed to your request, and the Cabinet, not without reservations, has endorsed my decision for I felt a moral obligation, which I believe the entire nation owes you, to honor your wishes and enable you to study for two years at the Hebrew University, Jerusalem." Dayan said he wanted to remain in the army with the rank of major general. Ben Gurion complied: "It was easier for us to reach a decision after you expressed your readiness to remain in the army with the rank of major general."

If Dayan thought for one moment—and indeed he did—that Ben Gurion would invite him to accept a senior position in the Cabinet, he was sadly mistaken. When Ben Gurion invited him for a talk, Dayan toyed with the idea that in the course of their discussion Ben Gurion might mention in passing that the elections of 1959 were at hand and that actually he had only a limited time to study. Or perhaps the "Old Man" would come right out and say that it might be better for him to start in on party work without delay. But Ben Gurion kept his thoughts to himself and displayed a profound interest in the course Dayan had chosen—Middle Eastern studies—extolling its virtues, stressing its importance, and deploring the fact that so few students delved deeply into the problems of the area. He did not offer the faintest hint that time was short until the elections—too short, in fact, for acquiring an academic degree. Their conversation ended with a warm handshake and the Prime Minister's good wishes for success at the University.

During 1958 the Hebrew University was frequented by several of the so-called "Mapai Youngsters," most of whom were in their late thirties. Dayan, now a major general on study leave, joined them at lectures and in the cafeteria. For a while he lived the life of a freshman. There were even rumors that he cheated on exams, and he verified them by commenting, "It's true. Avraham Ofer threw me some notes during exams. It's like cheating." But he did not retain his student image for long, for he did not complete his studies.

Ofer was one of the leaders of the Youngsters. In February 1951 he was the driving force behind the Convention for the Revitalization of Mapai, in which the Youngsters called for a revision of democratic practices in the party, the introduction of a constituent system of elections to the Knesset—instead of the existing system of proportional representation, and the institution of primary elections. All these proposals were a direct challenge to the power of the "Bloc" (or "Tammany Hall," as it was often called), the stronghold of the veterans, which had complete control over the party machine and the appointments committees.

Did Dayan, who in 1944 joined the Young Guard in Mapai, consider himself one of the Youngsters? This question was asked at the Youngsters' 1951 Convention for Revitalization. He supplied the answer when he took the floor and began his speech by saying that he had come out of curiosity. But the rest of his speech left no doubt as to his disapproval of the veteran Mapai politicians and their way of running the party. Clearly, Dayan accepted Ben Gurion's leadership and did not regard the faulty democratic practices of the party as an unfavorable reflection on its leader. Later, Dayan and Shimon Peres were to try to bridge the gap between their identification with Ben Gurion and their criticism of internal practices in Mapai.

At the 1951 convention, Dayan gave the first intimation of his concept of "pioneering statehood"; indeed, most of his address was devoted to this subject. Unlike the other Youngsters, he did not regard party life as an end in itself. He believed that the real measure of Mapai was the extent of its accomplishments in the service of the state, not its internal politics." If it were up to me, and if Nahalal agreed to dedicate itself to the present needs . . . [I would keep] only five families out of the seventy-five and divide up the other seventy among various [immigrant] villages and settle seventy new families in Nahalal." Security and national considerations strengthened his sense of the need for more successful integration of the new immigrants. Until his retirement from Zahal, it was the subject of immigrant absorption that informed his political thinking. As a military man he was aware of the social, economic, and cultural poverty of the new immigrant settlements scattered throughout southern Israel. In most cases the settlers were uneducated and unskilled Oriental city dwellers coming into contact with modern agriculture for the first time. Arab infiltrators played havoc with their property and often with their lives. As OC Southern and later Northern Command, Dayan knew that the immigrant settlements were not the defensive network they were meant to be, and his concern for the proper absorption of immigrants was based first of all on security considerations.

His approach to the problem of reinforcing the new settlements resembled his approach to raising the fighting fitness of Zahal—through personal example. Dayan wanted the members of Nahalal and others like them to disperse among the immigrant villages and like courageous officers lead the new recruits in tackling their day-to-day struggles. His call to disband Nahalal was reminiscent of his father's call in 1919 to disband Degania so that its members could settle the lands of the Horan. The situation in the immigrant villages gave him no peace. As the highest ranking military officer in the country, he came dangerously close to engaging in illicit political activity when he established a new movement among the second generation of the moshav movement, calling on them to leave their established farms, move to immigrant settlements, and guide the newcomers in agriculture and the Israeli way of life. In time, his call developed into the Moshav Youth Movement, which won the support of Ben Gurion.

Levi Eshkol, in addition to being Minister of Finance, was the Treasurer and Director of the Settlement Department of the Jewish Agency and was responsible for the establishment of new immigrant settlements. On the face of it, he should have hailed the establishment of the Moshav Youth Movement, which undertook to help the new arrivals; yet he was beset by doubts and gloomy forebodings. Aryeh Eliav, his assistant in the Jewish Agency, recalls that it was in reference to the Moshav Youth Movement that Eshkol likened Dayan to a Cossack ataman for the first time. Eshkol had grown up in the Ukraine and retained a vivid memory of the Cossack horsemen. He may have heard of the band of young riders in Nahalal, or may even have seen them in action on one of his visits there. At any rate, he feared that Dayan would lead the moshav youth like Cossack cavalry troops into his domain of settlement.

Eshkol was not so much against the help of the moshav youth as he was wary of the dramatic solutions which Ben Gurion so treasured. When the moshav youth came to him in the name of their recently established movement, he cooled their ardor with practical questions and drily told them that he would first like to see what they could do and whether "a tomato or a cucumber will eventually come of it." He feared that the moshav youth would disrupt the orderly work of the Jewish Agency's bureaucratic apparatus and do more harm than good. When the moshav youth did begin working in the settlements, he objected to their quasi-military methods.

In many respects Eshkol was the diametric opposite of Dayan. He loved company; it was as though he needed the constant presence of people about him to stroke his vanity. He was fond of small talk and jokes, unpunctual, unplanned, seemingly irresolute, yet effective in his own, roundabout, patient way. He did not make demands on the people who worked with him and was understanding of their weaknesses. His approach to life may have stemmed from his conviction that no man was without his shortcomings. Meetings with Dayan lasted no more than half an hour, with each participant being given only a few moments to express his views. In meetings with Eshkol, tea and pretzels were served and he addressed the participants as *Jungerman* (young man) or *Kinderlach* (children). He believed his aides were all good people—patient, tolerant, wordly—while Dayan's moshav youth were "Cossacks" who demanded budgets and said, "We'll decide, not the bureaucrats."

The moshav youth did much to aid the integration of the new settlers. There were some who paid with their lives for their involvement with the border settlements. Varda Friedman, a twenty-two year old girl from Moshav Kfar Vitkin who went out to the village of Patish in the Negev, was killed there on March 22, 1955 in an Egyptian attack during a wedding celebration. When Dayan took his leave of GHQ on January 28, 1958, he included Varda's name among the soldiers and security men. Weaving her into the wreath of Israel's heroes was an expression of Dayan's belief that absorption of immigrants is as much a front and demands as many sacrifices as a military battle. Mentioning the names of Varda Friedman, Ro'i Rotberg, and the Zahal heroes in his farewell address as C-o-S was also something of a pledge of faith upon entering politics. The aims that guided his term as C-o-S were now to guide him as a statesman. In a sense, he took it upon himself to act in the name of the fallen.

Dayan's plans for his political future were affected by his aversion to politicians in general and party functionaries in particular. He had no desire to be a leader among politicians, to resemble them or gain power through manipulating appointment committees. He regarded politicians as people who lived off the toil of others, without personally fulfilling the aims they ceaselessly exhorted others to achieve. It irritated him to hear ministry bureaucrats say that they understood the security problems facing Israel, for he believed the only person who really understood the meaning of security was the soldier who risked his life on the battlefield and personal achievement—not only professional ability—was the true gauge for assessing leadership potential. He demanded that army officers lead their soldiers with the call, "Follow me!" and he would have liked party people to experience at first hand the struggles and hardships of life in Israel.

Dayan's ambition was to lead a movement not of politicians but of young men who, like himself, had been in close personal touch with the pain and rigors of the creation and defense of the State of Israel. But this was to remain only an ambition, for the Moshav Youth Movement existed for only two years after completing its mission in the immigrant settlements, and the Mapai Youngsters were a far cry from his ideal. They included nearly as many politicians, untried in security activity or immigrant absorption, as could be found among the veterans. It may safely be said that Dayan never completely identified himself with the Youngsters or accorded their leaders the esteem he reserved for combat heroes. For lack of anything better, however, he continued to regard himself as one of them.

The main issue of the second session of Mapai's Eighth Convention in May 1958 was the far-reaching proposals of Pinhas Lavon, now Secretary-General of the Histadrut, to effect changes in the national union's industry. He demanded that the Histadrut's economic and industrial complex be split up into smaller divisions so as to increase the say of the individual member, though this actually meant increasing the power of the Executive Committee. The convention marked the beginning of a controversy between Lavon and Dayan, who strongly opposed the former's proposals. Politically speaking, this was the first convention at which the veterans came out openly against "the trend of the Youngsters to push their way into positions prematurely." It was at this convention too that Lavon hovered over Dayan like a bird of prey, waiting for him to make a false step. Ever since his unfortunate term as Minister of Defense, he harbored bitter resentment for Dayan and Peres.

It is difficult to say whether or not Dayan was deliberately using shock tactics, as he had done in the army, to publicize his entry into the maelstrom of Mapai politics. Supremely self-confident, and without consulting anyone, he made his maiden speech as a party man immediately after the Eighth Convention to a students' club in Tel Aviv on May 25, 1958. The subject of his lecture was "The Student and the State," and he held forth at length on economic problems—a sphere of domestic politics with which he was least equipped to deal. Dayan rambled on and expressed himself at inordinate length, without any apparent order. Later he admitted that anyone could have "improved on what I said and construed it to serve any purpose." He attacked everything: the establishment, the Histadrut, the kibbutz, the Nahal* units, bureaucracy, party functionaries, and the economic leadership of the country. He also embarked on what was called a "biological campaign" against the veterans: "The men of the last generation have reached an age where they can no longer carry out revolutions. Every source of energy ultimately spends itself. These man look back proudly on their achievements of 1902 ... before we were born ... but we are interested in 1962." Praising the younger members of the party, he added: "There are things that only the younger generation can do."

Dayan's desire for a "Greater Israel" colored every aspect of his political thinking and expression. If, after Sinai, Israel had not grown in size, he said, she must now grow in population, economy, technology, science, and culture. He advocated rapid development so that the country would be able to absorb Jewish immigration and reach a population of 3.5 to 4 million by 1970. This was a direct challenge to Lavon's proposals at the Eighth Convention, for Dayan did not believe the time was ripe for handing workers greater control over the economy. First priority, he felt, must be given to increasing the country's strength through economic development, guided by state criteria. "Let's say that $20 million are needed to achieve the desired development ... Are we not obliged to take this sum from the general budget and add it to the development budget without asking if we have enough powdered eggs? That is the question." He shook one of the foundations of the Histadrut by expressing doubts about the effectiveness of the Nahal units. This criticism was interpreted as an attempt to undermine the kibbutz movement and the principle of voluntary service held dear by the Israeli Labor movement. And as if all this were not enough, he came out in favor of what was called "efficiency dismissals" aimed at reducing the number of

* Special Zahal units that spend part of their National Service on kibbutzim.

superfluous, inefficient workers in public and government enterprises. This suggestion was absolute anathema to the Histadrut.

His address was regarded in party circles as a rallying cry for the revolt of the Youngsters and a clear challenge to the veterans, the Histadrut, and the party. In some circles his speech was dismissed as mere foolishness, the result of political naïveté. Ben Gurion blamed Dayan's action on ignorance. But if Dayan's intention was indeed to shock, there were some Youngsters who were no less stunned than the veterans. Ofer, the only professional politician among the Youngsters, hastened to extricate Dayan from "the veterans' ambush." He suggested holding a special meeting to clarify ideological differences with Dayan, so that critics could hear his views at first hand, rather than through garbled newspaper reports. Ofer hastily organized the "Ideological Circle," which was held on Saturday, June 7, at Beit Berl.

This was Dayan's first opportunity to outline his political credo within a party forum. He spoke mainly about what he termed "four main targets facing the state in the near future." Defense was not under discussion. The four were: strengthening the ties between Israel and the Jews of the Diaspora; in-depth absorption of immigration; economic development; and shaping the character of the nation in Israel. Not once did he mention socialism or the values of the Israeli Labor movement, or indeed any of the slogans used by Mapai speakers.

On the first issue, Dayan emerged as an unorthodox Zionist. He did not require every Jew to come to Israel. "I make no demands of the Jewish nation. Whoever comes will come, whoever does not come will contribute, and whoever invests will invest. And even he who opposes [all these] . . . who will not do anything, and even objects to what others do, there will still be no barrier between him and myself within the concept of nation. This is my people and [I] have no other." He felt that nothing was irreplaceable, that a substitute could be found for contributions, investments, immigration, "but there is only one thing for which no substitute can be found—if a million or a half a million people cut themselves off from the Jewish nation. This is a source that cannot be replaced. For this is all the nation there is." Israel's first obligation was therefore to consolidate the Jewish nation.

When he elaborated on the ways this consolidation could be effected, Dayan gave ample proof of how simplistic, untried, and naive was his view of the Diaspora and its relationship to Israel. One of his suggestions was to "send three hundred young men to the [Israeli] embassies to rally [Jewish] youth." He apparently believed that the heart-warming sight of healthy, straightforward Israeli youth could in itself explain to the better educated and more sophisticated youth of highly developed countries why they should proudly assert their Jewishness. What he overlooked was the fact that "Jewishness" was as controversial an issue among the youth of the Diaspora as among any three hundred men who might be sent from Israel.

On the subject of immigrant absorption—or, as he called it, the "assimilation" of new immigrants by the established population— he repeated his call for "pioneering statehood." His attitude was a great innovation from Mapai's point of view. One of the party's cornerstones was the spirit of volunteering. The Mapai veterans wanted to retain this spirit even after the establishment of the state and the founding of its national institutions. Dayan saw no need for volunteers to carry out what should have been state services. What he wanted was to preserve the spirit and essence of volunteering in the recognized institutions of the state. Just as he had developed voluntary units in Zahal, such as the paratroopers, he now wanted to nurture a spirit of volunteering in other state services. He also demanded that the country place the needs of settlement and economic development at the top of its list of priorities. His main criticism on this point was directed at education. Some delegates to the Mapai Convention claimed that students should be called upon to teach new immigrants. Dayan felt that "There is no need to call upon students to give an hour a week, because it is worth nothing. [What we should do] is call upon them to become teachers within the framework of the Ministry of Education, and then do what the ministry fails to do because the present teachers refuse to behave like volunteers."

In the sphere of economic development, Dayan's criterion differed from that of the party. He spoke exclusively in terms of efficiency. Propelling Israel toward economic autonomy warranted any method, as long as it was efficient. As a member of a labor party, and only a short time before elections, he exposed himself to fierce criticism when, referring to a recent strike in a large textile firm, he said: "If it is for the good of the firm to lay off workers, then the cloth can be manufactured with fewer workers. In this case it was not done. Yet if this principle does not guide our steps, it means that we are not even on the right track to economic independence." He also referred to a remark made by Pinhas Sapir, then Minister of Commerce and Industry, that there were two hundred superfluous clerks in his ministry, commenting, "I prefer unemployment tomorrow to keeping unemployed people in an office today, because if there are unemployed people outside an office we all take care of them, but if they are all just as unemployed inside the office, no one makes a fuss." He suggested that the savings which ensue from increased efficiency and money gained by a wage freeze be invested in development.

On the last issue, the shaping of the character of the nation, Dayan called upon the youth to develop a national consciousness. "They should know that they belong to a generation which is obliged to do something, for this is the aim of the present generation in this country . . . Their target today is to continue development." Dayan regarded himself as a perpetuator of the settlement movement and demanded a national plan, efficiency, development, and the identification of the individual with national aims.

Dayan's first appearance on an ideological platform was rebellious, and for Mapai even revolutionary. He cast doubt on the entire complex of pressures the party thrived upon and by virtue of which the party machine functioned. He also claimed that the veterans were too old, and as he said in an interview with the afternoon daily *Ma'ariv,* "Representation [in Mapai] is too indirect, there are too few elections, too many appointments." He also suggested that he might be the person capable of carrying out the correct policy without being swayed by pressures.

Ben Gurion apparently foresaw the commotion Dayan's speech would cause in the party, for he took Dayan under his wing, while politely refuting his ideas. Rising to speak at the meeting, he began by demanding respect for the former C-o-S. But he disagreed with the bulk of the address: the value of the kibbutz, individual volunteering, the identification of the youth with the country and its tasks. Nonetheless, Mapai regarded Ben Gurion's speech at Beit Berl as evidence of his complete support for Dayan, and it succeeded in toning down the party politicians.

But not for long. De Gaulle had recently risen to power in France with the help of the army, dissolving the Fourth Republic, establishing a Fifth tailored to his own dimensions, and curtailing democracy in the process. These developments deepened distrust of Dayan in Israel. In addition, Ben Gurion's strong support of Dayan aroused suspicion among the veterans that there was a secret plot afoot to leave them in the lurch and that the "Putsch" so often discussed years before—a takeover by Ben Gurion and his Youngsters—was now taking place before their very eyes. As one of the leaders of the Histadrut—the bastion of the Socialist left in Mapai—Pinhas Lavon regarded himself as Dayan's principal opponent. He regarded the former C-o-S's remarks as no less than an all-out attack on the Histadrut aimed at destroying it. He therefore fanned the flames of the anti-Dayan campaign. A wave of opposition followed Dayan's appearance at the ideological meeting. Secretaries of local labor councils, heads of trade unions, spokesmen of the kibbutz movement, organizers of political discussion groups, and others all joined the wave of antagonism against him.

The opposition parties, absolutely delighted with the internal squabbling in Mapai a short time before the elections, added fuel to the flames upon which the Mapai veterans were roasting the ex-C-o-S.

In the Knesset, five questions were put to the Minister of Defense on how it was possible that Dayan, still a general in the army (although on study leave), flouted Zahal's Standing Orders and involved himself in politics and affairs of state. At first Ben Gurion backed Dayan with feeble excuses, but he finally announced that he had instructed Dayan to "stop making speeches" for reasons of "state hygiene." Years later, Ben Gurion offered another reason: "When he entered politics in 1958, he did some foolish things. I could see that he did not know how to go about it. I told him to wait, and he listened. He had brains and he learned."

From then until November 1, when he was officially discharged from the army, Dayan made only a few innocuous, noncommittal appearances. But the battle between the Youngsters and the veterans was soon to be joined with greater ferocity than ever.

Nineteen fifty-nine was an election year. In anticipation, Mapai began preparing its campaign, which was to center on the 1956 victory in Sinai, the prestige and international contacts that had followed in its wake, and the economic boom. Ben Gurion was determined to further the careers of his Youngsters, Dayan, Peres, and more recently Abba Eban, who had just completed his tour of duty in the United States and returned to Israel. He believed that these men had proven their ability and could invigorate the ranks of Mapai. In retrospect, it appears that he did not exercise undue pressure to push the Youngsters into positions normally reserved for veterans, but in 1958 the veterans regarded his efforts as the momentum of an ax sweeping down to decapitate them. What Ben Gurion regarded as a light wristlock, they considered a stranglehold. The formidable power Ben Gurion wielded apparently had a great deal to do with the veterans' exaggeration of the danger posed by the "colts' " entry into the Mapai election stable. The slogan for the coming elections was to be "Say Yes to the Old Man." How were they to know that all Ben Gurion intended to do was open their ranks slightly to make room for three Youngsters? From their point of view, if Ben Gurion broke the rules of the game and jumped the "queue"—based on seniority, privilege, and position—by bringing in untried Youngsters over the heads of patiently waiting veterans, what assurance could they have that he would stop at a small opening in the front ranks? Not to mention the fact that Dayan had embarked on his "biological war," openly declaring that the veterans had had their day. A sense of impending doom spread through the ranks of the party veterans and intensified as Election Day approached. As the dispute between the veterans and the Youngsters grew hotter, Ben Gurion seemed more and more inclined toward the latter. He even went so far as to publish an article in Dayan's defence in *Davar,* thus fanning the veterans' envy still further. He had never done such a thing for any of the Mapai leaders who had been close to him.

Ben Gurion's protection of Dayan extended beyond the political sphere. Dayan's indiscriminate womanizing was well known in Mapai circles, where gossip was a favorite pastime. His amatory exploits were the subject of many a conversation between Mapai politicians, and because of his status as a military man, a general, and a victorious fighter, the gossips embellished his real escapades with imaginary ones. In 1959 the public first learned of a love affair he had been having with a woman named Haddassah Mor.

For the puritans, or hypocrites, in Mapai ranks, Dayan's freewheeling love life detracted from his eligibility as a party candidate. There were some who drew parallels between private and public morals and felt that a man who was unfaithful to his wife would be equally unfaithful to his party. It is possible that the entire issue of his extramarital relations would not have been brought up for discussion in the highest reaches of the party had Ben Gurion not been forced into a corner by the injured husband. He was none other than Dov Yermiyah, Dayan's classmate from Nahalal, who had served in the army and retired with the rank of lieutenant colonel. While still in service he divorced his first wife and married Haddassah Mor, who was much younger than he. Miss Mor, in pursuit of literary or other fortunes, wrote about her affair with Dayan in a book entitled *Passionate Paths,* and before she published it she gave Dayan occasion to repeat the phrase attributed to the Duke of Wellington, who in similar circumstances declared, "Publish and be damned!" In September 1959, Dov Yermiyah wrote Ben Gurion two letters. He remonstrated with the Prime Minister, asking how he could support a hypocrite who had caused him to separate from his young wife. It was far from being a personal matter, he claimed; Dayan was guilty of a grave public wrong which demanded redress.

Although Ben Gurion claims not to have been surprised by the pain, sorrow, and fury contained in these letters and conceded that the emotions of the heart were more profound than the reasoning of the mind, he was obliged to reply to those of Yermiyah's claims that touched upon the public aspect of Dayan's conduct, specifically the parallels drawn between private and public life. Ben Gurion saw them as separate provinces and drew a distinction between a man's intimate affairs and his public life. Moreover, he believed that Yermiyah should have railed not only against the man involved, but against the woman, and should have realized that a woman is not private property but a responsible individual in her own right. To bolster this point, he drew upon Jewish history, citing the case of David and Bathsheba, and English history, showing that the entire English nation knew of Lord Nelson's liaison with the wife of the English ambassador to Naples, but it did not in the least affect their fondness or admiration for the illustrious admiral. He also rejected the charge of hypocrisy, for he noted that Dayan was never, nor would he ever be, a preacher on the intimate matters in a man's life. On the other hand, everything Dayan had done in his public life had been characterized by skill and self-sacrifice; he always demanded of himself what he would demand of others, and in battle his place had always been at the head of his men.

This uncompromising stand put an early end to any attempts to exploit Dayan's private affairs as a weapon against him either within or outside the party. In point of fact, Dayan has had only one love outside the framework of his marriage and he has borne it for seventeen years. In his candid manner he left his wife the option of divorce, which she took up in December 1971. After thirty-six years their marriage broke up, and at Ruth's request they divorced.

In this state of internal dissension, Mapai could not expect a decisive victory in the elections. Ben Gurion set his sights on winning more than 50% of the seats in the Knesset—at least sixty-one—in order to set up a single-party government and consequently change the system of elections. He therefore wanted to clear the air in Mapai. Eshkol supported his efforts to effect a lasting reconciliation between the two sides of the generation gap. The first attempts at a rapprochement were staged at the Kfar Hayarok Agricultural School on November 22 and December 5, and on the face of it the session ended successfully. At the second conciliatory meeting, however, a dramatic confrontation took place between Ben Gurion and Golda Meir. According to one witness, "the picture as Ben Gurion drew it seemed to indicate to some of the veterans that they were superfluous. Suddenly Golda Meir announced that at the end of her term of office as Foreign Minister, she would not accept any post in the party, the Cabinet, the Knesset, or any other national institution. In other words, if Ben Gurion wanted posts for the Youngsters, she would willingly relinquish her own. This was a clear threat that the veterans would not give up without a fight. Thus, despite the rhetoric-encased resolutions, the so-called reconciliation achieved nothing and Ben Gurion was now forced to placate the rebellious veterans, for he had not the slightest wish to dispense with all the veterans in order to make way for the Youngsters.

December 1958, the last month before the elections to the Ninth Mapai Convention, at which the party was to launch its election campaign, was better remembered for the bitter internecine struggles in the party than for harmony between Youngsters and veterans. Dayan now permitted himself even greater license in his public statements. He demanded that 5,000 government and municipal workers be dismissed in order to streamline the Civil Service and that the money thus saved be used to give added impetus to development projects. He also demanded a wage freeze "until we achieve economic independence." On December 27 he joined issue with his opponents in the Histadrut Executive who accused the Youngsters of a lack of political understanding:

Do the youth of Israel, who for the past fifteen years have crawled over rocks and thorns, rifle in hand, who fought from planes and ships in two wars—during the War of Independence in 1948 and in "Operation Kadesh" in 1956—understand the problems of the Jewish people less than those men who have been sitting on the fifth floor of the Histadrut Executive building or other such places for the past twenty years?

Reaction was not slow in coming. *Davar* came out with an anti-Dayan lead article maintaining that an army sapper can quite conceivably be an incompetent economist, or vice versa, and that such comparisons are futile and self-defeating. While the article was polite though hostile, the paper's cartoonist portrayed Dayan as a small boy throwing stones at the windows of the Histadrut's headquarters. The caption read simply: "Naughty Boy."

At last, even Ben Gurion felt that Dayan must be stopped. On December 31 he invited all the top leaders of Mapai together with Dayan, to his office in Jerusalem. For six hours the veterans unburdened themselves of all their rancor against Dayan and his public utterances. Several of them demanded that Mapai pass resolutions condemning him, while others asked that he be forbidden to speak in public. Ben Gurion and Levi Eshkol merely remonstrated with him in a fatherly fashion. At the end of the meeting, Dayan promised to curb his public criticism of the Histadrut Executive. Finally, a five-man committee was appointed to formulate the party's economic and social policy, to which members would be bound in public appearances. Dayan and his opponents also agreed to end their personal attacks on one another.

There were many points of resemblance between Dayan's entry into politics and his entry into military life. In both cases he permitted himself a degree of recklessness, disobedience, and outlandish modes of attack. His campaign against the leadership of Mapai politicians was reminiscent of his raid into Lydda—a swift breakthrough, a burst of fire in all directions, and then a retreat. At first he seemed unripe for the highest positions and required a period of maturation before reaching his zenith. However, despite the setbacks he experienced at the hands of the veterans, he made progress. His reputation for fearless attacks on the party's "sacred cows" gained him many supporters, young and old, who saw him as a rebel capable of effecting dramatic changes.

With both the elections to the Histadrut and the general elections taking place in the same year, the campaign turned into a long, drawn-out affair that lasted from April to November, with most of the feverish activity taking place in the stifling summer months. For Dayan, public appearances had the exhilarating effect of a battle. He described them as such on a number of occasions. When the hall was noisy, hostile, panting in the heat, "I began to feel that this was my people, that this was what I was really dealing with. The fact that they were against me, that they did not want me, that they had complaints, and I was facing them—this was exactly as it should be."

At his first party meetings, Dayan declared repeatedly that Mapai should tell the voters the whole truth, without concealing what might be damaging to the party's prestige. He claimed that in 1958, for example, wages rose by 11%, but production rose by only 8%, and he was indignant that the head of the Trade Union Department of the Histadrut had not revealed this in his lecture on Mapai's policy in the Histadrut. Audiences flocked to his election meetings, which were among the largest in the entire campaign. In slum quarters, development towns, and immigrant settlements his admirers often rushed up to him and bore him aloft on their shoulders crying "Long live Dayan—Down with Mapai!"

21   THE RIFT (1960-1967)

In the elections for the Fourth Knesset, Ben Gurion won his greatest victory. Out of the 120 seats in the House, Mapai won forty-seven, seven more than in the previous Knesset. It was an impressive achievement by Israeli standards. Mapai entered the Fourth Knesset with renewed vigor and eleven new Knesset members. Among those in the Knesset for the first time with Dayan and Pinhas Sapir were Abba Eban and Shimon Peres.

The Fourth Knesset occasioned an unusual family problem for Dayan. Until then, his father had been a member of every Knesset. This time, however, Shmuel had only come in seventh among the moshav-sector candidates and therefore did not qualify for Knesset membership. Upon hearing this, Dayan said, "Pity." From the time Dayan entered the Knesset, Shmuel was never again voted in. He died on August 11, 1968, still a functionary of the moshav movement.

Disappointed at not having gained sixty-one seats in the house, Ben Gurion again had to form a coalition government. It should have been child's play after his party's resounding victory in the elections. But forming Israel's ninth government was no simple task because of strife within the victorious party itself. After the elections the veterans again closed ranks to fight the Youngsters. Since Golda Meir had announced that she would not accept any public or party position, Ben Gurion was left without a Foreign Minister. On the face of it he could have given the post to Dayan or Abba Eban. But he could not—and certainly did not want to—let Mrs. Meir go. To make matters worse, Zalman Aranne followed her lead and declared that he would not accept the Education and Culture portfolio which he had held in the previous government. Furthermore, it was unthinkable that other parties would agree to join a coalition in which Mapai was represented only by Youngsters.

Despite the difficulties he expected from the top ranks of Mapai, Ben Gurion was not prepared to reverse his decision to bring Dayan into the Cabinet. In lengthy, mostly indirect, negotiations with Golda Meir and Zalman Aranne, Ben Gurion discovered that the veterans would grudgingly agree to Dayan's appointment as a Cabinet minister, but only to the politically innocuous post of Minister of Agriculture.

On December 16, a month and a half after the elections, Ben Gurion finally presented his Cabinet to the Knesset. To all intents and purposes, it looked as though Mapai had set its house in order. Both Youngsters and veterans were represented, Golda Meir and Aranne had returned to their previous ministerial posts, and the differences were similarly smoothed over in the Knesset, the Histadrut, and the party institutions. Indeed, everything began functioning smoothly on the surface, with Mapai having the strongest government it had ever formed—ten out of the sixteen Cabinet portfolios were in its hands. However, internal dissension was too deeply rooted, and the suspicions aroused were too strong, to give the veterans any peace. Their fears of a takeover by Ben Gurion and his Youngsters had increased steadily. And now the "Troika"— which consisted of Golda Meir, Zalman Aranne, and Pinhas Sapir— hardened into a solid core of resistance that was prepared to challenge Ben Gurion.

The veterans' fears were not entirely self-generated. A district court that by chance tried a person implicated in the "unfortunate business"—later known as "The Third Man"—on another charge recommended that investigations be carried out to discover whether one of the officers who had appeared before the court had given false testimony to the Olshan-Dori Committee of Inquiry, which had investigated the "unfortunate business" in January 1955. Rumors of forged documents and false testimonies given by army men to the Olshan-Dori committee sprouted among Mapai leaders. Had it not been for the lies, the rumors had it, Olshan and Dori would have acquitted Lavon of all responsibility for the "unfortunate business," instead of apportioning the blame equally to him and the "Senior Officer." Lavon would then have continued to serve as Minister of Defense, Ben Gurion would not have been called back from Sde Boker, and things would have turned out entirely differently. This was the beginning of the frenzy called the "Lavon Affair," which infected the Israeli public with a fever that was to rage for at least five years.

Ostensibly the "Lavon Affair" centered on the question of whether sufficient evidence had been furnished by the army investigation ordered by Ben Gurion on August 28, 1960 to justify an official legal inquiry into the "unfortunate business," as Ben Gurion demanded, or whether it was enough for Ben Gurion himself, on the basis of the evidence furnished him, to clear Lavon of all responsibility for the order that led to the "unfortunate business," as Lavon demanded. To Lavon's great displeasure, Ben Gurion refused to acquit him since he claimed that he was not a judge. In the climate of suspicion and distrust of 1960, some felt that by demanding a legal investigation, Ben Gurion was trying to confuse the issue and place Lavon in an equivocal position, so as to weaken the veterans and strengthen the Youngsters. The supporters of the veterans believed that the rehabilitation of Lavon would discredit the Young-sters and check their "gallop to power."

Ben Gurion's opponents maneuvered him from one difficult position to another. At seventy-four, the "Old Man" seemed changed—weaker and less agile as in-fighter. It would seem, though, that his weakness was not the outcome of age, but of a personal crisis that concerned his public image. As Prime Minister he was authorized by law to set up a state commission of inquiry and deal with the "Affair" in any way he saw fit. But he did not take this step because he knew he was in the minority. Had he forced the issue in the government, he would surely have been labeled a tyrant. At that point, it was important for Ben Gurion—the strong man—to be regarded as a democrat and a liberal. He therefore expected the Minister of Justice, who was equally authorized by law, to set up the commission of inquiry for him.

But the Minister of Justice refused. Instead, the "unfortunate business" was raised before the Knesset committee on Foreign Affairs and Defense. In his appearance before this committee, Lavon stressed that he was not accusing Dayan or Peres of having had anything to do with the forgeries and false testimonies. His com-plaint was that their testimonies before the committee described him as untrustworthy, as one who gives orders and then denies responsibility for doing so.

Although Ben Gurion, Dayan and Peres were in no way involved in the "unfortunate business" of 1954 and none of them had anything to do with the relations between Lavon and the "Senior Officer," all three became principal targets of the inflamed public opinion that protested against the alleged injustice dealt Lavon. Several movements sprang up to save democracy from their clutches. One of these, organized by religious university students, even declared that it would continue "to fight for the expulsion of Ben Gurion, Moshe Dayan, Shimon Peres, and their like from the positions of power in the country." Such declarations were not uncommon at that time.

In the end, no evidence was found to prove that there had been forgeries or that documents had been concealed from the Olshan-Dori committee. As the "Lavon Affair" continued to gain momen-tum, the "unfortunate business" increasingly took a back seat. What concerned the public most was the claim insinuated by Lavon and inflated by opponents of Mapai and the Youngsters that under Ben Gurion as Minister of Defense, and Dayan as C-o-S, and Peres as Director-General of the Ministry of Defense, a phenomenon called "Defensism" developed in the country, that is, a political bias which served its own interests disguised as "the holy cause of national security." Overnight, Ben Gurion—a universally admired statesman, the guardian and savior of Israel, the leader who won the largest victory in Israeli election history—became a vindictive tyrant, an old man past his prime. Worse still, many began to believe that he had conjured up the notion of Israel's dire security position merely to reinforce his own rule.

This turnabout in public opinion was manna to the opponents of Mapai and the Youngsters. It was Levy Eshkol's hour. Employing his talent for compromise, he stepped in to save Mapai from itself. Instead of a commission of inquiry, he proposed a ministerial committee which, he believed, would satisfy both Ben Gurion—for it would be government sponsored, if not actually judicial—and Lavon—for it would be a public, rather than a legal body. Eshkol proposed establishing a committee of seven ministers to function as a Cabinet subcommittee, read the material touching on the "unfortunate business," and decide whether or not the appointment of a state commission of inquiry was warranted. In short, he meant to end the "Lavon Affair" once and for all.

Under Eshkol's guidance, the Committee of Seven broke every known rule of procedure, and it is difficult to imagine a greater hodgepodge of powers and jurisdiction. It inquired, interrogated, examined, judged, debated, chose to hear some witnesses and not others, and finally reached conclusions that were masterpieces of Eshkolian compromise. On the one hand, the seven ministers ruled that "Lavon did not give the order upon which the 'Senior Officer' acted, and the 'unfortunate business' was carried out without his knowledge." On the other hand, they failed to mention who did give the order. Against the credit side of Lavon's account, they posted a debit as well: their conclusions implied that as Minister of Defense, Lavon did not manage the affairs of the army in the best manner possible and his term was characterized by shortcomings "that stemmed from a lack of clearly defined limits of responsibility and authority on the highest level." In other words, even if Lavon were not to blame for the "unfortunate business," there was still reason enough to have him dismissed as Minister of Defense.

Ten ministers, including Eshkol, Golda Meir, and Pinhas Sapir, voted in favor of the committee's conclusions. Dayan and two others abstained. Ben Gurion was absent from the meeting and another minister was abroad. The results were a personal victory for Lavon. But contrary to Eshkol's calculations, Ben Gurion was not prepared to lay the issue to rest. On December 25, he announced that he could no longer remain in the government and that he refused to relinquish his principles for the sake of peace within Mapai. He embarked on a campaign that he labeled "the truth above all," aimed at rebutting the conclusion of the Committee of Seven by discrediting the committee's procedure and intended to establish a commission of

inquiry to uncover the truth about the "unfortunate business." Ben
Gurion launched a series of moves—all of which failed—to invalidate the Committe of Seven and rebuild his own good name on its
demise. On December 31, 1960, only thirteen months after forming
the new government, he resigned in the hope that the formation of
a new Cabinet would invalidate the findings of the previous Cabinet's Committee of Seven. Eshkol tried to placate him by dismissing
Lavon from his position as Secretary-General of the Histadrut on the
pretext of an anti-Mapai appearance in the Knesset Committee for
Foreign Affairs and Defense and his threat to disclose the contents
of a secret dossier. The dismissal meeting, held by the Mapai
Executive on February 4, 1961, was in effect a dress rehearsal for
the struggle between Ben Gurion and his opponents in Mapai.
Forty per cent of the members voted against the dismissal. This was
the largest group ever to oppose Ben Gurion, and it was a clear sign
of his decline.

Ben Gurion's resignation necessitated new elections. This time
Mapai lost five seats in the Knesset. A sharper blow, however, was
the demand by Mapai's four former coalition partners that a new
government be led by someone other than Ben Gurion. The task of
forming the coalition fell to Eshkol, who saw it as the beginning of
his rule within Mapai. He managed to overcome the opposition of
two former coalition parties to Ben Gurion and with their participation formed Israel's tenth government, with Ben Gurion as
Prime Minister. Ben Gurion's position, however, was very weak.
He headed a Cabinet that someone else had formed and he became
increasingly bitter about the growing opposition of the Mapai veterans, particularly Golda Meir. Ben Gurion contemplated retirement
for some time. Finally, on June 16, 1963—taking his Cabinet
colleagues by complete surprise—he announced that he was resigning
for personal reasons. He hoped to be more successful in his struggle
against the Committee of Seven outside the government than
within it. Ten days after Ben Gurion's resignation, Eshkol
presented his new Cabinet to the Knesset, calling it a "follow-up
Cabinet" to the one headed by Ben Gurion.

For five years, from December 1959 to November 1964 and in three
successive cabinets, Dayan served as Minister of Agriculture. During
that time the country was deeply involved in the "Lavon Affair" and
the break between Ben Gurion and the veterans, which threatened
the foundations upon which Dayan's career rested. Nevertheless, his
term as Minister of Agriculture had its own distinctive features. On
January 17, 1960 he outlined the four major problems faced by Israeli
farmers: water, export, profitability, and the socioeconomic status
of the farmer. Up to this point, he sounded like all his predecessors,

and for a time it looked as though he too would sink into the unspectac-
ular details of marshaling Israel's produce from land and sea. In
fact, the fireworks that generally attended his entry into a new post
were merely postponed, for it was in February 1961 that the first of
Dayan's sparks caught Israeli housewives and the public unawares.
He decided upon no less a revolutionary step than to replace the
tomato in the Israeli salad. At this stage, the local press began paying
attention to what they termed Dayan's "assault" on agriculture.

The Israeli's favorite tomato, the Marymond, is large, oval,
and juicy. Upon entering the Ministry of Agriculture, Dayan discovered that a few independent vegetable growers with private
export contracts had been experimenting with a strain called
Moneymaker—a cylindrical, fleshy, and almost juiceless tomato
which was thought to be particularly well suited to the English
palate. Dayan put his faith in this strain and chose it to spearhead
Israel's breakthrough into food markets abroad. Surpluses in the
local market suggested that the only way Israeli agriculture could
continue to develop was by turning to large-scale export. Avraham
Ofer, whom Dayan appointed Chairman of the Vegetable Board
and the Board of Agrexco (the national agricultural-export company) suggested that in the transition from one strain of tomato to
the other, 5,000 tons be grown in the first season (1960), half for
local consumption and half for export.

To Dayan, the transition seemed too slow. "Why not grow only
Moneymaker?" he asked. The taste buds of the Israelis were of
little concern when weighed against the spectacular national target
of enormous exports to world markets. Nor was the lack of experience in growing the strain over large areas, packing, transporting,
and marketing it in large quantities adequate reasons for restraint.
Let them start growing, start sending it out. Some of it will be lost,
some damaged; but it will be a start, and that is the main thing.

Apart from sheer "thinking big," Dayan did have one logical
reason for a total and immediate changeover. If farmers grew both
strains, there would be greater demand for the more popular Marymond, which would raise its price and lower that of the Moneymaker.
If only one strain were grown, the Israeli would have no choice but
to buy whatever was on the market at a good price, whether he liked
it or not. "If the English housewife likes Moneymaker tomatoes,
then we'll eat Moneymaker," he is reported to have said.

Ofer agreed and on the strength of Dayan's authority managed to
push through the Vegetable Board a unanimous decision forbidding
vegetable growers to raise any tomatoes except Moneymaker.
Farmers who disobeyed would be denied production quotas and
loans. And so, without any attempt to accustom the Israeli consumer
to the taste of the new tomato; ignoring dietary experts, who claimed

that the Moneymaker was good cooked or grilled as tomatoes are eaten in England, but not fresh in salads as the Israelis eat them; and making no attempt to help the housewives with recipes or advice, the Minister of Agriculture had Moneymaker planted over the greater part of the tomato fields in Israel.

The result was an absolute fiasco. Among the excuses offered by Dayan and the Vegetable Board was a blight that destroyed much of the new strain. But the fact is that packing houses were unprepared to deal with it, there were not enough ships to transport it, and the vegetable growers themselves were groping in the dark about ways of producing good yields. The Marymond regularly produced yields of 12 tons per dunam, while the Moneymaker in many cases produced no more than 5—not enough to cover production costs. Instead of 6,000 tons as forecast, only 500 were exported. Local housewives spurned the Moneymaker on the stalls and searched high and low for Marymond. The price of the Marymond skyrocketed to a point where the Vegetable Board had to create a special fund to help those farmers who had heeded the ministry order and grown only Money-maker. The farmers who lost on the new strain clamored, "The General ordered it—let the General pay for it!"

Dayan was alarmed by the outcry of the housewives and took what was for him a rare step: he denied responsibility for the entire affair. He told newsmen at the weekly press conference: "I am not responsible for this business. The Vegetable Board is responsible. They asked me to give them the appropriate legal means [to carry out the project] and I did." Strictly speaking this was true, but from a ministerial point of view it was a clear evasion of responsibility.

The Moneymaker affair had several repercussions. First of all, for better or for worse, everyone knew that there was a new Minister of Agriculture. Secondly, the farmers regained their professional self-confidence and plucked up enough courage to stand up to him. Another aspect of the affair was that despite the initial failure, Dayan managed to emphasize dramatically the need to export. Moreover, farmers saw that it was possible to change over quickly from one strain to another on a relatively large scale.

One of Dayan's chief concerns was hastening the completion of the National Water Carrier, which he considered not only a vital enterprise, but a symbol of his ideal of "pioneering statehood." As an indispensable condition for the continued existence of border settlements, the project's completion was warranted, in his opinion, by limiting public consumption and freezing the standard of living. At the rate the Carrier was being built, it would take at least five and a half years to complete it. Dayan demanded that it be completed in three. The accelerated pace was essential not only for developing agriculture, but also to forestall political opposition on the part of those Arab countries which shared the Jordan waters with Israel, as well as hostile public opinion in the UN. The Syrians had already begun experimenting with diversion of the Jordan headwaters in their territory. The Carrier was completed in 1965, exactly three and a half years after Dayan's decision to speed it up and six months after he left the Ministry of Agriculture. Today it is generally agreed that Dayan advanced its completion by at least three years.

Another achievement was turning the Center for Agricultural Planning and Development into an effective instrument for implementing his policy of "agriculture for the farmers," which meant production according to demand, priority to new areas of settlement, and reducing—or abolishing entirely—government subsidies (particularly to urban farmers), as well as reductions in land and water quotas to individual farmers and corresponding increases to collective agricultural settlements. Until his arrival at the Ministry of Agriculture, planning and execution were two completely separate fields. The Center for Planning produced blueprints and plans, while the farmers—as one of them quipped—produced crops and compromises. In some cases, the plans for a project were published long after the project itself had been completed.

To begin with, Dayan replaced the sector orientation of the Center for Planning with a functional, a-political structure. Then he linked the Center with the various Marketing and Production Boards, turning them into a mutually complementary system. He gave the farmers a powerful voice in planning by affording them a majority on the board of the Planning Administration, while the responsibility for implementing plans was virtually theirs alone, since they controlled the Marketing and Production Boards. Upon assuming his post he found that only two of the Marketing and Production Boards were functioning effectively—the Citrus Board and the Poultry Board. The others were still in their formative stages. He therefore provided every branch of agriculture with its own Marketing and Production Board and, with the aid of a law passed in the Knesset, granted them broad authorities, including the imposition of sanctions on farmers who did not implement the orders of their respective boards. Thus a unique cooperation developed between the Center for Planning (a government body in which the farmers had a majority) and its executive branch (the Marketing and Production Boards), which was controlled exclusively by the farmers.

Apart from closing the urban dairies, which made way for the development of dairy branches in new settlements, Dayan also suggested that expansion in poultry raising in the established settlements be suspended for five years and be permitted only in new settlements. A compromise reached with the poultry raisers stipulated that 20% of the poultry quotas of established settlements be turned over to new settlements. This move was undoubtedly prompted by Dayan's social awareness, for it was contrary to his stated intention of enslaving agriculture to efficiency. Taking 20% away from established settlements was like asking lawyers or construction workers in the large cities to give up 20% of their steady income for the benefit of needy colleagues in remote settlements.

Dayan's tried and tested method of staying out of others' area of responsibility and letting his subordinates do as they saw fit succeeded again. He felt that his work was done once he had provided all the branches of agriculture with Production and Marketing Boards and had supplied them with appropriate authority to implement their plans. From that moment on, he did not intervene in the way the boards carried out his instructions. He frequently told ministry officials who were used to interfering in the management of the agricultural branches, "Let the farmers do it their way. They know the soil and the production methods better than you do."

An entirely new set of relations sprang up between the farmers and the Ministry of Agriculture. Dayan's policy of "planned agriculture" and increased exports proved successful, as did his efforts to raise the farmers' income. In the first year of his term, farmers' income rose from IL 251 million in 1958/59 to IL 266 million in 1959/60 and IL 319 million in 1960/61, as opposed to a downward trend in the preceding years. By proper planning and trimming of surpluses, the farmers' income continued to grow throughout his term. When he resigned in 1964, even his critics acknowledged that he had been a successful Minister of Agriculture.

During Dayan's tenure as Minister of Agriculture, political developments set off in 1961 went on unabated. After Ben Gurion announced that he could no longer remain in the government because of the miscarriage of justice perpetrated by the Committee of Seven, he sent a letter to the Mapai Secretariat stating that his decision to resign was final. But the Mapai Secretariat, which conferred on December 31 until the early hours of the morning, was not certain whether or not he might still change his mind. The leaders of Mapai understood that Ben Gurion's implied condition was the establishment of a legally constituted commission of inquiry to investigate the "unfortunate business" of 1954. What he wanted above all was to invalidate the Committee of Seven's conclusions. If the public would see that he had been right from the start, he would regain its faith. On the other hand, such an outcome would amount to a virtual incrimination of Eshkol and the veterans, who had set up the Committee of Seven, participated in it, and supported its conclusions. Consequently, the words "commission of inquiry" and "Committee of Seven" acquired significance above and beyond the dispute between Lavon and the

"Senior Officer," and the former Committee of Seven became a strategic stronghold seized by the veterans to ensure their continued hold over the party.

Golda Meir quickly announced that she too was resigning. In so doing, she effectively blocked the way of any of the veterans who might consider giving in to Ben Gurion. Aranne, who had resigned a short time before, informed the Secretariat that should Golda resign, Sapir would follow suit, and he made it quite clear that these were planned moves against Ben Gurion. The party would then have to find replacements for them in the Cabinet, meaning that for the first time there would be a government without Mapai. This was obviously unacceptable to the Secretariat.

Because of his association with Ben Gurion, the pressures on Dayan steadily increased. He had reached a moment of truth in his political life, and found it imperative to make decisions that would define his political identity. Dayan did not approve of Ben Gurion's moves over this issue. He was convinced that Lavon had not given the order which led to the "unfortunate business," that it had resulted from the initiative of the person who became known as "the Third Man," and that Lavon gave the order to the "Senior Officer" only afterward. In any case, he felt that since Ben Gurion had appointed Lavon as his successor, he now had no alternative but to stew in his own juice. In principle, therefore, Dayan was in agreement with the Committee of Seven. Furthermore, he was against a legal commission of inquiry and felt that the entire affair should have been ended before it began. By the same token, however, he opposed the Secretariat's decision to appoint Eshkol as "peacemaker" and empowering him to appoint the Committee of Seven. Nor was he overly pleased with the way in which the Committee of Seven had functioned.

Quite apart from all these judgments, Dayan knew that the only way to ensure the perpetuation of a Ben Gurion line in the government, which he supported without reserve, was by ensuring that Ben Gurion himself continue to serve as Prime Minister. It was for this reason that he undertook to mediate between the sides. Despite his own objection to a legal inquiry, he proposed amending the Secretariat decision of January 20 stating that the affair of 1954 "must be dealt with in accordance with the demands of law and justice in the appropriate state institutions," and—to satisfy Ben Gurion—have it read that the affair should be investigated "in the appropriate national and legal institutions." The amendment was unanimously approved, but after the meeting Eshkol and the veterans bowed to heavy pressure from Lavon and had the word "legal" deleted again.

Dayan was probably aware of the increase in the veterans' strength and the decline of Ben Gurion's power. A novice in politics, he had to beware lest his political future be bound up with the future of one man. Actually, more of his lone-wolf disposition than political shrewdness came into play here.

Unlike Shimon Peres, who backed Ben Gurion to the hilt, Dayan let his own logic be his guide and consequently seemed two-faced: he tried to help Ben Gurion, but did not support him publicly until later, when the struggle involved Ben Gurion's entire political future; he even participated in some of the meetings in "Golda's kitchen," where important issues were resolved even before they were raised in the party institutions. In one of these meetings, he stated explicitly that in his opinion Lavon had not "given the order." In the circumstances of 1960, such a statement meant clear support for the veterans.

The Secretariat meeting of December 31 considered a proposal that Mapai members would not participate in a government headed by anyone but Ben Gurion. The only argument was whether or not it was fitting or wise to pass such a vote of confidence; there was no question about the fact that Ben Gurion was Mapai's only candidate for Prime Minister. The only one who did not come out against a government led by anyone but Ben Gurion was Dayan, who reasoned:

If a situation should arise in which Ben Gurion resigns and I think that it is in the interests of the state that a Mapai government should be formed, and if—God forbid—I am offered the post of Minister of Agriculture, I'll join the government. I say this in full knowledge of the pros and cons. I do not have to identify with Ben Gurion. My pro-Ben Gurion attitude is 96% not a personal "pro" but "pro" the identification that exists between Ben Gurion and the state. And the state comes before all else, even before Ben Gurion.

After reading the minutes, Ben Gurion commented: "I discovered that in all of Mapai there was only one man who knew what true state policy meant. Everyone says that without Ben Gurion, there can be no government. The only one who understood that the policy—not the man—is what counts was Dayan." Nevertheless, those who followed Ben Gurion closely felt that secretly the "Old Man" was deeply disappointed in Dayan. But there is no way of knowing when Ben Gurion discovered Dayan's stand on the question of whether or not Lavon had "given the order."

Since Mapai could find no way out of its predicament, Ben Gurion again wrote to the leaders of the party on February 26, 1961 suggesting they form a government without him. "The only possible Prime Minister is Eshkol," he added, thus anointing his successor. Since he felt that Eshkol was not capable of filling the post of Minister of Defense, he continued, "There remains the question of a Minister of Defense. I would agree without hesitation to be the Minister of Defense in Eshkol's government, but I shall not in this case, for reasons I do not want to go into." He did not name anyone he thought suitable as Minister of Defense; nor did he make the slightest reference to Dayan. A few years later, when an open rift existed between Ben Gurion and Eshkol, the former proposed a number of men for the position of Minister of Defense, but again did not mention Dayan.

In the middle of 1963, when Ben Gurion resigned for good, the Youngsters felt he had abandoned them. Some thought that Ben Gurion himself had advised Eshkol to take the Defense portfolio as well as the Premiership, thus blocking the way for Dayan or Peres to a top-ranking cabinet post. It was quite clear that Dayan was in a far weaker position than he had been before. As far back as the beginning of 1961, the veterans of Mapai began talking of bringing Achdut Ha'avodah, which had split from Mapai in 1942, back into the party fold as an effective means of consolidating a new political force to replace Ben Gurion and his Youngsters. Achdut Ha'avodah agreed and joined the Cabinet formed by Eshkol for Ben Gurion. This was the beginning of the Alignment that in 1968 became the Israel Labor Party. From Dayan's point of view, it was also the germ of a new force that was to oppose him on a political as well as a personal level. For it was in this Cabinet that Yigal Allon returned to a position of national prominence as Minister of Labor, after twelve years in the opposition. There was hardly any question about the fact that he would eventually aim for the positions of Minister of Defense and Prime Minister. And politically—especially where social and economic issues were involved—Dayan was the arch enemy of Achdut Ha'avodah.

Dayan's position in Eshkol's first Cabinet was in some respects a comedown from his previous political standing. While he remained Minister of Agriculture, on June 24, 1963 Eshkol became Prime Minister and Minister of Defense; Eban, who until then had been Minister of Education, was appointed Deputy Prime Minister; and Golda Meir, Zalman Aranne (who had returned to the post of Minister of Education), and Pinhas Sapir (now holding two portfolios, Treasury and Commerce and Industry) wielded immense power both in Mapai and Eshkol's government. Dayan was alone, outside—or kept outside—the corridors of power.

At first he fought for a position of influence. For an opener, he submitted his resignation—right after Ben Gurion had submitted his—at a time when Eshkol was still unsure of himself and needed the widest possible support, even from the Youngsters. Certainly that was the best time to extract concessions—to get closer to the decision-making circle—and Dayan was loath to let the opportunity slip. Hidden from the public eye, a political in-fight began. Dayan disclosed to no one the real reasons behind his resignation. The struggle took the form of meetings between Eshkol and Dayan and their intermediaries in which Eshkol proved himself a master tactician and eventually completely outmaneuvered Dayan. As a first step, he asked Dayan to postpone his resignation for a few months to "prevent crises in the government." Dayan agreed, thereby giving Eshkol time to improve his position. Eshkol used the time well and gained widespread party and public support. His attainment of political security was aided by two factors. First, he was Mapai's only candidate for Premiership and therefore indispensable to the party's integrity. Second, the country was permeated by a feeling that in the interests of democracy, Israel must overcome its total dependence on Ben Gurion and prove to the world, and to itself, that its leadership was not bound to one man. Moreover, the country was beginning to grow tired of Ben Gurion's powerful, centralized rule and began demanding a more lax, perhaps even collective rule, for which Eshkol seemed the ideal man. The fact that Ben Gurion supported Eshkol removed the final obstacle—any lingering doubts about his ability to serve as Minister of Defense.

Ben Gurion did not openly support Dayan when he turned to the public demanding a different Cabinet and challenging Eshkol's definition of his Cabinet as a "continuation" of the one before. When Dayan demanded that Eshkol's Cabinet present its political "identification card," the only support Ben Gurion offered was a promise from Eshkol and Golda Meir that Dayan and Peres (who stayed on as Deputy Minister of Defense) would retain their status in the new Cabinet. But Eshkol found it as easy to break promises as to make them. It was at that time that his saying "I promised but did not promise to keep my promise" became a byword.

From June 24, the day he presented his Cabinet, Eshkol's power increased steadily, while Dayan, rather than gaining support by virtue of his rebelliousness, invoked bitter criticism from top-ranking Mapai members and even his fellow-Youngsters. Shrewd a bargainer as he was, Eshkol did not reject Dayan's demands out of hand, but entered into protracted negotiations, letting time and circumstances be the villains while he continued to play the kind-hearted, amenable Prime Minister. A few well-timed leaks to the newspapers sufficed to create a situation in which Dayan's demands for a say in defense matters became inconceivable. The coalition began clamoring for clarifications and demanding assurances that Dayan would not be given access to or influence over defense matters above and beyond those accorded any member of the ministerial Committee on Defense Affairs and that he would not be, in Arrane's paraphrase, "more equal among equals."

Dayan emerged from his negotiations with lavish pats on the back but empty pockets. Eshkol and Sapir agreed to his demand that a ministerial committee be given control over the Economic Planning Authority. It was a hollow gesture, however, for even had such a committee been set up, Dayan would have been hopelessly overpowered by Eshkol and Sapir, the natural, all-powerful members of any committee on economic affairs. As a further gesture of condescending good will, the two agreed to increase the scope of the Ministry of Agriculture: Sapir agreed to transfer certain departments of the Ministry of Commerce and Industry to the Ministry of Agriculture, while Eshkol promised "greater coordination" between the Jewish Agency's Settlement Department (which he still headed) and Dayan's ministry. They thus dispatched Dayan not ignominiously, but with only a few token sweets to disguise the bitterness of his failure in the power play.

Yet no sooner were the three months Dayan had offered Eshkol over, and no sooner had Dayan declared his intention to remain in the government "after receiving clarifications on a number of issues, especially defense," than Eshkol and Sapir began reneging on the minor concessions they had made. Eshkol backed down from his promise to hold consultations of Mapai ministers on defense matters, and Sapir tied so many strings to his offer of transferring a department from the Ministry of Industry and Commerce to the Ministry of Agriculture that it became a farce. Promises were broken on a matter close to Dayan's heart and one of the mainstays of his agricultural policies—increasing farmers' incomes—for Eshkol and Sapir let it be known that any decision he made regarding prices of agricultural produce would have to be approved by the Sapir-controlled Committee for Economic Affairs. A few months later Eshkol simply ignored his promise of "greater coordination" between the Settlement Department and the Ministry of Agriculture by publishing his own plan for the establishment of settlement and rural centers in the Galilee, without showing Dayan so much as a preliminary draft.

Eshkol's most telling blow was his success in portraying Dayan as a man even more inclined to compromise than himself and far less aggressive or decisive than the public seemed to think. Eshkol's spokesmen leaked reports to the press that "Dayan gave in," and articles appeared entitled "Dayan Attacked and Retreated." Perhaps Dayan did gain something from his drubbing at the hands of Eshkol and Sapir. Not only did he learn a hard and valuable lesson, but an aspect of his image which at first seemed damaging—namely, his readiness to compromise—later became a valuable asset, for it was the belief in his flexibility that helped him gain a wide base of popular support.

These assessments, however, are in retrospect. At the end of 1963 Dayan was at the nadir of his political career. Realizing that he had been outmaneuvered, he adopted an increasingly independent stand and aired his views without restraint. Eshkol felt that this license was directed against him personally, and relations between the two deteriorated steadily until November 4, 1964, when Dayan finally tendered his resignation. He consulted no one before doing so, and even his closest aides were not let in on his decision. He handed Eshkol his letter of resignation at 9:55 a.m., just before the opening of the weekly Cabinet meeting. Only his close associates knew that the real reason for his resignation was a "lack of trust" between Eshkol and himself. A few years later, as Minister of Defense, he revealed something of the real background to his 1964 resignation: "Relations were fouled. Eshkol provoked me and made life a misery." He gave this piquant description of the way he viewed his position in Eshkol's cabinet:

There is a story about a Soviet forced-labor camp. To avoid sinking in the snow, the prisoners walked to work and back along the railroad embankment, which fell away steeply at the sides. The guards were under orders to fire at anyone who tried to escape. The prisoners marched five abreast, and among them there was a Jew who knew that the Gentile prisoners were after his blood for no reason other than sheer malice. They would push him from one to the other so that he would reach the edge of the embankment, lose his balance, and fall. Then he would be regarded as an escapee and the guards would shoot him. The day came when they succeeded, and the guards shot and killed him. In the Cabinet I felt like that prisoner, and I knew that I would end up as he did. They pounced on everything I said and did and ground me down. I realized that they wanted to roll me down the slope. Why should I wait until they succeeded in pulverizing me? I said good-bye and that was that. I told Eshkol, "There must be mutual trust between a Prime Minister and his ministers. I'm not a minister—or a person—after your own heart, and you're not a Prime Minister after mine."

Upon leaving the government, Dayan decided to devote his time to the "Yonah Fishing Company. As Minister of Agriculture he viewed fishing an important venture with tremendous potential that required further development. He needed Eshkol's approval to become the chairman of the company and requested an interview in order to obtain it. At first Eshkol postponed setting a definite date, but finally received Dayan and approved the appointment. Some of Eshkol's aides claim that in doing so the Prime Minister was openly condescending toward Dayan. One of Eshkol's associates claimed at the time that Eshkol deliberately forced Dayan out of the government. If that was the case, then Dayan's story about the Soviet prisoner was not as fanciful as it might first appear.

As Dayan was now convinced that Eshkol was firmly entrenched

above At his first press conference as Minister of Defense on June 3, 1967, two days before the outbreak of the Six-Day War

below With Prime Minister Levi Eshkol

With Prime Minister Golda Meir in 1970

opposite Entering the Old City of Jerusalem on June 7, 1967 with Chief-of-Staff Yitzhak Rabin (right) and OC Central Command Maj. Gen. Uzi Narkiss

Dayan seated in the archaeological garden of his home with Sheik Ali Ja'abri, mayor of Hebron, a major town in the administered West Bank

in the Mapai leadership, he did not feel it was worth his while to participate actively in establishing an opposition within the party. His thoughts ran along these lines: the overall situation "was not working in his favor," and everyone wanted the Ben Gurion era to be over, while Dayan was no less a symbol of that era than Ben Gurion himself. He admitted as much to one of his close associates, who deduced that Dayan intended to divorce himself from party activities, at least for the time being. He began writing his *Diary of the Sinai Campaign* and claimed that it kept him fully occupied. When one of his close aides visited him a week after his resignation, he got the impression that Dayan did not envisage a return to any government position in the near future, and that his departure from the national scene might last as long as five years. A week later, Dayan had a change of heart and decided to join the opposition within Mapai. Within a very short time, he was involved in it over his head.

Throughout this period, Ben Gurion was involved in preparing for his battle against the findings of the Committee of Seven. On October 22, 1964 he visited the Minister of Justice at his home in Jerusalem and personally handed him all the material on the "Lavon Affair" he had collected and prepared with the help of lawyers. The Minister turned it over to the government's Legal Adviser. In his report the Legal Adviser unreservedly supported Ben Gurion by declaring "The factual statement of the Committee of Seven would never stand up to the scrutiny of any Israeli court." In his concluding remarks, the Legal Adviser stopped just short of recommending that the government institute an investigation—this time a proper, full-scale inquiry—into that irksome affair. But Ben Gurion's victory was, in effect, only a moral one. Eshkol knew full well that if the government were to adopt the Legal Adviser's recommendations, his own political future would come crashing down about his ears. So Eshkol and the old guard once again rejected Ben Gurion's demands. Instead of justice, they opted for political expedience for their own good and—so they thought—for the good of the country, which was by now thoroughly tired of the affair.

Once again the Mapai Secretariat and Executive discussed the possibility of setting up a commission of inquiry into the "unfortunate business" of 1954. Opinions were split equally for and against Ben Gurion. In order to ensure himself a majority in the party, Eshkol employed the accepted practice in such cases. He convened an urgent Cabinet meeting on December 14, 1964 and announced his resignation. The Mapai Executive now had to decide whether to accept Ben Gurion's legally supported claims—and thereby hand over the business of forming a government to another party—or to perpetuate the rule of the party by rejecting them and giving Eshkol the oppor-

tunity to form a new Cabinet. In spite of Ben Gurion's threat to leave
Mapai and lead an opposition list to the elections, the Executive, by
a vote of 124 to 61, approved a resolution calling on Eshkol to head
a new Cabinet. Over 60% of the Executive's members therefore backed
Eshkol and the veterans, while only 40% backed Ben Gurion and the
Youngsters, who now became known as "the Minority."

Ben Gurion did not give up the fight. He began to attack Eshkol
personally and publicly, declaring that, "He is unfit to be Prime
Minister." It was not long before he was making charges that could
only be interpreted as accusations that Eshkol and his supporters
were liars. Eshkol, on the defensive, perceived a way to turn the
tide in his favor, for Ben Gurion's personal attacks offered him an
opportunity to tighten his hold over the Cabinet, and he forced out
some Ben Gurion supporters, Peres among them.

Without understanding these developments it is difficult to explain
Dayan's steps and frame of mind from the time of Ben Gurion's
resignation in June 1963 until the break of the "Minority" from
Mapai or Ben Gurion's decision to establish a new party—Rafi—on
June 16, 1965. During these two years Dayan wavered and struggled
with himself without making a definite move in any direction. This
was the first but not the last time the public was to regard him as a
person capable of changing his mind from one extreme to another
from one day to the next.

Despite his sharp criticism of Eshkol, Dayan did not give his
support to the Youngsters who, after the October 1963 Convention,
proposed establishing an active opposition faction within Mapai with
an independent political weekly. It is possible that he was neither
ready nor eager to lead an idependent faction. He may also have
thought that the Youngsters were not a homogeneous group. Indeed,
at this point their leaders entertained conflicting aims. Some felt
that Eshkol could be won over as an ally and turned against the other
veteran leaders. They saw Golda Meir, Pinhas Sapir, and Zalman
Aranne as the Youngsters' real enemies. Dayan, who had reached
some sort of understanding and rapport with Golda Meir (though
not with Sapir), considered Eshkol the Youngsters' most powerful
adversary and a lame-duck Prime Minister to boot.

In May 1964 Dayan changed his mind and displayed a sudden
willingness to set up a new political weekly. At that time, more than
any other, he also tended to regard himself as the leader of a separate
faction. Nevertheless, he opposed establishing a "shadow cabinet"
with himself as Prime Minister. Had he established the independent
faction and weekly then, his real ability to mold a political entity
would have been put to the test. But Ben Gurion's incessant pursuit
of the "unfortunate business" and the Committee of Seven put an
end to any such hopes, for the Youngsters'—and later the "Minor-

ity's"—moves were entirely dictated by Ben Gurion's actions. Dayan apparently understood that if there was to be an independent faction, Ben Gurion would head it, and by this time several points of conflict had developed between the two men. He was also irritated by the fact that as long as Ben Gurion believed he could use Eshkol in his battle against the Committee of Seven, all was well between them; but the minute Eshkol refused him on one issue—the Committee of Seven, which touched Eshkol personally—Ben Gurion became his sworn enemy. And while Ben Gurion felt that Eshkol was unfit to be Prime Minister and wished to see him replaced, Dayan continued to claim that the question was not a personal one but involved the way in which the party managed its own—and the country's—affairs. Ben Gurion called his campaign a battle for truth and justice, but Dayan did not think for one moment that this was a strong enough platform for a faction or a party. He told friends that he found it difficult to imagine himself belonging to a party which would enable any reporter to wake him up in the middle of the night and ask, "Dayan, what's your stand today on truth and justice?"

With the elections imminent, the "Minority" was forced to decide as quickly as possible whether or not it would break with Mapai and go to the polls as an independent list. On Saturday, May 26, 3,000 "Minority" supporters gathered at Avihail for a conference. Their intention was to allow the leaders of the "Minority" to observe the general drift of their supporters, that is, whether they wanted a break or a continued struggle from within the party. The participants at the conference were waiting impatiently to hear David Ben Gurion and Moshe Dayan. Ben Gurion did not even raise the question of a break in his speech. Privately, he had already decided to go ahead with it, but apparently his political wisdom counseled him that it would be better for this idea to develop spontaneously from the rank and file and not be imposed as a rallying call of the leadership.

The old leader had said nothing about the future of the "Minority." Would Dayan take it upon himself to mention it? Would he assume leadership? Would he call for a split? The crowd was intent and silent. The members of the "Minority" expected him to reveal himself as their leader, to heed their silent wish and call for a break.

Dayan's speech centered on the situation in Mapai: the lack of free debate; decisions made by a closed clique of leaders and carried out by an obedient party machine, rather than through the elected institutions; the disruption of the balance of power by packing the party institutions with supporters of the majority; the demand for blind loyalty to the veteran leaders. He accused Eshkol and Sapir of being unwilling or unable to draw up a viable economic program for the country, and worse, of letting personal political considerations color their decisions against carrying out even those improvements they themselves acknowledged were vital. The picture he drew of Mapai was far from appealing. When he did touch on the subject of the break, he uttered in the same breath what sounded like a direct contradiction: "I would like to tell you that this is not a breakaway conference, and, more important, it is not a conference of a threatened breakaway, which is worse. But I would advise all those who do not want a break not to turn this conference into one that is blind to the danger of the break which is at Mapai's doorstep." The implication was that although he himself did not want a break, he felt that Mapai might force the "Minority" into it. And the general feeling was that if a break should occur, Dayan would be with the "Minority." One month after the Avihail convention, therefore, the Youngsters were quite surprised—one might even say shocked—and certainly disappointed when Dayan announced that he would remain in Mapai and not join his friends in the "Minority," which split from Mapai and founded Rafi, the Israel Workers' List.

Dayan's decision, which seemed an extreme turnabout from his original stand, was contrary to all expectations. Was this the courageous leader who persevered until he achieved his aims? Was Dayan the daring soldier really Dayan the brave statesman? The disappointment of Dayan's followers was so intense, their pain at the sight of the hero who fell short of his promise was so deep, that the reaction of some was inordinately harsh: they accused him of treason. On June 27 the afternoon daily *Yediot Aharonot* printed the reactions to Dayan's move across its entire front page, quoting one of the leaders of the "Minority" as saying, "Dayan betrayed us." Others spoke in terms of a knife in the back. Zvi Brenner, Dayan's friend from the days of the Acre jail, accused him of abandoning Ben Gurion and hinted in a private letter that Dayan was seeking merely to further his own career. Three months later, Dayan announced that he was joining Rafi.

With characteristic frankness, Dayan explained in an interview to *Ma'ariv* why he had not joined at the outset: "I hesitated. I simply hesitated, because I hesitated. I didn't rush into a decision because I couldn't make up my mind . . . I didn't only hesitate. Perhaps more than any other member of Mapai I worked with my little hammer to prevent the construction of a dividing wall [between the majority and the "Minority"]." His hesitations stemmed partly from his loyalty to Ben Gurion's concept of statehood. Ultimately it prevented him from remaining in Mapai, where the process of "de-Ben-Gurionization" was at its height. During the time he was "perched on the fence," Dayan repeatedly declared that even if he remained in Mapai, he would vote for Ben Gurion rather than Eshkol. But how could he possibly reconcile this contradiction—belonging to one party and voting for the leader of another?

There seem to have been still deeper sources for his doubts. For had he really been the rebel, intent on fulfilling his ideas and confident of his ability to do so, he would have taken the reins of the "Minority" and led it any way he chose before Ben Gurion laid down the law. His supporters expected him to be as aggressive, decisive, and energetic in political affairs as he had been in Zahal. But the hesitations he revealed were characteristic of a follower groping for leadership, not of a leader. Still, they do not supply a satisfactory explanation of why he did not assume the leadership of the party at Avihail. As the leader of the "Minority," he could have fought a more effective battle for or against the split with Mapai. He could then have established Rafi as a political party, rather than "Ben Gurion's list," with less trouble and better chances of success.

Dayan's moves seem to have been motivated by personal factors. The first was his well-known trait of marking out his own area of responsibility and avoiding collective leadership. He did not want to be, nor could he be, responsible for Ben Gurion's steps vis-à-vis the Committee of Seven. He certainly did not want to be forced to answer for Ben Gurion on the issue and doubted his own ability to be Ben Gurion's leader. Furthermore, apart from two or three of the Rafi leaders, he was largely unimpressed by the list of Rafi candidates, and before joining the list he demanded that it be reinforced with a few names of his own choosing. He was none too eager to lead the group of candidates Rafi offered. In short, Dayan was guilty of an unforgivable shortcoming in a political leader—selectivity about the men he wanted around him. In the army he had been drawn to the choice of men of each unit, the "team." In Rafi he could not find men who had ventured and excelled in political life to the extent where he could consider them his political "team." It was for this reason that he placed himself seventh on the list.

Then there was Dayan's self-confessed pessimism. While some members of the "Minority" believed that a split in Mapai—or even the threat of one—would shake the party to its foundations, leaving the new list good chances in the coming elections, Dayan disagreed. When Rafi was established, he initially declared that it would not be able to achieve its aims, and later he was more pessimistic than the others about the number of seats it stood to win in the Knesset. While Ben Gurion talked in terms of a majority and Peres asserted that Rafi would win twenty to twenty-five seats and thus be an influential factor in any coalition government, Dayan estimated that Rafi might win six to eight seats—which was why, some claimed, he placed himself seventh on the list. Later he estimated the number might be eight to ten. The latter number proved accurate. Rafi won only ten seats in the Sixth Knesset and was thus utterly ignored in the negotiations to form a new Cabinet.

Dayan's tendency to believe that things would turn out worse than others expected must certainly have prevented him from becoming a leader on Ben Gurion's scale—borne on the wings of a vision and fully convinced he held the power to realize it. Without such a vision and faith, he felt unworthy of leadership. Dayan the soldier, who believed that small forces could defeat the massed Arab armies, was not Dayan the statesman, who did not believe that Mapai and its alignment with Achdut Ha'avodah could be defeated by a small political force.

Asked by a reporter if he did not feel his doubts and hesitations had damaged his image, Dayan replied, "Perhaps. But if there are people who do not want to support me as one who hesitates before making a decision to join another party, then I accept it regretfully." It seemed that Dayan wanted to put his relations with the voting public on the basis of fair play: you know who I am and I know who you are. You know what you can expect in return for your vote, and I, for my part, promise to give you just that—no more, no less. Finally, as a pragmatist, rather than a visionary, Dayan always tried to leave options open. He tried as far as possible to delay burning all his bridges, either back to Mapai or back to Rafi.

All these factors influenced his activities within Rafi, from September 1965 to May 1967. Whereas Shimon Peres bore the brunt of the administrative work raising party funds, Dayan hardly did anything to help the party. He seldom appeared in public and did little to help bring about the change Rafi had promised the voters. He did not create a single program for changes or innovations in the system. In the Knesset, he was more a party of one than the leader of Rafi. On several occasions he took a stand opposed to that of his colleagues. One instance of this sort occurred after the retaliatory action in the Jordanian village of Samoa in November 1966. Ben Gurion and Peres attacked Eshkol in the Knesset, vehemently criticizing him for the action, while Dayan supported it.

In April 1966, the press learned of an invitation Dayan had received to visit Vietnam and cover the war there for several foreign newspapers. The Knesset was unanimous in its opposition to this trip, fearing that it might be interpreted as Israeli support for America in the Vietnam War. Dayan confided to a friend:

Today after twenty-five years in defense work and five in agriculture, I have no consuming interest. This is the only war going on in the world now. Hardly any of us has ever seen or fought in a war this size and which makes use of so many new technologies. My speciality is security. Just as specialists in botanical diseases travel abroad to observe plant diseases and find out how they are treated, I want to see and learn about the war in Vietnam and study its possible applications to war in our area. I don't understand what's wrong with that. It amuses me to hear people claim that my trip means support of America. Whether or not that is so will only become clear after I return.

The entire Rafi faction in the Knesset was opposed to his journalistic assignment, but he took little notice. A few days before he left for Vietnam, a Knesset member commented, "I wouldn't go in your place." To which Dayan replied, "You'll be surprised to hear that in your place, I wouldn't go either. But I'm going in my place, while you're staying here in yours."

The trip to Vietnam and the subsequent series of articles on the war there gained Dayan international recognition as a political-military authority. He was invited to meet government and military officials in the United States, England, and France. Upon his return to Israel in the summer of 1966, he asked to be relieved of the chairmanship of the Rafi faction in the Knesset. From that time on, his political activity came to a virtual standstill, while his independence continued to grow.

It was generally believed that Dayan had only one foot in Rafi. He did not conceal his disappointment with the party and some of its leading figures, and even questioned the effectiveness of a party with only ten Knesset members. Yet he did not leave, perhaps once again to leave his options open. Though he criticized the government, and particularly Pinhas Sapir's recession economy, his criticism was no more biting than that of any other politician. The hesitations which apparently damaged his image were soon to become an asset, marking him as a person who would always be open to negotiations. The change in his political fortunes came much earlier than he or anyone else expected. In May 1967 all the shortcomings he had displayed in Rafi turned to advantages when Mapai began to review the candidates who could replace Eshkol as Minister of Defense.

22   THE SIX-DAY WAR

(May-June 1967)

At the age of fifty, Moshe Dayan found himself off course for the second time in his life. His party was being pushed further and further off the road to power, and he moved increasingly away from active involvement within the party. If he had pinned any hopes on Rafi, they had been in vain, and by the same token Rafi's expectations of him came to naught.

Generally speaking, there are two questions that judge the measure of a potential leader: can he lead himself and his colleagues to power? And, if he can, will he then be an able Prime Minister? It would seem that even Dayan's staunchest supporters did not have to rack their brains for an answer to the second question, for their reply to the first was an unequivocal no. He was not built to organize and lead a party. Dayan was the first to admit this. He complained that people bored him, especially party politicians. Their conflcts, their day-to-day problems in the party branches, their questions on issues other than foreign affairs and defense, their complaints, petty crises, and vexations simply did not interest him. He shunned parties and rarely stayed after eleven o'clock at those he could not avoid. His appearances at top-level Rafi meetings were equally rare and just as brief. Dayan's companions knew that fifteen or twenty minutes in their company was about the limit of his patience. When he began shifting restlessly in his chair, they knew their time was up. Anyone who misread the signs and tarried would soon see him rise and summarily take his leave.

Dayan explained his behavior by saying that he had no ambition to be Prime Minister. Perhaps it would be more accurate to say that his ambition had a price: he was willing to go only so far to see it fulfilled. If he became Prime Minister at that point—fine; if not, then it was not too great a loss. The position and the power were not the be-all and end-all of his political existence.

Dayan's expectations dwindled with the fading of Rafi's hopes to win over a sufficiently large body of voters to bring its men into the Cabinet and with the strengthening of the Mapai alignment with Achdut Ha'avodah. The great hopes Dayan inspired as leader of the rebels inside Mapai began dying out when he became one of the leaders of the very same rebels now organized in a new party.

The main obstacle to Dayan becoming a party leader was his inherent inability, or unwillingness, to work as part of a team. One of the people who felt this most strongly was Shimon Peres, the

Secretary-General of Rafi, who carried the main administrative burden of running the party. He frequently complained of the impossibility of arriving at a complete and committing "understanding" with Dayan. He could reach agreements with him on one move or a single stage, but never on an entire, multiphased, long-term political policy. His colleagues in Rafi discovered, or confirmed their assumption, that Dayan was a man unto himself; "lone wolf" was the name most frequently applied to him by friends and foes alike.

At the same time, Dayan continued to display natural leadership and aroused in many the desire to work for him. The riddle of his personality was only partly explained by "charisma," although sometimes his smile alone was enough to captivate people and inspire them with devotion. His strength was manifest in his person, not in his qualifications or political or social vision. With his inherent realism, clearsightedness, and ability to analyze developments correctly, Dayan was his own chief asset. His character was no less important than his views, and his personality no less relevant than his ideas.

Always controversial, Dayan's personality was equally a source of envy and admiration. The closest verbal description of it is the word "sovereign." He spoke, acted, and behaved exactly as he pleased. Much as a military uniform and the rank of major general did not prevent him from wearing sandals in Southern Command and "lifting" oranges from the nearest orchard, so the status of political leader did not bind him to conventions. On the national plane he said what he felt to be true, even if it was in painful contradiction to widespread public sentiments. Thus he could say that he did not expect Israeli Arabs to be loyal to the state, but at the same time demand that they be brought into the Civil Service; he wrote about the "boastfulness" of Israelis in Africa; and stated that he had nothing against Israelis who emigrated. He voiced his private opinions during appearances in the Knesset, even when they were out of line with, or directly opposed to, those of other Rafi members, such as Ben Gurion or Shimon Peres. His membership in Rafi did not prevent him from showing open approval for members of rival parties, or from leveling criticism at his own colleagues. That he was one of the leaders of Rafi did not prevent him from saying he would be prepared to return to Mapai.

In his *Diary of the Sinai Campaign,* Dayan wrote so provocatively about Zahal, the apple of Israel's eye and so highly regarded as to be almost unassailable, that Golda Meir described the book as containing the most serious charges against the army and its top officers ever published and demanded that a man such as this, in whom the "grandeur of statehood" throbbed, should be made to explain himself to the nation. He was equally frank about his family and once said that were he to live his life over again, he would not marry and raise children. He did as he pleased in his private life, whether or not his behavior offended accepted social mores, as was the case in his indiscreet love affairs or when he broke the law.

The incident of "moving the barrels" became something of a symbol of his indifference to public order, despite the expectations that a political figure—and a minister at that—should serve as an example to the public at large. The incident occurred in November 1961, when Dayan was Minister of Agriculture. Driving along a road, he reached a stretch that was under repair and entry to it was blocked by a row of barrels. A long line of cars inched along the dirt detour, but Dayan, too impatient to wait until the bottleneck cleared, asked one of the workmen to move the barrels so that he could drive along the section under repair. When the workman refused, he got out of his car, moved the barrels, and drove through the barrier.

His illegal quest for antiquities became something of a public scandal. His favorite site was Azur (ancient Azor). It was known to be rich in relics from the Calcolithic Age onward and had never been properly excavated. Yet before any systematic digging could be done there, contractors began clearing the land for housing, and in the course of their work bulldozers opened up ancient graves. Dayan, then still C-o-S, hastened to Azur to excavate the graves. Ten-year-old Aryeh Rosenbaum, one of the immigrant children who lived in the area, watched him at work and soon began helping. Within a short time, a friendship developed between the two. They often exchanged finds, and when Dayan discovered that the boy had a knack for finding antiquities, he took him to other sites far from Azur to help him uncover relics. Aryeh became a sort of "spotter" for Dayan and always notified him of any new finds brought to light by the builders in Azur. The friendship lasted through the years, and on March 20, 1968, Aryeh Rosenbaum was given the opportunity to save Dayan's life. A mound of limestone, estimated at a ton and a half, collapsed while Dayan was digging in a tomb and covered him completely. Aryeh immediately called the drivers of the bulldozers and the local Red Magen David (equivalent of the Red Cross). There is no doubt that had Dayan not been extricated from the limestone immediately, he would have suffocated to death.

Dayan claimed that in digging at Azur he was saving antiquities that would otherwise be destroyed by the bulldozers or vanish forever beneath the new housing projects. But the papers carried numerous reports of his illegal excavations and published scores of letters from indignant readers. Ultimately, on January 15, 1965, Dayan was summoned by the police following a complaint lodged against him for digging without a permit. He declared that he was willing to forgo his parliamentary immunity in order to be questioned or even brought to trial. On January 25 the police questioned him, but instead of a trial a settlement was reached between Dayan and the Department of Antiquities. Yigael Yadin, by now a full professor and head of the Department of Archaeology at the Hebrew University, labeled the heads of the Department of Antiquities "criminals." When they tried to explain the awkwardness of their position in dealing with the misdemeanors of a former Cabinet minister, the hero of the Sinai Campaign, and now a Member of the Knesset, Yadin told them, "You're the criminals, not he! If you allow him to dig, what will all the small fry do?"

Dayan rejected admonitions about behavior unbecoming to a public figure or that "a leader must restrain himself and serve as an example." His replies were generally based on the rules of "fair play." He did not invoke parliamentary immunity when charged with reckless driving or questioned by the police about illegal excavations and was fully prepared to accept any punishment meted out in a court of law. As an individual, he was free to do as he pleased; society, for its part, was free to react in accordance with its laws and the judgement of its courts. And if people did not want him, they need not vote for him.

The fury he aroused as a "grave robber" and "barrel mover" was counterbalanced by the fact that the public came to acknowledge the "sovereignty" of his personality. Dayan was an individual who did as he pleased, but because of the inherent weakness of the society in which he lived, as well as the respect and admiration he commanded, he seemed beyond the reach of the law. His friendship with Aryeh Rosenbaum gave his exploits an added touch of charm. The public was enchanted to learn that Dayan, who was so easily bored in the company of dignitaries, ministers, and celebrities, could find boundless interest in a boy with a knack for finding antiquities and always found time to hear what Aryeh had found or what he thought.

Quite conceivably, side by side with their respect for his positive traits, many Israelis felt a certain envy, or perhaps admiration, for some of Dayan's more questionable qualities. To a great extent, he was the image of what many men would like to be—a person capable of leading his life according to his real wishes, unmindful of the conventions, circumstances and obligations that society imposed on him. Dayan's philosophy of giving full expression to his real self and satisfying his personal desires found more devotees than might have seemed likely at a time when he was under heavy fire and his political standing seemed to be on the decline.

It seems that Dayan's image as a man who would do what had to be done, regardless of personal or party considerations, ultimately

wrought a miraculous change in his fortunes. A great wave of
faith and support swept him back into the Cabinet and gained for
him the prize office of Minister of Defense.

Whatever the interpretations of the events of May 1967, one thing
is quite clear: the sudden massing of the Egyptian Army in Sinai,
the expulsion of the UN Emergency Force from the Gaza Strip
and the Straits of Tiran, the renewed blockade of the straits against
Israeli shipping on May 23, and Nasser's declaration to pilots in
Sinai*, all combined to throw the Israeli public completely off
balance. They suddenly discovered that Zahal's deterrent capacity—
upon which the country depended for its security—disappeared
overnight. Moreover, Nasser's self-confidence vis-à-vis Eshkol's
hesitancy aroused in all sectors of the Israeli nation a real fear of war
and its consequences. Within a few days, the continuing survival
of the state was placed in question. The horrors of the Nazi holocaust
came vividly to memory in the public consciousness, conjuring up
the specter of extermination anew. Eshkol ordered a general mobilization of Reserves. Ostensibly, Israel was prepared to meet any danger,
but she lacked a clear determination to employ this mobilized force.
The long wait also bred doubts about Zahal's ability to win an easy
victory over the Egyptian Army.

In Zahal's field units, a general mood of self-confidence prevailed.
But the Chief-of-Staff, Yitzhak Rabin, was unable to transmit this
spirit to the government or the civilian population. He himself felt
faint** on May 23, the day Nasser announced the closing of the
Straits and his readiness for war with Israel, and was kept in his
bed for two days under doctor's orders.

A faint C-o-S, an indecisive Prime Minister and Minister of
Defense, the increasing impudence of the President of Egypt, and
the incessant reinforcement of the Egyptian Army in the eastern
sectors of Sinai combined to create an unprecedented state of
emergency. A feeling ran through the country that in order to unite

* "The waters of the Straits of Tiran are our territorial waters. If Israel's leaders
and General Rabin want war, *ahalan wa-sahalan* [hello and welcome]. Our troops are
waiting for them."

** There were several versions of the C-o-S's illness. The French daily *Le Figaro*
wrote on January 19: "The day after President Nasser closed the Straits of Tiran,
Rabin underwent a crisis and fell into a nervous depression." M. Gilboa in *Six Days-Six
Years* and S. Nakdimon in *Toward Zero Hour* both quote the *Le Figaro* article and add to it
from other sources. The former writes: "[Rabin's] friends believe that the fact that
ministers asked him if Israel can allow herself to become involved in a war had a
telling effect on him." The latter adds: "At the [GHQ] meeting [called to discuss the
closing of the Straits of Tiran] the C-o-S fell ill . . . He was taken home and examined
there by the Chief Medical Officer, Col. Eliyahu Gilon, who prescribed complete
rest for two or three days until such time as he should recover from his exhaustion.
The telephone was disconnected and no visitors were allowed."

the nation to face the danger, a wall-to-wall coalition government must be set up. From May 23 on, most of the parties began demanding the formation of a Government of National Unity. The opposition parties, however, were willing to join such a coalition under Eshkol only on condition that changes be made in the handling of the defense affairs of the country.

For ten days, from May 23 until June 1, a fierce public struggle was waged to introduce changes in the Cabinet. There was a universally acknowledged need to restore the self-confidence of the army and the people and to bolster their faith in the government. It was hoped that this could be achieved by placing the Defense portfolio into strong, capable hands. Five basic proposals were forwarded toward this end, and each one was rejected. One of them, suggested by Eshkol, stipulated that he would continue to hold the Defense portfolio but added three alternatives: he would be assisted either by a committee of army officers, an expanded ministerial Committee for Defense Affairs (which would include representatives of the opposition parties), or a special assistant for military affairs, Yigal Allon. A second proposal, backed by the Herut Liberal Bloc and the National Religious Party, was that Ben Gurion should return to the government as Prime Minister or Minister of Defense. A third, put forward by the same parties, was that Dayan be appointed Minister of Defense. The fourth was proposed by the leader of the National Religious Party and suggested that Yigael Yadin be appointed Minister of Defense. The fifth, supported by Mapai veterans and Achdut Ha'avodah, was that the Defense portfolio be given to Yigal Allon. There were also several variations on these five basic proposals. Among the ideas suggested and dropped were that Dayan be made Deputy Prime Minister, Foreign Minister, or one of three advisers to the Prime Minister.

Dayan was surprised by the developments of May 14. Like Rabin, he believed that war with Egypt was still a long way off. On a visit to the United States in April 1967, he told a group of Harvard University professors that he did not foresee war within the next ten years. This was the official evaluation of Zahal and the government, based on the calculation that Egypt's involvement in Yemen left her army in no condition to launch a war against Israel. Unlike others, however, Dayan was quick to modify his position. While Eshkol's government was still explaining the flow of Egyptian troops and arms into Sinai as mere display, he recognized the inevitability of war. Dayan publicly criticized the Cabinet during a tour of ex-Chiefs-of-Staff in the Armored Corps on May 15, stating that "Nasser will resort to extreme measures, and after the withdrawal [of the UNEF] from the Israeli borders, he is capable of closing the Straits of Tiran." This was a prophecy that was soon to be fulfilled.

On the same occasion, Dayan told his colleagues that Eshkol's government would "swallow" the blockade of the straits.

Characteristically, at that point he removed himself from the steaming cauldron of party activity. When the "Lavon Affair" broke out, Dayan was out of the country, and when the struggle between the majority and the "Minority" reached boiling point in the summer of 1965, he was sailing to Eritrea in a fishing boat. This time, instead of leading his party or taking an active part in its deliberations or campaign for the establishment of a Government of National Unity, he asked Eshkol for permission to visit Zahal units in the south, "To see things at first hand." Eshkol politely complied, giving him military transport and a lieutenant colonel as an escort. In a uniform bearing the rank of lieutenant general, he toured army units stationed along Israel's southern borders, far from party activity and sometimes out of touch with the leaders of Rafi. Above all, he wanted to learn about Zahal. Ten years had passed since he left the army, and during this time many innovations and improvements had been introduced. Perhaps in the back of his mind he entertained thoughts of a military posting to which he could contribute his own experience and knowledge. Be that as it may, he instinctively took the right step.

Consciously, Dayan left the centers of political activity because of his utter pessimism about the prospects of a meaningful change in Eshkol's Cabinet. His reading of the situation led him to advocate immediate military measures—before the Egyptian Army managed to complete its deployment in Sinai. Ben Gurion opposed him on this. He proposed that the Reserves be sent home, the closing of the straits be temporarily "swallowed," and Israel wait until a better opportunity presented itself to reopen them. He claimed that Israel should choose the time most fitting to her needs, and not be pushed into an untimely action by Nasser's machinations.

Ben Gurion's proposals for dealing with the situation were dictated to a great extent by his personal animosity for Eshkol and a burning desire to see him replaced. But he was also motivated by a very real fear that Eshkol was incapable of guiding the nation in time of war or through the political struggle that was bound to follow. This concern spurred Peres to work for the formation of a Government of National Unity and to seize the opportunity of returning Ben Gurion to power. But Peres was unsuccessful. Mapai went up in arms, fearing that heads would roll should Ben Gurion be reinstated. Of the five proposals designed to unite the nation, the first to be dropped was that advocating the return of Ben Gurion to the post of Prime Minister or Minister of Defense. This left Rafi with only one alternative: to seek Dayan's appointment as Minister of Defense in Eshkol's Cabinet. The option created new waves of tension in Rafi, particularly between Peres and Ben Gurion. The latter demanded above all else that Eshkol be ousted. His desire to settle his score with Eshkol guided and distorted every move. Even after he agreed to have Dayan, not himself, appointed Minister of Defense, it prompted him to state that "If Eshkol should offer Dayan only the post of Minister of Defense, it must be turned down."

Golda Meir claimed that Eshkol's government could be strengthened and the public's faith in it restored without changing the Minister of Defense or setting up a Government of National Unity. Her objection to expanding the Cabinet, and in particular to having Rafi join it and handing the Ministry of Defense to Dayan, were based on party as well as personal interests. She firmly believed in Zahal's ultimate victory and did not feel inclined to share its glory with other parties or other individuals. As for her personal reasons, she hinted to her close associates that the Cabinet could be strengthened from within, for instance by appointing her as Deputy Prime Minister. Be that as it may, Golda Meir was the most powerful, and ultimately the last, stronghold of opposition to opting Dayan into the new Cabinet as Minister of Defense. When she finally acknowledged that the nation's trust in the present government could not be regained unless the Minister of Defense was replaced, she strongly backed the candidacy of Yigal Allon. When this move failed, she brought the entire weight of her considerable influence to bear upon Eshkol and convinced him to make Allon his Deputy Prime Minister.

Eshkol's position was unenviable, to say the least. He apparently had no idea of the extent to which his personality generated a sense of insecurity in all those around him. At first he tried to maneuver his way out of the trap. On one occasion, he agreed to appoint Allon, then changed his mind and proposed a whole string of alternatives, backpedaling furiously in order to outwit all those who had exercised pressure and retain both his posts intact, without advisers, assistants, or deputies. He went from one meeting to another like a chain-smoker, hoping that in the ultimate confusion only he would be left on his feet, while all the others would be too dazed to catch their bearings. From a distance, Eshkol's maneuvering gave the appearance of nimble footwork. At closer quarters, it was abundantly clear that he was dancing in a desperate effort to avoid the hot coals under his feet. The responsibility for crucial decisions fell increasingly on Rabin, whom Eshkol took to all his Cabinet meetings and even to meetings with party and public figures. It may have been this burden—the sole responsibility for the fate of Israel—that wore Rabin out to the point of collapse.

Allon-and Dayan, the two candidates for the post of Minister of Defense, reacted completely differently to the events of those hectic days. Like the others, Allon was convinced that Eshkol must be relieved of the Defense portfolio, but he was quite prepared to serve as Eshkol's adviser on defense matters—a sort of Acting Minister of Defense—and thereby "slide" into the post. Later, he began openly demanding the post for himself. He worked hard to win the appointment and at one point even began introducing himself as Acting Minister of Defence.

Dayan behaved according to the maxim: "The work of the righteous is done by others." He stayed far from the centers of political activity, spending most of his time visiting the troops in their bases and along the front lines. Occasionally he agreed to come to Tel Aviv for consultations, but he never declared his candidacy for the post of Minister of Defense. Eshkol and others were forced to deduce his willingness to serve as Minister of Defense from his actions. Dayan himself categorically turned down any other post. On May 31, Eshkol asked him if he would be prepared to serve as Deputy Prime Minister in the Government of National Unity and, if not, to name the position he might be prepared to assume. Dayan replied, "That's a hypothetical question; therefore, the answer will be too. I am prepared to be Prime Minister or Minister of Defense or both. If I cannot be in charge of defense affairs, then I would like to be mobilized, but this would be outside any political negotiations. In that case I would be prepared to assume any post the C-o-S decides upon." Eshkol asked, "Which post, for example?" And Dayan replied, "OC Southern Command, because I know Sinai and the Egyptians well. But in the army, I would even be willing to drive a half-track."

At this point, Eshkol had already agreed to give up the Ministry of Defense in favor of Yigal Allon. But Dayan's reply suddenly offered him a new way out. He pounced on Dayan's words as if all his problems had been solved in a flash. He would no longer have to keep his promise to give Allon the Defense portfolio, for should Dayan become commander of the Egyptian front, the nation would again put its trust in the army and the government, while he would be able to retain both his posts. He hastened to announce to his colleagues in Mapai, and to the leaders of the parties clamoring for Dayan, that the problem was solved and the Government of National Unity could be established.

On the face of it, by agreeing to accept a military post, Dayan was working against those who were trying to bring him into the Ministry of Defense. But the rapidly snowballing circumstances in the Middle East brought Eshkol's maneuvering and fancy footwork to naught. The daily growth of Egyptian might in Sinai and the hesitant steps of the government in dealing with the crisis aroused a strong public movement throughout the country demanding Dayan's appointment as Minister of Defense. Eshkol was inundated with telegrams and petitions from all walks of Israeli life clamoring for Dayan. When Golda Meir made a stand against the appointment, she found herself in the minority. In the Knesset Mapai faction, support for Dayan ran so deep that its chairman asked Eshkol to explain his position and warned that there would be "mutiny" on this issue. At a conference held by the faction on May 30, the Knesset Speaker, Kadish Luz, said, "They want Dayan. I think this is the only thing that will calm the public."

The women of Israel, now the majority of the civilian population, also rallied round Dayan. In letters from the front, their husbands and sons described the enthusiasm with which Dayan was received when he visited their units. As a result, they also began to believe that the only way to raise the morale of the country was to appoint Dayan Minister of Defense. The group known as the "Women Voters' Circle" decided to organize a petition demanding his appointment, but before embarking on their campaign they tried to ascertain if Dayan would be in favor of it. Mrs. Herzla Ron telephoned him at his home late one evening and told him of the planned petition. Dayan replied, "You haven't spoken to me," and ended the conversation. Mrs. Ron, a lawyer in the Ministry of Defense, understood that Dayan was not against the plan but was reluctant to back the "Women's Circle for Dayan" openly. The group got down to work, drew up a petition, and by June 1 had collected tens of thousands of signatures.

Ultimately, the support of the soldiers and the women, together with the strong stand of the National Religious Party, the Herut-Liberal Bloc, and the majority of Mapai, the persistent unflagging efforts of Shimon Peres, and even the support of Yigael Yadin, an a-political figure with no personal stake in the issue, created a weight of public opinion that Eshkol and Golda Meir could not withstand. At a meeting with representatives of the Herut-Liberal Bloc, Eshkol was deeply impressed when Menahem Begin said, "Mr. Prime Minister, you can have the entire nation united behind you within half an hour if only you will agree to appoint Moshe Dayan Minister of Defense." After the meeting, Eshkol decided, by his own account, to "swallow the bone." On Thursday evening, June 1, he invited Dayan to his office and proposed that he join the government as Minister of Defense.

Later, at a meeting in Ben Gurion's house, Peres told Rafi leaders the details of the negotiations with Eshkol and asked them to approve Rafi's incorporation in the Government of National Unity. Most of the leaders tended to agree; only two demurred. One was Ben Gurion, who disguised his opposition in an impossible condition: "I am in favor of Rafi's agreement to Moshe Dayan's appointment as Minister of Defense. I suggest that Rafi should also inform Eshkol that he must quit the Premiership and serve as Deputy Prime Minister to Moshe Dayan." If Ben Gurion had established Rafi with the sole aim of bringing Eshkol down for the sins of the Committee of Seven, he utterly failed and was now a minority in the party he had created out of the "Minority" of Mapai.

With the confidence that he would receive an affirmative answer from Rafi, Eshkol called the first meeting of the Government of National Unity for 8 p.m., when it was decided to acquiesce to Eshkol's request to be relieved of the post of Minister of Defense and to appoint Moshe Dayan in his stead. Dayan arrived at the meeting only after the Rafi vote, which took place close to midnight. The debate on the situation along the Egyptian-Israeli border was referred to the Ministerial Committee for Defense Affairs that was due to meet the following day, Friday, June 2.

The first Cabinet meeting in which Dayan participated from beginning to end took place that Friday in GHQ and was devoted entirely to reports given by C-o-S Rabin; the Chief of Intelligence Branch, Maj. Gen. Aaron Yariv; and the Commander of the Air Force, Maj. Gen. Mordechai Hod. On Sunday, June 4, the Cabinet met again and authorized the enlarged Ministerial Committee for Defense Affairs to react to the situation along the Egyptian border. That afternoon, in its capacity as a War Cabinet, it decided to declare war on the following morning, Monday, June 5.

This decision ended a process of feverish debate, begun on May 21, on the merits of diplomatic efforts versus the use of military force and a United States-led attempt to open the Straits of Tiran with the aid of a multinational flotilla versus military action by Zahal. Dayan's opinion on military action was taken for granted, and no one was surprised that upon entering the Cabinet he demanded that war be launched immediately. The Cabinet had previously been divided, and at a night-long session on May 27, it reached a nine-to-nine deadlock; but after Dayan joined it, the decision was passed quickly and effortlessly, with only two objections. Dayan's appointment seemed to change the entire mood of the Cabinet, making it easier to reach so fateful a decision.

Why did the nation want Dayan and no one else? Certainly not because of his conduct as a statesman in the ten years that had elapsed since he left the army. Actually, Dayan was simply preferable to the three other candidates considered experienced in military matters— Ben Gurion, Allon, and Yadin. Ben Gurion had maneuvered himself into a position that made his appointment well-nigh unimaginable. Of the two others, Yadin's and Allon's combat experience went back to 1948, while Dayan enjoyed the advantage of being familiar with Zahal up to the Sinai Campaign and for some time after.

Moreover, he was remembered as the molder and leader of a victorious Zahal, a man fired with a profound will to fight. To the Israeli public, Dayan was the nation's number one soldier. The same negative qualities he had displayed during his ten years of political activity now reinforced his image as a military leader. It was clear to all that he would be tough and carry out his duty without mercy. In war, unlike peacetime, effectiveness is the only criterion. There was no one who met this demand of the Israeli public better than Dayan.

Dayan's visits to Zahal units and his willingness to serve as OC Southern Command did not help the public campaign to have him appointed Minister of Defense and actually almost ruined its chances of success. But from the moment he was appointed to the post until the end of the war, they became his greatest asset. The extent of the army's trust in him became apparent, and he was greeted enthusiastically wherever he went. When news of his appointment reached the units, there were spontaneous outbreaks of exuberant and even hysterial celebration. Everyone was now certain that Dayan would take decisive, correct, and wise steps that would lead Zahal to victory. The decision to go to war seemed implicit in his very appointment. During his visits to the units and along the front, he had learned much about the army's weapons, material, and planning. He was therefore well prepared to assume his post and on his first day as Minister of Defense, Friday, June 2, could give Rabin explicit orders on the plan to be followed.

Dayan's main contribution to the brilliant victory over Egypt, Jordan, and Syria was the fact that he restored Zahal's confidence in its ability to win. The army that went to war on Monday, June 5, was confident both in itself and its ultimate victory. An incident that seems to explain the change of mood in Zahal occurred at his first meeting at GHQ, which was devoted to a review of plans. Dayan arrived on time, at 7 p.m., but routine and punctuality in the army had grown somewhat lax, and some of the participants had not arrived yet. When he was told, "We're not ready yet. It'll take some time"—as though such tardiness were a matter of course—he replied, "You told me to come at seven. We begin now." Ezer Weizman relates: "He sat down and right off the bat said, "Well, let's see your plans. I have my own plans.'" Rabin remembers Dayan as saying, "Show me your plan—that is, if you have one."

The nation had retained an impression of Dayan as a brave man, and this image was corroborated by his appearance on the front lines. Before he knew he would be Minister of Defense, he had ensured himself a place in the command half-track of Col. Shmuel, the commander of the armored brigade singled out for the toughest breaching assignments in Sinai. This fact quickly became widely known, as did the order he gave on his first day as Minister of Defense to prepare a half-track and have it ready at all times, so that he would be able to leave for the front at a moment's notice. Courage is infectious, and Dayan infected everyone around him with his own fearlessness.

His leadership was demonstrated not only in minor episodes, however. In his first public appearance at a large press conference called for June 3, he handled the barrage of questions like a seasoned Cabinet minister with a sense of humor and ready replies.

Q: Do you believe that a diplomatic solution can be found?
A: The government of Israel has taken diplomatic steps and it must now be given a chance.
Q: Until when?
A: Until the government decides.

This simple, seemingly flippant reply contained information that most of the reporters overlooked, namely, that the Cabinet had not yet decided on military action. Many reporters interpreted the mere fact of Dayan's appointment as a clear decision to go to war, but it was only on Sunday, June 4, that the entire Government of National Unity met and authorized the Prime Minister, the Minister of Defense, and the C-o-S to decide on the timing of military reaction to the Egyptian build-up in Sinai.

One correspondent asked if Dayan did not think Israel had weakened her military position as a result of its agreement to lengthy diplomatic negotiations. Clearly, Dayan thought she had, and the reporters hoped to catch him off guard and elicit some criticism of the Cabinet he had recently joined or force him to retract some of his own previous statements. Dayan replied: "At this moment, we are more or less in a position of being a bit too late and a bit too early: too late to react with force to the closing of the Straits of Tiran, and too early to come to any final conclusions about the diplomatic efforts applied in this matter." In reply to the question of whether or not time was working in Israel's favor, he remarked that he did not believe nations live with a stop watch in hand. In the Arab countries these replies were understood to mean that Israel was not yet prepared for war. Consequently, although purely by chance, he restored to Zahal the element of surprise in the war that was launched only thirty-six hours later.

Dayan's greatest contribution to the nation's self-confidence was his total rejection of offers of military aid from outside. Up to the time of his appointment, Eshkol's government had attempted to reopen the Straits of Tiran with the help of diplomatic activity that centered on Washington. Israel claimed that when she withdrew from the Straits of Tiran, the Sinai peninsula, and the Gaza Strip in 1957, she received explicit promises from President Eisenhower's administration that the straits would be kept open to Israeli shipping. This was included in the document—signed by Eisenhower—which Golda Meir called "Expectations and Clarifications." Dayan, then C-o-S, had little faith in the document. Following Israeli appeals, President Johnson tried to set up a multinational fleet which, by its mere presence in the straits as a sort of merchant marine armada, would honor Eisenhower's promise and ensure free passage for Israeli shipping. The attempt was doomed from the outset, but up to a point, Eshkol believed in its ultimate efficacy. In a broadcast to the nation on May 28, he stated that "Zahal's mobilization has been, and is now, a crucial factor in hastening international action" for a swift removal of the blockade. At the end of his address he reported that the government had formulated directives for continued diplomatic activity in the capitals of the world aimed at urging international bodies to take steps to ensure universal free passage in the Straits of Tiran. Eshkol therefore regarded the mobilization of Zahal as an added incentive to the diplomatic efforts. Dayan opposed this reasoning on several counts, the most important of which was his fear that if this attempt to open the straits with the help of the Great Powers succeeded, it would amplify the error inherent in calling for outside help, for Israel would then appear to be a nation living by the grace of the Great Powers. Just as Dayan was opposed to having the United Nations guard Israel's borders, he now opposed international action which could turn the country into a permanent protectorate of the Powers involved.

The diplomatic moves brought another issue in their wake—the possibility of American military intervention on Israel's behalf. This was the devout wish of some Israelis, and to others beyond despair it was a last hope of salvation. At the press conference on June 3, Dayan rejected both the illusion of a multinational maritime force and the prospect of American military intervention. In this respect, it was the first time in 1967 that anyone had heard a clear-cut statement from a minister in the Israeli Government: "I do not expect, nor do I want, anyone to fight or die for us. Of this I am certain." He made no secret of his complete confidence that Zahal could handle the Egyptian Army on its own. Asked whether he had considered the possibility of the Egyptians using missiles in case of war, he replied, "Let them try."

Dayan's concept of war was quite different from Eshkol's, and this difference also helped restore the army's self-confidence and influenced the way the war was run. Eshkol's plan in case the diplomatic efforts failed was that Zahal would strike the Egyptian Army in one sector, Eastern Sinai or the Gaza Strip, and then hold the territory until the Egyptians agreed to open the Straits of Tiran. He never conceived of total war, and the preliminary plans of Zahal therefore made no mention of conquest for its own sake, but only conquest as a means of acquiring a trump card to be used in the negotiations that would follow the war (which was estimated to last a day or two). Zahal would retreat from the limited area it had captured only in return for a satisfactory resolution of all the points of conflict. One direct result of this concept was the defensive nature of what were essentially plans for an offensive action. OC Southern Command and GHQ had a contingency plan which was substantially identical, but involved the capture of larger territories than Eshkol envisioned. There were, then, two plans: the "limited plan," favored by C-o-S Rabin and Eshkol's Cabinet before Dayan's appointment, and the "extended plan," which was more ambitious but did not set its sights any further than the middle of the Sinai peninsula. It would seem that by the very act of joining the government, Dayan weighed the scales in favor of the "extended plan."

It was not only the possible extension of the military action that pointed out the differences—and even contrasts—between Eshkol and Dayan. At a meeting of the Ministerial Committee for Defense Affairs, before his meeting with GHQ and OC Southern Command, Dayan made it clear that the destruction of the Egyptian Army was far more important than seizing territory. This marked a change in his thinking, for in 1956 his "collapse" theory had stipulated merely disrupting the Egyptian deployment and not killing its soldiers. By specifying the customary war aim of "destroying the enemy's forces," he lent the coming war its sense of totality. His order was to hit the Egyptian Army as hard as possible, regardless of the areas marked out in the "limited" or the "extended" plans for negotiation purposes. However, at this stage he did not have a more comprehensive, or even a different, concept of the nature of the war than that of the government. The country was certain that Egypt had made war inevitable by massing almost its entire army in Sinai and closing the straits. Israel was preparing for a war of survival. The order to destroy the Egyptian Army stemmed to a great extent from the desire to prevent a similar threat in the near future, which is exactly what would have happened had Zahal stopped at holding certain areas as bargaining cards for the opening of the straits.

Minister of Defense Dayan was not Chief-of-Staff Dayan. In the ten years that had passed, his hair had thinned and his forehead had joined the bald patch in the middle of his head; inches had been added to his waistline and a paunch was in evidence. But military men noticed a change in him beyond his external appearance.

He was no longer the headlong, precipitate Dayan who swept higher ranks along with him in the power of his momentum. This time he directed his war with the utmost sensitivity to world public opinion and a remarkable caution in all his military moves. Almost throughout the Six-Day War, he served as a brake both on Zahal, which was under his command, and on the Government of National Unity, to which he was responsible.

This new facet of Dayan came to light before the outbreak of the war. In the discussion that followed OC Southern Command Isaiah Gavish's presentation of his "extended plan" at GHQ, the question arose to what point in Sinai the troops should be allowed to advance. Earlier plans had mentioned Jebel Libni as the limit. Once the "extended plan" was approved and the directive about destroying the Egyptian Army had been issued, the limit had to be modified. GHQ regarded the Suez Canal as the natural line to stop and dig in. Dayan objected: "What do you need the Suez for? It's political madness," he told the C-o-S and went on to mark out the two passes—the Mitla and the Jidi—some 20 to 40 kilometers from the Suez, as the stopping point. This was more or less what had been agreed upon in the tripartite Anglo-French-Israeli plan as Israel's western limit in the Suez War. Apparently the memory of the political struggle that followed the military victories of 1956 was still fresh in his mind. This time he feared even greater international pressure should Zahal dig in on the eastern bank of the Canal, and he wished to obviate this possibility before the outbreak of hostilities. He had other, equally important, reasons for his choice of a limit. Dayan believed that the Egyptians would not admit their defeat and would continue fighting. He thought that the war would never end and explained that the Canal was vital to Nasser's prestige, economy, and power, not to mention the fact that it was an important factor in the Soviet build-up of naval forces in the Mediterranean and their contacts with Yemen and Vietnam. Dayan therefore told his colleagues in the Cabinet: "Anyone with an ounce of sense should keep away from the Canal. If we reach the Canal, Nasser will never agree to a cease-fire and the war will go on for years."

As it happened, the war that began on June 5 turned out quite differently from all the forecasts. It lasted only four days—not two or three weeks as Dayan had estimated—and its outcome was decided in the first half of the first day, when the greater part of the Egyptian Air Force was destroyed by the Israeli Air Force in three hours and Maj. Gen. Tal's armored division penetrated the fortified defense network of Rafah-El-Arish. Furthermore, it became clear from the very first day that Israel's losses would be smaller than anticipated and, in view of the Egyptian Army's rapid disintegration and flight, the order to destroy the army physically no longer applied. On the contrary, after the first three days of battle, Zahal began searching for Egyptian soldiers wandering about the sand dunes and helped them find their way back to Egypt.

Zahal's advance was so swift that on the third day GHQ was under the mistaken impression that the northern arm of Tal's division had reached the Suez Canal opposite the city of Kantara. Dayan issued an order that the unit be moved back to the stopping line near Romani. However, the units had not crossed this line and the order was unnecessary. Yet the fact that such an order was issued underscored Dayan's caution.

It was only on Wednesday, June 7, that Dayan authorized an advance all the way to the Canal, apparently because the forward momentum of the army was difficult to stop. Dayan is quoted as saying after the war, "I did not want, under any circumstances, to reach the Canal. I issued orders to stop some distance from it. But the army established facts in the field and I had no choice." It is likely that his reasoning was influenced to some extent by GHQ claims that the Canal was the most convenient defense line in the entire peninsula, while any limit east of it would preclude the possibility of achieving a complete victory and ending the hostilities. This new caution also led Dayan to postpone by one day the attack on the Gaza Strip. And even when it transpired on the morning of the 5th that Zahal had complete superiority in Sinai, he maintained his moderate stance and forbade Central Command to move from the defensive to an offensive, despite the fact that Jordan had already opened fire in the Jerusalem area. Initially he tried to avoid involving Zahal on two fronts and ordered OC Central Command, Uzi Narkiss, "Grit your teeth, and don't ask for more troops from GHQ." Narkiss told Dayan that the Arabs might seize two strategic points: the Kastel Hill overlooking the western approaches to Jerusalem and Mount Scopus, the Israeli enclave east of the Old City. Dayan was skeptical but added that even if such a danger existed, he preferred ending the war in Sinai first, then reinforcing Central Command and "recapturing Mount Scopus and the Kastel." At the same time, he did consider the possibility of the war spreading to the Jordanian front and ordered GHQ to send the Harel Armored Brigade as a reserve force for the battle along the mountain ridges leading to Jerusalem. This turned out to be one of his most important decisions in the Six-Day War. Only after it was clear that the battle in Sinai was virtually over (on Tuesday, June 6) did Dayan order Central Command to mount its offensive. Yet here too, he imposed limits and marked out the mountain ridge as the stopping line. So strict was the obedience he demanded to this directive that when the Harel Brigade surged eastward almost to the Jordan River, it was ordered to return to the mountains. There it heard that the restriction had been lifted and could now turn back to the Jordan. To ensure that no Central Command units cross the Jordan to the East Bank, he instructed Narkiss to have the bridges on the river blown up. According to one story that made the rounds at the time, when Dayan was told that the Harel Brigade had blown up the Abdullah Bridge, he asked, "From which side?"

Dayan's restraining hand in the war was nowhere more evident than in East Jerusalem (the Jordanian sector of the city, outside the walls of the Old City) and the Old City. His first order to Central Command concerning Jerusalem was, "We'll surround it if necessary, but will not enter." After the stunning successes in Sinai and other sectors of the Jordanian front, however, the other ministers excitedly demanded that Jerusalem be "liberated" and made an undivided city again. Yigal Allon and Menahem Begin were the most extreme, while the Minister of the Interior, an orthodox Jew, was more moderate and expressed his concern that the world would object to Israeli occupation of the Old City. Dayan was similarly concerned. On June 5 Eshkol concluded the Cabinet meeting by saying that above all else, "The Old City must be taken, to avert the danger of incessant bombardments [on Israeli Jerusalem]," but Dayan still did not hasten to order entry into the city. He held back for so long that Eshkol was forced to telephone him at midnight to reiterate, "The government wants the Old City!" Dayan replied that theoretically the Old City could be taken the following day, June 6, but added that he felt it should be taken by siege rather than by frontal attack. In seeking a formula that might appease world public opinion, Dayan preferred to wait and have the city surrender. On Tuesday morning, June 6, the Cabinet met again, and at that time both Yigal Allon and Menahem Begin complained of "the hesitancy on the political-security level that has stopped the drive for the liberation of Jerusalem." Dayan replied, "I'm willing to wager that the inhabitants of the Old City will come out waving white flags within a few hours or days." With half the ministers supporting Dayan and the other half against him, the meeting ended in a draw.

The ministers who demanded the immediate capture of Jerusalem were spurred by their fear that the UN Security Council would impose a cease-fire before the Old City was taken. Menahem Begin recounted that at dawn on Wednesday, June 7, after hearing on the BBC news that the Security Council was to vote on a cease-fire, he phoned Eshkol, woke him up, and demanded an immediate meeting of the Cabinet because, "Jerusalem is not like the Golan Heights or anywhere else, in the country or the world. It is impossible to capture Jerusalem after a truce has been called . . . after the Security Council has set a definite hour for a cease-fire." Eshkol called a Cabinet meeting for nine o'clock that morning, at which Begin demanded steps be taken immediately to capture the Old City. By this time, however, Dayan was able to tell the Cabinet that he had already given the order during the night. There was to be no artillery or air support, and the utmost care was to be exercised so as not to damage the city's many holy places. At 8:30 on the morning of Wednesday, June 7, the Paratroop Brigade launched its offensive to seize the Old City.

As Zahal's successes mounted and the territories taken by Israel multiplied, Dayan's restraining influence on the government and the army increased. But while the caution about attacking the Old City was supported by half the Cabinet, his delaying the attack on Syria and the Golan Heights was backed by no one. As the war was not over in Sinai and the West Bank, he was opposed to opening a third front in Syria. This was indeed a curious reversal. Eshkol, who as Minister of Defense had been unsure and hesitant, became aggressive and decisive from the moment Dayan assumed his post and Zahal reaped its first victories. On the very first day of the war, June 5, he demanded that "the sources of the Jordan be seized," in other words that war be launched against Syria. On the other hand, Dayan, who as C-o-S was known for his eagerness for battle and had been appointed Minister of Defense because the nation had faith in his leadership in time of war, now became so moderate and wary as to arouse bitter resentment in the government, the army, and large sections of the population.

The situation on the northern border was indeed bizarre. While the Egyptian Army was being routed in the south, and the Arab Legion had retreated back across the Jordan, the Syrian Army had the best of two worlds. It could display solidarity with the Arab war effort by firing down on Israeli settlements below the Golan Heights while not suffering any of the consequences of a full-scale war on her territory. Dayan's order concerning the Syrian front was quite explicit: do not get involved in a war with the Syrian Army. Thus Syria, clearly Israel's most bothersome enemy since 1956 and actively instrumental in precipitating the Six-Day War, came close to emerging from the war unscathed. The Syrian Army had suffered no casualties at all, still retained the Golan Heights, and with it the means of seriously disrupting life in the border settlements below.

Fearing that the opportunity to be rid of the Golan nightmare would slip through their fingers, the inhabitants of the northern settlements met to find ways of influencing the government. These meetings in the north were dubbed "The Galilee Rebellion." On Thursday, June 8, when the war against Egypt and Jordan was to all intents and purposes over, a representative of the northern settlements phoned Eshkol and demanded that Zahal attack the Syrians. While they were talking, the Syrians opened fire again, and Eshkol could hear the sound of explosions in the background. That evening, the chairman and secretary of the Upper Galilee Local Council and one other representative of the settlements drove to Jerusalem. The three met with Eshkol and requested permission to speak to the Ministerial Committee for Defense Affairs, which was in fact an inner Cabinet. Eshkol not only let them know he was completely on their side, but even undertook an unprecedented step: at 8 p.m. he invited the two to the meeting of the Ministerial Committee for Defense Affairs. Yigael Yadin claims that this was the second time in the history of Israel that citizens were given the opportunity to have a direct say in government and army decisions. The first was in May 1948, when Ben Gurion received a delegation from the Jordan Valley settlements. He had not, however, invited them to speak at a Cabinet meeting.

There is an ironic reversal in this episode, for in 1948, when representatives of Degania and Kinneret asked Ben Gurion and Yadin to send immediate aid against the Syrian Army, Dayan was sent to the area as if he alone were a whole troop of reinforcements. That fateful mission brought him back into the mainstream of army life and was the starting point from which he rose to the two pinnacles of his career—Chief-of-Staff and Minister of Defense. And now it was he to whom the representatives of the Galilee settlements appealed for help against the same Syrian Army. Eshkol undoubtedly took the rare step of bringing the three men into the Cabinet meeting in order to force Dayan to change his mind about attacking the Golan Heights. In bringing him face to face with the settlers who had suffered from Syrian bombardments for so long, Eshkol was deliberately putting Dayan's convictions to the test.

Dayan was under very heavy pressure. Most of the Cabinet ministers favored an immediate attack on the Golan Heights, and now representatives of the Galilee settlements added their voices, even hinting that should the Syrians be allowed to continue harassing them from the positions on the Golan Heights, they would be forced to abandon their settlements. Dayan, however, did not bow to the pressure and told the settlers that he would not budge from his stated policy, even if some settlements along the Syrian border would have to be moved.

This remark raised eyebrows in the Cabinet, for here was Dayan, one of the zealots of the settlement movement who had always maintained that the borders of Jewish settlement were the borders of the Jewish State, suddenly prepared to give up territory and accept the withdrawal of settlements. It would seem that apart from logical considerations and the readiness to bear the full responsibility of his post, his decision also contained something of his own un-willingness to make decisions under pressure. His associates knew this trait well. Now, cornered by Eshkol and the representatives from the Galilee settlements, he leaped to his own defense. Returning to their respective kibbutzim, the Galilee farmers were convinced that they had failed and that the Golan Heights would not be attacked.

Dayan had several reasons for refraining from attacking the Golan Heights. First, he wanted to avoid involving Zahal on a third front. After the defeat of Egypt and Jordan, he claimed, the Soviet Union would not sit idly by while the Syrian regime—so dear to its heart—was attacked. He feared that Israel, exhilarated by its successes, might go too far. In 1949, when Zahal routed the Egyptian Army, Ben Gurion forbade it to throw its entire weight against the Arab Legion for fear of British intervention and in the belief that everything has its limit. It was for these reasons that he had ordered the withdrawal of Zahal from eastern Sinai. Dayan also subscribed to this concept of a bird in the hand.

Another important consideration was that assaulting the Golan Heights—which loomed over Israel like a rock fortress—would cost many lives. Dayan claimed that the Air Force—by now "worn out"—would not be able to give the land forces the full close support they would need to keep their losses down. The ministers left the meeting on Thursday night with the understanding that another meeting would be called should there be any change in the situation or in the position of the Minister of Defense.

Within a few hours the situation changed radically. At 3 a.m. on June 9, Dayan was informed that the Egyptians were prepared to ask the Security Council for a cease-fire and that they had advised Jordan and Syria to follow suit. This move ran completely counter to his predictions, and he had to rethink his position. Egyptian agreement to a cease-fire meant the southern front would be quiet and Zahal would be able to transfer troops to other fronts. The prospect of simultaneous involvement on three fronts would there-fore disappear. The Egyptian move thus allayed Dayan's earlier fears of Soviet intervention and the inability of the Air Force to give adequate support. He decided to attack.

There was no time to lose. If the Syrians were to follow Egypt's lead and agree to a cease-fire, Zahal would miss the opportunity of liberating the Galilee from the perpetual terror of bombardments from the Golan. Never a stickler for protocol and—so he claimed—unable to locate the C-o-S (Dayan was told Rabin was asleep at home), Dayan called OC Northern Command, Maj. Gen. David Eleazar, at 7 a.m. and ordered him to launch Northern Command's attack on Syria and to destroy the fortified emplacements on the Golan Heights. Only later did he inform the Prime Minister. Eshkol immediately called a Cabinet meeting for that morning, at which the government retroactively approved the Minister of Defense's decision to launch a war against Syria.

Dayan offered two explanations for contravening protocol and launching the war against Syria on his own initiative: the first was the acknowledged support of such an attack by the majority of the Cabinet ministers. The second was that between the time he gave the order at 7 a.m. and the time the troops would actually begin fighting (the first units crossed the border only at about 11:30, four and a half hours would elapse, and that was time enough to stop them or have them turned back should the government decide against attack.

Dayan's first instruction to Eleazar was "to advance throughout the Heights" with the aid of substantial air support; but after the action began, he decided that it was preferable not to go beyond the demilitarized zone demarcated by the former Mandatory borders, where the Syrians had constructed bunkers in violation of the 1949 Armistice Agreement. At a Cabinet meeting held on Friday morning, he reiterated his fears that the Syrians would raise a panic, claiming that Zahal was gaining on Damascus, and would drag the Soviet Union into the hostilities. The Cabinet met four more times over the question of the limit of advance in the Golan Heights, which was now bound up with the Security Council's call for a cease-fire: twice more on Friday—at seven and eight in the evening—and twice before dawn on Saturday, June 10. At 4:30 in the afternoon, Dayan personally flew to Eleazar's Command Headquarters and suggested that he stay out of the southern sector of the Golan and concentrate his forces in the area of the Banias.

Even after he had changed his mind about the attack on Syria, Dayan did not want to set definitive rules about the stopping line. His stance was motivated by the fear that the Soviets might intervene if Zahal movements were interpreted as the first steps toward an attack on Damascus and by the expectation of a Syrian collapse. He wanted to ensure limited casualties and even stated that "it would be a pity if fifty boys were to lose their lives" in the event that the impending collapse did not materialize. But it came about quickly.

On the following day, June 10, Dayan ordered the Deputy C-o-S, Lt. Gen. Bar-Lev, to reach Kuneitra by 2 p.m. At 11:30 he met with Eleazar for a second time and ordered him to complete the conquest by reaching a point parallel to the Kuneitra highway, a necessary condition for defending the conquered territory. From this meeting he flew to another with General Odd Bull, head of the UN Observers, and succeeded in "extending" the deadline for a cease-fire to 6:30 p.m., instead of the original hour of 2 p.m.

He thereby afforded Zahal another four and a half hours of action, which sufficed for the forces of the Northern Command to get a firm grip on their conquests.

On June 12 Dayan visited the conquered Golan Heights and canceled his prohibition regarding one of the peaks of Mount Hermon. At the request of Dr. Yuval Ne'eman, who was serving in the Reserves, he ordered the capture of the highest peak in the area, which would be important to furthering the science of astronomy in Israel. By generally restraining the Northern Command, however, Dayan succeeded in convincing world public opinion that Zahal had no designs on Damascus, and thereby made the capture of the Heights possible. Later C-o-S Rabin remarked of Dayan's restrictions, "In the Six-Day War we all had our traumas. For Moshe Dayan it was the Russians; for me it was all the Arab armies fighting against us."

23 MINISTER OF DEFENSE

(1967 and After)

Immediately after the war, Dayan was criticized for the restraining influence he exercised and for his fear of the Soviet Union. As time went on, however, it transpired that he had foreseen more clearly than others the outcome of the war and the developments that would follow. His fear of a protracted war and Soviet intervention proved uncannily accurate, for the Six-Day War was not to be the last war, as most Israelis had hoped, but only the opening round. During the "War of Attrition" which followed, Soviet intervention reached such proportions that Dayan called it the "Sovietization" of the Egyptians' war against Israel.

Soon after the hostilities were halted, Dayan repeated what he had said in GHQ and the Cabinet when the question of a limit in Sinai was discussed, namely, that "If Zahal reaches the Canal, the war will never end. The Egyptians will not be prepared to accept Zahal's digging in on the banks of the Suez, nor will the Soviets reconcile themselves to it." On June 29, 1967—a year and a half before the beginning of the "War of Attrition," he reiterated this theory at a Rafi convention in Tel Aviv:

I can say that I am not sure, that I am quite far from being sure, that the actual fighting has come to an end, and I certainly do not believe that the political battle is over. We are at the beginning, in the first phase of the political battle, after only one step—an important and glorious step, but only a first step of the military engagement . . . Israel's army is now stationed along the Suez Canal, in Sharm e-Sheikh, on the Jordan, and in Kuneitra, on the Syrian Heights. We are only one operative move away from all the Arab capitals, less than 100 kilometers from Cairo, Damascus, Amman, and Beirut. We have no aggressive intentions. But our presence along these borders . . . is more than just a challenge to the countries around us—it virtually imperils their foundations. Will they accept these borders? Will they be reconciled to them?

On several other occasions he termed Zahal's occupation of the East Bank of the Suez Canal "keeping a foot on Egypt's neck" and believed it to be a situation Egypt would find untenable.

In the latter half of June it was unanimously agreed that in return for a peace treaty drawn up in direct negotiations between Egypt and Israel, Zahal would withdraw from Sinai to the Mandatory borders; in other words, Israel would relinquish all of Sinai except the Gaza Strip. Dayan agreed to this policy, as did Yigal Allon and the leaders of the right-wing Herut-Liberal Bloc. Though contrary to Dayan's early predictions, this concept fitted in well with the restraining role he had taken upon himself. At the same time, however, he was the first to regard the Six-Day War and its results in a different light. Here began a series of contradictory public utterances that may have been a sign of his own confusion.

Even before the war broke out, the impending hostilities were viewed by Israel as a fight for survival. Dayan shared this view, but he was also among the first Israeli statesmen who stressed the significance of the nation's yearning for the land of its historical heritage. At the Wailing Wall, on June 7, while the war was still raging in other sectors, Dayan stated: "We have returned to our holiest places. We have returned never to be parted from them again." Later, on August 3, at the reinterment on the Mount of Olives of the men who had fallen in the defense of the Jewish Quarter in the Old City in 1948, he said:

Our brothers who fell in the War of Independence: We have not abandoned your dream, nor forgotten the lesson you taught us. We have returned to the Mount, to the cradle of our nation's history, to the land of our forefathers, to the land of the Judges, and to the fortress of David's dynasty. We have returned to Hebron, to Shechem [Nablus], to Bethlehem, and Anatoth, to Jericho and the fords over the Jordan . . . Our brothers, we bear your lesson with us . . . We know that to give life to Jerusalem we must station the soldiers and armor of Zahal in the Shechem mountains and on the bridges over the Jordan.

Dayan's declaration about the return to "the land of our forefathers is reminiscent of Ben Gurion's statement at the close of the Sinai Campaign (November 7, 1956) on "a new revelation at Mount Sinai" and "freeing" the Bay of Shlomo (a biblical name used for the first time in modern times), actually proclamation of a new kingdom of Israel from Dan in the north to the island of Yotvat (Tiran) in the south. Ben Gurion, who expressed his opposition to a preventative war before the Sinai Campaign, who promised the Knesset and the world (November 2, 1955) that "We do not covet one inch of foreign territory," and who opposed using force in order to ensure free access to Mount Scopus and to drive the Syrian Army out of positions it had taken up in the Israeli sector of the demilitarized zone, was so taken aback by Zahal's victory in 1956 that the momentum of his emotions swept him away from his own basic positions. There is, therefore, some resemblance between Ben Gurion and Dayan as Ministers of Defense in time of war. Both fulfilled roles of exercising restraint and both possessed the strength to uphold their cardinal rule: do not stretch the rope to the breaking point. But Dayan learned from Ben Gurion's bitter experience. Thirty-six hours after his original statement, Ben Gurion was forced to announce to the Knesset the conditions in which Israel would be prepared to withdraw from the "new kingdom of Israel."

Dayan chose his words carefully, saying "returned" and not "conquered," "annexed," or "liberated." In a limited perspective, this could be taken to mean merely the principle of free access to all the holy places mentioned in the Bible to be maintained in a confederacy—which Dayan regarded as the solution to the Palestine problem, if and when such a confederacy would be set up. In a broader perspective, his speech could have been taken to mean a permanent return by force of arms.

When he said at the Wailing Wall, "We have returned to our holiest places," he added in the same breath, "And to our Arab neighbors we extend, even now, and more emphatically, the hand of peace." Dayan quickly grasped the contradiction between his two statements. Uniting Jerusalem and extending a hand of peace were in Arab eyes irreconcilable opposites. The same was also true about the essential differences between a war for survival and a war in which a nation's longing for the land of its forefathers was a powerful motive.

The coincidences that were Dayan's personal history lent the term "land of our forefathers" a palpable personal significance for him, beyond the national or the historical. His father, whose ambition it had been in the twenties to "conquer" the lands belonging to Baron de Rothschild in the Horan by cultivating them, had not abandoned his dream even after the establishment of the state. When word was received that these lands had been expropriated by the Syrian Government, Shmuel entered into correspondence with the Foreign Minister, Moshe Sharett, urging him to take action. On March 17, 1953, Sharett replied, " . . . I doubt very much if we can effectively claim ownership of these lands as part of peace negotiations with Syria, for as far as I know the Syrian authorities have arbitrarily and administratively seized these areas, but have also seen to it that the expropriation . . . should have the appearance of legality . . . Nevertheless, time will tell." Shmuel replied, "We have not lost our hope"* and continued to harass the Legal Adviser of the Foreign Ministry with the issue of the lands in the Horan. After the Six-Day War, Shmuel was one of the first civilians to hasten to the Golan Heights. On June 24, 1967, equipped with a special permit to enter military areas and with a military escort, he traveled across the Heights in search of the Baron's lands. He wrote later in his autobiography, "We found that these lands lie only 6 kilometers beyond the cease-fire lines. Therefore the Baron's lands are still beyond our

---

* A quote from the Israeli national anthem.

reach. What a pity!" Naturally, had his son subscribed to the view that the entire southern part of Syria should be taken, Shmuel would have fulfilled his life's ambition, and the lands of the Horan would also have been included in Dayan's concept of "the land of our forefathers."

Finally, while Dayan was able to impose some limits on a war for survival—to prevent it from becoming a war that would slowly consume Israel itself—he was powerless to act as a restraining force once he himself reformed the definition of the war as one to regain the land of Israel's forefathers. It would seem that this inner discord detracted from his ability to run the war in the light of his basic comprehension of the situation.

The events following the war made Dayan, as Minister of Defense, the Cabinet minister in charge of the occupied territories. In this sense he became the Supreme Military Governor, a task at which he excelled. Arabs who for years had been taught to hate Israel accepted his terms for cooperation without losing face or being subjected to any form of oppression. His task was unique in its complexity and seemingly impossible, for he was charged with establishing a military government not in a country whose army had been defeated and whose people had surrendered, but in a territory whose inhabitants—the Palestinians—were part of a greater Arab nation which outnumbered Israel by many millions and still possessed large armies. Furthermore, in a Summit Meeting held at Khartoum in August 1967, the Arab leaders declared their firm resolve to continue the war against Israel. Maintaining military rule over a million and a half Arabs while virtually 80 million of their brethren continued the war and terrorist organizations for the liberation of Palestine incited them to rise against Israeli rule was like trying to hold on to and control the thrashing tail of an agitated whale.

The secret of Dayan's success may have been his long-held attitude toward the Arabs of Palestine. Since the war itself had been so short, prewar concepts vis-à-vis the Arabs acquired great significance. Statesmen and army officers had no time to arrange their thoughts on how to exploit the military victory in order to achieve a political settlement and therefore fell back on their earlier terms of reference. Those who wanted Israel's borders to include all of pre-1948 Palestine set up what became known as the "Movement for Greater Israel," demanding that the Administered Territories be fully annexed. Others were apprehensive about Israel losing its predominantly Jewish character because of the greater rate of natural increase among the Arabs and demanded that the Administered Territories be returned as soon as possible. Dayan vacillated between these two poles, while politically his attitude toward the Arabs of Palestine was based upon the concept of a confederacy. On December 21, 1966, at a time when he—like many others—believed that a military confrontation in the area was still a long way off, he told a students' meeting in Jerusalem that a confederacy including "Israel, Jordan, and the Palestinians of the West Bank could be the solution to the Israel-Arab problem." The basic condition for establishing such a confederacy, he then thought, was that each country should retain its autonomy in foreign and defense affairs, while the cooperation between them would be mostly economic.

A second component of his attitude toward the Palestinian Arabs was an aspect of his approach toward the Arab minority in Israel. He was far more liberal than Ben Gurion on questions of military rule in the Israeli-Arab sectors, and his view on the question of the Arab minority's allegiance to the state was highly unorthodox. On October 11, 1965, during the election campaign for the Sixth Knesset, he addressed an election meeting in the village of Tirra and in the process provoked the ire of a considerable number of Jews. He called upon his Arab audience to do one of two things: those who wanted to live in the Jewish State should be loyal citizens; those who did not should pack up and leave. But before saying this he stressed repeatedly that those Arabs who did want to remain in Israel must not be assimilated into Jewish society; on the contrary, they should retain and nurture their social and cultural values.

These basic attitudes influenced Dayan's initial steps as Military Governor. From the very first, his aim was to establish good neighborly relations between Israel and the Arabs of the Administered Territories, whom he considered potential allies. To do so he strove for a liberal military rule that was strict only on matters of security. His basic idea was that the military government should interfere as little as possible in the daily affairs of the populace or, as he put it in English, "would not 'boss' them." He strove to let them manage their own affairs and allowed them a great measure of freedom in contacts with their relatives and friends on the other side of the cease-fire lines. These were the cornerstones of his approach to military government even before the initiation of his "Open Bridges Policy."

Dayan quickly took advantage of the aftermath of the war—the Israelis' shock after their stunning victory and the Arabs' astonishment over their crushing defeat—in order to establish certain facts before public opinion or politicians could recover sufficiently to obstruct them. While others were still confused and had not found their bearings, he took his first steps toward establishing a military government to his own taste.

His first order was normalization, in other words doing everything possible to return life to normal throughout the Administered Territories. The army took the order at face value and understood it to mean renewing public services and the supply of foodstuffs without altering the military situation that had emerged in the Administered Territories. Thus the first orders were the conventional postwar precautions—strict curfews, restrictions on travel, and roadblocks. In the West Bank, for example, the Army Spokesman announced on June 8 that a 50-meter wide strip of land along the former armistice line was closed, and anyone found crossing it would be doing so at the risk of his life. Later, the same order was applied to all the Administered Territories. In addition, each military governor set up his own system of curfews, roadblocks, and controls as he saw fit. This was caused partly by the fact that the military government was still in the process of being set up, and it was feared that allowing Arabs from the Administered Territories free entry into Israel after their prolonged exposure to violent anti-Israel propaganda would result in riots and outbreaks of violence.

It is impossible to say how long the Administered Territories would have been caught in a hopeless tangle of entry and exit permits, restrictions, and curfews had there been another Minister of Defense. But Dayan refused to wait until the military government had rallied sufficiently to deal with all the problems. He had never had much patience for paper work and did not believe that a proliferation of papers, permits, and documents would solve any problems. At the sight of the roadblocks and the idle *fellaheen* who were unable to work their lands because of strict restrictions on their movements, he immediately demanded that all roadblocks be lifted and curfews reduced to the hours of darkness only. Normalization, as he saw it, meant freedom of movement, not only a proper supply of electricty, water, and flour.

His first move in the direction of removing roadblocks was in Jerusalem, when he demanded that Maj. Gen. Narkiss open the gates of the Old City. Narkiss, who as OC Central Command was now Commander of Zahal forces in the West Bank, faced problems of great complexity. The closed gates made it easy for the army to keep the Jewish population out of the Old City and the Moslem population out of the Israeli sector. He believed there were two good reasons for controlling traffic from one part of the divided city to the other. First, the entry of large numbers of Jews into a hostile Arab city would necessitate the deployment of strong security forces to maintain order and prevent any disturbances or bloodshed. Secondly, the entry of so many Jews, including unruly elements, would necessitate increasing the security forces guarding Arab property. Looting is part of any war, and in Jewish Jerusalem there were some who were out to seek revenge. To control such phenomena, Dayan sought a commander who would have the courage to open fire. Should the gates now be opened, only strictly controlled passage, guarded by soldiers, could be instituted. The army authorities considered this an inadequate arrangement, but Dayan's mind was made up: he demanded the gates be opened. Two weeks later he ordered all the soldiers and guards removed from the control points, and on June 29, when East Jerusalem was formally annexed by Israel and the city was united, he ordered all the control points between the two sectors abandoned.

The swift removal of the barriers was manifestly designed to strengthen Israel's claim to the Old City. At the same time, it was an expression of Dayan's desire to remove all the barriers between Jew and Arab. He had always believed that once the physical barriers fell, the two nations would meet, feel each other out, struggle, and ultimately find a way to peaceful coexistence. A barrier of any sort—a UN Emergency Force, an international army, or even merely a fence—would assure that the two nations would never meet and reach any kind of agreement and would only perpetuate the mutual lack of understanding.

In this rapid series of first steps, Dayan decided to restore the control of the Waqf (the High Moslem Council) over the Temple Mount and its two mosques—the Dome of the Rock and El Aksa—thereby removing the possibility of religious overtones in any future clashes and cutting the ground from under any possible call for a holy war. Only two weeks after the war, he decided to allow all the Arabs in Israel and the Administered Territories to pray in the two mosques on the Temple Mount. This was to be the first time the Arabs of Israel would be allowed to pray in one of the holiest places of the Moslem religion. The army was again apprehensive that the mass pilgrimage would end in bloodshed; but again Dayan refused to be dissuaded. He claimed that after the defeat, civilians, who had not fought in the war, would hardly be likely to take up arms or resort to violence. His assumption proved correct. Removing the blockades and the consequent "exchange of population" passed without incident.

Characteristically, Dayan carried out all these steps independently, by-passing regular channels. He gave the order to remove the roadblocks and allow prayers in Jerusalem directly to Narkiss, instead of having it issued via the C-o-S; on a visit to the cities of the West Bank on June 17 and 20, he told brigade and battal-

ion commanders to remove the roadblocks they had set up, return vehicles they had confiscated, allow farmers out to their
fields, and restrict the curfew to the hours of darkness. Likewise,
he ordered that the refugees from Kalkilya be allowed to return
home and instructed that the city be rebuilt. When he visited
there on June 28, he was received by the inhabitants with enthusiastic cries of *Ya'ish Dayan!* ["Long Live Dayan!"].

In establishing "facts" in the Administered Territories before the
aftereffects of the war had completely worn off, Dayan established enduring patterns of military government. One example of the good
neighborly relations he aspired to achieve centered on the Cave of the
Machpela in Hebron, the traditional burial place of the Patriarchs
and their wives. A holy place to the Jews, it had been taken over
by the Moslems in the early years of the spread of Islam and Jews
were allowed no further than the seventh step of the mosque built
over the cave. Dayan allowed the Moslems in Hebron to retain the
mosque, but he also permitted Jews to enter the holy place and establish a synagogue there. In a sense, it became a model of religious coexistence.

At first Dayan treated the Administered Territories, particularly
had begun spontaneously—the marketing of West Bank agricultural produce across the Jordan. Later, bridges and new approach
roads were built to replace those destroyed during the war. Restoring the bridges over the Jordan came to be known as the "Open
Bridges Policy." In some ways this move seemed to be a practical step
toward his vision for the future: the Palestinian Arabs living in a
confederacy with Israel while maintaining contact with the rest
of the Arab nation.

At first Dayan treated the Administered Territories, particularly
the West Bank, as a pledge given to Israel for safekeeping until the
signing of a peace treaty. Consequently, he did whatever he could to
expunge the Arabs' hate for Israel and instill the realization that coexistence was not only possible, but beneficial. His aim was to create
the kind of relations that would be needed in peacetime. When early
hopes of a quick peace settlement faded, Dayan tried to operate as
though a peace settlement did in fact exist and transferred most of the
administrative responsibilities to the municipal authorities. This policy gave birth to the idea of creating two independent administrative districts in the West Bank, one centered around Nablus and the
other around Hebron. In turn, these might form the core of a Palestinian state, strengthen the moderate Arab leadership, who favored
a peaceful settlement with Israel, and eventually lead to a confederacy.
For a while it seemed as though the idea stood a good chance of succeeding. But while the Hebron area, led by the Mayor of Hebron,
Sheik Ali Ja'abri, gladly embraced the idea of independent adminis-

tration, Nablus rejected it. This was reason enough to abandon the initial plan, but not to drop the entire concept. Dayan therefore tried to bring about the confederacy in another way.

By the summer of 1968, Dayan's approach to the Administered Territories underwent a change, for it became quite clear that peace was still a long way off and the territories would remain in Israeli hands for some time. As long as he could regard the Administered Territories as a short-term pledge, he opposed economic cooperation and objected to Israeli investments there. His main concern was that Arabs not be dispossessed of their businesses, which would lead to resentment toward Israelis who moved into their province. With this condition in mind, he declared that even if it was obvious that a Jewish doctor would run a hospital better than an Arab, it was preferable to let the Arab do it. In upholding the principle of Israeli nonintervention, he even prevented the Ministry of Education and Culture from interfering in the education system of the Administered Territories, despite the fact that they were permeated by hate for Israel. His stance was motivated by the desire to dispel any impression of "Israelization" of the Administered Territories.

At this point, Dayan felt that the time was ripe for a new phase. Liberal though a military government may be, it nevertheless deals with an enemy and consequently has few obligations. In his own words, he wanted "to bring about a situation in which the military government would be a passing episode, not a permanent institution," that is, the government would assume complete civil responsibility for the inhabitants of the Administered Territories. He now stressed that in order to improve medical services, a Jewish doctor should definitely be appointed director of a hospital, if he proved superior to an Arab doctor, and he called for maximum cooperation between Israel and the Administered Territories. A Five Year Agricultural Plan drawn up for the West Bank dovetailed with a corresponding Israeli plan, thus reducing the West Bank's dependence on markets east of the Jordan. The citrus groves of the Gaza Strip were incorporated into the Israeli Citrus Marketing Boards, and local packing houses were built with Israeli capital. He called for an integration of the labor forces and increased Israeli investment in the Administered Territories, labeling this phase of his policy "economic integration."

In 1967 Dayan opposed Israeli-Arab partnerships and demanded that the Arabs manage their own affairs and provide the public services they were accustomed to, even if these were on a much lower level than those provided in Israel; in 1968 he maintained that Israel was obliged to develop the public services in the Administered Territories and raise the standard of living as much as possible. He demanded that the government double the sums spent on services in the Territories.

It was against the background of this demand that the first public confrontation occurred between Dayan and Pinhas Sapir, the Minister of Finance.

Sapir put all the weight of his considerable influence against the duplication of the Services Budget and objected to opening the entire Israeli economy to the Arabs of the Administered Territories. In the end, he managed to thwart Dayan's plan. The Cabinet, led by Eshkol, was mostly in Sapir's favor and limited the development of public services and investment in the Administered Territories. Permission to employ labor from the Territories was restricted and temporary, designed only to ease immediate problems of unemployment in the West Bank and the Gaza Strip. At first the government set a limit: no more than 5,000 workers from across the "Green Line."

Sapir was candid about the reasons for his objections. He had no need of the confederacy Dayan was striving for and was quite content with a Jewish State with borders very similar to the "Green Line." He feared that employing Arabs from the Administered Territories in industry and manual labor within Israel would change the country's image, and the Israelis would cease to be a "nation of workers." Sapir was also concerned that a million and a half Arabs would threaten the demographic status of the country's Jewish majority. In a meeting of functionaries of the Labor Party (created out of the union of Mapai, Achdut Ha'avodah and Rafi) held on November 11, 1968, he stated: "I am against adding a million Palestinian Arabs to the 400,000 Israeli Arabs in the country, who would then constitute a minority of 40% in Israel's population. And if their rate of natural increase continues to be three or more times greater than that of the Jewish population, it is not too difficult to calculate when there will be an Arab majority in the country."

The differences between Dayan and Sapir were clearly a function of their different outlooks on Israel. In Dayan's view, the two nations in the area formerly called Palestine could function within a single economy, even though they belonged to different cultures and sovereign states. The basic principle in his approach was neighborliness, or, in his phrase, "a joint way of life." Sapir's concept of a Jewish State was modeled on the first twenty years of Israel's existence, and even if peace came in the future, the marked differences that existed between Israel and its Arab neighbors would serve as a guarantee for the survival of the Jewish identity. Sapir would apparently have been content to dig a giant trench along Israel's borders and cut the country off from the Middle East. Dayan envisioned a land of many dimensions; Sapir relied on the conventional concepts that a Jewish State meant congruent geographical, demographic, political, and cultural borders. Dayan saw the country as an integral part of a region and only its geographic and economic borders were identical. They contained two distinct demographic and cultural entities whose political demarcation did not follow strictly demographic lines. Thus an Arab from Jerusalem and an Arab from Nablus, though belonging to the same demographic and cultural group, could belong to different political entities. Both would work in the same economy but would vote for representatives in different countries and enjoy different civil rights. Dayan's overall aim was to blur the identification between the geographic and the demographic lines of demarcation. He therefore proposed that the government establish four Jewish cities along the mountain ridge extending from Hebron and Nablus, thereby breaking up the Arab demographic continuity. When he presented part of his plan to the public for the first time, he suggested that the Hebron-Beersheba area be turned into a single economic-administrative region. Another integrated area, in the north, could include Afula and Jenin.

The Jewish State Dayan envisaged was not defined by a geographical border but by demographic and cultural criteria. The same applied to the Palestinian entity, although he had not yet decided whether it should be a state in its own right or a part of the Hashemite Kingdom of Jordan whose inhabitants live in Israel. He did not care whether the Palestinian inhabitants of the West Bank temporarily remained Jordanian citizens or whether his "country-as-part-of-a-region" concept was complicated by the fact that Arabs living in a sovereign Israeli framework would be the citizens of and vote in another sovereign framework.

The weak point of his concept was the question of sovereign allegiance. His critics asked how long the country would remain a Jewish State if it embraced a sector whose inhabitants were not Israeli citizens. How could both nations operate within a single economy and infrastructure of utilities, yet each owe allegiance to different cultures and sovereign states? They claimed that in time, economic integration would bring about unification of the civilian populations, and the result would be a country with a large and rapidly increasing Arab population. The Arabs would thus be able to achieve by demographic means what they had failed to achieve in war. Dayan's reply to these questions was at best provisional. He argued that as long as a state of war existed between Israel and the Arab countries, there was no threat of total civilian assimilation, and an asymmetrical solution, such as the one he proposed, would remain valid.

Despite its weaknesses, Dayan's concept facilitated the implementation of various joint activities, while Sapir's concept of a Jewish State in isolation was unrealistic. But Eshkol's government did not decide in favor of either one. The intensification of the "War of Attrition" and increased Soviet penetration into the Middle East made a clear-cut decision difficult. However, events themselves gradually created a process that tended toward Dayan's reading of the situation: the economy of the Administered Territories became increasingly integrated with that of Israel. Electric power, water, roads, transport, agricultural coordination, marketing of agricultural produce, control over plant and livestock diseases, preventive medicine, and particularly the exploitation of manpower were all shared with Israel. On June 14, 1971, Dayan was able to report to the Knesset that unemployment in the West Bank had been drastically reduced and stood at only 3.5%; 25,000 inhabitants of the Administered Territories (30,000 one month later) were working within the borders of Israel. In the West Bank, private consumption had risen from IL 618 per annum in 1965 to IL 800 in 1969 and was continuing to rise. In the summer of 1971, some 100,000 Arab tourists were expected to visit the Administered Territories and Israel.

The "Open Bridges Policy" and the economic integration that Dayan proposed as the official government line came into being almost of their own accord. Just as the pioneers in Ottoman Palestine determined the borders of the future state of Israel by establishing settlements, the *faits accomplis* of the post-1967 era began defining the future relations between the Administered Territories and Israel.

While Dayan was considered liberal in economic, social, and cultural matters, he was equally as intransigent in matters of security. Attacks perpetrated against Israel and her inhabitants by the terrorist organizations brought swift and harsh Israeli reactions. Dayan authorized the exile of *provocateurs* and administrative detention for anyone suspected of terrorist activity. He did not shrink from demolishing the houses of those accused of terrorist activities in Israel, even if they were officially the property of innocent relatives. He announced the rules of his game to the inhabitants of the Territories on several occasions. On October 11, 1967, for example, after a large-scale school strike thoughout the West Bank, he formulated the policy thus: I do not expect you to love us or to reconcile yourselves to our rule. You lost the war and I do not know what will happen in the future . . . I want there to be peace. But quite clearly, you, the inhabitants of the Territories, can do nothing to change the situation one way or another. The choice is yours, either to rebel or to accept the present situation. I expect the population and the civil institutions to lead a well-ordered, normal life and to fulfill the administrative obligations in your areas, while we will fulfill our obligations of government and rule. The choice facing you now is either normal life or rebellion. But you should be aware that if you choose rebellion, we will have no choice but to break you.

Dayan's strength was his crystal-clear formulation of the rules and his strict adherence to them. It was as though he held a stick in one hand and a carrot in the other. As long as the inhabitants of the Administered Territories refrained from rebellion, they would taste only the carrot. Dayan wanted to feed them more and more sweets of this kind so that they would feel they had something to lose if they were caught engaging in hostile activities. In effect, the undisguised threat of taking away what had already been generously handed out was more of a deterrent than the stick. When he found it necessary to apply the stick, however, he did so accurately, forcefully, and without remorse.

The clarity of his rules and his unwillingness to back down one inch on the civil, cultural, and economic liberties he demanded for the Territories or on the swift punishment he meted out for hostile activities helped Dayan realize his policy successfully, as seen by the fact that the Arabs of the Administered Territories opted for normal civilian life. The terrorist organizations failed to incite the Territories to rebellion. The population clearly rejected them and their organizations were forced to wage war from the Arab side of the cease-fire lines. Eventually they failed even from there.

Dayan extended his willingness to coexist with the Arabs to Israel's neighbors as well. Although he employed the same iron hand, on questions of security, he could not achieve the relaxation of tension won in the Territories. Exchanges of small-arms, artillery, and tank fire, aerial bombardments and skirmishes, commando raids, destruction, and sabotage were daily occurrences on both sides of the Suez Canal until August 1970, when the Egyptians again agreed to a cease-fire.

On the surface, the reason for the renewed outbreak of hostilities between Egypt and Israel was simple: Israel was unwilling to withdraw from the territories captured in the Six-Day War until such time as the Arabs would enter into direct negotiations on demarcating borders designed to ensure Israel's security. As he had opposed the withdrawal from Sinai in 1957, Dayan now emphatically opposed the withdrawal of Israeli forces from Sharm e-Sheikh, in order to prevent a third blockade of the Straits of Tiran; from the Gaza Strip, to prevent its reverting to a convenient base for the Egyptian aggression against Israel; and from the Golan Heights, so that the Syrians could not renew their bombardments of the settlements below. He also demanded that Israeli forces remain on the mountain ridges of Judea and Samaria and that united Jerusalem remain the capital of Israel. Several other ministers shared these views, but it was Dayan who saw to it that they became a central part of the Labor Party's platform in the 1969 elections and made them the basic principles guiding Golda' Meir's Cabinet. He also established the principle that Sharm e-Sheikh and overland contact with it must remain in Israeli hands whatever the terms of the final settlement. Egypt demanded total Israeli withdrawal to the armistice lines of June 4,

1967 and rejected any arrangement that did not ensure the rights of the Palestinian people. Thus while Egypt regarded Israel's demands as an expression of her expansionist ambitions, Israel regarded Egypt's demands as an attempt to improve her positions for a final war of annihilation. The stalemate was complete.

President Nasser tried to bring about an Israeli withdrawal by the use of military force and launched what he called the "War of Attrition" in the belief that Israel would be unable to bear the high price of indefinite mobilization and a high casualty rate. Dayan's reaction to the "War of Attrition" echoed his reaction to similar provocations in his youth or during his term as C-o-S. His rule from the days of the reprisal raids still held: "We cannot prevent the murder of workers or families . . . but we can put a high price on our blood." Just as the paratroopers had carried out deep penetration raids behind the armistice lines in the fifties, Air Force jets now penetrated Egyptian skies and bombarded installations deep inside the country. This military policy was not an innovation but a continuation of the process of escalation. According to Israeli estimates, some ten thousand Egyptian soldiers were killed in the "War of Attrition," and ultimately it was Egypt that suffered the worst consequences.

Another of Dayan's rules from the fifties no longer held true: "The Arabs will decide against clashing with Israel only if they have reason to believe that if they do otherwise, they will meet with severe reactions and be drawn into an armed conflict in which they will be the losers." The Egyptians no longer feared being drawn into armed conflict. Moreover, the threat to Israel's existence, which until the Six-Day War had been posed mainly by the Arabs, became a Russo-Arab threat after June 1967, and the Middle East conflict became a focal point in the global confrontation of the two Superpowers. In some respects this period was the opening of a new chapter in Israeli history. From then on, protecting the existence of the State of Israel became an issue with world-wide ramifications. Israel was now being besieged not only by the Arab nations of the Middle East, but by the might of the Soviet Union as well.

Dayan's life also seemed to enter a new phase at this point. Protecting the country became an increasingly complex undertaking and the focus of Israel's day-to-day life. Unlike 1948 and 1956, when defense became a secondary issue after the fighting ended, this time, after the greatest victory, defense became the axis around which Israeli life revolved. Dayan's position as Minister of Defense gained him a special status. On several occasions, both in Eshkol's Cabinet and Golda Meir's, he alone held the fate of the government in his hands. His opinion was so highly regarded that at times he carried the Cabinet even though he was in the minority.

The most difficult part of the struggle for survival—bearing the responsibility for the continued loss of life—fell upon his shoulders. The number of fatalities from the end of the Six-Day War until the cease-fire in the "War of Attrition" was 721, of whom 127 were civilians. This was close to the price paid in the Six-Day War itself (790 dead). Yet the losses of the Six-Day War could at least be understood as the cost of a war for survival forced upon Israel. The same was not true of the losses in the "War of Attrition," which was no longer a war of "no alternative." Some felt that it was a war for Israel's policies, rather than for her survival; others could not understand why Israel was paying with soldiers' lives for territories she was in principle prepared to relinquish; still others believed that Israel had fallen into a bloody, inescapable maze. The constant loss of lives was so much more significant in a nation permeated by the sense of a dwindling tribe. Each Israeli casualty seemed to reduce the life span of the nation as a whole. It was as though the nation's days were numbered by the amount of losses it could sustain. Dayan had to account for the heavy price and simultaneously continue to demand it of the nation. It was he who signed the letters written to the families of the fallen, and it was to him that bereaved parents, widows, and orphans turned for reassurance that their sacrifices were not in vain. Finally, it was Dayan who had to instill courage in a small nation whose enemies, far from dwindling, were growing stronger and more numerous each day.

In effect, Dayan had become a sort of Minister of Survival. His self-confidence and belief in the future and his spiritual strength to withstand the difficult, complex struggle had to serve an entire country. The task that circumstances had forced upon him was not at all the one he had prepared himself for. He had neither the prophetic vision with which Ben Gurion had sustained the nation in the forties, nor the religious faith upon which the Jews of the Diaspora had drawn throughout the centuries of exile. In fact, his personality was restricted by his efforts not to overreach his own narrow area of personal responsibility. Ben Gurion called upon the nation to be a model of justice and truth and to live for the realization of a great mission—to be "a light unto the nations." Dayan was suspicious of rhetoric and scrupulously avoided it. He preferred talking in concrete terms; not of the great truth with which the nation had to arm itself but of the types of planes and missiles it needed to survive.

The contrast between Dayan's nature and his task produced a change in him. At first his nature held sway and he shied away from collective responsibility. As he had done many times in the past, he tried to breed courage through personal example, not by vision and prophecy. Although his status no longer demanded it, and physically he was no longer equal to it, he visited the front lines frequent-

ly, reaching the most remote and dangerous outposts. On one occasion he even crawled to an observation post, taking pleasure
in the realization that he could still do so like any other soldier. The
old stories recurred. A brigade commander in the front line tried to
forbid him to climb up an embankment that was a habitual target
of Egyptian artillery, saying, "We have a lot of soldiers, but only
one Minister of Defense." Dayan replied: "You'll be surprised
to learn the number of candidates waiting for the opening."

In his free time Dayan continued digging for antiquities, which
again almost cost him his life. His greatest fear was that age
would prevent him from pursuing his hobby. Not long before his
fifty-fifth birthday, he said, "The only thing about old age that wor-
ries me is that I might not be able to dig with a pickax from morning till night. Not that I will grow bald, not that I'll have pains in
my stomach and not that I will have no physical stamina at all. Old
age does not worry me, and if anyone were to ask me if I would like
to be eighteen again—no!"

If Dayan consciously altered his image to suit his position, at first
the difference was felt only in those aspects of his public personality he found easy—and was perhaps even glad—to be rid of. It
was extremely easy for him to shed the skin of the rebel. In December
1967, at the last Rafi convention before the breakaway party rejoined
Mapai, he still raised the banner of rebellion and promised a
fight. "If I go to 110 Hayarkon Street [to carry out the merger in Mapai's office there] . . . I shall do so with pleasure, because I shall go
not in order to acquiesce but to fight: to propose that Eshkol be removed from the Premiership and to fight for it; to see that the present economic policy be changed and that the Minister of Finance
be someone other than Pinhas Sapir." But it now seems that he made
these statements mainly to appease Ben Gurion (who opposed the merger), for Dayan cooperated with Eshkol in his daily work in the united
party. When Eshkol died, Dayan did not submit his candidacy for
the Premiership and willingly accepted Golda Meir as Prime Minister. Likewise, he did not lift a finger to have Sapir replaced. Either
because of the circumstances or because of the advent of middle age,
or perhaps even because it ran against his true nature, Dayan completely dropped the image of the rebel. He no longer criticized the
veterans and was completely loyal to Golda Meir. He even discussed with her such purely military matters as the appointments of
generals in the front commands and GHQ.

Yet these changes were not enough. His position demanded more
than a mere display of personal courage, practical solutions, the calm
of a self-confident citizen, and the image of a national leader who
was above political rivalries and personal quibbling. The renewed war
with Egypt, the aggressiveness of the Arab terrorists, daily reports

of Israeli losses, and above all the realization that peace with the Arabs was a distant, almost unattainable, goal created a deep depression in the country. Dayan was one of the first of Israel's leaders who realistically perceived and openly expressed the limited prospects of peace in the near future. With peace seemingly out of reach, the nation asked, "What will be the end?" Until when would Israel have to fight for her life, and what was her life without peace? In a convention held at the Chief Rabbinate, a tourist from America asked Dayan the same question in Yiddish, as if to prove that even outside Israel he was considered the man to whom questions concerning the continued survival of the Jewish people should be addressed. That he was prepared to reply to that question was a clear sign that the demands made upon him by his position had begun to gain on those of his nature.

On August 7, 1969, in an address to the graduates of the Staff and Command School, he dealt for the first time with the ultimate question of Israel's existence:

The question "What will be the end? has been with our people for four thousand years . . . and it can be said that the concern over "what will be" is an organic part of our people. You undoubtedly noticed that in my last sentence I omitted "the end"; I said "What will be?" not "What will be the end?" I did so because I feel that the emphasis should be placed on the road we take, and not on the final destination. Rest and peace for our nation have always been only a longing, never a reality. And if from time to time we did achieve these goals, they were only oases—a breath that gave us the strength and the courage to take up the struggle again . . . I therefore think that the only answer we can give to the question "What will be?" is "We shall continue to struggle." I feel that now, as in the past, our answer . . . must center upon the assurance of our ability to face difficulties, our ability to fight, more than on expectations of final concrete solutions to our problems. We must prepare ourselves morally and physically to endure a protracted struggle, not to draw up a timetable for the achievement of "rest and peace."

In searching for the significance of Jewish survival, Dayan became more a true son to his father and forefathers than he ever thought likely. Like his grandfather, Reb Avraham, and his ancestors, the Rabbis of Squira and their fathers from the "court" of the "Grandfather" of Spola and Reb Pinhas of Koritz, he used the Bible as a tool to understand the Jewish essence, and like them he believed in what God said to Abraham: "Arise, walk through the land in the length of it and in the breadth of it; for I will give it unto thee" (Genesis 13:17). Like his father, who exhorted his comrades in Degania not to regard their kibbutz as their "rest and peace," he urged his country to continue its struggle.

Dayan read the Book of Kabbala*, the *Zohar,* and the books of one of the founders of the Kabbala, Rabbi Yitzhak Luria (Ha'ari). He recalls being deeply impressed by Ha'ari "as a human phenomenon, not by the wondrous miracles. I don't believe in Jewish mysticism, but rather in the culture and history of the Jewish people, in the fact that over the years national gifts and character are passed down from one generation to the other." Without becoming religious, he searched for his own interpretation to the Jewish essence and claimed that the Jewish people were endowed with "two resources which would enable it to bear up in its incessant struggles." The first is faith: "I do not mean religious faith, but rather faith as the antithesis of despair; as an element . . . that was injected into the spirit of the Israeli nation, that was mixed in its blood from the very first day; a faith in its direction, its justice, its future; a faith that protects it and hardens it against spiritual depression, weakness, inaction and destruction." The second was courage, "which is the basis and the *sine qua non* of its ability to endure the struggle . . . throughout the generations and in changing circumstances."

For Dayan, the path and the struggle were the essence and transcendent aim of the Jewish individual and nation as a whole. His own life was an unbroken chain of war—from the burning of Degania B, through the Ya'akobi murder in Nahalal, shepherds' fights, the Haganah, Wingate, the Second World War, and Israel's wars, the terrorist onslaught, and the "War of Attrition." Such were the lives of most Israelis. Death was his constant companion, and more and more he turned to death to discover the significance of life. How to die, he said, was an inseparable part of how to live. In his address at the memorial meeting to mark the anniversary of the poet Natan Alterman's death (March 21, 1971), he set out this idea as part of an attempt to interpret Alterman's poems in the light of the "fighting spirit":

Death in combat is not the end of the fight but its *peak,* and since combat is a part, and at times the *sum total,* of life, death, which is the peak of combat, is not the *destruction* of life, but its fullest, most powerful *expression* . . . Man goes to his death in battle not in order to bring *salvation to others,* not in order to sacrifice himself for the future; man goes to battle because he, personally, is unwilling to surrender, to be defeated; he does not wish to fight for his *survival,* but for him the content of his life and death is merely the supreme expression of the ferocity of his struggle. This is not a death in war, in an historical event; it is a personal, dyamic death, intrinsic in the *struggle,* in the combat, not in the *war* . . . Most of my years have been spent, in one way or another, in the company of fighters. These men lived in the shadow of death, yet it did not darken their lives or brand them

---

*A system of theosophy based on a mystical interpretation of the Scriptures.

with a stamp of grief. The opposite was true; these were men driven by an immense *life force,* and it is this *life force* that makes them *fighters* (italics in the original).

A resemblance had developed between Israel and Dayan. Both were solitary, dynamic, energetic, and disabled. Just as Dayan's eyesight was impaired, so Israel's vision of the future was impaired by her severed hope of peace. This resemblance was particularly striking when Dayan eulogized comrades and soldiers who fell in the ongoing war. At such times, his one eye sparkled with a great and vital passion for life, while the other remained darkened and dead under the black eye patch. It was as though Moshe Dayan symbolized Israel, teeming with life and death; ready to die in order to live.

LIST OF ILLUSTRATIONS

Between pages 118 and 119

Moshe Dayan at the age of five (courtesy I.P.P.A., Tel Aviv)
Sixteen-year-old Moshe on horseback (courtesy I.P.P.A.)
Moshe and Ruth Dayan soon after their marriage (courtesy I.P.P.A.)
Moshe as commander of the armored car at Hanita in 1938 (courtesy
I.P.P.A.)
With Yitzhak Sadeh and Yigal Allon at Hanita in 1938 (courtesy I.P.P.A.)
With members of the "Forty-three" in the Acre Fortress (courtesy I.P.P.A.)

Between pages 150 and 151

With men of the 89th Raiding Battalion (courtesy I.P.P.A.)
With Col. Abdullah el-Tel in 1948 (courtesy I.P.P.A.)
The Chief-of-Staff demonstrates throwing a grenade (courtesy Israel Government Press Office)
With officers of the Paratroop Brigade (courtesy I.P.P.A.)
With Maj. Gen. Chaim Laskov (courtesy I.P.P.A.)

Between pages 278 and 279

Searching for archaeological finds in the desert (courtesy I.P.P.A.)
With troops after the victory in Sinai (courtesy Israel Government Press Office)
Meeting with General Burns about Zahal's withdrawal from Sinai in 1957 (courtesy Israel Government Press Office)
With Pinhas Lavon (courtesy Israel Government Press Office)
With David Ben Gurion and Shimon Peres (courtesy David Harris)
With American troops in Vietnam (courtesy I.P.P.A.)

Between pages 310 and 311

At first press conference as Minister of Defense (courtesy I.P.P.A.)
With Levi Eshkol (courtesy Israel Government Press Office)
Entering the Old City of Jerusalem on June 7, 1967 (courtesy Israel Government Press Office)
With Golda Meir (courtesy I.P.P.A.)
With Sheik Ali Ja'abri (courtesy I.P.P.A.)

Maps on pages 156 and 267 by Alex Avnon; drawn by Carta, Jerusalem.

MAJOR EVENTS IN MOSHE DAYAN'S LIFE

May 4, 1915	Born in Degania
1922	Moves to Nahalal
1929	Joins the Haganah
July 12, 1935	Marries Ruth Shwarz
November 5, 1939	Arrested and later sentenced to five years' imprisonment in the Acre Fortress
February 16, 1941	Released from the Acre Fortress
June 7, 1941	Loses his left eye in action in Syria
May 18, 1948	Appointed commander of the Jordan Valley sector and returns to active military service
May 25, 1948	Begins command of the 89th Battalion with the rank of major
August 1, 1948	Becomes commander of the Jerusalem Brigade with the rank of lieutenant colonel
November 21, 1949	Receives the rank of major general
November 25, 1949	Becomes OC Southern Command
May 26, 1952	Becomes OC Northern Command
December 7, 1952	Becomes Chief of G Branch in the General Staff
December 6, 1953	Becomes Chief-of-Staff
December 16, 1959	Becomes Minister of Agriculture
November 4, 1964	Resigns as Minister of Agriculture
June 2, 1967	Becomes Minister of Defense
December 12, 1971	Divorced from Ruth Dayan

ISRAELI PRIME MINISTERS, MINISTERS OF DEFENSE, AND CHIEFS-OF-STAFF, 1948-1972

Prime Minister	Minister of Defense	Chief-of-Staff
David Ben Gurion May 1948–December 1953 (on leave July 20–November 17, 1953)	**David Ben Gurion**	**Ya'akov Dori** May 1948–November 1949
		Yigael Yadin November 1949–December 1952
	Pinhas Lavon Acting Minister of Defense, July 20 November 17, 1953; Minister of Defense, December 1953–February 1955	**Mordechai Maklef** December 1952–December 1953
Moshe Sharett Acting Prime Minister, July 20— November 17, 1953; Prime Minister, December 1953–November 1955		**Moshe Dayan** December 1953–November 1958
David Ben Gurion November 1955–June 1963	**David Ben Gurion** February 1955–June 1963	**Chaim Laskov** January 1958–January 1961
		Zvi Zur January 1961–January 1964
Levi Eshkol June 1963–March 1969	**Levi Eshkol** June 1963–June 1967	**Yitzhak Rabin** January 1964–January 1968
	Moshe Dayan June 2, 1967	**Chaim Bar-Lev** January 1968–January 1972
Golda Meir March 1969–		**David Eleazar** January 1972–

INDEX